"*Building a Sustainable Kitchen* is a refreshing, down-to-earth guide that cuts through the noise and brings clarity to the conversation around sustainability at home. With a thoughtful, evidence-based approach, Naomi empowers everyday Canadians to take practical steps toward a greener kitchen, without guilt or overwhelm. Her chapter on managing food waste is especially powerful: packed with smart, achievable strategies that align with Second Harvest's mission to prevent perfectly good food from going to waste. From shopping smart to making the most of leftovers, this book is a must-read for anyone who wants to nourish their family while nourishing the planet. Inspiring, informative, and rooted in real-life experience, *Building a Sustainable Kitchen* proves that sustainability starts right where we gather most, around the kitchen table."

—Lori Nikkel, Chief Executive Officer of Second Harvest

"*Building a Sustainable Kitchen* is a refreshing, evidence-driven antidote to the noise surrounding sustainability. Naomi Hansen cuts through greenwashing and guilt with a clear, practical roadmap for creating a more planet-friendly kitchen—one realistic step at a time. Drawing on extensive interviews, academic research, and her own lived experience as a regular Canadian cook, Hansen demystifies the science behind everyday choices with honesty and humility. This book is grounded, accessible, and most importantly, useful. It's a timely guide for anyone seeking sustainable habits without the hype."

—Sylvain Charlebois, Senior Director of the Agri-Food Analytics Lab at Dalhousie University and co-host of *The Food Professor* podcast

"Looking to make your home and the world more sustainable? The kitchen is where your actions have the power to make the biggest impact and Naomi Hansen has done all the legwork to find out where and how you should prioritize your efforts. This is a fantastic, well researched reference guide for all of us."

—Bea Johnson, best-selling author of *Zero Waste Home*

"Reducing food waste is one of the most powerful individual actions you can take. This book is your A to Z on how and why these simple everyday shifts in your kitchen can help reduce our carbon footprint. Going zero waste is impossible but it is something we all need to work towards."

—Christine Tizzard, creator of Zero-Waste Kitchen, author of *Honest to Goodness*, and ambassador for Love Food, Hate Waste

"Eating sustainably can feel overwhelming! Naomi's book breaks down complicated concepts into practical, doable steps that have real impact. *Building a Sustainable Kitchen* offers people flexibility and meets them where they are, at every stage of their sustainable living journey. With region-focused advice, easy-to-follow takeaways, and 'What You Can Do' sections scattered throughout, this book is an essential guide to building a sustainable future for all. Buy this book now—you'll love it!"

—Puneeta Chhitwal-Varma, author of *Good Food, Healthy Planet*

Building a Sustainable Kitchen

Also by Naomi Hansen

Only in Saskatchewan:
Recipes & Stories from the Province's Best-Loved Eateries

Building a Sustainable Kitchen

A Practical Guide to Prioritizing the Planet from the Heart of Your Home

Naomi Hansen

Foreword by Elizabeth May, OC, MP

TOUCHWOOD

For more information, contact the publisher at:
TouchWood Editions
touchwoodeditions.com

Edited by Nara Monteiro
Copy edited by Meg Yamamoto
Proofread by Kate Kennedy
Cover illustration by Sara Oliveira
Cover and interior design by Alex Hennig

CATALOGUING DATA AVAILABLE FROM LIBRARY AND ARCHIVES CANADA

ISBN 9781771514736 (softcover)
ISBN 9781771514743 (electronic)

TouchWood Editions gratefully acknowledges that the land on which we live and work is within the traditional territories of the Lkwungen (Esquimalt and Songhees), Malahat, Pacheedaht, Scia'new, T'Sou-ke and W̱SÁNEĆ (Pauquachin, Tsartlip, Tsawout, Tseycum) peoples.

We acknowledge the financial support of the Government of Canada through the Canada Book Fund and the Canada Council for the Arts, and of the Province of British Columbia through the British Columbia Arts Council and the Book Publishing Tax Credit.

This book was produced using FSC®-certified, acid-free papers, processed chlorine free, and printed with soya-based inks.

Printed in Canada

30 29 28 27 26 1 2 3 4 5

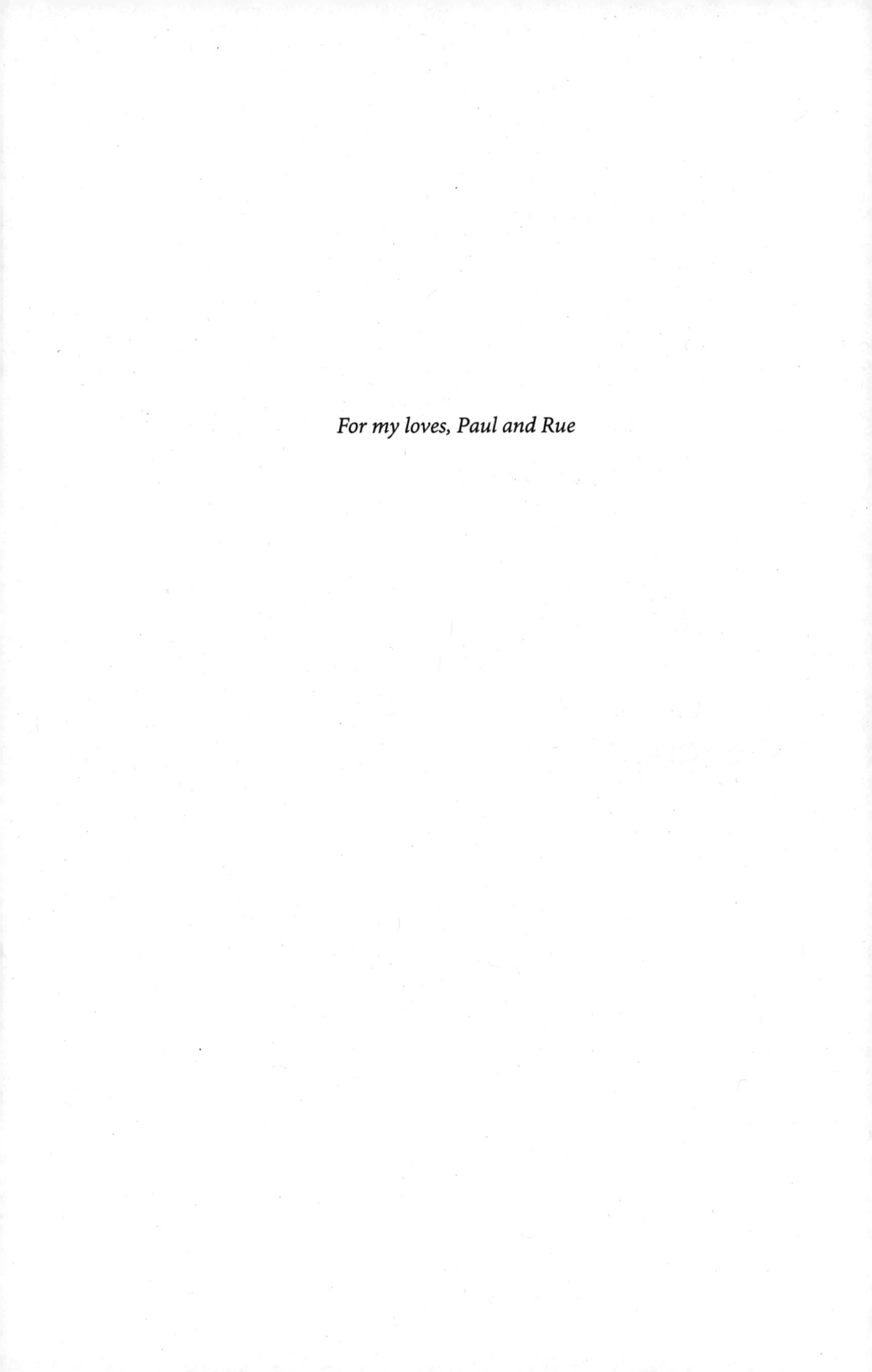

For my loves, Paul and Rue

AUTHOR'S NOTE

I researched and wrote *Building a Sustainable Kitchen* on Treaty 6 territory, which is the traditional territory of the Cree, Saulteaux, Dakota, and Nakota, and the homeland of the Métis Nation.

As a descendant of eastern European settlers, I acknowledge that I am a guest of this territory. I offer my gratitude to the Indigenous Peoples who have cared for and protected Treaty 6 territory for generations. Their understanding and knowledge of the land illuminates a path where the Earth and all its boundless beauty evokes deep respect, reciprocity, wonder, compassion, and appreciation. There is much to learn from this approach.

It is with both humility and reverence that I offer this book, knowing that any path forward must always take into account, and reconcile with, the past and its resounding impacts in the present.

TABLE OF CONTENTS

Foreword

AS I READ *Building a Sustainable Kitchen* I felt hope rising. Not since the best-selling, awareness-raising *Diet for a Small Planet* has an unassuming book been poised to revolutionize world views.

Back in 1971, Frances Moore Lappé's book made people aware that starvation was more about food distribution systems and inequity than about a lack of food. Her book, sprinkled with recipes for eating low on the food chain, was like manna from heaven for me. I had been a vegetarian since 1964, when at ten years old I stopped eating meat. There were no vegetarian cookbooks, or if there were, I had not found one. *Diet for a Small Planet* gave me an ethical justification for my vegetarianism. I had stopped eating anything that loved its mother. But reading *Diet for a Small Planet* gave me a more grown-up answer for why I was refusing to eat animals. Truth was, I had decided to stop eating meat after watching the Disney movie *Bambi*. More than that, Frances Moore Lappé's book launched a revolution in thinking about the waste of resources in society being committed to meat-based diets. More people could be healthy all around the world if we ate lower on the food chain.

Naomi Hansen has outdone Frances Moore Lappé! She has done the deep research to answer questions for the curious and ethical shopper. How does one make the right choice between recyclable or recycled? Between new gadgets and sticking with the old ones?

For a book that is built around the idea of the kitchen, she has delivered a revolutionary road map to changing our food systems, reducing waste, and improving health, with each chapter throwing light on subjects that are of deep interest to the climate-conscious consumer.

The message here is needed, and needed urgently. It is a profoundly hopeful book. Every choice we make can make a difference in the wider world. And her essential advice does not stop with the kitchen. It is my hope that it takes you to the ballot box, where the choices we make most profoundly impact our future. If we are to have a livable world in one hundred years, we need to cook up a storm—both figuratively and literally. We need citizen action and community resilience, and a kitchen is not a bad place to start!

As a woman political leader, my work life started in the kitchen. Literally. Cooking and waitressing in my family's restaurant was my pre-law background. Our restaurant, on an old schooner on the Cabot Trail, Cape Breton Island, was open in the summer months and closed up for the winter. I went from fighting against toxic pesticide spraying in the off-season, to cooking for a living all summer. Running a kitchen with an ethical lens has always been a challenge.

For many of us, the kitchen is the heart of the house. It gathers us all around the same table. It gives us a place for sharing. We share food and we share ideas. The heart of a global movement for resilience lies in connection, in social cohesion. Sustainable food means community in the same way that a fast-food drive-through increases alienation. Knowing how to cook is a powerful tool to cut household costs as well as to build community.

Reading the solutions built into every chapter will inspire every reader.

Live well, eat well, and change the world!

Elizabeth May, OC
Member of Parliament, Saanich—Gulf Islands
Leader, Green Party of Canada

Introduction

IF YOU'RE READING these words, I would venture a guess that you are concerned about what the future holds for both us and this beautiful planet. I am concerned about that too. I'm also going to make a second guess here: At various points in the past, you've probably wondered if there was any action you could personally take that would make a dent in climate change. If that's true, then we also have that in common. I often feel helpless when I hear about extreme weather events or read up on climate news. No matter what angle you approach it from, climate change seems like a problem almost too enormous to tackle. Although I want to be informed, I've often questioned whether it's even possible for anyone to inspire meaningful and lasting change in this realm. If it's not doable, then why bother trying?

But then I go outside. I look up at the towering elms that line the streets in our neighbourhood. Their grand trunks and outstretched arms tell a story of trees that have stood tall for decades. I see wildflowers poking up from our front flower bed, with more shades of pink and purple than you'd think possible for such tiny blooms. The big blue sky extends endlessly above, while the sun shines bright, sharing its warmth. Even in my small corner of the world—on a random day in Saskatoon, Saskatchewan—it's easy to see that the Earth is astonishing. There's no denying that nature is exquisite. The tiniest bug or a blade of grass is a wonder in its own right. So despite my feelings of despair, I can't help but think there must be some way to protect and save it all—the trees, the flowers, the bugs, and beyond. I simply cannot accept that nothing we do in this realm matters, or that our only option is to lament climate change's inevitability. I won't take these notions as reasonable excuses. There has to be more to the story.

My Journey to *Building a Sustainable Kitchen*

For years now, I have felt a gnawing need to do something—*anything*—to chip away at the problem that is climate change. Back in 2018, I felt this gnawing more keenly than ever before. That summer, smoke from wildfires near and far seemed unrelenting. I can remember a time when wildfire smoke was essentially non-existent in Saskatoon's summertime forecast. That now feels like a distant memory. But in the summer of 2018 in particular, when going outside meant being greeted by a persistent smoky haze, I realized I could no longer ignore the reality that climate change was happening. And if climate change was happening, there was only one thing to do. I had to become more engaged.

At the time, living low-waste seemed like the most obvious way to become more engaged in an individual, everyday sense. This solution was plastered everywhere, once you started looking for it—books, blogs, and social media alike. Ready to do my part, I willingly hopped on board. I began to spend my spare time reading about low-waste and minimalist lifestyles. I started a backyard compost. I bought cloth produce bags and used them at the grocery store. At a local sustainability shop, I stocked up on reusable kitchen items: beeswax wrap, stainless steel straws, cloth napkins, and more. I switched to a shampoo bar and a bamboo toothbrush and started buying natural deodorant in a refill format. Paul, my then-partner, now-husband, joined me in these changes. We even picked out matching reusable and collapsible silicone coffee cups, vowing to never use a disposable coffee cup again.

I began documenting the whole effort on my personal Instagram account for a small audience of family and friends. I called it "the sustainability project." At first, I thought the videos would just be a fun way to track our progress. Then my family and friends surprised me by showing great interest in the project. People started asking questions, so I started investigating the answers. Was there anywhere in Saskatoon where you could recycle plastic grocery bags? Where could someone drop off a light bulb that had burned out? Could you purchase non-plastic garbage bags anywhere in the city? Did such a thing even exist? These questions and more began to occupy my time, and I became increasingly intense about recycling, composting, and analyzing—okay, *overanalyzing*—anything we threw away.

Then came the COVID-19 pandemic. Almost immediately, everything I had been doing was put on pause. Bringing your own reusable mug or cloth produce bags into a café or grocery store was understandably no longer an option. Although I was initially pained about the overnight halt on most of my sustainability efforts, I have to be honest with you here. As time went on, I stopped caring. I was both defeated and preoccupied by the reality of the pandemic. Paul and I had to cancel our wedding, and he spent long days finishing up his university degree from our kitchen table. We were both at home around the clock, and I was anxious about everything. I constantly refreshed the news, searching for some sort of explanation or resolution that simply did not exist. Sustainability took a serious back seat during this period of my life, and it stayed there for much longer than I care to admit.

I don't need to explain to you that the pandemic was terrible though. So let's fast-forward to a couple of years later. With the publication of my first book under my belt, and the pandemic gradually fading into a foggy bad dream, I had time and space to think. I knew that summer wildfires weren't getting any better. If anything, they seemed to be getting worse. One day, while I was brushing my teeth with my bamboo toothbrush—I never quit buying the bamboo toothbrushes—it dawned on me to examine the link between climate change and reusable, low-waste items. The fact that I was a bit older now (read: wiser) certainly aided in this cross-examination. How did my bamboo toothbrush relate to larger problems like wildfires, if at all? The link between these two things did not appear overly direct, and I craved more information. Was there a tangible connection between low-waste living and climate change? Were some individual actions more hard-hitting than others?

I began reading more broadly on sustainability and climate change. Then, I began writing about it too. I pitched article ideas to various news sources and magazines, because I wanted to research the topics anyway. I was assigned articles on lifestyle topics like reducing food waste, explaining compostable plastics, and exploring whether or not beef could be sustainable. As I dived into these topics and more, I discovered that my previous sustainability project had fallen a bit short. While I had been on the right track, I had missed or maybe even ignored important details. In hindsight, I had not properly done my homework before hopping on board. Now that I was reading, researching, and writing more, I discovered a number of facts that surprised me. For starters, being more sustainable wasn't really about stocking up on reusable stuff, like cloth produce bags or stainless steel straws. Being more sustainable wasn't about creating a more intense home recycling set-up either. These actions aren't bad—don't get me wrong. We will dive into all of this and more in the chapters to come. But these actions merely scratch the surface of both the depth and reach that individual action can have. While these actions are on the right track, the track in question is long and complex.

Meanwhile, I had a second realization: Other people were interested in these topics too. When push comes to shove, many people genuinely care about the trees, the flowers, and even the bugs. Many also view nature as exquisite, something to be saved and protected. And many people understand that we are not separate from nature; instead, our very well-being is directly tied up with that of the environment.

But people are busy with everyday life. They simply do not have time to research the climate impact of individual actions. Without this information, or even a sense of where to find it, they may not know how to start or what to do. As my own knowledge expanded, it occurred to me that sharing what I had learned with others was an important piece of the puzzle. When faced with a problem as big as climate change, there is simply no sense in not sharing solutions. We are truly all in this together, whether we like it or not.

These realizations eventually turned into the idea for *Building a Sustainable Kitchen*. There's a large intersection between food, climate change, and what we do in the kitchen. I decided that I wanted to explore that intersection in a way that made it easy for other people to understand. I knew kitchens, and I knew food—and I knew I could figure out the rest.

We're going to zoom out from food and kitchens for a moment here, just so I can explain a few key concepts. Understanding sustainability and climate change will help form the foundation for the rest of this book. Then we'll get back to the kitchen, I promise.

Understanding Sustainability

Sustainability is a word that gets thrown around a lot. I sometimes hesitate to use this word in the first place, because it can admittedly seem like a bit of a buzzword. *Sustainability* can be applied to food, health, fashion, finance, agriculture—you name it, there's probably a sustainable version. But I think part of the reason *sustainability* is used so frequently is because it's an incredibly fitting way to describe whether something is working long-term or not.

There are many different definitions of sustainability out there. For example, in 1987 the United Nations defined the term as "meeting the needs of the present without compromising the ability of future generations to meet their own needs." I like this definition because, while straightforward, it encompasses a lot. Other, more lengthy definitions often focus on the three pillars of sustainability, which are economic, social, and environmental factors, along with how these elements overlap. Environmental sustainability is the one factor I'm primarily concerned with in this book, but the environment does not exist in a vacuum. So economic and social factors inevitably appear here and there throughout this book as well.

Environmental sustainability is rooted in the belief that we are both intricately linked to and dependent on nature and other living things. This notion acknowledges that if we want future generations to be able to fulfill their needs, we have to ensure that we don't exploit the environment or natural resources in the interim. Overall, I think the simplest way to think about environmental sustainability in its ideal form is like this: We can continue to do whatever it is we're doing now, into the future. In doing so, we won't cause harm to the environment. That continuity doesn't mean that environmental sustainability is rigid or static—quite the opposite. Sustainability is inherently adaptable on an ongoing basis to ensure that it consistently delivers on its future promises. At its core, sustainability is proactive and forward thinking. If something is sustainable, then it makes sense both in the here and now, and further down the road.

The problem is that many things about the way our world operates are unsustainable. In other words, we *are* causing harm to the environment. If we keep this up and don't change anything, it will serve only to exacerbate climate change.

Understanding Climate Change

What is climate change, anyway? If you already know the answer to this question, feel free to skip ahead. If not, I'll give you a brief primer.

When people talk about climate change, they are talking about significant, long-term changes in weather patterns. This includes changes in temperature, precipitation, humidity, and more, measured over extended periods of time, typically decades. Historically speaking, natural events like a massive volcanic eruption can trigger these types of significant climate change. But current climate change is not happening because of a massive volcanic eruption—it's happening because of human activities.

The human activities in question are primarily those that cause greenhouse gas emissions. When we burn fossil fuels like gas, oil, or coal, greenhouse gases are emitted into the atmosphere. Burning fossil fuels is the number one source of human-caused greenhouse gas emissions. The greenhouse gas we emit most is carbon dioxide, which is the gas that tends to get the most attention. There are other greenhouse gases, though, like methane and nitrous oxide, for example, both of which will come up later on.

Greenhouse gases are aptly named because they essentially absorb heat and then re-emit that heat back to the surface, warming the Earth. One analogy commonly used to explain this likens greenhouse gases to a blanket. The blanket wraps around the Earth, absorbing heat and making things warm. But when too many greenhouse gases are emitted, the blanket becomes increasingly thick, making the Earth warmer than it should be. This then causes the Earth's surface temperature to rise.

I'm going to run with the blanket analogy here. Imagine that your entire body is wrapped tightly in a wool blanket. You'd probably be feeling pretty warm. Then, let's say someone else is actively knitting the blanket, adding more and more wool while it's still wrapped around your body. What would happen? You would get progressively warmer and your body temperature would rise. If you were wrapped in that ever-growing blanket for an extended period of time—say, decades—the outlook for you in this situation would obviously not be good.

The wool in this example represents the greenhouse gases we continue emitting, largely from fossil fuels we keep burning. The more greenhouse gas that's emitted, the warmer it gets. Guess what the rise in the Earth's temperature from warming is known as? You got it—global warming. Increased global warming leads to increased climate change. All of this shows up in our lives as escalating weather events like droughts, floods, fires, heat waves, and more. The Earth is a system, though, so any given climate impact inevitably has ripple effects. From melting polar ice to water scarcity to negative consequences for plant, animal, and human life, these impacts are all connected.

To reiterate, the root cause of all of this is *human activity* from emitting greenhouse gases. The Intergovernmental Panel on Climate Change (IPCC)—which is part of the United Nations and regarded as the global scientific authority on climate change—reports that between 2011 and 2020, the Earth's average surface temperature reached 1.1°C above its recorded average temperature between 1850 and 1900. The IPCC also reports that since 1970, the surface temperature has risen much faster than at any other point in the last two thousand years. Although a temperature rise of 1.1°C might sound minor, it's absolutely not. The world is already experiencing many of the impacts I mentioned—droughts, heat waves, flooding, and more. Furthermore, since the IPCC released these numbers in the early 2020s, other organizations have noted that the Earth's average surface temperature has already inched past 1.1°C and continues to rise. But continued increases in temperature will only make these impacts worse. It has been widely stated that every single fraction of a degree in warming will quite literally make a difference here. What type of difference? The difference in how extreme the impacts of climate change become. Meaning: the difference in whether or not future generations inherit a livable Earth and can meet their own needs.

Much of the world has agreed that in order to prevent the worst of the worst, warming needs to stay below 2°C but ideally be limited to 1.5°C. This was formally agreed upon in a legally binding international treaty—known as the Paris Agreement—which came into effect in 2016. Nearly all of the countries in the world have adopted the Paris Agreement, including Canada. Like other countries, Canada has committed to reducing its greenhouse gas emissions to net zero by 2050. Net-zero emissions means that no greenhouse gases are being emitted, or that any emissions are somehow being offset. To make net zero a reality, we need to stop adding more greenhouse gases—or, in the blanket analogy, more wool. We also need to start unravelling the blanket, by improving and inventing ways to remove greenhouse gases from the atmosphere. If we don't do this, and warming surpasses 1.5°C or even

2°C—which it is on track to do by the end of the century—the world is looking at a future of unimaginable loss. Certain areas of the planet could become uninhabitable by humans and a whole host of other species.

No matter how you look at it, achieving net-zero emissions will require enormous change in how the world operates. This includes how we produce food, how we make goods, how we use energy, and how we travel and transport ourselves. In short, net zero requires a full-scale shift from the unsustainable to the sustainable. But that full-scale shift should have started yesterday—to put it lightly. We do not have unlimited time to tackle this. And some climate impacts will be irreversible. If we lose the polar ice, for example, there is no way to get it back in any sort of fathomable timeline.

Before we move on to how all of this relates to food and the kitchen, I want to quickly address two other related concepts that will come up later on. Given carbon dioxide's prominence as a greenhouse gas, it's typically used as a reference point. One widely used reference point is the concept of a "carbon footprint," which you've probably heard of before. A carbon footprint refers to how much greenhouse gas is being emitted by any given entity, usually measured on an annual basis. You and I can calculate our carbon footprints to measure our own personal greenhouse gas emissions—there are many online calculators that do this. Carbon footprints can also be used to measure emissions from many other entities, like families, buildings, organizations, products, and businesses.

A second and related concept is "carbon dioxide equivalent," which is a measurement that's used to compare greenhouse gases. Different greenhouse gases vary in both their ability to trap heat and their lifetime in the atmosphere. Let's say that, hypothetically, a company emits *x* amount of carbon dioxide and *x* amount of methane. This company needs to be compared with a different company that emits *x* amount of nitrous oxide. Rather than measuring these gases and their impact individually, they can instead be converted into their carbon dioxide equivalent. Doing so makes it easier to both compare and measure emissions overall.

Explaining climate change could take hours or days if you wanted to do the topic justice. That's why other books are dedicated to this topic alone. If you want to understand climate change in greater depth, I highly recommend exploring other sources. Throughout *Building a Sustainable Kitchen*, I mention many of the concepts we just discussed—climate change, carbon dioxide equivalent, greenhouse gas emissions, and more. Feel free to come back to this section for reference as much as you need. These are big concepts, so the more familiar you become with them, the easier they'll be to digest.

Why Food and Kitchens?

All right, back to the kitchen. What, exactly, is the intersection between climate change, food, and kitchens? Although burning fossil fuels is the main source of human-caused greenhouse gas emissions, it's not the only one. Many elements of food and kitchens have a part to play, particularly when they're considered on a collective and cumulative scale. For example, greenhouse gases are generated when food waste rots in landfills, through the production of food itself, or any time something new is manufactured—from a glass bottle to a small appliance.

Many food- and kitchen-related actions also appear on acclaimed lists of climate solutions. Project Drawdown, for example, is a highly regarded non-profit organization that works to map out climate solutions that are effective, efficient, and rooted in science. It has a list of nearly one hundred climate solutions, which revolve around how the world can reduce greenhouse gas emissions to achieve "drawdown." Drawdown refers to the point at which intentional human efforts will begin to trigger a decrease in the amount of greenhouse gases in the atmosphere. And guess what? Many of Project Drawdown's proposed solutions have to do with food and kitchens. Some of these solutions require broader system changes, involving agriculture and fisheries, for example. But other solutions have a clear and direct link to individual, everyday action, like composting, curbing food waste, and changing the type of food we're eating. Therefore, many of Project Drawdown's solutions overlap with the topics covered in this book. This means that many of the solutions in this book have an impact on reducing greenhouse gas emissions—which ultimately reduces your individual or household carbon footprint too.

Another way to frame the intersection between all of these things is to think of the kitchen as a portal. Aside from my home office, I spend a lot of time in the kitchen during the day, whether I'm cooking, eating, putting away groceries, doing the dishes, or dealing with our household waste. This makes the kitchen a sort of window to a number of wider problems and solutions. For example: Household kitchen garbage is linked to landfills. Daily use of plastics is related to plastic pollution. The type of food we buy and eat is connected to the wider impacts associated with how food is produced. When we use appliances that draw on non-renewable sources of energy, this involves fossil fuels. Gardening is related to building climate resilience. The pervasiveness of single-use, disposable food and kitchen items tells us a lot about our throwaway economy. I'll stop here because I'm sure you get it, but the list could go on and on.

Of course, none of this is to suggest that other areas of your home are any less important than the kitchen. As we move through the chapters, you'll come across many instances where I've noted that a given solution can be applied to the rest of your home. Some solutions can also be applied outside of the home—like in the workplace, for example. There's plenty of crossover, because it's not like the kitchen is the only place where food, plastics, and waste appear. But starting with a specific area and then scaling up helps make it less daunting to implement sustainable changes. And given its prominence in our daily lives, I think the kitchen is a good place to start.

But Does Individual Action Really Matter?

I have to address this question, because I know many people seriously doubt the effectiveness of individual action. The reality is that this is too complicated a question to have a single, clear-cut answer. Although I'm going to give you my own take here, in the end, you have to decide how you want to answer this question for yourself.

Let's imagine that climate change is a gigantic, unmoving boulder. One day, I decide to approach this boulder to see if I can do anything about it. Once I get close to the boulder, I can barely see the top or sides of it—it's just so massive. But I've brought along a small hammer, so I start chipping away at the rock anyway, hoping to make even a dent. At first, nothing happens. The boulder seems impenetrable, and it's not like I have any sort of flashy tools or technology in tow. Still, I keep showing up and hammering away. Slowly but surely, a small dent appears. Encouraged, I keep going. With time, my small dent gives way to a larger dent. It's still a dent, to be sure, but it's a dent nonetheless.

Now, what if I am joined in this scenario by a million other people? A million people chipping away at the boulder means that eventually, it will crack. Plus, every now and then, someone who comes along will inevitably cause a crack on their own—perhaps due to a certain perspective or the amount of force they approached the boulder with. The Swedish climate activist Greta Thunberg is a great example of this: Greta's efforts have caused much more than a crack in the metaphorical climate change boulder, to say the least.

In actuality, you have no way of predicting what your own small dent may turn into. You also have no way of foreseeing if your efforts will inspire anyone else, or lead to further collective change. Other people may join the endeavour, simply from observing you out there labouring away. Maybe one of the people who joins happens to have a tool that's better than a hammer, which makes the process that much easier. But if nobody chips away at the rock, and everybody waits for someone else to do the work, then we can be sure the boulder will remain unchanged.

So my personal answer to the question is that individual action does matter. However, this does not mean that individuals alone can fix climate change by themselves. I am not operating under the pretense that my own food waste or packaging reduction efforts at home will single-handedly stop climate change. They won't. Because while individual changes can do a lot, larger system changes can do much more. By this I mean changes to industry, infrastructure, and government or corporate policy, for example. These types of shifts are essential to getting the world to net zero and beyond. But while the burden of addressing climate change shouldn't rest on individual shoulders alone, if individuals don't demonstrate that they care about the boulder in the first place, larger system changes are much less likely to happen.

Both of these types of changes can and should happen at the same time—I don't see why we need to pick one or the other. As noted earlier, Project Drawdown's list of nearly one hundred climate solutions includes both individual *and* system-level changes. Of these solutions, one-third can effectively be addressed by individuals and households in particular. *One-third*. That's far from insignificant.

We honestly don't have time to get stuck in the mud debating this or that anyway. Remember: Every fraction of a degree in warming matters. I don't mean to freak you out by repeating this fact, but I do mean to stress the importance and severity of this moment in time. So if I were to answer "No" to the question of whether or not individual action is relevant, where does that leave me? It leaves me feeling anxious, helpless, and hopeless. It leaves me filled with an overwhelming sense of dread. It leaves me feeling like there's no option but to sit back and watch climate change happen, despite the fact that the Earth is astonishing. Frankly, none of this is helpful for climate change or my own mental health.

At the end of the day, we all live within the systems around us and we're all part of the collective—again, whether we like it or not. We have to remember that the collective is not some sort of amorphous, elusive being. It's *literally* made up of individuals. Therefore, any changes that happen on a collective scale can typically be traced back to individual changes at some point. This is the difference between one person chipping away at the boulder, and a million other people joining them. It's also the difference between thinking of individual action as being isolated, versus being a part of something bigger. In an isolated scenario, it's much easier to feel like nothing you do will help change the situation. In the second, collective option, you trust that you are not alone and that what you do can have an impact as part of a greater whole. From there, you just keep going and doing what you can. Personally, I choose the second option.

How to Use This Book

Each chapter of *Building a Sustainable Kitchen* features a different topic related to sustainability in the kitchen. The chapters include background information on the "why," which dives into the environmental issues and impacts associated with each topic. This part of the chapter is where I show you that everyday things—like what we eat or what we throw in the garbage—are related to larger challenges. The depth and length of this first section varies from chapter to chapter, because some actions have a larger overall impact than others.

From there, each chapter has a "What You Can Do" section that moves through various solutions. Most chapters have multiple solutions, but know that these are *not* ranked in order of importance. In some cases, the solutions simply build on one another. Whenever possible, I have provided solutions that are realistic and affordable and take into account differences based on where readers live. You might want to apply all of the solutions in a chapter, or there may be one or two that are a better fit for you. When we talk about grocery shopping, for example, you'll see that there's no such thing as a one-size-fits-all solution. Sometimes I also mention products or brands in the solutions. However, I am not affiliated with any of the products or brands I note in the book; all recommendations are genuinely my own.

Although each chapter is a different topic, I strongly recommend reading the book in order. Each chapter builds on the previous ones, and many concepts that come up early in the book will appear again later on. So even though there's a full "Plastics" chapter, for example, plastics also appear in the "Recycling" and "Disposables and Reusables" chapters before it. There is a lot of crossover between the topics in this book, because in some ways, each topic is connected to the next one. I've put the chapters in a specific order to help make sense of that.

It was important to me to write *Building a Sustainable Kitchen* from a distinctly Canadian perspective. I have included Canadian statistics, information, and solutions whenever possible. I also conducted over eighty interviews for this book, and I tried to prioritize speaking with Canadian experts whenever I could. Of course, climate change and sustainability are global topics, so there are many cases where the book takes a wider view. But on the whole, if there was an opportunity to bring the examples or the information back into a Canadian context, I did that. I hope this book is as useful for someone living in Yukon or Nova Scotia as it is for someone living in Ontario or Saskatchewan.

As a companion to this book, you can find a Resources List online, linked on page 309. I collected the materials for the Resources List as I did my research, and I used many of the noted resources myself as I made changes in my own life. Throughout the book there are plenty of recommendations from me on when to check the Resources List for further reading. I hope you'll find these resources as helpful as I did.

On that note, I hope you'll consider *Building a Sustainable Kitchen* a resource in itself. What I'm about to say may sound blasphemous coming from an author, but I encourage you to write in the margins, fold down the corners, underline sentences and paragraphs, and take notes throughout. I do this all the time with the books I read, and I find it helps me learn more effectively. Doing so also makes it much easier to come back later on and reread or reference certain sections that stood out to you. So please, treat this book like a guidebook or a resource in its own right—I implore you to do so.

As you read, keep in mind that this is meant to be a journey. I did not mean for you to implement all of the solutions within the span of a few days or even weeks. Researching, writing, and implementing the solutions in this book took me over a year. I had already been using some of the solutions for years prior to that anyway. So keep in mind that having a sense of *personal* sustainability is important too. The point of this book is not to change everything immediately. If you attempt to tackle everything in a short amount of time, you may end up just giving up. Instead, the point is to make changes on a consistent, ongoing basis so that you can successfully sustain those changes in the long run. Start with something that makes sense to you, and then scale up from there.

The Journey Begins

If I had to sum up *Building a Sustainable Kitchen* in one phrase, it would be this: one person's journey to making their kitchen more sustainable. That's it. I'm the one person here. I am not a scientist or a climate expert. I am just someone who is concerned about the changes that are happening to our Earth, and I'm interested in how my own actions play a role in that. My driving question throughout the entire book is this: How can I reduce my own environmental impact and carbon footprint as much as possible, within the realm of all things food and kitchens? At its core, this journey is really about understanding how the kitchen and food connect us to wider issues of climate change. This journey isn't fancy or elaborate. It's tangible, realistic, and down to earth. I promise that I'll be as honest as possible with you, every step of the way.

Although I'm not a scientist or a climate expert, I firmly believe that sustainability is not a topic reserved for those with accolades or credentials in the matter. Sustainability is for everyone. You and I are both part of the collective, which means we both belong here. But it also means that we both have a responsibility to learn from scientists and climate experts. Thankfully, it's never too late to start learning.

So please know that this is not an exclusive club, and there are no prerequisites for becoming informed and engaged. If you are concerned about climate change, then sustainability is for you. If you believe the Earth is astonishing, then sustainability is for you. If you are willing to try making even a dent in the boulder, then trust me when I say *sustainability is undoubtedly for you.*

Allow me to officially welcome you to my journey—I sincerely hope it becomes your journey too.

CHAPTER 1:

Food Waste

I DECIDED TO START *Building a Sustainable Kitchen* with a chapter on food waste for three reasons. First, food waste is one area where it's easy to see how individual action matters. Although throwing away some long-gone leftovers might not seem like a big deal, the environmental toll of wasted food adds up significantly when measured on a collective scale—so every little bit really does count.

Second, focusing on food waste is a win not only for the environment, but for you too. Reducing food waste will save you money, and it's relatively easy to do, especially when compared with some other climate-conscious actions in this book.

The third and final reason is that writing about food waste felt like a natural starting point for me personally. A few years ago—before I even began daydreaming about *Building a Sustainable Kitchen*—I wrote an article for *Canadian Living* that detailed tips on how to prevent food waste at home. After that article was published, I was cleaning out our fridge on a random Sunday afternoon, when I realized rather suddenly that I too had something to learn from the article. I had just thrown some slimy cucumbers and wilted spinach into our compost bin for no good reason, other than that I had forgotten about them over the course of the week. In that moment, it was immediately clear to me that the article's takeaways were applicable to my own daily habits. And so, that food waste article became a catalyst for making changes in my own kitchen.

When I started consciously reducing our household food waste, I was taken aback by the quantity of food we were throwing away. I honestly didn't think we wasted that much food. But once I started paying attention, I quickly realized I had been grossly underestimating the amount.

At our house, the household garbage, recycling, and compost bins are all located in the back alley, so if I take any waste out to them, I can't see it after that point. Unless they work in waste management, most people don't just hang around the municipal landfill or compost on a regular basis. As a result, it's easy to forget about waste once you've dropped it into your household bins. I believe that we waste food, in large part, because once that waste is out of sight, it's also out of mind. If we're not being mindful about food waste on an everyday basis, it's easy to either ignore or overlook how much food is actually being thrown away—which is exactly what I had been doing for years.

What Is Food Waste and Why Does It Even Matter?

At this point you may be wondering what I mean by food waste. Some definitions include both the edible and inedible parts of food—say, the orange and its peel—while other definitions concentrate on edible waste that is otherwise avoidable. I want to be clear on this: The food waste I'm talking about here is entirely avoidable, meaning that I am not suggesting you chow down on a chicken carcass for dinner in the name of sustainability. Instead, when I say "food waste," I am referring to food that could have been consumed at some point. This includes beverages too. If you take a look in your fridge or freezer on any given day of the week, chances are there are a few food items lurking in its depths that have been there well past their prime. Or perhaps there is food just sitting pretty in your fridge door—the unofficial place for all things used once and forgotten. Food waste includes the avocado that got mushy unexpectedly fast, the spaghetti leftovers that nobody felt like eating, and the milk that sat in the fridge too long and curdled. Eventually, you will likely notice these items, sigh at the fact that they're long gone despite your best intentions, and toss them into the trash or compost.

What Food Waste Costs Us

It's estimated that around 63 percent, or nearly two-thirds, of the food that Canadians throw away could have been eaten at some point. This means that on average, every household in Canada wastes approximately 140 kilograms of food per year, which is about $1,300 worth of food. In grocery terms, 140 kilograms is the weight equivalent of thirty-one 4.54-kilogram bags of potatoes, or 308 standard-sized loaves of bread. I am confident that nobody would knowingly purchase 308 loaves of bread and then immediately throw them in the garbage. But what about throwing away a few pieces of bread every day for a year? Maybe, especially if you're not really paying close attention. The total waste that results from throwing away a little bit of bread every day makes clear that food waste is a cumulative issue. When we think about what that quantity of food actually looks like over time, it's staggering.

I wanted to see for myself if this $1,300 number was accurate, so I conducted a week-long experiment where I paid absolutely no attention to reducing our household food waste. I ignored my usual waste-reducing tactics and just let the fridge do its thing. At the end of the week, prior to my next grocery shop, I tallied up the avoidable food waste. I had to chuck out half of a large container of spinach ($4), three-quarters of a loaf of bread ($3), one leftover serving of a ground turkey and pasta dish ($4), a large container of mushrooms ($5), and a jug of kefir ($4). In total, the food I threw out came to approximately $20.

While this might not sound like much, if every week I throw out $20 worth of food, that is $80 per month, or $1,040 per year, just a couple of hundred dollars shy of $1,300. With that same amount of money, I could easily pay for a lovely weekend getaway with Paul or buy myself a brand new bike. You can visualize this however you want—308 loaves of bread, a brand new bike, or some other item of a comparable cost that is being purchased and thrown out every year. Again, and again, and again.

On a global scale, about one-third of the total food produced worldwide for humans to eat is either lost or wasted. Yes, you read that right: *one-third.* All throughout the food supply chain there is potential for food to be wasted, from the moment the food is grown or produced to the moment it lands on a grocery shelf. Food waste that is generated during these initial phases of the supply chain is considered "food loss" and can result from a variety of causes like incorrect harvest timing, poor weather, or lack of proper storage.

Once it's at the consumer end, food waste generally comes from three sources: households, food service, and retail. The United Nations Environment Programme's Food Waste Index Report noted that in 2022, global food waste amounted to just over one billion tonnes. Of that, 60 percent came from households, followed by about 27 percent from food service, and, finally, 13 percent from retail.

While it's clear that there are problems to address in a number of areas, avoidable household food waste *does* account for the majority. And if it seems like food waste is a problem that only people with excessive disposable income could possibly have, what's surprising is that it's not. That same United Nations report also noted that the rate of household food waste per capita is similar in lower-middle-, upper-middle-, and higher-income countries, indicating that this truly is a global problem.

What Food Waste Costs the Planet

Household food waste is not only wasteful when it comes to the food itself; think about all of the resources that are wasted in the process by association. Take carrots, for example: The seeds are planted, the crop is tended to, the vegetables are harvested when ready. Then the carrots are stored and transported, making their way to the final destination. Once there, the carrots are displayed for sale and purchased by someone, and if they're not eaten, they will be either composted or tossed into a garbage bin. If they're destined for the latter, they will likely end up there with their packaging intact too—most often plastic. So when we throw those carrots away, we also throw away all of the resources and time that went into the process of growing, producing, harvesting, packaging, transporting, storing, distributing, and retailing them.

What happens next is not any better, I'm sorry to say. When food waste makes its way to the landfill—as it often does if organics or composting programs do not exist in a given location—it generates greenhouse gas emissions, specifically methane gas.

Why does this happen? Because when organic waste like edible food, inedible food scraps, or even yard waste is put into the landfill, it will not break down or decompose properly. To properly decompose, organic waste needs oxygen, which is certainly lacking in a landfill, where the waste is usually in plastic bags. Even if it's unbagged, it's still packed down tightly like sardines. As a result of the lack of oxygen, organic waste in landfills naturally produces methane.

What's so bad about methane? It's an incredibly potent greenhouse gas, and the second most common greenhouse gas caused by human activity—remember, carbon dioxide is the first. Methane is short-lived by comparison; its lifespan is up to twelve years, compared with carbon dioxide's lifespan of centuries. But during its lifetime it packs a heat-trapping punch. When methane and carbon dioxide are compared over a twenty-year period, methane's ability to trap heat in the atmosphere is eighty times more powerful than carbon dioxide's, meaning that it has a clear impact on global warming.

Methane accounts for about 16 percent of Canada's overall greenhouse gas emissions. Just under a fifth of those methane emissions comes from landfills, while the rest comes from sources like agriculture, and oil and gas. For context though, emissions from annual food waste in Canada are estimated to equal those caused by 2.1 million cars. That's just for Canada, in one year alone. On a global scale, food loss and waste combined are responsible for 8–10 percent of the world's total annual greenhouse gas emissions. Which is, needless to say, a lot. But this also means that if efforts were made to cut global methane emissions from food loss and waste, it would have a significant impact on reducing greenhouse gas emissions. This is especially true given how potent methane is, combined with its shorter lifespan.

This is where we can see the direct impact of our actions: The food we throw in the garbage produces methane in landfills, contributing to greenhouse gas emissions and global warming. Meaning that food you or I have thrown into the garbage in the past might have already generated methane, might be producing methane right now, or will cause methane in the future. The same can be said of your neighbours, friends, and family—and anyone anywhere who has ever thrown food into the garbage.

Composting food waste is certainly a better option than putting it in the garbage, given that the food will properly decompose. Municipal organics programs are largely put in place for this very reason. Diverting organic waste away from landfills both saves landfill space and reduces methane emissions (we'll dive into this more in the "Composting" chapter starting on page 117). Unfortunately, municipal organics programs do not exist everywhere in Canada, home composting is not an option for everyone, and composting alone cannot solve the food waste problem.

To illustrate this point, let's go back to those carrots once more. We have to remember all of the resources—and the subsequent environmental impact—used during the process of getting the carrots from the farm to your fridge. If you throw those unused carrots into the compost rather than the garbage, they will properly decompose—which is a good thing. But either way, all the water, energy, labour, and more it took to make the carrots have still been wasted. Which is why we need to prioritize reducing that waste in the first place.

What You Can Do

Take Stock: Build Awareness of Your Food Waste Habits

The recipe for change starts with mindfulness. But in order to bring mindfulness into the equation, you have to understand how much food you are wasting. The best way to figure this out is by conducting your own weekly food waste experiment.

Prior to your next grocery shop, take stock of your fridge, freezer, and pantry to see what food needs to be thrown out, and pile everything that is avoidable food waste onto your kitchen table. Then add up approximately how much money you are about to throw away. Multiply the dollar amount by four to get a sense of the monthly amount. Then, multiply the original weekly amount by fifty-two to get a sense of the yearly total. Write this down somewhere—put a sticky note on the cupboard or the fridge—so it serves as a visual reminder. You can repeat this exercise as often as you want to really drive home the point and track your progress.

The second reason this experiment is useful is that you will get a sense of what types of food you are wasting. In Canada, the most commonly wasted foods are vegetables, fruit, and leftovers, followed by bakery items and then dairy/eggs. This is in line with my own food waste experiment where two of the items I wasted were produce, one was leftovers, one was bread, and one was dairy. This also makes sense logically because these types of foods are much more perishable than, let's say, a can of beans.

Once you have a visual of how much food you're wasting and what types of foods you're wasting most often, you can choose to incorporate solutions that work best for you. No two weekly food waste experiments are going to be the same because no two households are the same, so your own journey to reducing food waste will probably vary from your neighbour's.

Take Stock Again: Check In with Your Fridge, Freezer, and Pantry Regularly

Part of ensuring you don't waste food means frequently checking what's going on in your fridge, freezer, and pantry. I wish I could tell you this is the type of task you can put on a list, complete once, and then cross off forever—I love those types of tasks. But it's not. Instead, checking in with your fridge, freezer, and pantry is an ongoing task that you must turn into a habit. There is no way around this. If you don't know what's happening in your fridge, freezer, and pantry, and you continue adding more food to these three areas, you are going to end up wasting food.

In my experience, the fridge needs more regular checking than the freezer or pantry. I like to check my fridge two times a week—usually mid-week and then again near the end of the week—to see what needs to be used up. Then I make a mental note of this information, along with a plan of what to do. You can be as formal or informal as you want about these regular fridge checks. Maybe you make a 10:00 AM date with yourself on Wednesdays and Saturdays where you check your fridge, or maybe you just check "mid-week," which might vary in day and time. There's no specific way to do this, so choose what makes the most sense for you.

When it comes to the pantry and freezer, both of these areas are particular problem spots because—just like the household waste bins in my back alley—they are often out of sight and out of mind. Plus, it's nearly impossible to simply remember everything you've bought and stored in the freezer or pantry over time. Instead, you have to be intentional about checking both of these locations at regular intervals.

Here's what I do: Every four to six months, I do a full inventory of my pantry, my freezer, and the items in my fridge that I don't buy regularly—like the condiment and sauce gang hanging out in the fridge door. I go through *everything* and write a list for myself of the food I have in each place that needs to be used up within the coming weeks or months. If needed, I also mark down a timeline for using these items up. Examples from my current list: "a few leftover lasagna noodles in the top pantry," "chicken carcass frozen upstairs for stock," and "two bags of frozen apples from last summer in the basement freezer." Then I tack these lists onto the fridge so I can see them easily. Before I head to the grocery store, I always check my inventory lists to see what I could make that week that incorporates some of the foods I already have. I find making this inventory list actually saves me work and time down the road, especially when it comes to frozen leftovers. I might otherwise forget about a random serving of stew I tossed in the freezer a few months ago, but when I see it on the list, I remember to heat it up and then I don't have to make dinner.

As I use up the food on the inventory list, I cross it off—not only because it's a great visual for seeing where you're at, but also because it's fun. If I'm being honest, I've turned this into a little game for myself. We could call this the "How much food can I *not* waste?" game board. Bring out the fancy pens, use headings, create bonus points for meals that cross two items off the list, use images, make it colour-coded, make a spreadsheet—make it whatever you want. Because how you decide to take regular inventory doesn't matter. What *does* matter is that you do it.

Plan Ahead, at the Store and at Home

Planning is genuinely one of the most helpful tools in the tool box when it comes to reducing household food waste. Without a plan at home, you're more likely to waste food, and without a plan at the store, you're more likely to rely on in-the-moment judgment, which isn't always our best friend. Listening to in-the-moment judgment typically results in purchasing more food than we actually need, which leads to more waste. To illustrate this point, I'm going to tell you a sad story about some mint chocolate chips.

Once upon a time, I was in the bakery aisle of the grocery store when I happened upon the chocolate chip section and saw some mint chocolate chips. The Christmas holidays were right around the corner, and the mint chocolate chip bags were marked "limited edition." I never use mint in baking because neither Paul nor I really like it, but I thought to myself, "These are limited; I might need them at some point." That day, marketing got the best of me. I tossed one bag of mint chocolate chips into my grocery cart.

A couple of months later, when I was making my regular inventory list, I noticed the mint chocolate chip bag, checked the best-before date, and saw that it was only a month away. So I wrote down "mint chips" on my list of items in the pantry to use up soon. But even though the mint chips were on my inventory list, I did not use them. I read the list regularly and I thought about baking some mint chocolate chip cookies. But I made no attempt to actually do this. Why? Because I don't like mint chocolate.

Five months later, when the mint chips were still in my cupboard and their best-before date had long since passed, I happened to receive a mint dark chocolate bar from a family member. I ate that particular bar, and to my surprise, I really enjoyed it. Then, suddenly, I remembered the mint chips sitting in my cupboard. I figured that if by that point I wasn't going to bake something with them, I might as well just eat them plain. So I went to the cupboard, opened the bag, dumped a handful into my palm, and popped them into my mouth.

I was flooded with instant regret. Not only were the mint chips incredibly stale, but I could tell immediately that they would have been too sweet for my taste buds anyway. And so, after all that, the mint chips ended up in my compost pail.

I am telling you this story because we all have some version of a mint chocolate chip bag hiding in our cupboards. We buy things we do not need, we buy things because they're new, we buy things we do not like because they're a good deal, and we buy things we don't know how to use but promise ourselves we'll figure it out. And then we throw these things away. I cannot stress this enough: *Buy only what you need.* Regardless of how noble our intentions may be when it comes to buying any given food, good intentions do not equal less food waste.

While you don't need to make any sort of master plan, it's important to at least create a loose list and a general plan for how you're going to use what you buy. From there, I've outlined various strategies that can help—many of which I use regularly. There are also plenty of wonderful resources out there with even more tips; I've noted some in the Resources List.

Before the Store

- Before you go to the store, check your fridge, freezer, and pantry. I cannot count the number of times I bought something, went to put it away at home, and realized I already had that item, which I would have known if I had checked first. If you have created your own inventory list, you can skip checking your freezer and pantry and just refer to the inventory—which also saves you time in the moment.
- Plan your grocery list around what you find in your fridge, freezer, and pantry (or on your inventory list), so that you can incorporate any items that need to be used up into your meals and snacks for the week.
- Make a meal plan for your week. Meal planning is an extremely effective tool, and there are many resources online that can assist with this. I've outlined a couple of helpful meal planning tools in the Resources List.

- If you're making something that requires an ingredient you don't normally buy and are unlikely to use again, try to find a substitute for it. A quick online search for an ingredient substitution might just save you a trip to the store. We will also look at ingredient substitutions in more depth in the "Low-Waste Cooking" chapter (page 31).

At the Store

- Stick to your list at the store. No, seriously, *stick to the list.* Only ever buy things not on your list if you know you will truly use them, and be as honest as possible with yourself about this. Your inventory list should help you stay accountable too.
- Only buy an amount of any given food that you actually need, which might mean buying a couple of loose tomatoes, rather than five in a prebagged portion, for example. If you need only a small amount of an ingredient for a recipe—like a spice—see if you can purchase a smaller amount from a bulk bin store.
- If you tend to buy large amounts of food but then don't actually eat the stockpiled food, take note of that tendency. Avoid stores where you will be tempted to engage in overbuying. While it's great to get a good deal on a larger quantity of something, if you end up chucking it out, this isn't really a good deal for you or the environment in the long run.

Back at Home

- Strategically use ingredients first that are going to spoil faster than others. A crisp spinach salad on day one or two is always preferable to a salad made of wilted spinach that's already been in your fridge for six days.
- Even if you have a meal plan, reducing food waste is something that can require a bit of flexibility. If you planned to make squash, but the squash is holding strong and instead the broccoli you have needs attention, then change your plans—leave the squash and cook something with the broccoli first.
- Make only reasonable-sized portions that you will eat. If you do make too much food, freeze the leftovers right away before they go bad. For help with portion sizes, you can use the portion planning tools noted in the Resources List.
- Label and date everything you put into your freezer. A freezer full of frozen containers of food with no dates or labels is a total nightmare

and means you'll be unlikely to eat the food later, if you don't know what or how old it is.

- Store food in the fridge, freezer, and pantry in clear containers, like glass jars, whenever possible. This way it will be much easier to see whatever is in the container, making it less likely that you'll forget about it.
- If you have food that you know you're not going to use, send out a message and offer it up to family and friends. What you have might just be what someone else needs.
- I have heard of some people putting an "eat first" bowl or container in their fridge where food can be placed accordingly. Plus, then you have a visual reminder to reduce food waste every time you open the fridge.
- Have a "clean out the freezer and pantry week" when you eat only foods from those two places. In reality, at any given time I probably have enough food in my freezer and pantry that Paul and I would not actually need to go to the store. We wouldn't have fresh produce or milk, but we could certainly live off what we already have for at least a week. This strategy can be a good way to get the entire family involved too.
- You can use an app to help with reducing food waste. I've noted a few different ones in the Resources List.

I do find that there is a delicate balance when it comes to planning yet not *overplanning*. I meal plan every week, but I plan for one meal less than we need. This is because, usually, something comes up later in the week that will fill that meal—whether we decide we want to eat out, someone invites us over for dinner, or we have more leftovers than expected. If none of those things happen, I almost always have a meal in the freezer or pantry I can pull out to fill the space—as per my inventory list. Otherwise, meal planning for every single day of the week usually results in too much food for us.

When planning doesn't go as planned, I rely heavily on freezing food, whether it's leftovers, fruit, or bread. These foods typically freeze well, and then I mark them on my inventory list and use them later on. However, while freezing food to reduce waste is generally a good plan, this is true only if you use the frozen food later. Otherwise, you are not really reducing food waste, just delaying it.

As you try out different planning strategies, be patient with yourself. Consistently reducing food waste can be a bit of a learning curve. I am by no means perfect at reducing food waste, and some weeks are simply better than others. But overall, I waste much less food than I used to, and that can be attributed to consistently using a number of helpful planning strategies. Try out different options, use what fits, ditch what doesn't, and over time you will figure out what works best for you.

Understand Best-Before Dates

One reason people waste food is that they don't use it by the best-before or expiration date. There is also a general sense of confusion about what these terms mean. Best-before and expiration dates are actually not the same thing.

Best-before dates refer to how long food will keep for peak freshness, taste, and nutritional value—but only if the food is unopened and stored properly. In reality, best-before dates are not really about whether the food is safe to eat; they are more about the assumed potential quality and shelf life of unopened food. This means that you can, in fact, purchase and consume unopened foods even after their best-before date has passed. The taste and freshness of those foods just might not be at 100 percent. I'm going to quote the Canadian food rescue organization Second Harvest here, because they make an incredibly valid point worth repeating: "'Best before' does not mean 'bad after.'"

It's worth emphasizing that best-before dates apply to unopened foods. The shelf life of any given food can change after you open the product. Sometimes how long food lasts once opened is also listed somewhere on the packaging—for example, "Consume within 10–14 days after opening." Whenever I see something like that written on a product, like a container of vegetable broth, for example, I take a permanent marker and write the date I opened it on the packaging, because I know I will not remember otherwise. Alternatively, if you can't use certain foods fast enough, you can freeze them after opening. For example, vegetable broth can be transferred to an airtight container and then frozen. Just remember, if you do freeze anything, be sure to label it, date it, and then follow through by using that food later on.

While we can think of best-before dates as a guideline to the shelf life of unopened products, expiration dates are more final. Expiration dates are listed on food that has nutritional and compositional specifications, like infant formula or nutritional supplements. In these cases, once the expiration date has passed, the food should not be eaten. I think part of the confusion here is that food is commonly referred to as "expired" even if it doesn't have an actual expiration date. But yogurt that still looks, smells, and tastes fine a day or so past its best-before date is not "expired" in the technical sense of the term.

In doing my research, I came across a fantastic resource from Second Harvest—drumroll, please—a Consumer Best Before Timetable, which provides guidelines on how long certain foods are typically safe to eat once their best-before date has passed, so long as they are unopened and have been stored appropriately. With their permission, I have reprinted this timetable in the book, on page 28. Thank you, Second Harvest, for sharing this gem!

I find that by using the various buying and planning strategies noted previously, I rarely have food on hand that reaches too far beyond the best-before date anymore. If you feel uneasy about best-before dates, then focus on planning and keeping regular tabs on the food that you buy, which will help ensure it's used up well in advance of any potential spoilage.

Improve Your Food Storage Habits

I don't need to tell you that how and where you store food makes a difference in moving the needle on your household food waste. This one might require some homework, depending on your own food storage needs. Essentially, if you are keeping regular tabs on your fridge, freezer, and pantry, you may notice certain items going bad faster and more frequently than others. That's when it's worth figuring out if how you're storing your food has something to do with how long it lasts.

For example, I was recently struggling with storing green cabbage. We subscribed to a local food box over the winter (we'll talk more about this local box later, on page 85), and one of the items that arrived monthly in the box was a massive green cabbage. These cabbages were consistently huge—think award-winning farmers' market cabbages. Although we were sharing this local box with another couple, that still left us with half of the said massive cabbage every month. And I simply could not use the cabbage fast enough. It kept getting black dots all along the sides, and I had to cut off spoiled chunks every time I went to use it. So I took to the internet. I learned that I should be storing it in the crisper, which seems obvious in hindsight. But because it was so large, I hadn't been keeping it in there. So I moved some things around to accommodate. I also put it in a plastic bag and added one square of paper towel to the bag, to help soak up moisture. And voila! The cabbage lasted longer, by about a week.

Second Harvest's Consumer Best Before Timetable

BBD = Best Before Date

FOOD CATEGORY	ITEMS	CONSUME BY
PRODUCE	Perishable fresh fruits and vegetables	No spoilage, blemishes, visible decay, mold or bio-degrading smell
	Shelf stable canned fruits and vegetables, pickles, sauces, or pastes	1 year past BBD
DAIRY	Perishable milk (including dairy alternatives), butter, yogurt, cheese, ice cream, sour cream	2 weeks past BBD IF FROZEN 2-3 months past BBD
	Shelf stable evaporated, powdered, or milk alternatives	1 year past BBD
	Shelf stable baby formula, supplemental beverages (i.e.: Ensure)	Expiry date
MEAT & FISH / EGGS & SOY / LEGUMES / NUT PRODUCTS & NUTS	Raw meat and fish	BBD or IF FROZEN: Beef, lamb, pork, whole poultry: 1 year past BBD Poultry pieces: 6 months past BBD Ground meat: 2-3 months past BBD Fish: 2-6 months past BBD
	Cooked luncheon meats, tofu, eggs	1 week past BBD
	Shelf stable canned meat, fish, beans, chickpeas, nuts, nut butter, peanut butter, seeds, spam	1 year past BBD
BREAD / CRACKERS & CEREAL / GRAIN	Perishable bread, buns, bagels, pitas, tortillas, flat bread, na'an, matzah	No spoilage, blemishes, visible decay, mold or bio-degrading smell
	Dry, shelf stable cereal, crackers, flour, oats, pasta, rice, quinoa, meals or sides, energy bars	1 year past BBD
	Meal replacement or supplement bars	Expiry date
BAKED GOODS / SNACKS / DESSERTS	Perishable cakes, cookies, pies, danishes, chocolate, pudding	72 hours past BBD IF FROZEN 1 month past BBD
	Shelf stable cookies, chips, popcorn, bagged snacks, snack cakes, granola bars	1 year past BBD
PREPARED	Pre-cooked or ready-to-eat meals; deli salads, pizza, sandwiches	72 hours past BBD IF FROZEN 1 month past BBD
	Frozen dinners, microwavable meals	1 year past BBD
	Shelf stable canned soups, stews, meals	1 year past BBD
	Shelf stable baby food	1 year past BBD
CONDIMENTS	Frozen sauces, gravies	6 months past BBD
	Shelf stable mustard, relish, ketchup, jam, margarine, mayonnaise, oil, salad dressing, vinegars, spices, sauces, toppings	1 year past BBD
BEVERAGES	Juice, water, coconut water	3-6 months past BBD
	Other drinks; coffee, tea, sport or energy drinks, crystals	3-6 months past BBD

As a general guideline for food storage, Health Canada notes that leftovers containing cooked meat, poultry, fish, eggs, and/or vegetables will last in the fridge for three to four days. Freezing greatly extends the life of most foods. Frozen leftovers are generally good for two to six months, depending on what they are. Frozen fruit and vegetables are generally good for eight to twelve months, again depending on what they are. In the Resources List I have noted several sources you can refer to for a quick reference on how and where to best store food, along with how long it will last once stored. You can also find information online about how to optimally organize your fridge to make food last longer—like which fruits and vegetables shouldn't be stored together, as doing so can speed up spoilage. If this interests you and seems like something that would be helpful, then mastering the art of food storage might be your calling. But even generally staying mindful about the food in your fridge, freezer, and pantry will mean that you are more aware of what's happening there. When you notice food spoiling that could be solved with better storage techniques, take action. Little changes can have a big impact here.

Be Mindful of Food Waste Beyond Your Kitchen

Since food waste is not just a household problem, many of the solutions noted in this chapter can be applied to other scenarios. For example, food waste can be an issue in the workplace, when hosting gatherings and events, or when dining out.

Just to give you an example, let's briefly touch on dining out. Food waste in eating establishments can happen for a number of reasons: if food was prepared or plated but never ended up being served, if too many ingredients are ordered and don't get used, or—and this is where you and I come in—if uneaten food is returned to the kitchen from a customer who doesn't want to take it home. This is already a waste of resources, but on top of that, if the uneaten food is not composted by the restaurant and gets tossed in the garbage, it produces methane when it eventually gets to the landfill.

So, what can you do? Try to order only an amount of food you will actually eat, and if you don't eat it all, take it home. When you get home, store that food properly so it doesn't immediately go bad. If you took home a paper takeout box, for example, transfer the food to a reusable food storage container that's airtight. And here's the key part: *Eat the food.* Transferring it to a reusable container that's clear, like a glass one, is especially helpful because then you can see the food when you open the fridge, making it less likely that you'll forget it's there. In a worst-case scenario, if you don't eat that food before it goes bad, then compost what's left. All of this also applies to food you ordered for pickup or delivery—store any leftovers properly, eat the leftovers, and compost what's left if necessary.

Takeaways

- Conduct a weekly food waste experiment to learn how much food you waste, and note any particular problem spots.
- Take regular inventory of the food in your fridge, freezer, and pantry to keep tabs on what you have and avoid wasting food.
- Check what you already have and make a list of what you need before grocery shopping. Resist impulse buying and implement planning strategies as needed.
- Understand best-before dates to avoid throwing away edible food.
- Store food efficiently so that it stays fresh longer.
- Bring your tactics to reduce food waste beyond your own kitchen, like when dining out.

CHAPTER 2:

Low-Waste Cooking

LOW-WASTE COOKING is pretty much exactly what it sounds like: Cook to use up as much of the food you have on hand as possible, and waste as little as possible. Low-waste cooking is a key part of preventing food waste, and since cooking is what we spend most of our time doing in the kitchen, it's not surprising that it needs its own chapter.

But I will start by saying I am not a chef. My credentials for providing low-waste cooking tips are that I try to cook as low-waste as possible in my own kitchen and have been doing so ever since I moved out of my parents' house in university. At first, this was largely out of necessity. Food was expensive, and I was in school and living on my own, so I tried to simply use everything I bought. A decade later, food is still expensive—even more so—and along the way I have developed a deep enjoyment of cooking, particularly without a recipe.

I grew up in a household where both of my parents cooked regularly, and we ate the dreamiest homemade meals. Fresh pizza with soft, pillowy crust, savoury vegetable soups, and baked macaroni in a creamy cheese sauce were the stuff of my childhood. If this sounds like a gourmet set-up, it really was. Upon moving out, I discovered that both time and skill were necessary to make these homemade meals—which I was totally unprepared for. Although I knew how to follow a recipe and cook the basics, I quickly realized that homemade macaroni and cheese does not just appear. Quite the opposite, in fact. Who knew that the question "What should we eat for dinner?" could be so exhausting! Feeding yourself and potentially the other people in your household is both demanding and never-ending. And let's be honest—boxed macaroni and cheese is always going to be easier. It just is.

But developing the ability to cook at home—and, in particular, to cook without always using a recipe—is going to make it easier for you to waste less food, save money, and implement other solutions in this book. I say "developing the ability" because while not everyone is naturally gifted in the kitchen, I believe this is a skill you can learn. Cooking at home without using recipes is something you build slowly through trial and error over time. It's also probably something your elders and ancestors did out of necessity, using whatever food was on hand to feed their family. Nowadays, we often find new and sometimes elaborate recipes from every corner of the internet and then head out to buy ingredients. While this approach has pros, if you don't have all the ingredients on hand for a given recipe, then you just end up buying more food, which potentially results in more food waste. Cooking without a recipe is kind of like reversing this process. I find there is something freeing about cooking intuitively, because it allows a lot of creativity, and really, there are no rules aside from the ones I create.

I'll pause here and note that not everything can magically be done without a recipe. I do use recipes for baked goods and only make simple substitutions when baking, given that baking requires more of an exact science than, say, soup. I have many cookbooks and often look to them for inspiration—plus, the first book I wrote *was* a cookbook, so they do have a special place in my heart and on my bookshelf. I typically don't attempt to make complicated or unfamiliar dishes for the first time sans recipe either, as that is just asking for trouble. But I can look in my fridge, assess a variety of ingredients that need to be used up, and whip them into something that tastes good. This is what I hope for you too.

What You Can Do

Learn to Cook Intuitively with What You Have

To illustrate how I cook intuitively, I'm going to walk you through a recent corn chowder I made without a recipe. We had an unusual amount of potatoes and frozen corn, and Paul is a big fan of corn chowder. I started by looking at recipes online to get a sense of what other people were putting in their corn chowder. I looked at six different recipes from various blogs, making a mental note of the common ingredients they used, and how they differed.

I already had onions and garlic, which were in all six of the recipes. I did not have any celery or cream, which were in most of the recipes, but I had carrots, parsnips, and canned coconut milk instead. I didn't have any ready-made stock or broth, but of course, I had water. I also didn't have any ham or bacon—two corn chowder classics—but I did have some farmer's sausage in the freezer, which seemed like a reasonable substitute.

First, I popped the sausage into the oven to cook. Meanwhile, I chopped onions and crushed garlic, and then added them to my Dutch oven to sauté in oil on the stove as I chopped the rest of the vegetables. Then I added some water, enough to fill about one-third of the Dutch oven, and tossed in the ingredients that were going to take the longest to cook: the chopped potatoes, parsnips, and carrots. Once those vegetables were soft, I added the frozen corn, cut up the cooked sausage and tossed that in, and then added salt, black pepper, and a bit of onion powder. I was unsure if one or two cans of coconut milk were going to do the trick, so I opened and added only one can to start. I tasted the soup and decided one can was enough. Finally, I looked in the fridge and saw some spinach that was on the verge of wilting, so I chopped it up and tossed it in. I tasted the soup again and felt like it needed more salt and pepper, so I added more.

Was this an award-winning corn chowder? No. But it tasted good, we both enjoyed it, and I made it out of ingredients I already had. If I think about what else I could have put in this soup, I suspect a number of ingredients would have worked just fine: chives, rosemary, thyme, leeks, peas, finely chopped kale, bell pepper, green beans, turnip, jalapeños, cooked chicken, chickpeas, or white kidney beans. If I hadn't had coconut milk, I could have used any sort of dairy or non-dairy milk and added cornstarch or flour to thicken it. None of this makes for a traditional corn chowder, but that's not the point.

The guiding principle here is thinking intuitively about what tastes good to you. If you can do that, you can learn to cook without a recipe. Think about it: When you look at a photo of a dish on a blog or in a cookbook, you instinctively know if it's appetizing to you or not. Same goes for working without recipes. Picture the ingredients together, and if they seem like they would taste good, they probably will. On the other hand, if they seem off-putting, they probably will be.

If it helps, you can practice or experiment with this without cooking anything. Wander over to your kitchen and take a look in your fridge, freezer, and pantry. What could you make right now out of what you already have? At the moment my fridge is fairly empty, but I have carrots, onions, mushrooms, and a block of marble cheese. These vegetables seem unrelated to the cheese, but if I take a couple of pantry staples like pasta and a can of crushed tomatoes, I can make a baked pasta dish. Option two: Sauté the mushrooms and onions, and then use them in a loaded grilled cheese sandwich with frozen bread—another staple I like to have on hand. Then, serve the sandwiches with the most basic side dish ever: carrot sticks. None of this has to be fancy—in fact, the more modest, the easier.

If you want to cook on demand without a recipe, it's important to always have some reliable staple ingredients you feel comfortable working with. For me that typically includes garlic, onions, a variety of canned and dried beans and lentils, some sort of canned tomatoes, canned coconut milk, lemon juice, frozen bread, white vinegar, olive oil, stock or broth (sometimes ready-made, sometimes homemade and frozen), a variety of dried spices and frozen herbs, a few kinds of pasta, and a couple of grains like quinoa or rice. There's a lot I can do just having these ingredients waiting in the wings.

When you begin cooking without a recipe, regardless of what you are making, it's a good idea to start small. Don't freestyle a massive batch of something, as you don't want to be throwing out an enormous pot of an experiment gone wrong. Starting with smaller portions also means it's easier to control the spices and seasonings, especially if you're unsure how much you should add. As a general rule, you can always add more of something, but fixing it once you've added too much can be a bit more challenging. So add a little, taste it, and, if needed, add more. This also helps with understanding how certain ingredients change the flavour when you're not measuring them out. Remember that can of coconut milk in the corn chowder? One can made the soup creamy without even the slightest coconut taste. Had I immediately dumped in two cans, I would have had to compensate by adding more of everything else to make it not taste like a coconut corn chowder—which I can't imagine would have been very good.

That said, I have learned the most from having to fix things gone wrong. Paul and I still sometimes talk about the wonton soup I tried for the first time without a recipe—it was not a crowd-pleaser, to say the least. But if you are starting small and working with random ingredients in your fridge that you may not have eaten anyway, then this possibility will be a bit easier to digest. You might want to try freestyle cooking when you're cooking only for yourself or the people you live with. Cooking for guests is not a great time to go rogue, because it will probably end up being a stressful experience. It's also important to pick a day when you're not in a rush, so that you can allow yourself the space and time needed to have a successful end result.

Get Comfortable Substituting

If starting from scratch with no recipe feels too intimidating, then start by substituting ingredients in a familiar recipe. You could follow the method portion of the recipe and just change some of the ingredients, or leave others out altogether if you don't have them. Substituting ingredients is much easier with dishes that have a number of ingredients and more complex flavours, and can therefore handle variation. Most soups, stews, chilis, stir-fries, curries, casseroles, pasta dishes, and even salads are all easier to work with when changing out ingredients. This is less easy with extremely specific dishes. If you are craving broccoli cheddar soup, for example, and you swap broccoli for cauliflower and cheddar for feta, it will probably be a letdown.

Although substituting ingredients can sometimes change the texture, appearance, taste, or overall time required for a recipe, I still tend to be extremely liberal with food substitutions. This is mainly because in my late teens, I began reacting to gluten and cut it out of my diet. I now eat gluten whenever I'm doing food writing work that involves it, but on an everyday basis, I avoid gluten because I feel physically better without it. Cooking and baking gluten-free has taught me a lot about working with food substitutions and modifying recipes. Over time, as I pushed the boundaries in the kitchen by substituting various flours and grains to accommodate a lack of wheat, this practice naturally spilled over into other types of food.

It helps to think about ingredients in categories, based on similar flavour or function in a recipe. For example, I regularly swap fruits and vegetables that are similar. So I will use blueberries, raspberries, strawberries, blackberries, and even cranberries in place of each other. I use shallots, leeks, and red, yellow, and white onions interchangeably. I substitute similar root vegetables like carrots, turnips, beets, or parsnips, and so on.

You can also add ingredients to a recipe that are not listed but that you want to use up. Making a stir-fry but have some leftover cooked quinoa or couscous? Toss it in. Making a bean chili but have a bunch of dark, leafy greens? Chop them up and add them in. Making muffins but have a few soft apples? Chop and add, baby. In general, adding one or two ingredients in small to medium quantities to any given recipe is unlikely to upset the recipe as a whole. As you gain more experience with this, you will gradually get a sense of how far you can push it—which, I would say, can be pretty far.

If you are new to substituting ingredients or cooking without a recipe, consulting trusted resources is a great option. If you've ever asked a family member how to re-create a favourite recipe, only to be met with something like "Oh, just add a little bit of this and that," then this person probably knows their way around freestyle cooking. That makes them the ultimate trusted resource. Spend time with them in the kitchen, ask questions, watch them cook, and you will tap into a wealth of information.

Apps can also be a useful resource if you're not sure where to start. For example, there are apps where you plug in the ingredients you already have, and then the app provides recipe options that match those ingredients. Zero-waste and low-waste cookbooks can also be helpful because they often list substitutions in the recipes, so you can easily make modifications. I have noted several low-waste apps, cookbooks, and food blogs in the Resources List, along with some other useful food substitution resources.

Ingredient substitutions can range from more basic changes, like some of the ones I've outlined, to ones that are incredibly specific—like how to make brown sugar out of white sugar and molasses, or how to make buttermilk from milk combined with lemon juice or vinegar. In short, there are countless ways to work with food substitutions. Which means that, lucky for us, there are countless ways to adjust recipes to suit the food you already have. As you gain more experience with substituting ingredients and cooking without a recipe, you will naturally build your own repertoire of substitutions you enjoy.

Use Foods in Their Entirety

A number of foods have edible parts that typically don't get eaten—for no good reason either. This is especially true of produce. Some common edible fruit and vegetable parts that are often trashed include: greens from beets and radishes (cook similarly to spinach); watermelon rind (pickle it); kiwi skins (can be eaten raw); green carrot tops (sauté or make pesto); kale stems (sauté, steam, or add to soups); cauliflower leaves and stems (roast or use in salads or soups); celery leaves (add to soups or salads); broccoli stems, leaves, and stalks (roast or use in salads or soups); pumpkin flesh (turn into purée or soup); seeds from squash like butternut or spaghetti (roast similarly to pumpkin seeds); and citrus peels (use as zest, candy them, or use to infuse vinegar or oil). Just note that some parts of foods may require longer cooking times to soften, for example, kale stems, which take longer to cook than the leaves.

Similarly, I rarely peel produce if it has edible skin. Unless there's a really severe blemish, I keep the skins on for potatoes, sweet potatoes, beets, carrots, parsnips, cucumbers—you name it, I'm probably not peeling it. Same goes for fruit. Even when baking, I don't peel fruits like apples or pears. Just be sure to wash all skins, rinds, stems, and leaves thoroughly prior to using. You can also hang on to parts of foods you don't eat and use these items for homemade stock, putting scraps to good use. I keep a bag of vegetable discards in my freezer—like carrot ends, garlic peels, and onion skins—and add to the bag on an ongoing basis. Once it's full, I make stock, giving these discards a second life prior to composting them.

Eating and using parts of foods you usually throw away might seem odd, but unless one specific part is truly inedible, there is nothing wrong with doing this. Food often gets thrown away simply out of habit—but habits can change. When you think about it, there's no reason not to use foods in their entirety, or to their fullest potential. If you are unsure whether part of a specific food is edible or usable, look for a reliable source that has an answer. I find online encyclopedias fairly useful for this purpose; they often list plant parts and whether they are edible or not.

Find "Anything Goes" Recipes That Work for You

I make a few things regularly that I would consider to be "anything goes" recipes. One example is a fruit crisp. I follow the same method for the crisp portion, but I change up the fruit to fit whatever I have. This can include a mixture of fresh or frozen apples, pears, berries, rhubarb, and more. Two of my other "anything goes" recipes involve vegetables. The first is a hamburger soup, which I make with the same soup base but use a variety of vegetables alongside lentils or ground meat. The second is a tomato spaghetti sauce, which also follows the same method every time, but with an ingredient list that can be modified to use up any vegetables I have on hand. Hamburger soup and spaghetti sauce also freeze well, which is like icing on the cake when you're trying to save food. Another simple option I rely on is sheet pan meals, which are incredibly versatile. You can easily make a delicious meal out of a protein like leftover sausage or chickpeas, roasted in the oven until crispy alongside a host of random vegetables.

Your "anything goes" recipes can be whatever you want, but it's best to pick recipes that maximize the food you often have left at the end of the week. For me, that is most often vegetables and fruit. I asked a few friends what their "anything goes" recipes were, and the responses included compote, stir-fry, pizza, smoothies, vegetable soup, and meat sauce. Having a couple of staple "anything goes" recipes not only will help you reduce waste but, over time, will help you practise substituting ingredients as well.

And remember, for your next meal, you can also just eat whatever needs to be used up in your fridge. Is this sexy? No. Is it random? Yes. But does it work? Absolutely. Not every meal we eat needs to be photo worthy, and you can easily put dinner on the table in a matter of minutes with a meal built around the principle of "It's gonna go bad, we need to eat it." If you want to really get into it, lay the food out nicely on a wood board and make up a fun name, like Anything Goes Charcuterie. Who knows—you might just start a new weekly thing.

Repurpose Leftovers to Create Something Even Better

Here's a great example of how you can turn leftovers into an upcycled dish: In the cookbook *Cook More, Waste Less*, by Canadian chef Christine Tizzard, there is a recipe for rice pudding that uses up leftover rice. Sure, you could turn leftover rice into fried rice or use it as the base of a burrito bowl, but warm rice pudding seasoned with cinnamon and nutmeg? Now, that's gold.

Applying this to other scenarios is simple: Think outside the box to repurpose food from its original use and create something delicious. Here are examples from my own kitchen: I'll freeze bread and buns if we're not eating the fresh version fast enough. While these make great sandwich bread and toast later on, they also make fantastic baked garlic bread, croutons, and French toast. If you have seasoned bread products like an Italian loaf or cheese buns, even better. Cheese bun croutons are an incredible creation. Vegetables that need attention could be boiled or roasted, or form the base of a soup. But they could also become refrigerator pickled veggies, which don't require canning equipment or processes. If I have leftover beans, I bake desserts with them; black bean brownies are my current obsession.

Leftover baked potatoes are another gold mine. They can become hash browns for breakfast, potato skins, or crispy smashed potatoes.

The only thing to note here is that if you have something like cooked quinoa already sitting in the fridge for three days, turning it into a new dish doesn't mean its food safety clock starts over. That quinoa will be good for only three to four days from the day you originally made it. It's also not recommended to reheat leftover food more than once, so if you're using previously cooked foods in a new dish, you'll want to make sure you eat that newly prepared dish right away.

When it comes to low-waste cooking, the sky's the limit. I truly believe cooking should be fun, and if you approach low-waste cooking with a creative mindset and a "why not" attitude, there is no end to what you can do. But know that none of this has to be elaborate. The overall goal is simply to cook in a way that's less wasteful, whatever that looks like for you. In doing so, you will inherently reduce your household food waste, meaning that this is a process where every step along the way matters—or, should I say, every bite.

Takeaways

- Practise cooking intuitively with ingredients you already have at home. Be sure to start small and work your way up.
- Try substituting or adding ingredients in recipes to work with the foods you already have.
- Use up all the parts of an ingredient by cooking with green carrot tops, pumpkin flesh, celery leaves, and more! If it's edible, it's usable.
- Find some staple "anything goes" recipes that work well with the types of foods you most often have on hand.
- Don't like leftovers? Turn your leftovers into delicious new creations.

CHAPTER 3:

What We Eat

In this chapter I discuss calories, dietary guidelines, and other related topics as they pertain to food and sustainability. As such, I would like to offer a trigger warning for disordered eating.

THE KITCHEN IS COMMONLY called the heart of the home—but really, the reason the kitchen is so important is because it revolves around food. Therefore, there is just no way to talk about sustainability in the kitchen without doing a deep dive into what we eat. Not only does the type of food you put on your own dinner table matter, but on a wider scale, how the world grows, produces, and distributes food is a key part of the conversation on addressing climate change and reducing greenhouse gas emissions.

The Impact of the Global Food System

When I think of greenhouse gas emissions, I tend to picture cars. I imagine millions of cars all over the world, sending up emissions as they speed along. That, of course, is part of it. But guess what makes up another part of the emissions story? The global food system. A quarter of all human-caused greenhouse gas emissions—about 26 percent—are from the food system.

These gases include carbon dioxide, nitrous oxide, and methane, which result from several different processes. Examples include fuel for agricultural machinery and fishing boats (carbon dioxide), the use of fertilizers (nitrous oxide), the use and management of manure (methane and nitrous oxide), and transportation (carbon dioxide). Agricultural greenhouse gas emissions are also caused by something called enteric fermentation, which is a natural part of the digestive process in ruminant animals. This is mainly a problem of cows, but sheep, goats, and bison are ruminants too. Ruminants produce methane gas as a sort of digestive system by-product. When they burp, that gas is released, causing emissions. This is the same methane gas we already talked about that results from food waste sitting in landfills, just coming from a different source.

The food system uses a significant amount of resources too. Agriculture—of both crops and animals—requires a lot of water. It also requires a lot of land. About 43 percent of all global land that is not a desert or covered in ice is used for agriculture. Agricultural expansion is typically bad news for the living things that made their home wherever the expansion takes place. When natural ecosystems like a forest, for example, are turned into pasture or cropland, this leads to biodiversity loss. Biodiversity is a shortened term for "biological diversity" and refers to the number of species in any given area, like plants and animals. Globally, biodiversity loss is occurring at alarming rates. It's estimated that approximately one million species are facing extinction, unless drastic measures are implemented to turn things around. For some species, this isn't a faraway problem either—extinction could happen within a matter of decades. And up to 80 percent of biodiversity loss is a result of the global food system. Converting land and cutting down forests—also known as deforestation—for agricultural purposes is another cause of greenhouse gas emissions. Forests and the soil are both examples of natural carbon sinks, which means they store carbon over time. But that means that when a tree is chopped down or the soil is disturbed, the stored carbon is lost and emitted into the atmosphere.

Not all foods are created equally when it comes to environmental impact. I'm going to cut to the chase and give you the key point of this chapter right now, so that you know exactly where we're headed. Then I'll work backwards and explain.

Here it is: On the whole, plant-based foods have a significantly lower environmental impact than animal-based foods. The most environmentally intensive food of all is beef—by a long shot. Therefore, the ultimate conclusion of this chapter is that building a sustainable kitchen involves drastically reducing our consumption of animal-based foods; that is, shifting either partially or fully to a plant-based diet. Experts widely agree that shifting to plant-based diets on a global scale would be an effective way to cut down on the food system's greenhouse gas emissions overall.

Before I started writing this book, I was reasonably aware of the environmental impacts of plant versus animal foods. I had done other writing that opened my eyes to the impact of beef in particular, when I wrote an article for *Chatelaine* titled "Is There Such a Thing as Sustainable Beef?" But at that point in my life, I didn't eat much beef anyway. As a result, when I wrote that *Chatelaine* article, I did not make any changes to my diet. When I started working on *Building a Sustainable Kitchen*, I assumed the same would apply. Since beef is the highest-impact food and I rarely ate it, my work in the animal-based foods reduction department was done. Right?

Wrong. Quite wrong, actually. About two months into the research for this book, I was confronted with a stark reality. If I wanted our kitchen to be more sustainable, and if I wanted to implement the information I was writing about authentically, then I had to eat fewer animal-based foods overall and shift to a plant-based diet. There is no way around this. So, in March 2024, I began to shift away from animal-based foods. Fast-forward to January 2025, ten months later, and I am now eating a diet that is 85–90 percent plant-based, depending on the week.

But I want you to know that I did not start this transition—or this chapter—from any sort of meat-hating standpoint. Although I may not be a beef lover, I do like bison and certainly enjoy other animal-based foods. In particular, I like bacon, seafood, and chicken, and I will always jump at the chance to assemble and eat a charcuterie board. But the writing was on the wall for animal-based foods, and I simply could not ignore this fact. If I wanted my environmental beliefs to inform and guide my actions, I had to get my diet on board. No ifs, ands, or buts. Let's look at why.

Plant-Based and Animal-Based Foods by the Numbers

First, let's talk about how greenhouse gas emissions compare between plant- and animal-based foods. Although there is a range in the amount of emissions that result from any specific food, emissions from most plant-based foods are generally lower than those from animal-based ones. Here's an example to illustrate this difference. Producing 1 kilogram of beef results in 60 kilograms of carbon dioxide–equivalent greenhouse gases being released. Producing 1 kilogram of soy milk or corn, on the other hand, results in only around 1 kilogram of carbon dioxide–equivalent emissions.

What does that measurement actually mean? Beef's 60 kilograms of carbon dioxide equivalent is equal to the amount of greenhouse gas emissions that would result from driving 246 kilometres in a gas-powered vehicle. Again, this is just the emissions that result from producing 1 kilogram of beef, or about four 250-gram steaks. In contrast, you'd need to drive only 4 kilometres to equal the greenhouse gases emitted from producing 1 kilogram of corn or soy milk.

For a visual representation, I've included a helpful chart on page 45, which lists several other foods. The chart reveals a clear hierarchy in how much greenhouse gas is emitted when various foods are compared per kilogram. The foods in the high to middle range tend to be animal-based ones, whereas plant-based foods fall in the middle to low range. As with any rule, there are exceptions—don't worry, I see coffee and rice on there too—which I'll get to later on.

Part of the problem here is that almost 60 percent of the food system's greenhouse gas emissions come from meat, dairy, eggs, and farmed fish and seafood combined, but these foods provide only 18 percent of the calories that are consumed globally. What's more, when taken together, meat, dairy, eggs, and farmed fish and seafood use a whopping 83 percent of all global farmland. That means that the majority of global calories come from all other foods, which require far fewer resources and cause significantly lower emissions.

The hierarchy that appears in the greenhouse gas chart is generally the same when other environmental impacts are considered. So foods that have one high environmental impact, like greenhouse gas emissions, often have high impacts in other categories, too, like land or water use. Beef and cheese are near the top of the list whether we're talking about land use, water use, or greenhouse gas emissions. Similarly, pork, eggs, and poultry have consistently moderate impacts across all three categories. Apples, soy milk, and root vegetables have consistently low impacts.

A few foods don't follow this pattern, including nuts, which produce low greenhouse gas emissions but require high water and land use. Another

Food: Greenhouse Gas Emissions Across the Supply Chain

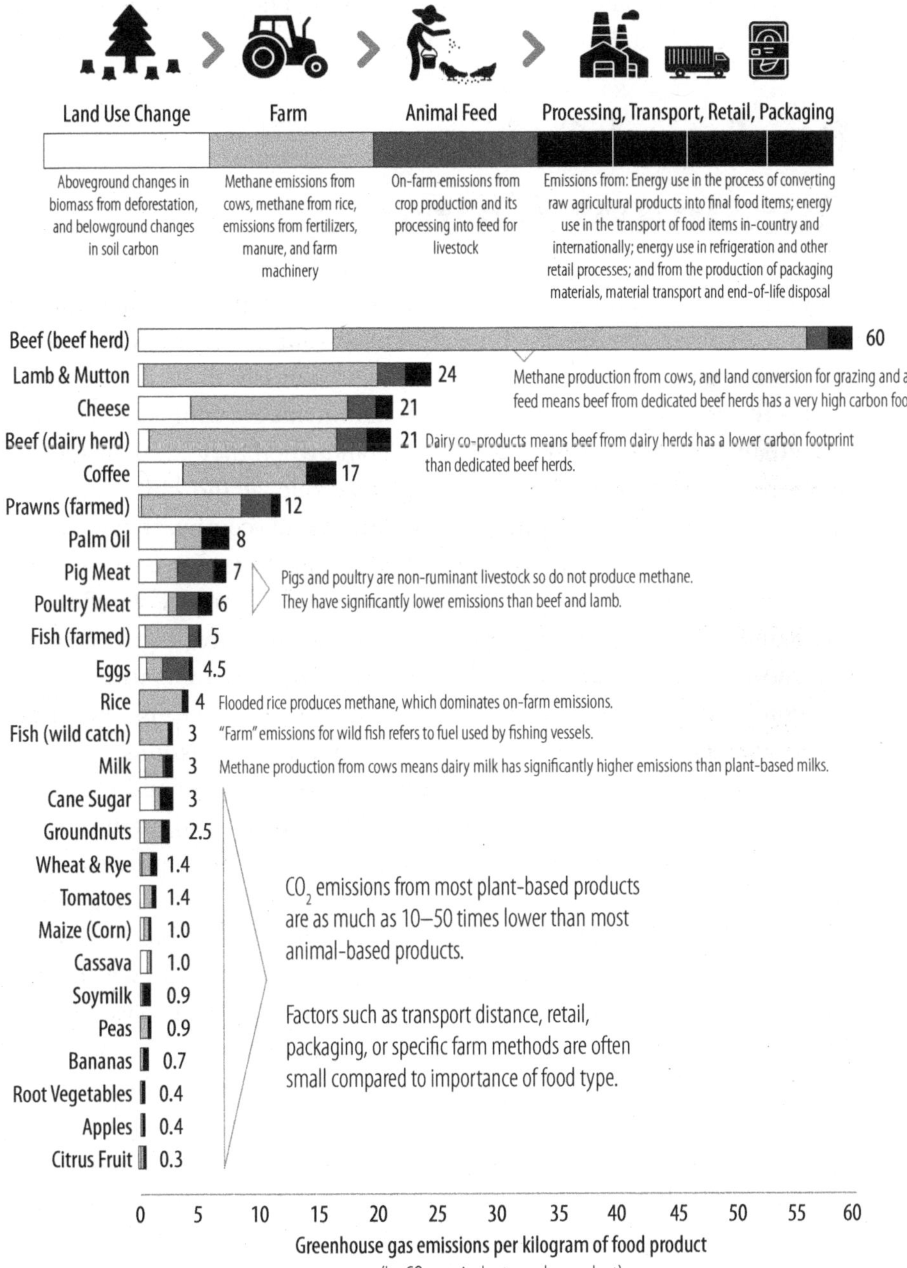

exception is rice, which involves high water use and greenhouse gas emissions but moderate land use. If you're interested in exploring the impact of specific foods in greater detail, interactive resources are available online where you can play around with various foods and impact indicators. I've noted where to find these in the Resources List.

Beef and Other Ruminant Animals

Why do ruminant animals like cows top the charts, especially when compared with other, moderately impactful meat sources like pork or poultry? This largely comes back to how ruminant animals' digestive systems work—the enteric fermentation process. Ruminants are defined as having more than one chamber in their stomach, and when they eat their food, they repeatedly chew, swallow, and bring it back up, all the while burping up methane. If you're wondering how significant some cow burps can really be though, you're not alone. I must admit this thought has crossed my mind in the past too. But it turns out ruminant methane emissions are significant. For example, in Canada, nearly 4 percent of the country's overall greenhouse gas emissions are specifically from enteric fermentation. In contrast, pigs and poultry do not produce methane through digestion because they are not ruminants, which means they naturally have lower emissions.

Another reason for the impact difference between beef and pork or poultry is the sheer amount of food required to feed animals of different sizes. You need up to ten kilograms of animal feed for a cow to produce one kilogram of body weight. In comparison, pigs need up to five kilograms of animal feed and chickens need up to two kilograms to produce one kilogram of weight. Animal feed is also a contributing factor in why most plant-based foods have lower impacts. When we grow plant-based protein, for example, we can eat that food directly. But in order to eat animal protein, we need to feed those animals while they're alive. Although not everything that animals eat is potentially suitable for human consumption, we're still essentially using food to feed our food, when we could just eat some of that food instead. Eating crops directly not only saves resources and reduces environmental impacts along the way, but also is just much more efficient.

Of course, the way any given food is produced can vary depending on a number of factors. For example, chicken that comes from a factory farm may have different impacts than free-range chicken. However, although the environmental impacts for any food may vary, plants remain victorious. Animal-based proteins with the lowest possible impact still have larger impacts overall compared with plant-based proteins. There is simply no situation where beef is produced in a way in which its impact dips below that of plant-based proteins. This pattern also holds true when beef is compared with moderately impactful pork or poultry. Pork and poultry that is produced in the highest-impact way possible is comparable to beef that is produced in the lowest-impact way.

What About Local or Sustainably Raised Food? How About Packaging?

I know that I said no ifs, ands, or buts, but a few come to mind right about now. So here we go: But what if the meat is local? What if it's grass-fed? What if it's sustainably raised? What if I bring my own packaging? All of these questions are totally fair. If we look at what widespread, popular sustainable living tips suggest, it would be safe to assume that buying ground beef from a local farmer in your own reusable packaging is the number one way to lower your carbon footprint. Unfortunately, it's not.

If we go back to the food system's overall greenhouse gas emissions—which are about 26 percent of all human-caused emissions—this percentage can be further broken down. There is a visual on page 48 to illustrate this. If we look at all of the parts that make up 100 percent of the food system's greenhouse gas emissions, we can see that 18 percent of these emissions come from the supply chain, with retail at 3 percent, packaging at 5 percent, transport at 6 percent, and food processing at 4 percent. All other emissions—82 percent of the food system's overall emissions—are from factors related to the *production* of food. These are the factors I mentioned earlier, like enteric fermentation, fuel use, manure management, turning natural landscapes into agricultural land, and so on. What this means is that most of any food's greenhouse gas emissions

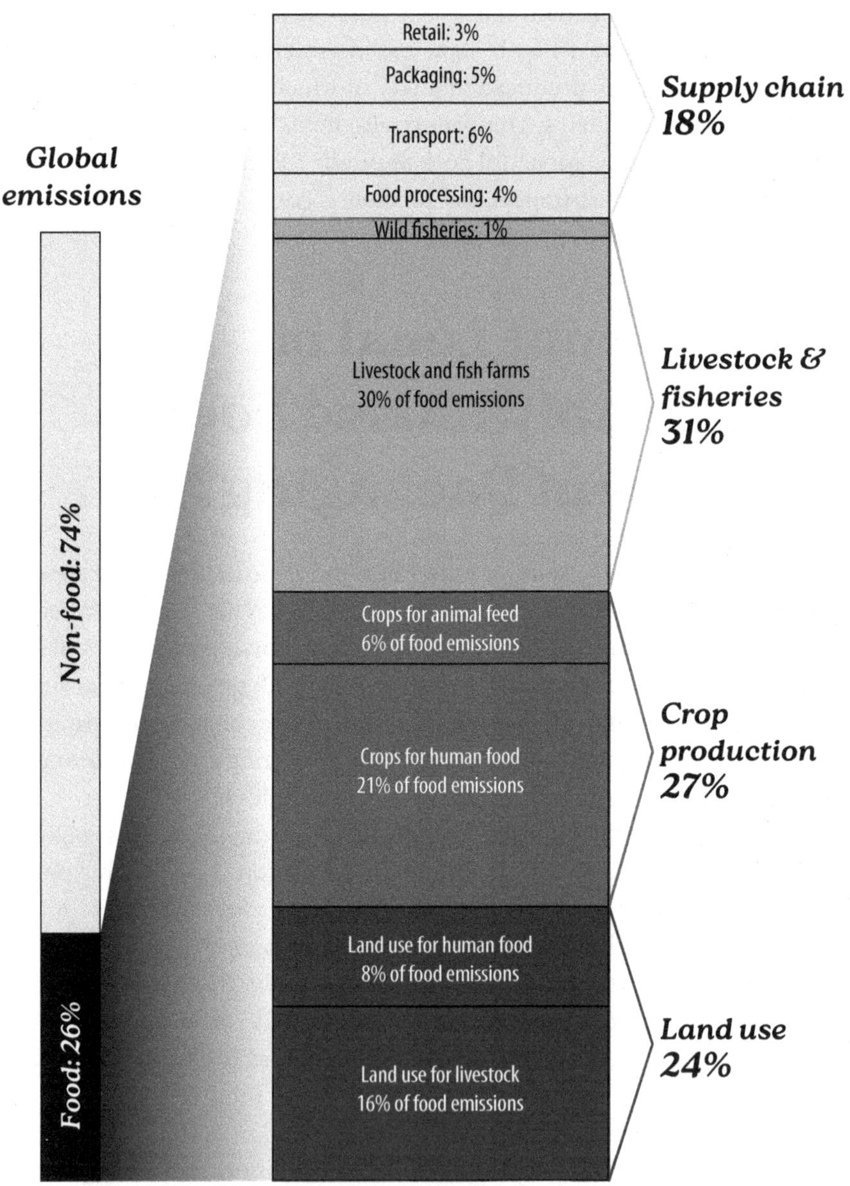

Global Greenhouse Gas Emissions from Food Production
Global emissions
Non-food: 74%
Food: 26%
Retail: 3%
Packaging: 5%
Transport: 6%
Food processing: 4%
Wild fisheries: 1%
Livestock and fish farms 30% of food emissions
Crops for animal feed 6% of food emissions
Crops for human food 21% of food emissions
Land use for human food 8% of food emissions
Land use for livestock 16% of food emissions
Supply chain 18%
Livestock & fisheries 31%
Crop production 27%
Land use 24%

come from producing the food itself—not from how far the food has travelled or how it's packaged.

To put this in perspective, let's say that someone who eats a typical North American diet featuring animal-based foods decides to purchase all of their food locally. The impact this person could have from this action would be the same as if they simply swapped beef and dairy for either plant-based protein or a moderately impactful animal-based one, like chicken, on *less than one day each week*. To put it another way: If you bought all your food locally, the maximum impact it would have in reducing greenhouse gas emissions would be about 4–5 percent. Unless you walk to get the food or someone delivers it to you via bicycle, local food still has to be transported to an extent. Plus, this example comes from a study in *Environmental Science & Technology* that's talking about buying *all of your food* locally to achieve the maximum reduction in emissions. Meaning that if you bought only certain grocery items, like meat, locally, the reduction in emissions would be less than 4–5 percent.

Don't get me wrong here. I believe that buying food locally and reducing packaging are both incredibly important for a variety of reasons, which we will discuss in the coming chapters. But if we're concerned with reducing the greenhouse gas emissions associated with what we eat, the crucial point lies in the *type of food* we're eating.

Let's look at the details: What if the beef is grass-fed? What about meat that's sustainably raised? The first issue I want to point out is that the term *sustainably raised* doesn't necessarily mean anything. This term is largely subjective, and its application and environmental implications may vary from one farm to the next. This is not just a problem of meat. I always exercise caution when I see any food—meat, vegetable, or otherwise—that's being advertised as "sustainably raised" or "sustainably grown." You have to go beyond the face value of that claim and ask what they mean by it. If you're shopping at a farmers' market, it's easier to inquire with producers directly. If you're buying an item that has additional information on the packaging, or on a corresponding website, this may also be helpful. But if you're buying food that is simply marked "sustainable" and no further information is provided or anywhere to be found, then it probably doesn't mean much. The word *sustainable* and other iterations of it do not have standard definitions in Canada—or in many other places—so their interpretation and application can vary.

Grass-fed is more specific and is often used to distinguish cattle that eat grass from those in feedlots where they eat mostly grain, like corn or barley. This term can apply to other animals like bison or sheep too. There can be positive benefits to raising cattle on grass from a couple of different perspectives. Cattle that spend most or all of their life eating grass are typically in much better situations from an animal welfare perspective. Farmers raising grass-fed beef may also implement other practices on their land that prioritize environmental stewardship, like making efforts to support biodiversity, or considering the health of the grasslands via rotational grazing. If you are going to eat any beef at all, buying beef from these types of scenarios is probably the best option.

The term *grass-fed* can vary in practice, though. In Canada, many cattle actually eat grass for the first portion of their lives and are then finished with grain in feedlots. So the term *grass-fed* may mean that the animal was raised either partially *or* fully on grass during its lifetime. If animals are raised entirely on grass, they're actually considered "grass-finished." But in practice, these terms are often used interchangeably, even though they don't technically mean the same thing. I have also seen the label "100 percent grass-fed," which would mean the beef is grass-finished. Part of the difficulty with grass-finishing beef, however, is that it requires consistent access to grass. In Canada, the winter months can make this tough. So this terminology is something you'd also have to ask an individual producer about. How are they using these terms, and what does this look like in practice on their farm? If someone is advertising their beef as grass-fed or grass-finished, you can usually find out the specifics by asking them directly at a market or if there's further information on their website.

However, there are still a few issues with grass-fed beef in general. Since grass-finished cattle grow at a slower rate and live longer lives—six to twelve months longer than cattle that are finished on grain—they produce more methane emissions from enteric fermentation over the course of their lives. This means that the overall greenhouse gas emissions per unit of beef can actually be higher when the beef is grass-finished. Another issue is land. Although feedlots may be problematic for a number of reasons, they produce more beef using less land. As it stands, the world eats a lot of beef. Switching all cattle to grass-finished operations would require that additional natural landscapes be used for agriculture. And we do not want to be converting more land. This would have negative environmental consequences, like causing more biodiversity loss and additional greenhouse gas emissions. So it's not a realistic solution for everyone to eat grass-finished beef as a means of reducing beef's environmental footprint, while continuing to consume high amounts of it. A reduction in consumption is still necessary overall.

All of this goes to show that there are numerous impacts associated with food beyond those that are visible. Packaging, for example, is both obvious and tangible, and therefore easier to fixate on. But what we really need to focus on is the food itself. Then, following that up by purchasing food locally, and with little to no packaging whenever possible, serves to further reduce the impact. Consider this the foundation—I'm going to call it the cake, if you will. Priority number one, the cake itself, is eating plant-based foods like lentils instead of animal-based foods like beef. The icing on the cake would be if those lentils are local. If those lentils are local *and* can be bought without packaging, that's the cherry on top. We'll revisit these concepts in greater detail in the next two chapters, "Local, Seasonal, Organic" and "Grocery Shopping."

What About Fish and Seafood?

It might seem like fish would be a more obviously sustainable choice, given the impacts of meat. But fish is honestly a bit tricky. Fish and seafood come from one of two sources: either wild-caught or farmed, which is also known as aquaculture. Both of these methods are associated with various environmental concerns.

One of the primary issues with wild-caught fish is the risk of overfishing. Overfishing basically means we are catching and eating any given species much more quickly than it can repopulate itself, leading to a decline in population levels. There is a clear end to this process if overfishing continues without limit. About 65 percent of global fishery stocks are considered biologically sustainable, while the rest are considered overfished. For comparison, in the mid-1970s, biologically sustainable stocks were at 90 percent. Another problem is fishing practices themselves, some of which are more concerning than others. For example, let's say you go out and catch some fish recreationally on a nearby lake, using a line and pole. As long as you are fishing in a way that complies with local fishing regulations, this is fairly sustainable in the grand scheme of things. Large-scale, commercial fishing operations are more concerning because they may use practices that have negative environmental consequences. Bottom trawling, for example, is one fishing practice that can tear up the ocean floor, which affects habitat. Large-scale fishing operations may also catch a number of other, unintended species in the process—commonly referred to as bycatch. Depending on the regulations in a given area, bycatch may be repurposed for human food or fish meal, or it may simply be discarded.

With this in mind, aquaculture is sometimes considered a positive development. Aquaculture essentially allows humans to continue eating fish and seafood without increasing our reliance on wild catch. On the other hand, there are still environmental concerns associated with aquaculture, which can vary depending on how individual farms operate. Some of these impacts include converting natural ecosystems into aquaculture farms, polluting the surrounding area with contaminants like antibiotics or feces, and negatively affecting the health of wild fish species in the region through the spread of disease. Farmed fish may not be native to the area where an aquaculture farm is located; if non-native farmed fish happen to escape, this can be a problem when those fish inevitably interact with native wild fish. In addition, farmed fish have to be fed directly. Some of the fish that's wild-caught globally is turned into fish feed and used for this purpose. Fish feed for aquaculture includes other ingredients, too, like corn or soy.

Part of the reason it's tricky to make any sweeping recommendations here is that "fish and seafood" is a very broad category that includes a number of species—compared with something like "chicken." The sustainability of any given fish or seafood depends not only on the species in question but also on how it was caught or raised. If you refer back to the chart on page 45, farmed prawns and fish rank high for greenhouse gas emissions per kilogram. Wild-caught fish have lower emissions. But if everyone decided to eat more wild fish as a means of lowering their emissions from food, this would not be good news for wild fish populations. Eating farmed fish avoids much of the overfishing issue, and it's also better than eating animal-based foods with higher impacts, like beef or cheese. But aquaculture still has a bigger impact than most plant-based foods. Using soy or wild-caught fish to feed farmed fish also means we're stuck in the wheel of producing food to feed our food. So overall, the lowest-impact option is still a plant-based diet.

However, if you are interested in making more informed choices about the fish and seafood that you do eat, you can refer to a couple of helpful online sources. One is Seafood Watch, which has comprehensive and user-friendly guides to sourcing more-sustainable fish and seafood. For example, Seafood Watch's list of some of the most sustainable options includes farmed mussels, clams, and seaweed. I've noted where to find Seafood Watch, along with a few other, similar sources, in the Resources List.

What About Dairy?

How about dairy specifically, versus plant-based alternatives? If we compare the impacts of cow's milk with plant-based milks—like soy, rice, almond, or oat milk—cow's milk doesn't do so hot. Cow's milk requires more land and water than any of the four plant milks. Unsurprisingly, it also generates more greenhouse gas emissions in the process. When soy, rice, almond, and oat milk are compared with only each other, though, there are also some differences. For instance, oat milk uses the most land but has lower rates of water use and greenhouse gas emissions. Rice milk causes the most greenhouse gas emissions but uses the least amount of land. Even with these differences, all four plant milks still have lower environmental impacts and require fewer resources than cow's milk overall. This is positive news for variety's sake, because it means that any plant milk you prefer is a solid option for replacing cow dairy. Other plant-based dairy alternatives for yogurt, cheese, and more follow a similar pattern: They have lower environmental impacts than their cow-dairy counterparts. Plant-based dairy alternatives are often made from ingredients similar to those in plant milks—including oats, nuts, coconut, vegetable oils, or soy.

Soy often comes up as a red flag, though. I was curious about this myself, as I have been a devout soy milk drinker for years. I prefer soy milk to any other dairy or non-dairy milk option, although I would say oat milk is a solid runner-up. But I have heard other people remark in the past that soy is no better than beef because it's a leading cause of deforestation. I decided to include this in my research and investigate whether it was true.

Here's what I found: Soy is linked to deforestation—that much is true.

The main food-related commodities associated with deforestation are beef, soy, and palm oil. Since the 1960s, the amount of soy produced globally has increased significantly, which of course requires more land. However, deforestation from soy is not the result of the world gobbling up tofu or guzzling glasses of soy milk. Over three-quarters of the soy that's grown globally—77 percent—is turned into animal feed. It's then used for poultry and pigs, and, to a lesser extent, aquaculture. Comparatively, only a meagre 7 percent of the soy that's grown globally is actually used for soy products like tofu, tempeh, edamame beans, or soy milk. What that means is that if you are worried about deforestation from soy, once again, the concern lies primarily with animal-based foods.

The Prominence of Animal-Based Foods in Society

Although I have been blunt about the environmental impacts of animal-based foods in this chapter, I have not done so to vilify farmers or ranchers in any way. Agriculture is a livelihood with real people involved. It's also hugely important in Canada, particularly in rural communities. All four of my grandparents lived on farms in rural Saskatchewan before moving to urban centres. On Paul's paternal side, some of his family members operate a cattle farm in Alberta, which has been in the family for decades. If broad shifts are going to happen in how the world eats, farmers need to be involved in that conversation. There are farmer-led organizations working to address this already—including in Canada. I've noted a couple of these organizations in the Resources List.

Similarly, nothing in this chapter has been meant to vilify animals. Animals can be an important part of agricultural systems, working in tandem with the landscape by adding nutrients to the soil as they graze and excrete. So I don't think it's fair to discount animal agriculture entirely and say that meat has absolutely no place in the future. But it does need to have a dramatically reduced place. This is especially true for countries like Canada where consumption of high-impact animal-based foods is widespread and frequent.

Globally, the production of meat—including poultry, pork, and beef—is now four times higher than it was in the early 1960s. Although there are more people living on Earth today than there were in the early 1960s, the amount of meat consumed per person has also jumped since then. There is also a strong link between high-income countries and high rates of meat consumption. In Canada, about 44 percent of the population eats beef one or two days every week, while 17 percent of Canadians eat beef three to four days each week. On the plant side of things, only 3 percent of Canadians are vegan—meaning they do not eat any animal-based foods at all—and a combined 11 percent identify as either vegetarian, flexitarian, or pescatarian, meaning they don't eat meat but may eat eggs, fish, or dairy.

During my research for this chapter, I came across some sources calling veganism and plant-based eating a privilege for people who can afford it in high-income countries. One reason for this assessment lies in having the option to pick between plant- and animal-based foods in the first place. Being able to choose plant-based foods out of a colossal number of options at the grocery store is a privilege—no doubt about it. There's also some truth to the idea that plant-based eating is a privilege if you are eating large quantities of specialty plant-based products with a higher price tag—like nut-based cheese, for example. However, it's fair to say that meat is generally more expensive than many of the less glitzy plant-based protein staples, like lentils and beans.

A second reason for this assessment is that in some parts of the world, small-scale subsistence fishing and animal agriculture practices *are* sustainable. This is also true of certain parts of Canada. In northern regions, for example, foods like fresh fruits and vegetables can be harder to come by, so Indigenous communities in particular may rely on small-scale hunting and fishing practices. And small-scale subsistence practices simply do not have the same impacts that industrialized meat, dairy, and fishing do.

But with that in mind, choosing to eat a diet that's heavy in industrialized meat and dairy could also be considered a privilege for people who can afford it. This is especially true if there are a variety of options available and affordable to you any time you stroll through the sliding doors of the supermarket. So if you *do* have a choice in whether your diet consists primarily of animal- or plant-based foods, then I think there's a certain level of responsibility there. How could there not be?

It's fair to acknowledge that hearing about the environmental impacts of different foods can sometimes be uncomfortable or inconvenient—particularly if you're hearing it for the first time. This information is unlikely to be cheerful news to anyone who eats animal-based foods several times a day. In a book like this, you probably expected me to talk about low-waste cooking tips, the problems of plastic, or why composting is important. But these types of topics don't hit home the same way that finding out about the impact of your favourite hamburger does. However, there is no way to address making your kitchen more sustainable without talking about what we eat. The impacts of the food system are far too great to be ignored in a discussion like this. The topics we've looked at in this chapter are incredibly complex; there is plenty of nuance involved. So if you're interested in further reading, see the Resources List.

The Impacts of Plant-Based Foods

At this point, you may be wondering if there is anything wrong with plant-based foods at all. It seems like plant-based foods can do no wrong. I told you earlier that I'd get to rice and coffee, which rank highly on the chart on page 45—and I keep my promises. Given the popularity of coffee in Canada, though, I decided to give the beloved bean its own chapter. So we will do a deep dive on coffee and tea starting on page 211.

Rice has higher environmental impacts than many other grains because of how it's produced. During the growing season, rice fields are often submerged—a process that requires a lot of water. Flooded rice fields are basically an ideal environment for certain micro-organisms to create methane gas, which then leads to emissions. About 1.7 percent of all global greenhouse gas emissions are the result of methane from rice. However, if changes are made to how rice is grown, these emissions could be reduced.

At the end of the day, all food has some sort of environmental impact, regardless of whether it's plant- or animal-based. Even low-impact plant-based foods still have an impact—it's just less than that of other foods. For interest's sake, though, what would happen if the world started eating a plant-based diet? In terms of greenhouse gas emissions, there are massive savings to be made—a 49 percent reduction, to be exact. It's also estimated that shifting to plant-based diets could cut the total amount of land used around the world for agriculture by 76 percent. That's an incredible amount of land. What might happen to that land if it's not being used for agriculture? This is an important question. A perfect solution would be to give that land back to Mother Nature and let her do her thing. Trees grow tall, biodiversity levels increase, and ecosystems restore themselves. The beauty of letting nature rewild is that it requires little of us. Nature knows how to recover; we just have to get out of the way. Maybe this is wishful thinking, but what if it's not?

Furthermore, many top environmental organizations, activists, and others highlight plant-based diets as both a major opportunity for addressing climate change and one of the most effective ways to take personal climate action in an everyday sense. This includes Project Drawdown, Greta Thunberg's *The Climate Book*, and the Intergovernmental Panel on Climate Change. Eating little to no animal-based foods often appears alongside other hard-hitting actions, like going car-free, reducing air travel, and using renewable sources of energy.

Now it's time for the big question: How exactly do you go about shifting to a plant-based diet? Well—let me tell you.

What You Can Do

Shift Toward a Plant-Based Diet

All of the other chapters in this book offer two or more solutions. In this chapter, however, there is really only one solution: shifting away from frequent consumption of animal-based foods and toward more plant-based ones instead. The rest of this chapter is about helping you get there. Some people may be inclined to cut out all animal-based foods cold turkey—minus the turkey, in this case—but others may favour a gradual approach. Changing your diet can sometimes be easier said than done, so keep in mind that this is a journey. To give you some guidance, I'll also get into the nitty-gritty of my own plant-based shift as we go along.

Take Stock of Your Starting Point

The specifics of implementing a plant-based shift will vary from one person to the next, largely depending on your starting point. Before you dive into adding more plant-based foods, it can be helpful to reflect on how much of your regular diet is made up of animal-based ones. There's no need to extensively track what you're eating—unless you feel it would be genuinely helpful—but it is useful to have a basic grasp of what you eat in a typical day or week, so that you have a clear understanding of how extensive your shift will be.

We're going to do a bit of time travelling here and go back to March 2024, so that I can walk you through my own starting point.

For most of my childhood, I drank a glass of cow's milk with breakfast and dinner—no leaving the table until it was finished. Then, when I was a teenager, my sister, Aunya, was diagnosed as lactose intolerant. As a result, our family gradually began eating more plant-based dairy alternatives. Given that I was not lactose intolerant, I regularly ate a combination of cow and plant dairy. I never saw much of a distinction between them; they just tasted slightly different. I still view dairy through this lens. I prefer soy milk in my coffee and smoothies. I prefer cow cheese on my nachos. I bake with whatever we have in the fridge—sometimes that's cow butter, sometimes it's plant butter. So my starting point with dairy was flexible, and I had similar feelings about eggs. I've never really been an egg person, so I didn't eat eggs very often, aside from using them in baking.

Meat was a bit of a different story, however; I felt more attached to it. Even before undertaking this shift, all of my breakfasts and snacks throughout a typical week were plant-based, but my lunches could go either way. On average, my lunches were plant-based three times a week, animal-based four times a week. Dinners in our household almost always included animal-based foods, though. I had a few plant-based recipes in my regular dinner rotation, but these recipes were the exception. Our dinners often featured a protein like chicken, fish, pork, or bison, either in a soup or stew, or alongside some sort of vegetable, starch, or grain. When I considered my starting point, it became obvious to me that dinners were going to be the biggest change. Paul and I had been eating dinners together with an animal-based protein for years by this point, so I wasn't about to simply reverse this overnight.

This is exactly why taking stock is helpful; it will give you an indication of how much time you need to shift toward a plant-based diet. It's possible the transition could take weeks, months, or even longer, especially if it requires more drastic changes or you face additional challenges, like cooking for a large family, major dietary restrictions, or living in a remote area, for example. As I mentioned before, I'm now eating 85–90 percent plant-based, but it's been ten months since I started this shift. It was not an immediate transition by any means. Later on in this chapter, we'll talk more about finding a balance between making dietary changes and being realistic about your circumstances.

Before you make any changes to your own diet, I would recommend having a chat with the health professionals in your life. Changing what you eat can have an impact on your health, especially sudden changes. And given that I'm not a doctor, none of the information in this chapter is meant to be used as health, nutritional, or medical advice. For example, depending on the extent of your plant-based shift, you may need to take a vitamin B12 supplement. Plant-based foods do not contain vitamin B12 unless they're fortified with it. Again, speak to a health professional about this. Before and during my own shift, I got my vitamin B12 levels checked—which is done via a blood test—just to confirm all was well.

Invite Your Loved Ones into the Process

If you live with other people who will be affected by this shift, talk to them in advance. There are two key things that I think are important to address in this conversation.

The first is explaining why the shift matters from a sustainability perspective, but also why it matters to you. Set aside some time together for a discussion, and then explain the various impacts of plant versus animal foods. Alternatively, you could ask your loved ones if they would be willing to read the first part of this chapter for context.

The second key thing to address is what can be gained from shifting toward a plant-based diet. It can be helpful to frame this shift as increasing your consumption of plant-based foods, rather than reducing your consumption of animal-based ones. How you view this shift will shape much of your experience. This is an opportunity to add, not take away. The reality is that if you are the one initiating a plant-based shift in your household, then you are also the one marketing it to your loved ones. "Let's eat more plants and try some different types of beans!" is much more enticing and inviting than making a demand like "We need to stop eating beef and cheese right now!" I would put money on the fact that most people would not react well to the second statement—which is fair.

In my case, the loved one in question was Paul. To be honest, I'm not sure if Paul knew what he was in for when I started working on *Building a Sustainable Kitchen*. Over the years and prior to writing this book, I'd made various sustainable changes in our home—like reducing food waste, for example. To his credit, Paul accepted these changes willingly. But Paul enjoys meat—and it would be safe to say that he enjoys meat more than I do. At the same time, he's incredibly supportive of me and my writing career. So when I approached him about this plant-based shift and explained my reasoning, he agreed to try it.

Paul is a good example of how other people in your household may have a different starting point from you. What that means is that the extent or time-line of their plant-based shift may be different from yours. For example, Paul doesn't usually eat breakfast, and his lunches consist of either leftovers from the night before or whatever's on the menu at the school cafeteria where he works. Dinners are the same as mine, since we eat together every night. Any plant-based changes he was going to make would therefore mainly involve our dinners, which would then spill over into his leftover lunches. I was not about to start monitoring his lunch food from the school cafeteria—there was no way that doing so would be good for our relationship. Paul's main comment about the plant-based shift was that he didn't mind if any given food was plant- or animal-based as long as it tasted good. This stipulation was fine by me—I had no intention of preparing plant-based food that tasted bad.

Keep in mind that your family may be less keen on shifting to a plant-based diet than you are. This also may be more or less challenging if you have children. In practice, you might have to navigate a bit of a transition period. Perhaps you provide both plant- and animal-based options at meals, at least for a little while. As I dived more heavily into the plant-based shift than Paul did, I ended up doing this every now and then with our dinners. For example, taco salad with ground chicken for Paul and black beans for me. At the end of the day, you can't force other people to eat or not eat certain foods. Everyone has to choose this path for themselves.

Set Reasonable Goals

Once you've decided to proceed with a plant-based shift, the next step is deciding how much of your animal-based food consumption to reduce. Because I was initiating this shift for environmental reasons, I wanted to see what was recommended from a research perspective. In other words: How much of a reduction is necessary to make a difference?

While there are many climate-friendly dietary guidelines out there, I decided to go with the Planetary Health Diet. This diet was first published in 2019 by the EAT-Lancet Commission on Food, Planet, Health, a global non-profit foundation involving scientists and researchers from across the world. The diet essentially outlines a path forward where we can feed the global population projection of ten billion people by 2050 in a way that is sustainable for the Earth.

I was drawn to the Planetary Health Diet largely because of its flexibility. Given the variety in what people eat around the world, the guidelines are meant to be malleable. The recommendations focus on food groups or categories but do not prescribe specific foods. Additionally, the Planetary Health Diet is widely esteemed for its emphasis on the health of *both* humans and the planet. Beyond environmental concerns, there are many other reasons to eat more plant-based foods—one of which is better human health. So the Planetary Health Diet is primarily focused on whole foods. It's not a junk-food diet by any means.

If the Planetary Health Diet takes the shape of a plate, half of the plate is fruit and vegetables. The other half is mainly whole grains, plant-based proteins like legumes and nuts, and unsaturated plant oils like olive oil. Small amounts of meat, dairy, eggs, and fish are also included on the plate, but they are optional. A visual of this plate is included below, for reference.

How much optional meat, dairy, eggs, and fish are we talking about here? When combined, all animal-based foods make up about 12 percent of daily or overall calories—it's 12.14 percent, to be precise. The Planetary Health Diet outlines an example based on 2,500 calories per day, which means that about 300 calories each day come from animal-based foods. The rest comes from plants.

Here's what that looks like on a weekly basis: The guidelines allow 98 grams of red meat (which they define as beef, pork, or lamb), 203 grams of poultry, 91 grams of eggs, 196 grams of fish, and 1,750 grams of dairy. In grocery terms, this is approximately one 100-gram steak, one chicken breast, one and a half eggs, one can of salmon, and about seven cups of cow's milk—every week, per person. If you eat fewer than 2,500 calories a day, these amounts would be lower to adjust for your overall caloric intake. So the key here is that animal-based foods make up about 12 percent or less of overall calories. In other words, the diet is at least 88 percent plant-based.

What's interesting is that Canada's Food Guide isn't all that different from the Planetary Health Diet. When Canada's Food Guide takes the shape of a plate, fruits and vegetables comprise half, while one-quarter is whole grains and the remaining quarter is proteins. But the food guide also recommends consuming plant-based proteins like legumes, nuts, seeds, and tofu more often than animal-based proteins. If a quarter of the plate is for protein, and let's say that even half of that protein comes from plants, then that would make Canada's Food Guide a largely plant-based diet.

Taking these guidelines into account, I decided to set an initial target of 80 percent plant-based within the first few months. My final goal would be the lucky number of 88 percent plant-based or higher, in line with the Planetary Health Diet. Paul did not set any sort of reduction goal. He was just willing to eat more plants. Given that this was my project, I considered his willingness a step in the right direction.

When setting your own goal, consider how extensive your shift will be and what a realistic timeline is for you. You can do this individually, or if everyone in your household is fully on board, you could set a household goal instead. Both the Planetary Health Diet and Canada's Food Guide can be useful guidelines, but you could also approach this more generally. For example, if you currently eat a lot of animal-based foods, you might start by aiming to just cut that amount in half within the first few months. Then you could scale up from there and adopt a set of guidelines like those of the

Planetary Health Diet later on. Either way, it's important that any changes you make are personally sustainable, so that you can actually commit to them long-term. If starting slowly with smaller goals feels more manageable, then do that. In the Resources List, I have noted where to find information on both Canada's Food Guide and the Planetary Health Diet.

Start with What's Easiest for You

I think the best place to start your shift is with whatever feels like low-hanging fruit—or, more accurately, whatever feels like low-hanging meat and dairy. This might be a specific meal, or it might be a specific ingredient. If it seems like breakfast would be an easy swap, or if you've never been a fan of pork anyway, then start there. This approach is helpful because it means that even small shifts will make it feel like you've been successful almost immediately.

This was exactly what I did: I cut out dairy and eggs. Dairy and eggs felt like the easiest changes to tackle, given my long-standing approach toward them. I soon found myself baking with blended beans, using flax eggs (ground flaxseed mixed with water to create a mock egg), and "baking" without actually doing any baking at all—many vegan treats can simply be frozen. On the dairy front, I swapped cow butter for plant butter more consistently, and I bought yogurt made from oat milk and kefir made from coconut milk. All of these products were easy changes—I didn't find them overly different from cow-dairy versions. The one thing that I think cows do better is cheese. Plant-based cheese can admittedly be a little disappointing, although it will likely improve in the future. So I decided that when I did eat cheese, it would be the cow variety and included in my 12 percent of animal-based foods. The other low-hanging fruit I went for was my weekday lunches, which were easy to tackle because changing them affected only me. I found some reliable one-pot plant-based pasta dishes and also started bulking up salads with lentils, beans, and grains.

What's easiest for you to tackle first may not align with the big-ticket foods, and that's okay. Remember, it's going to be better in the long run if you make changes you can actually commit to and then work your way up. Here's what I mean: Since the highest-impact food is beef, cutting consumption of beef and other ruminants will have the biggest impact. But if you eat a lot of ruminant-based foods and find it difficult to envision yourself enjoying lentils in their place, start by swapping high-impact beef for moderate-impact chicken or pork. Choosing animal-based foods with moderate impacts over those with high impacts is still going to reduce the overall impact of what you eat. This is especially true if you eat high-impact foods several times a day. The environmental jump from beef to plants is a large one, but the jump from beef to chicken is still significant. If it feels easier to take smaller steps in the meat department first—rather than heading straight to the plant-based department—then start there.

Learn to Cook with Plant-Based Protein

Eating a plant-based diet does not mean you don't eat any protein—quite the opposite, actually. But I think one of the barriers to adopting a plant-based diet is simply not knowing what to do with plant-based proteins like beans, lentils, or tofu. This was certainly the case for me. I knew that cooking with plant-based protein was going to be the biggest hurdle—especially for our dinners—largely because I was a much better cook in the animal-based protein department. I wasn't totally unfamiliar with plant-based cooking, but there is a certain level of skill involved in preparing something like tofu in a flavourful way. However, I consoled myself with the knowledge that at one point in my life, I was not particularly good at cooking animal-based foods either. I make a mean roast chicken dinner now, but when I first moved out of my parents' house, I didn't have a clue what to do. I have come a long way since then, so I tried to keep this in mind as I approached beans, lentils, and tofu. It was going to be a learning curve, and I allowed myself to be okay with that.

You could approach learning to cook more plant-based in a number of ways. But after doing some reading online, I concluded that the simplest option was to take recipes we already ate and modify them to exclude meat. This is fairly common advice, because it's one of the least disruptive tactics—you're just swapping one protein for another in the same recipe. So I made our usual hamburger soup but used lentils instead of ground turkey. I tried tofu in tacos and swapped chicken for chickpeas in a noodle soup. While this was largely fine, after a few weeks Paul said something that made me pause. He noted that when we ate our favourite meals without meat—like hamburger soup, which we've been eating the same way for years—it was much more obvious that the meat wasn't there. This made it easier to compare the meat version with the meatless one. Once I gave this some thought, I realized I agreed. Shouldn't this be about more than just substituting plants for meat? What if I cooked so that plants were designed to be the star of the show? Why not make plant-based foods the centrepiece, rather than just the replacement?

I changed my game plan. I combed through vegan blogs and cookbooks for inspiration. I started an ongoing list on my phone of recipe ideas and meals I wanted to try. Over the course of several months, I tried numerous plant-based dishes, at a rate of about three to four new ones each month. There was a range to the complexity of these recipes. Some were quick and simple, but others were more involved, particularly when trying them for the first time. For example, there was a bean chili we both really liked and a spiced lentil and kale soup that was superb. I kept going: falafel bowls, Thai red curry with tofu, edamame bean stir-fry, tempeh peanut bowls, chickpea curry, bean and veggie burritos, and more.

I went rogue with many of these recipes and modified them along the way. While I enjoy looking at recipes for inspiration, I wanted to teach myself how to cook plant-based intuitively. I also wasn't about to leave my usual food waste reduction habits at the door either. I took many of the tactics we discussed in the "Low-Waste Cooking" chapter and simply applied them to plants. I thought intuitively about what might taste good together, I made small batches to start, and I taste-tested the food along the way. On the whole, Paul and I approached this thoughtfully, as a sort of experiment. We ate the meals together, and then we discussed them in depth. What did we like? Was there anything we didn't like? We talked about the texture of various proteins and brainstormed ways that meals could be changed or improved. For example, I had tried cooking tofu in cubes, which seemed like the obvious way to cook it. But neither of us was crazy about the cubed texture. So I tried shredding a block of tofu and then crisping it in the oven, which we agreed gave a better end result.

As time went on, I gradually developed a better understanding of how to best cook beans and create perfectly crispy tofu. But while trying new dishes is both interesting and enjoyable, it's not always a realistic strategy for a busy weeknight. So in between trying new recipes, I implemented other tactics. I found ways to add plant-based protein to simple dishes—like blending a can of cannellini beans into pasta sauce, or blending a block of tofu into a smoothie. I also continued to make some of the animal-based meals we particularly enjoyed but cut the amount of meat in half—like spaghetti and meat sauce. Rather than making a full meat sauce, I made a sauce of half ground meat, half lentils. This was an easy way to cut the amount of meat in a dish by 50 percent without having to change the dish entirely. Replacing half of the protein in any dish with canned beans or lentils in particular also requires no additional work, other than opening the can.

Other plant-based protein options you can explore are meat alternative and substitution products. This may be particularly helpful if you really love the taste of meat. The brand Beyond Meat, for example, makes plant-based versions of sausage, ground beef, hamburgers, and more. I find that the hamburgers in particular from Beyond Meat are so flavourful and juicy, it makes you wonder whether you're actually eating meat. You're not, but it's a striking comparison.

But are these types of products still environmentally preferable to meat? Yes. For example, in a study in *Sustainability* that compared a regular beef burger patty with an equal serving of two different plant-based burger patties, the plant-based patties had lower impacts than the beef. The two plant-based burger patties in the study were from the popular brands Beyond Meat and Impossible Foods. The results showed that both of the plant-based patties caused fewer greenhouse gas emissions and required less water and land than their beef counterpart. This reduction ranged from 87 to 96 percent across the various categories—which is to say, a lot. So if you feel like these types of alternative plant-based products would be helpful for you, try incorporating them into your diet.

One other thing I will say here is that while tofu often comes to mind as an obvious plant-based protein, you certainly don't have to eat it exclusively. There's a whole wide world of beans and lentils out there. I buy both dried and canned beans and lentils, and I find them incredibly versatile. Dried chickpeas, for example, can be turned into falafel, ground into flour, or cooked and used in soups, stews, salads, curries, and baking. So don't be afraid to explore a range of plant-based protein foods as you tackle your shift.

As I taught myself to cook plant-based, I discovered that plant-based proteins have so much to offer—much more perhaps than what meets the eye. This realization certainly helped the cause. Plant-based proteins are both delicious and versatile. I have found both delight and pleasure in shifting to a plant-based diet, which makes plant-based eating personally sustainable in the long run. Flavour is not something to be sacrificed in the slightest. There are many other incredible resources out there that highlight this sentiment—from cookbooks to blogs, plants are certainly having a moment. In the Resources List, I have outlined other sources you can refer to for recipe inspiration, cooking techniques, and more. If there are any plant-based cooking classes being taught near you, this could also be a helpful way to jump-start the learning curve.

Prioritize Progress over Perfection and Reflect on the Process

If you're making drastic changes to your diet, I think it's important to reflect on those changes, take note of your progress, and acknowledge how far you've come. Has shifting to a plant-based diet been easy? Has it been challenging? What foods have you come to appreciate that you never bothered with previously? Your experience may surprise you—mine certainly did.

As the months passed, I noticed that my palate started to shift. I began to thoroughly enjoy the taste and texture of lentils and beans, in particular. I appreciated how creamy cannellini beans were, and how meaty dark red kidney beans could be. Some days for lunch I simply opened a can of beans, seasoned them, and ate them alongside vegetables and crackers. I also began to view animal-based foods as more of an every-now-and-then thing, rather than an everyday one. All in all, I leaned much more fully into the plant-based shift than I had expected. Previously, I would never have imagined myself eating a can of seasoned beans for lunch and being happy about it. Yet there I was, genuinely debating whether I was more in the mood for Romano, kidney, or lima beans. All of which are excellent choices, by the way.

It is now January 2025. Any meals I eat that do contain animal-based foods are typically dinners. Out of seven dinners each week, Paul and I eat four that are entirely plant-based, two that have an animal-based protein, and one that typically includes a plant protein for me and an animal protein for him. For our animal-based dinners, we primarily choose from the moderately impactful meats, like chicken or pork, and sometimes fish. On an average day I eat about 2,200 calories, which is 15,400 calories each week. In a typical week now, about 1,000 of my calories come from animal-based foods. This makes my weekly diet about 6.5 percent animal-based, 93.5 percent plant-based. But there's a caveat: Any time a family dinner, holiday, or celebration comes up, my consumption of animal-based foods increases. On Thanksgiving weekend, for example, I probably eat closer to 15 or 20 percent of my calories from animal-based foods. Or if we're going to visit family for a weekend and I know I'll have less control over the type of food I'm eating, then I don't worry about this. I just get back to plants once I'm home. Which is why I would say, all things considered, my diet is now, on average, 85–90 percent plant-based.

Although this calorie and percentage breakdown is helpful to see how my diet has changed in retrospect, throughout my own plant-based shift, I didn't think about it like this at all. Instead, I thought about it more generally—like how a more sustainable diet looks when it's mapped out on a dinner plate. You can choose to approach this however you want. Just know that tracking exact percentages is not necessary to be successful.

In a similar vein, shifting to a plant-based diet does not need to be perfect to have an impact. This is not about a handful of people eating perfectly plant-based. This is about millions and millions of people choosing to consistently eat more low-impact foods, which would collectively move the needle on our food system's multi-faceted environmental impacts. Choosing to eat a more plant-based diet also doesn't mean that you can't enjoy animal-based foods when you do eat them. Enjoy the meat, fish, and dairy that you do eat—just eat less of these foods. We don't need perfection or shaming here. We need everyone doing what they can on a regular, long-term basis.

Given that I did not set out to eat 100 percent plant-based, I have found plenty of flexibility within this shift. If my friends get together for a wine and cheese night, that's no problem. If I go cover a restaurant for CBC that's renowned for its barbecue eats, I can still try the food and write the article. The bottom line is that if only about 12 percent of your diet is coming from animal-based foods, for example, then you get to choose where and when you are eating that 12 percent. Prioritizing a drastic reduction, but not total elimination, of animal-based foods makes shifting to a plant-based diet much easier.

I enjoy eating certain animal-based foods from time to time, but I also feel strongly about living more sustainably. I know I'm not the only person who feels both of these sentiments. Furthermore, animal-based foods can be an important part of both cultural and traditional practices. They often feature prominently around the holidays and special occasions. And, simply put, there has to be room for all of that and more. I think the fact that adopting a sustainable diet doesn't require going full-on vegan to make a difference helps make plant-based eating much more approachable overall.

As a final note, let's go back to the loved ones in the picture. After ten months of eating more plant-based, I asked Paul what he thought of the experience, to gain a second perspective. He did not miss eating dairy or eggs—he said this was barely noticeable. He also didn't mind that he was eating less beef and bison. While he still sometimes orders a steak if we go out for dinner, on the whole, he eats beef less regularly now. The main challenge Paul felt from this experience was that he grew up eating dinners that featured meat, alongside potatoes and a vegetable. Therefore, he thinks of meat-based meals as being more inherently satisfying, which is something he didn't realize until undertaking this shift. He had a hard time with tofu, in particular. We agreed that meals featuring lentils and beans were our preference—they were filling and hearty.

At the same time, I think perhaps Paul has leaned into this experience more than he realizes. Recently, we went out to eat at a local restaurant for a family dinner. This particular restaurant has several succulent meat-based main dishes on the menu. And Paul ordered a plant-based beet ravioli. This surprised me. But then again, maybe it shouldn't have. He's been open to eating more plant-based all along—as long as it tasted good, right? And I could tell by the smile on his face that this beet ravioli certainly fit the bill.

Takeaways

- Consider your starting point so you have a sense of how extensive your shift will be, and prepare by talking to your doctor.
- Talk to the people you live with about shifting to a plant-based diet before you make any changes. Invite them to be involved in the process.
- Figure out a reasonable target for reducing animal-based foods. Take a look at the Planetary Health Diet, for example, as a guideline.
- Pick whatever feels like the easiest change, and start there. You can always scale up!
- Lean into the experience of learning to cook with plant-based proteins. Explore new recipes, make simple protein swaps, or try plant-based meat substitute products.
- Remember that progress, not perfection, is the goal. Take some time to reflect along the way and recognize that this is a journey.

CHAPTER 4:

Local, Seasonal, Organic

WE'VE JUST ESTABLISHED that the *type of food* is the most important factor when it comes to reducing the environmental impact of what we eat. But whether we're eating a forkful of plants or animals, it still leaves unanswered questions. Where should we buy our food? Should it be local and seasonal? Should it be organic? This is exactly what we're going to talk about in this chapter.

It's mind-boggling that I can walk into a grocery store in Saskatoon at any time of the year and purchase food that was not grown or produced anywhere near the Prairies. I can get lemons and avocados in September, January, or May. If one grocery store doesn't have them, it's highly likely the next one will.

At one point in time, however, eating food that was local or seasonal to you wasn't a choice—all the available food was inherently local or seasonal. So while eating locally and seasonally are not really new concepts, they have both undergone a resurgence, particularly since the early 2000s. In Canada, over the past ten years, a heightened interest in food that's produced locally has also led to an increase in the number of farms that do direct-to-consumer sales. Direct sales can include online stores with delivery, farmers' markets, or on-site farm stores, for example.

But what do I mean by local or seasonal food? Let's get into it.

Eating Local

The term *local* doesn't necessarily have one single definition and can be subject to interpretation. Statistics Canada, for example, collects information about local food sales, and in doing so it defines those sales as taking place within the same province or territory that the food was produced in. But its definition also notes that any food that's sold within 50 kilometres of where it was originally produced would count as local, even if it crosses a provincial or territorial border. The bestselling book *The 100-Mile Diet: A Year of Local Eating* by Alisa Smith and J.B. MacKinnon, published in 2007, popularized the idea of eating only food from within a 100-mile (160-kilometre) radius of where you live. As a result, local food is often considered within this framework: If it was produced within 100 miles of you, it's local. This is also sometimes referred to as "food miles," which measures the distance that food travels between where it's produced and where it's consumed. The key here is that local food usually refers to food that was both produced and consumed either within a certain distance or within the same geographic boundary on a map. Sometimes it means both.

I have also seen some definitions of local food that use the place of purchase, or the vendor, as a defining factor. For example, if you bought the food from a farmers' market or directly from a farm. Although place of purchase may be one important element of local food, I don't think it's necessarily as accurate as defining local food by distance or geographic boundary, because local food is now showing up in conventional grocery stores, and some farmers' markets may also sell food that is from other locations. Here in Saskatoon, throughout the summer there are often fruit vendors from British Columbia selling cherries, peaches, and more. These situations blur the lines of using place of purchase as the sole defining factor of local food. Geographic location and distance travelled are a bit more clear-cut. Either the food falls within the boundary or it doesn't.

When I seek out local food, I am mainly looking for food that was raised, grown, or produced in Saskatchewan. I tend to think about local food first in terms of geographic location and second in terms of distance. The goal is really just that the food be produced as close to me as possible. Food produced in Alberta is outside of that boundary for me—it's local to Alberta. How you define local food is somewhat up to you, though. If you live in a border city like Flin Flon or Lloydminster, local food may be less about province or territory and more about food miles. For the purposes of this book, I am going to consider local food in the following way: Food that is produced within the province or territory that you live in and, secondly, sourced *as close as possible* to you within that boundary.

Eating Seasonal

Seasonal is much more straightforward. During the time of year when any given food grows naturally in a specific place, it's *in season*. When people talk about seasonal food, they're mainly talking about fruits and vegetables, because other foods like meat and dairy can be produced any time of year.

The outdoor growing season in Canada for fruits and vegetables is not a constant year-round process, despite the fact that conventional grocery stores make it appear that way. Instead, eating with the seasons means that what you eat will fluctuate throughout the year. For example, in Saskatchewan, rhubarb and asparagus are in season in the spring, raspberries and corn in the summer, and apples and pumpkins in the fall. The outdoor growing season essentially drops off in Canada during the winter, which makes practices like preserving, dehydrating, cold storing, and freezing helpful.

When rhubarb shows up at the Saskatoon Farmers' Market in June—looking all fresh and cheery in bright shades of pink and red—that makes it both local and seasonal in Saskatchewan at that point in time. You might be able to buy fresh rhubarb at the grocery store in Saskatoon in January, but it would not be seasonal at that point. Given that most grocery stores don't stock food based on when it's in season locally, it can be hard to know which foods are in season where you live, unless you seek this information out yourself. In the Resources List, I have noted a few sources where you can learn more about seasonal food.

Why Eat Local and Seasonal?

Local food and seasonal food both have several benefits, many of which overlap. The economic benefits of eating local food are typically the ones that get the most attention—and rightly so. When you buy local food, you are directly supporting the farmers, growers, ranchers, and producers who live and work nearby. This helps keep money within your town, city, or province. When local food is produced and distributed all in the same geographic area, it helps create and sustain jobs in the community. In Canada, small-to-medium-sized farms are also more likely to engage in direct-to-consumer sales than larger ones, which really just means that by buying local food, you're often supporting small-business owners. All of this contributes to a more resilient local food system—the importance of which should not be understated.

There isn't a more obvious example of why local food systems are important than the COVID-19 pandemic. When grocery shelves were suddenly devoid of their typical unbounded selection, the global food system and our reliance on it were laid bare. But we don't want to have strong local food systems just for the sake of falling back on them in times of crisis. Instead, it's important to support and engage with local food systems on a consistent and frequent basis. Doing so also helps to address wider issues like food security, economic stability, and building resilience in the face of a changing climate.

Other benefits of eating locally and seasonally include the overall quality and freshness of the food. When you buy produce at a farmers' market, for example, that produce is typically picked a couple of days or fewer before it's sold—and only once it's ripe. You are getting the freshest produce possible, which also means it's at its nutritional peak. This makes the food taste much better. It also means the produce is more likely to last longer once you bring it home—which is good news for reducing food waste. Because non-local produce is often travelling long distances to its final destination, it can get picked before it's ripe. Although it's better for fruits and vegetables to ripen along the way, rather than arrive in a mushy, overripe mess, this does affect the quality and flavour. You can absolutely taste the difference between a pale grocery store tomato picked too early, and a vibrant garden tomato that has been plucked from the vine in season. Produce that is going the distance is also more likely to require additional packaging than local food, since there is a larger window between when it's harvested and when it's consumed.

But I told you in the "What We Eat" chapter that packaging and the distance food travels are both less important than the type of food we eat. This is still true. So why do we often assume that buying local food is the best way to reduce greenhouse gas emissions? I think this likely has something to do with the belief that most of our food is flying around the world. This logic makes sense, given that reducing or avoiding air travel *is* associated with a lower carbon footprint. However, the vast majority of food does not actually come by air—it's incredibly expensive. Over half of the world's food, 59 percent, is transported by water, followed by road at 31 percent, and rail at 10 percent. Air travel makes up less than 1 percent of all global food miles.

Flying food around the world does have a large carbon footprint though. If you take the exact same amount of food and compare the impact of transporting it by air versus by water in a temperature-controlled situation, air transport causes about fifty times more greenhouse gas emissions than water transport does. If you didn't eat any food that was transported by airplane, you could actually cut down on your food's greenhouse gas emissions. Unfortunately, it's a bit tricky to know exactly which foods to avoid, because they're not labelled. Food that comes by air is often produce with a shorter shelf life, like cherries, berries, or green beans, for example. At the same time, there may be cherries, berries, or green beans available at the grocery store that were not flown in. To avoid air-transported foods, you could prioritize buying perishable produce in particular from local sources, when in season.

At the end of the day, air travel accounts for a very small percentage compared with food that's delivered by other transportation methods. On top of that, most environmental impact comes from food production, not food transportation. This is why the *type* of food we're eating—plants or animals—is still priority number one, followed by considerations about local and seasonal. The most straightforward way to reduce the overall environmental impact of what you eat is to focus on the cake, remember? This doesn't mean that the icing or cherry on top of the cake is unimportant. In fact, I think we can all agree that the icing and cherry on top actually make the cake *better*. Eating local and seasonal still makes a difference, and it can be especially worth the effort when you take into account supporting local food systems near you.

Eating Sustainably Looks Different in Every Climate

I want to mention one other thing before we move on to organic. So far, this discussion of local and seasonal food has been about food that's grown outdoors. You can buy local food from greenhouses too, though. Greenhouses make it possible to grow food like fruits and vegetables outside of their natural growing season and in geographic areas where the growing conditions might be difficult to work with. However, greenhouses sometimes get flagged as more of an environmental problem than a solution. This is because it requires ongoing energy to keep greenhouses warm and bright. This impact varies from one greenhouse to the next. If a greenhouse happens to rely on a renewable energy source like solar, for example, this brings the impact way down.

Either way, if you buy food from a local greenhouse, you're still supporting and receiving all of the other local food benefits we've talked about—the economic side, the quality of food, and the creation of a more resilient food system. Greenhouses can also be crucial for food security, especially if it's hard to grow fresh produce in a given area. I'll give you an example of this.

A couple of summers ago, Paul and I were in the town of Inuvik, Northwest Territories, and I saw first-hand just how essential a greenhouse can be. The produce situation at the town's two grocery stores was dismal; the quality of the fruits and vegetables was poor, and yet they were still incredibly expensive. On all fronts, I would have been paying more for less. I've since learned that this produce quality issue becomes even more challenging during the winter months. There are a number of reasons for this, one of which is how far food has to travel to get to Inuvik in the first place. While we were there, though, I happened upon the most magical place: the Inuvik Community Greenhouse.

Formerly a hockey arena, the Inuvik Community Greenhouse is a non-profit organization that has been around since 1998. The greenhouse operates on a seasonal basis, greatly extending the natural growing window in Inuvik. It also has a seasonal farmers' market, so I was able to buy some produce from them. I purchased deep red, juicy tomatoes, massive, dark green zucchinis, and the most fragrant, crisp purple basil. The quality of this greenhouse-grown produce was a stark contrast to the grocery store offerings. And the best part? The Inuvik Community Greenhouse is solar-powered. All in all, it's a gem of a place.

But even if the Inuvik Community Greenhouse weren't solar-powered, it would still be a gem of a place. Why? Because the greenhouse helps provide access to fresh, quality produce. It also runs workshops and serves as a community centre. I'm telling you this because greenhouses are the first example in this book of a sustainability trade-off. Some greenhouses may require more energy to operate, but what if the greenhouse provides improved access to fresh and local plant-based foods?

There's no black and white answer here. The answer is that there is nuance to absolutely everything. Although it's good to be aware of the potential environmental impacts any greenhouse may have, it's also important to be aware of the role it can play in building local food systems. And those benefits cannot be discounted as we work toward a more sustainable future for everyone. Trade-offs like this are everywhere, so you'll see this concept repeatedly as we go along here. If you do buy produce that's greenhouse-grown, the one thing you can do is start asking questions. Is the greenhouse solar-powered? Does it recycle its water? Can the community get involved somehow to switch the greenhouse to renewable energy? And so on.

Eating Organic

What Makes Food Organic?

Organic agriculture is a system of farming that puts nature at the centre. In doing so, it takes a holistic approach to how food is grown, raised, and produced, compared with conventional, or non-organic, agriculture. The Canadian Organic Standards list four general principles that form the foundation of organic agriculture: health, ecology, care, and fairness. These four principles take into account everything from the soil, plants, and animals, to humans and the Earth more broadly. This means that organic farming is not just about producing food. It's about producing food in a way that works *with* nature, all the while taking care of both living things and the surrounding environment—now and into the future. These principles apply to producing both plant- and animal-based foods.

Organic food may be local, seasonal, or both—but it also might not be. Local food is not automatically organic, nor is it automatically grown in a more sustainable way, for that matter. *Local* refers to where the food comes from and how far it has travelled, but that doesn't necessarily tell you anything about how it's grown or produced. So there may or may not be crossover between these terms.

One of the major differences is that organic food is regulated in a way that local and seasonal food are not. In order to use the Canada Organic logo on any given food, a producer or grower has to have successfully completed the rigorous Canada Organic certification process. The transition period takes about three years, and it requires regular audits and extensive documentation to prove that food is being produced according to the Canadian Organic Standards. The standards are enforced at the federal level, and they're also reviewed and updated every five years. They encompass a number of different elements; I'll touch on some of the big ones here.

People often buy and eat organic food for health or environmental reasons, but when you look at the Canadian Organic Standards, it's clear that these two concerns are intertwined. The standards prohibit the use of the following: synthetic pesticides, synthetic fertilizers, routine antibiotics for animals, genetic engineering (GMOs), cloning animals, artificial food flavouring, colouring, preservatives, and more. The element that often gets the most attention here is the lack of synthetic pesticides and fertilizers. That's not to say that pests are totally unmanaged on an organic farm, or that the soil is left unattended. It just means that fertilization and pest management in organic agriculture has to align with what is approved as per the Canadian Organic Standards. There are Permitted Substances Lists that go alongside the standards. On the lists, for example, are numerous substances approved for fertilizer use, including animal manure, compost, worm castings, and bone meal, all of which can be used to add nutrients to the soil and improve soil health.

I think it's important to emphasize that this isn't just about what organic farmers are not doing. It's also about what they *are* doing to take care of the land and living things, while producing food. This environmental stewardship can include a number of different practices that may vary from one farm to another. Examples include rotating crops to balance the soil's nutrients and manage pests or weeds naturally, selecting specific crops that may either attract or repel certain insects, avoiding or reducing tilling to promote soil health, and leaving sections of land simply as they are in an effort to increase biodiversity. One thing that sometimes gets missed from these benefits is that the Canadian Organic Standards include animal welfare considerations as well. For example, animals need to be raised in living conditions that are aligned with their natural behaviour, with adequate space to move around freely and go outside. Animals also need to have access to high-quality feed, fresh water, and fresh air. It's also worth highlighting that non-organic farmers may be doing some or all of these things as well. Outside of official organic certification, much of this comes down to how individual farms operate. Organic or not, this is why engaging directly with the people who grow and raise your food is important—which is something we'll talk about shortly in the solutions.

In addition to the farm itself, the Canadian Organic Standards apply to the rest of the supply chain, from processing and packaging to storage and transportation. When you see the Canada Organic logo on something—whether it's fruit, grains, meat, or anything else—it means that the product has met these standards and is 95–100 percent organic. You have probably seen other organic logos on food before too. In Canada, one of the most common of these is for USDA Organic. Canada and the United States have an organic equivalency arrangement that regards both countries' national organic standards as equal. So if you're looking for organic food in Canada and spot a product that has the USDA Organic seal, you can rest assured that it's comparable to Canada Organic. Canada has organic equivalency arrangements with other countries, too, including Costa Rica, Mexico, Japan, the United Kingdom, South Korea, Switzerland, and Taiwan, as well as with the European Union. If you see any of these organic logos in Canada, it means their organic standards are comparable as well.

Is Eating Organic More Sustainable?

Organic agriculture and interest in it are both on the rise. In 2024, Canadians spent about $9 billion on certified organic food, which was up from just over $8 billion in 2021. It's likely that some of this rising interest comes from increasing concerns about climate change. So the real question is whether eating organic food is the best way to reduce your environmental impact. Prior to working on this book, I assumed it was. But I must admit that I have never prioritized buying organic food in the past, mainly because of the cost. If I ever came across organic food that cost either the same or less than non-organic food, I would buy it. But otherwise I made no effort to seek it out. When I started working on *Building a Sustainable Kitchen*, I figured that purchasing organic food was probably going to feature prominently in my future if I wanted to reduce my carbon footprint. As with most things, though, I have discovered that it's a bit more complicated than that.

What happens when organic agriculture is compared with conventional, non-organic agriculture for various environmental impacts? Some differences emerge. Organic wins for energy use. It requires a lot of energy to manufacture synthetic pesticides and fertilizers. Since organic farming does not rely on these synthetic products, it uses about 15 percent less energy than conventional farming. When compared for land use, however, organic farming requires more land. This is largely because conventional agricultural systems tend to have higher yields. Producing the same amount of food in an organic farming situation can use anywhere from 25 to 110 percent more land than what's required in a conventional situation. When the two systems are compared for greenhouse gas emissions, there isn't much difference between them. Both systems cause greenhouse gas emissions, just for different reasons. For example, in conventional agriculture, the use of synthetic fertilizers is a cause of nitrous oxide emissions. But in organic agriculture, using manure as fertilizer also causes nitrous oxide emissions, even if it's from a natural source. It's worth noting that all of the information in this paragraph comes from a meta-analysis published in *Environmental Research Letters* that compared organic and conventional agricultural systems over ninety different foods—everything from fruit and vegetables to pulses and meat. So these conclusions span organic and non-organic systems as a whole, rather than being specific to any single type of food.

However, other impacts have to be considered. One is the fact that organic farming systems often support greater biodiversity than conventional systems do, thanks in part to the lack of synthetic pesticides. Of course, the extent to which biodiversity is supported on any given farm will vary based on a number of factors. On average, though, organic agriculture increases biodiversity by approximately one-third when compared with conventional, non-organic agriculture. This increase tends to be greater for some species, like plants and pollinators, than others.

But people often buy organic food because of health concerns as well—and this is also an important consideration. Although I'm not going to get into the health side extensively here, one of the main health-related concerns is about synthetic pesticide residues on food. It's nearly impossible for humans to avoid synthetic pesticide exposure entirely at this point—pesticides are ubiquitous in the environment. But eating organic food can reduce this exposure. Organic fruits and vegetables, for example, have been shown to contain about one-third the amount of synthetic pesticide residues that conventional, non-organic fruits and vegetables have. Why would organic produce have any synthetic pesticide residue at all? Because there are factors beyond any organic farmer's control—like the wind. Still, if you want to minimize your synthetic pesticide exposure from what you eat, certified organic food fits the bill. Some of the sources I noted in the Resources List for this chapter also touch on health and pesticides, if that interests you.

All of this information taken together leads me to approach organic food similarly to how I approach local and seasonal food, which is why I put these three topics together in one chapter. In the end, it still holds true that reducing consumption of animal-based foods and increasing consumption of plant-based ones is the best way to reduce the overall environmental impact of what you eat. But the close seconds here are local, seasonal, and organic food, all of which have a number of positive impacts that are both important and relevant, even if they don't cut down your carbon footprint to the same extent that shifting to a plant-based diet does. Once you are eating a majority plant-based diet with smaller amounts of animal-based foods, there is plenty you can do within that framework to purchase food that is local, seasonal, organic—or all of the above.

At the end of the day, it's fair to say that all of this is complicated. Once you zoom in on any given aspect of the food system, there are a million tiny details at play that result in larger trade-offs. Organic farming might use more land, but it can do a better job of supporting biodiversity. Greenhouses might require more energy than growing food outside, but they can help improve food security. Eating plant-based protein from across the world might have much less impact than eating meat from a ranch down the road, but buying even a small amount of meat supports the rancher. It's admittedly tough to navigate all of this. But my driving question for this book is how I can reduce my own environmental impact and carbon footprint as much as possible, within the sphere of all things food and kitchens. So that's what I keep coming back to. Which means, first and foremost, eat plant-based foods as much as you can. From there, buy and eat local, seasonal, and organic foods as much as you can, based on what is available and affordable to you. How that looks in practice is going to vary, because there are many different options for how and where to buy food. This is where this part of the book becomes a choose-your-own-adventure story. As you implement your own changes in how you buy and source food, don't be afraid to try out different things. Remember: This is a journey.

What You Can Do

Reframe How You Think About Local and Seasonal Food

The default response to buying local or seasonal food—whether it's organic or not—is to take our usual grocery list and see what we can buy from that list that's local, seasonal, or both. Doing so typically involves no changes to your list. Instead, you're changing where you buy the food, which in turn changes how far it's travelled relative to you. There's nothing necessarily wrong with this; I've done this plenty of times myself. However, you can take it one step further by shifting your grocery list mentality to be more flexible, and shopping and eating based on which foods are actually abundant near you at any given time.

Here's an example of what I mean: Let's say you go to the farmers' market armed with a list. You need potatoes, onions, and beets—you're making borscht for dinner. But when you get to the market, it's clear that tomatoes are in season. Plump, shiny tomatoes in all shapes and sizes line farmers' display tables as far as the eye can see. It's a beautiful exhibit of bounty, with every imaginable shade of red, orange, green, and yellow. After walking around the market, it becomes clear that nobody has potatoes, onions, or beets for sale that day. What do you do? Should you just go to the grocery store and get the potatoes, onions, and beets you planned to buy? Or can you change your plans to work with what's in season—what if you made a roasted tomato soup instead?

Buying and eating local and seasonal food can and should be reciprocal. It's good for you *and* it's good for the farmers. There has to be some give and take here. Otherwise, if everyone wants to buy potatoes, onions, and beets, but farmers have an excess amount of tomatoes, what happens to the tomatoes? Ideally they get eaten, but if nobody buys them and the farmer can't process the excess fast enough, then those tomatoes may end up going to waste. We already know food waste is a huge problem, which is inherently related to how we grocery shop.

However, I'm not suggesting ditching your list entirely or leaving your food waste reduction habits in the dust. Shopping lists are great for reducing food waste—this is a non-negotiable for me. In practice, though, if I go to the farmers' market with a list, I keep it flexible. The list might read: some sort of root vegetable (four meals' worth), herbs (any kind), something pickled (two jars), and any ingredients to make stew with. Then I go from there. I get to the market, I see what's available, and I shop in a way that takes into account both what I need and what the farmers have. This makes the whole experience mutually beneficial. The low-waste cooking strategies we discussed already are going to help here as well, since working with what's available will involve modifying recipes or substituting ingredients. If you can align what you buy and eat with the abundance of food that's available near you throughout the year, you are cutting straight to the heart of what local and seasonal food is all about.

Visit a Farmers' Market Near You

If you're new to buying and eating local and seasonal food, one of the best places to start is a farmers' market. The extent to which you can shop at a farmers' market is going to vary based on where you live. You might live down the street from a bustling farmers' market where local, seasonal, and organic food is on offer year-round. If not, then you have to take a bit more of a patchwork approach. If you're unsure if there's a farmers' market near you, do a quick online search. In the Resources List, I've included numerous sources that can help you find a farmers' market. Some operate only on a seasonal basis to coincide with the growing season—usually starting in April or May and running until late fall. Others operate year-round, but typically with reduced vendors throughout the winter months. The Saskatoon Farmers' Market, for example, is a year-round market, but over the winter the number of vendors and the variety of food both decrease.

When you go to a farmers' market for the first time—or any time, really—start by taking a look around to see what's available. Farmers' markets offer a clear picture of which foods are seasonal near you at a given time. There will also be non-seasonal foods at a farmers' market, like meat, dairy, eggs, preserves, and baked goods. Another thing to observe at the farmers' market is the packaging situation. Can you buy loose fruits, vegetables, or dry goods? We will discuss the logistics of shopping with your own bags and jars in the "Grocery Shopping" chapter shortly, but if you're heading to the farmers' market, this is something to keep an eye on. Sometimes foods are vacuum sealed in plastic or prewrapped in other packaging. But in many cases, I have found that producers are often able to accommodate me using my own containers. The chances of a farmer or producer being able to remove or swap certain packaging are much higher at a farmers' market than at a conventional grocery store. Some vendors may also take back packaging. For example, at the Saskatoon Farmers' Market, a vendor I frequently buy pickles and preserves from collects empty glass jars to wash and reuse. So once I'm done with their products, I save the jars and bring them back on my next market trip.

When you visit a farmers' market, you often have the opportunity to speak directly to the person who grew or produced the food. You don't get this opportunity at a conventional grocery store. I think this is such an important aspect of eating local food that often doesn't get the attention it deserves. When you can ask someone face to face about how they raise their chickens or grow their vegetables, it leads to both increased transparency and a greater understanding of the food system. You will probably learn many things you didn't know. For example, if you want to buy garlic, but week after week nobody at the farmers' market has any garlic even though it's supposed to be in season, you can ask someone about this. You may learn that it was a bad year for garlic, which you never would have guessed shopping at the grocery store. In chatting with producers, you will also learn more about how farms operate. I have had conversations with producers at the farmers' market where I learned that they implement various organic practices on their farm despite not being certified, like avoiding synthetic pesticides in their garden. Ultimately, these types of discussions will serve to deepen your understanding and appreciation for local food.

People at farmers' markets are usually not in a mad dash to grab their groceries and get out the door, which leads to a more relaxed environment where conversation can happen naturally. This means that shopping at a farmers' market is much more of an experience in itself. When I go to the farmers' market, I tend to take my time. I chat with people, I browse what's there, and I may even get a coffee or invite a friend to come along. All of this points to the fact that farmers' markets are a hub not only for local, seasonal, and often organic food, but also for community and connection. Farmers' markets provide a tangible link between the farm, the producer, and the consumer, in a way that's much more direct than buying food from the grocery store. The more often you frequent farmers' markets, the more you'll see what I mean.

Subscribe to a CSA or Local Food Box

Community Supported Agriculture programs—commonly referred to as CSAs—are essentially local and seasonal food subscription boxes, often focused on fruits and veggies. There may also be a CSA program near you that includes certified organic foods. The logistics of any CSA program will depend on the specific farm or market that's providing the service—your box might be delivered, you might have to pick it up, it might be month to month, or it could be prepaid for the growing season.

What you get in a CSA box will depend on what the farmer or grower has at the time. Some programs may be customizable to a certain extent, but the benefit of these boxes is that they facilitate reciprocity. So if a farmer has tomatoes, all their CSA boxes get tomatoes. This cuts down on the possibility of surplus harvest going to waste. It also means that farmers get a guaranteed amount of money during the growing season and have a consistent market for their harvest, rather than having to guess what people may or may not buy at the farmers' market. I think the name sums all of this up rather nicely—Community Supported Agriculture. As in: You are choosing to support the farmer and committing to work with whatever food you get in your box.

Here in Saskatchewan, we're lucky enough to be one of the places in Canada where you can find winter box programs, in addition to the spring, summer, and fall harvest. Back in the fall of 2023, I was searching online for winter CSA options near Saskatoon. I stumbled upon a winter box program called the Instant Locavore, which is run through the Wandering Market in Moose Jaw, SK. The Wandering Market works with over two hundred producers, growers, and farmers, and they bring it all together at their market store, which serves as a hub for local food. They also run several other box programs throughout the year and do regular deliveries to many communities across the province.

After taking a good look at the Instant Locavore program, I was intrigued. The boxes were available in a few different sizes and were delivered monthly. It was an eight-month commitment, from November to June. Each box offered a full range of locally sourced grocery items. Some were set items included every month, like whole chickens, eggs, ground meat, oats, honey, potatoes, and bread. Other *categories* of foods—like frozen fruit and vegetables, grains, spices, cooking fat, and more—were included each month, but the *specific* food you received in that category varied based on what was available. One month the frozen produce might include saskatoon berries, green peas, and tomatoes, while another month it might include strawberries, kernel corn, and garlic scapes. The bigger the box you signed up for, the more money you saved. The large Instant Locavore box was $600 per month, but you received $800 worth of food.

I knew the amount of food in the large box was going to be too much for Paul and me alone, but it was an incredible deal. So I asked my brother-in-law, Luke, and his wife, Jaz, if they wanted to split the box with us. They looked it over and agreed to give it a go. We decided that each couple would pay $300 per month, and then we would divide up the box's contents based on who needed what. The first month we received a delivery, I honestly wasn't sure what to expect. When it arrived, I was completely overwhelmed—in the best way possible. There was much more food than I'd anticipated. It was not just one box. It was actually three huge boxes plus four reusable grocery bags' worth of food. And it was all locally sourced. Much of it was seasonal, and some of it was even organic.

While most of the food in that first delivery was familiar to me, there were some items I had never cooked with before. As time went on, this pattern continued. For example, over the months we received chokecherries, fiddleheads, stewing hens, flaxseed oil, oat groats, tallow, chanterelle mushrooms, and several varieties of squash. None of these foods were items I had ever bought at the grocery store before. But this wasn't a bad thing—the fact that I had to do *something* with these foods pushed me out of my comfort zone. I wasn't about to waste it, so I had to figure it out. The bonus was that we thoroughly enjoyed trying these different foods. I particularly liked a grow-your-own-pea-shoots kit, which I kept close to the kitchen window and got several small harvests out of.

Subscribing to this box dramatically changed how I thought about both grocery shopping and local and seasonal food. I was no longer basing our meals on a list that I made each week, nor on any short-sighted impulses at the grocery store. I was basing our meals on what we got in the box, which was based on what farmers and producers in the province had to supply. It was a completely different way of eating, cooking, and sourcing food. For example, in late spring, we did not receive any fresh onions in our delivery. Up until that point, we had been receiving fresh onions on a monthly basis—and I had been counting on getting those onions. I sent a quick email to ask about the missing onions, and I found out that fresh onions were done for the year. Duh! I felt silly—of course that was the reason why. But this just spoke to the fact that I had gotten so used to being able to buy any given produce at the grocery store, regardless of whether or not it was in season in Saskatchewan. Subscribing to the Instant Locavore box married the concepts of local and seasonal food for me, in a way I had not necessarily experienced before.

This program had several other benefits, one of which was the quality of the food. Overall, it was superb. One of the monthly staples, for example, included four whole chickens, which meant two chickens for us and two for Luke and Jaz. I had initially figured that these chickens would be a typical size—but no. They were on par with what you'd expect from a small turkey. Other items like steelhead trout, garlic sausage, potatoes, beets, parsnips, and more were all jam-packed with flavour. The frozen fruit was a delectable reminder of a Saskatchewan summer: saskatoon berries, haskap berries, raspberries, and strawberries, all picked and frozen at their peak.

Along the way, however, there were a few items I found challenging to use up. Green cabbage was one—every month we got 4.5 kilograms of cabbage in the box. I had never bought or eaten that much cabbage in my life before. We had coleslaw, vegetable soup, and deconstructed cabbage roll casserole on repeat. I had to ramp up my food waste reduction habits to ensure none of it went to waste. The excess seasonal cabbage also gave me a newfound understanding of why my Prairie ancestors had eaten so much damn sauerkraut. I was even briefly tempted to resurrect the antique crock on display in our living room, which my great-grandmother had made sauerkraut in, once upon a time. Doing so would have knocked out several of the cabbages, to say the least.

As time went on, we did make a few requests to change some of the contents in our box. Our entire box was gluten-free, for example, and while Luke and Jaz didn't want pork, I wanted fewer eggs and no beef. The box was customizable only to a certain extent, however, because the whole point of it revolved around sourcing food more reciprocally. So subscribing to this box did become a bit of a complicating factor because there was overlap between when we started the box, in November 2023, and when I started my plant-based shift, in March 2024. I knew I wanted to proceed with the plant-based shift regardless, but I certainly wasn't about to back out of the box program. Once Paul and I started reducing our consumption of animal-based foods, however, we could not keep up with the amount of meat we were receiving. Luckily, I managed to cram the excess into our basement freezer. It's not a very large freezer, but I have always been rather good at

Tetris. It took us an incredibly long time to eat our way through the meat, though. Months after the program ended, we still had meat from the box.

As a result—and given the permanency of our plant-based shift—I decided to switch our box subscription for year two. The Wandering Market also offers a Box of Crop winter option, which features only seasonal produce for the same eight-month period. Paul and I signed up for the medium-sized Box of Crop, which is $80 per month, and physically speaking, it's one huge box of food. The monthly delivery includes produce like potatoes, beets, carrots, parsnips, cabbage, squash, and onions—in line with whatever is available from local producers and growers that month. I decided this medium box, supplemented with food from a couple of other sources, was a better fit for us. I started visiting the Saskatoon Farmers' Market on a monthly basis to buy bread, honey, preserves, additional seasonal produce, and any of the meat that we were eating. My monthly trips also turned into a regular opportunity to chat with producers and to purchase other home essentials, like bar soap.

Although this may not be true of every CSA or local box program out there, I found that subscribing to this box was extremely affordable. The Wandering Market is able to keep its box prices low because it's purchasing food from farmers in bulk, mainly when it's ready to go in season. Since customers are making a commitment to purchase the boxes for a defined period of time, it's much easier for the market to plan ahead and keep the prices consistent. I think this is an important point, because local food sometimes gets a reputation for having a higher price tag than non-local food. If you are cherry-picking buying certain local foods, this may be true. But buying more local and seasonal food through something like a box program has shown me that it can actually cost *less*. We will talk more about cost in the coming chapter on grocery shopping. Given the affordability though, it's certainly worth exploring the options for these types of programs near you, even if they're offered only on a seasonal basis.

To find similar programs, start by doing an online search for CSAs in your area. Any farmers' market is also a good place to learn about these types of programs. Some vendors may have both a market stall and a CSA program, or they may know of other producers who offer something similar. Certain provinces also have CSA directories; I have included this information in the Resources List. If you can't find a CSA program nearby, you can try reaching out to individual farmers or growers in your area to inquire about this possibility. Perhaps they can even customize a regular order that you can pick up on a monthly basis—you simply never know until you ask.

Asking questions is really central to all of this. About a month into our Box of Crop subscription, I found out that the Wandering Market has criteria for the farmers and producers it works with. One of these criteria is that vegetable and fruit suppliers can't use any synthetic pesticides or fertilizers. They don't have to be certified organic—although some of the market's producers are—but they have to declare that they don't use synthetic products. The Wandering Market has other criteria that are in line with organic agriculture, like animal welfare considerations for the meat it sells and not allowing artificial flavourings, dyes, or colours in any products. The key point is that we had been subscribing to the Wandering Market's programs for over a year before I knew any of this. I would have signed up for the Box of Crop either way, but knowing this information made me appreciate both the program and the farmers and growers even more. This was also a telling reminder of why asking questions about the food we buy and eat matters—local, seasonal, organic, or otherwise. The more you know about your food, where it comes from, and the people behind it, the better.

Buy Your Animal-Based Foods Local and Organic

The main priority is still eating fewer animal-based foods overall. But I want to specifically touch on animal-based foods here to give you an idea of how to approach the meat, fish, seafood, or dairy that you do eat, within the context of supporting local and organic.

If you are buying ruminant meat like beef or bison specifically, you can look for meat that comes from farms where there's an emphasis on environmental stewardship of the land. If a farm can provide specific information about grass-finishing, grazing practices, or biodiversity considerations, for example, this is typically a good sign. Environmental stewardship is also something you can consider when purchasing other types of meat, like pork or poultry, for example. However, be mindful about claims on packaging that may not actually have any sound backing, particularly at the grocery store. Words like *sustainably raised* and *regenerative* do not have standard definitions in Canada. Unless you can actually talk to someone about this or have a way of tracking down additional information, I would not take these claims at face value.

What do I mean by tracking down additional information? This could include a website with a *thorough* explanation of their on-farm practices. Or, if the business has a social media account where you can actually catch a glimpse of what's happening on the farm, that may also be helpful. If there's a listed phone number and you can call them to ask questions, even better. Cold-calling a business to ask questions seems odd in a world where texting is the norm, but this is truly the most straightforward way to get to the bottom of something. If the person who answers the phone has immediate answers to your questions, this is an excellent indicator of legitimacy. The opposite is also true. If you cannot speak to someone or find information about what a producer means when it advertises that its meat is "sustainably raised," then you have no way of verifying this claim.

Canada Organic can be particularly helpful here because organic gets a lot of things right in the meat and dairy department, and the organic logo is one of the most easily identifiable food labels with a specific and consistent meaning attached to it. One thing to note, however, is that certified organic beef does not necessarily mean it's grass-finished. Although cows on certified organic farms need to have access to pasture, they may have eaten a combination of grass and organic grains. So if you are looking for grass-finished beef, you have to look for that distinct wording.

I'll give you an example of how I approach all of this. In our Instant Locavore box, meat and dairy were provided from a number of provincial producers, one of which was Original Family Farm. Located outside of Saskatoon, this farm sells bison, chicken, pork, and beef. They also have a year-round booth at the Saskatoon Farmers' Market. Although Original Family Farm is not certified organic, they implement a number of practices that I value: their bison are grass-finished, their pigs and chickens eat high-quality feed that is produced using crops both grown and milled on their farm, and their animals are not given any unnecessary medications during the course of their lifetime. Because I can actually talk to someone from Original Family Farm at their Saskatoon Farmers' Market booth, I feel confident in these claims.

I take this same approach with other animal-based foods, like fish and seafood. Buying fish and seafood locally is more or less difficult depending on where you live in Canada, but doing so provides many of the same benefits as buying other food locally, including the fact that the producer should be able to tell you more about how their fish and seafood were caught or raised. If there is a local fish market or a fishmonger near you, check with them as a starting point.

If I am ever in a situation where I am buying meat, fish, seafood, or dairy and I am unable to talk to someone or find additional reliable information online, then I now choose certified organic whenever possible. In a perfect world, you would be able to buy all of your food from a source that's local and implements organic practices, *and* you'd be able to talk to the producer as well. But we do not live in a perfect world, so you just have to do what you can with the options available to you.

Find Your Region's Unique Ways to Source and Support Local, Seasonal, and Organic

Beyond farmers' markets and CSA programs, there are other options for how and where to seek out local, seasonal, and organic food. Check with any specialty stores near you, like health food stores, organic food stores, food co-operatives, and bulk bin stores. There are stores in Saskatoon, for example, that are dedicated to all things Saskatchewan. These stores sell a mix of food, gifts, home goods, and personal care products, bringing a variety of local producers together under one roof. These types of local hubs exist in many other places across Canada. Try searching online for local stores near you. If you know of such a store but have never actually been there before, pay them a visit.

Some farms, gardens, and orchards have seasonal U-picks for fruits and vegetables. This can be a great way to purchase local produce when it's in season and then freeze or preserve it yourself for the winter—provided you have enough freezer or storage space. You can also buy local food from some farms directly, like at an on-site farm store. Depending on where you live, there may also be an online farmers' market that does delivery or pickup. The Wandering Market has an online store, for example, so I can add other foods to my monthly subscription that then get delivered alongside my box.

You may also be able to find local food at conventional grocery stores. For example, at one particular chain grocer in Saskatoon, I have noticed there are now designated areas in the produce and natural food sections for local products. You can absolutely find certified organic food at most conventional grocery stores, which may or may not be local as well. Of course, another option for eating more local, seasonal, and organic food is to grow it yourself. We'll chat more about this in the "Gardening" chapter (page 229).

Beyond grocery shopping, another way to support local food is to eat at local eateries. Supporting local eating establishments helps create and maintain jobs for people in the community, ensures money stays within a given region, and can have spill-over effects too. For example, if a local eatery makes an effort to source its ingredients from other small businesses—like a bakery or farm in close proximity—this can help strengthen local food systems overall. Eateries that source ingredients locally will often use those ingredients to their fullest potential, which can help reduce waste—like practising whole animal butchery or preserving excess produce when it's in season. Practices like this are often referred to as "farm to table" or "farm to fork." I had the absolute pleasure of gaining backstage access to all of this when I wrote my first book, *Only in Saskatchewan*, which is a collection of recipes and stories from eateries across the province. Travelling around Saskatchewan and working with chefs, bakers, and business owners showed me that the role of local eating establishments in our communities cannot be overstated.

None of this is possible, however, if nobody is dining at local eateries—regular customers are necessary to ensure doors stay open. So whenever you dine out or order takeout, make it a priority to support local establishments. Choose the deli on the corner over a fast-food chain; buy your morning coffee at a small sidewalk café over a big-name coffee shop; pick the quaint downtown eatery over a franchise establishment. You can also apply this to a number of other scenarios beyond an everyday sense. For example, if you need to order cupcakes for a birthday party, place an advance order with a local bakery. If you require catering for a wedding or a reunion, hire a local business. If your workplace is planning to order food for a business meeting, suggest a local restaurant. And so on.

All of the options in this solution point to the fact that it's never been easier to source and support local, seasonal, and organic. It might require some initial effort on your part to source food this way, particularly if you don't have a bustling farmers' market down the street. Is it easier to just go to the grocery store and fill up your cart with whatever's there? Sure. But this isn't a book about how to have an easy breezy time at the grocery store. Plus, I must say that getting a local food box delivered to our doorstep every month couldn't have been simpler. I didn't even have to leave the house or fill out any sort of regular order form. But this is a choose-your-own-adventure story, right? So how you implement these considerations is up to you. We've talked extensively about what to eat and how to consider local, seasonal, and organic food within that framework. Now it's time to go one step further, as we take packaging, alternative grocery stores, and more into account.

Takeaways

- Build flexibility into your kitchen habits so that you can become more integrated with your local food systems. Which foods are in abundance near you at any given time? How can you build your meals around them?
- Visit a nearby farmers' market and chat with producers to learn about local food systems.
- Subscribe to a CSA box or local food box program in your region. Box programs encapsulate local and seasonal reciprocity, and they may even be organic, too.
- When you do buy animal-based foods, try to purchase from local and organic sources whenever possible.
- From U-picks and on-site farm stores to local eateries and more, find other ways to source and support local, seasonal, and organic food in your area.

CHAPTER 5:

Grocery Shopping

GROCERY SHOPPING is essential to building a sustainable kitchen. How we shop for food is inherently tied to food waste, what we're eating, how far the food has travelled, and whether it's organic or in season. You know this by now. But how we grocery shop also sets up many other sustainability considerations, like the amount of garbage we end up with and whether we can recycle or compost whatever we bring home.

I think there's an automatic assumption that sustainable grocery shopping has to look a certain way. It goes something like this: You shop exclusively at a local farmers' market and at a zero-waste store. You bring your own reusable bags and containers to transport everything home in. When you get home, you store your food in glass jars in the cupboard, while fresh produce stays wrapped in cloth bags in the fridge. If you have an open shelf or pantry in the kitchen, even better. In that case, the whole thing doubles as decor, and everyone who comes over can admire your lovely plastic-free display of oats, pasta, and nuts.

While this is certainly a pretty picture, I don't think it's realistic for everyone. Canada is a very large country, and where you live will determine much of what's available to you. Not everyone lives close to a bustling farmers' market or a zero-waste store. Not everyone has a local Community Supported Agriculture box. Cost is a factor here too; more-sustainable grocery shopping needs to take into account different price points. And we can't forget about time. Buying food that's both local and package-free may require visiting a number of different stores. If you have time to do this every week, that's not a problem, but what if your work schedule and family life leave you with just enough time for a quick weekly shop at a conventional grocery store? Sustainability has to be an option in that case too.

Hear me out: I have nothing against the pretty picture I painted. We just talked about why farmers' markets are great. Hauling your groceries home in your own jars and bags to reduce packaging waste is also great. But my point is that it's not the only way. If it's not available to everyone, then it can't be the only way. Which is why my approach to grocery shopping is broad—it encompasses a little bit of everything.

The Principles Behind Sustainable Grocery Shopping

During the process of writing *Building a Sustainable Kitchen*, I tried out a number of different grocery shopping options. Paul and I shifted to a plant-based diet, which meant buying more plant-based foods. We subscribed to two different local food boxes. I went to the Saskatoon Farmers' Market on a monthly basis. I also started doing a monthly trip to a bulk bin store to buy certain foods without packaging—like dry goods, baking staples, and spices. I brought my own reusable grocery bags, cloth produce bags, and a mix of plastic and glass jars to transport the food home in. Then I scoped out other options: a health food store, an organic food co-operative, and a smaller seasonal farmers' market. I still went to a conventional grocery store as well, and I tried to seek out more-sustainable options there. I was partially doing research as I went about all of this, so I probably tried more options than necessary. But I think the range in what I experimented with demonstrates that this is a journey, and that there's no one right way to do things. Sustainable grocery shopping is more of a mosaic than anything.

We still need to keep in mind the order of our priorities. The most important part of sustainable grocery shopping is, first and foremost, the type of food you're buying. If the biggest way to reduce the environmental impact of what you eat is to eat more plant-based foods than animal-based ones, that means buying more plant-based foods. This one factor alone upstages everything else. What you eat is also a bit easier to change from a practical standpoint, in comparison to changing the fact that you may or may not live near a farmers' market or a bulk bin store.

Next, support and buy local, seasonal, and organic foods whenever you can. From there, reduce the amount of packaging as much as possible. This may mean shopping for food at a bulk bin store, a zero-waste store, or the farmers' market, or it may mean reducing packaging at a conventional store. The entire time you go about any of this, be mindful about food waste: Buy only what you need. When you get home, store your food well to ensure it lasts, and then incorporate other habits to reduce food waste on an ongoing basis until your next grocery shop.

Here's the thing: You can implement many of the noted priorities while shopping at a conventional grocery store. Many of the plant-based staples I buy, like tofu, soy milk, canned beans, and frozen vegetables, come from a conventional grocery store. You can also cross many of these items off the list by having your groceries delivered. Big shocker—I know. But my local food box was delivered to my doorstep, after all. So if you just can't seem to paint that typical pretty picture, not all hope is lost. You can still make sustainable changes in how you buy and source food. Although much of what I've said in this chapter so far goes against popular information about sustainable living, I think this approach ultimately simplifies things. If sustainable grocery shopping doesn't have just one single definition, then there's a lot of freedom to find what works for you.

No method is perfect. There are going to be a million little trade-offs involved in grocery shopping, regardless of what you do. Realistically, at some point you're going to have to pick between packaging and plant-based, or food waste and local—or some other combination of priorities. If you're buying frozen edamame beans that come in an unrecyclable plastic bag, and there's nothing you can do about that bag, then that's the trade-off you make in prioritizing plant-based foods. Edamame beans wrapped in plastic may look less sustainable than beef in a reusable container, but looks can be deceiving. Even when you put your best foot forward, these trade-offs are still going to bubble up. I think this reality speaks to the fact that although individuals can do a lot, systems also need to change. But more on that later.

There is one bonus benefit I experienced from trying out all of these grocery methods that is worth mentioning here. I went from feeling like my weekly grocery shop was a necessary but somewhat repetitive life task, to feeling more connected to food on several levels. From learning to cook plant-based, to working with seasonal foods in the Instant Locavore box, to visiting a variety of stores and markets to get a sense of what was available nearby, I can honestly say I've never felt more informed, engaged, and interested in food and where it comes from. I traded my time in exchange for all of that, of course, but I don't think that's necessarily a bad thing. I now spend much more time thinking about and sourcing food than I ever did before. But I also view all of this as enjoyable and educational in a way that rushing around the grocery store simply never was. Not everyone has time for this—I absolutely understand that. Which is why I have provided options in this chapter that take time, pricing, and more into account.

Even if you make small changes, you will probably notice a shift in how you connect to food in certain ways. And know this: You do not have to do everything all at once. Start by considering the aforementioned grocery shopping principles, reading through the following solutions, and factoring in all that we learned in the previous chapters. If those three elements made up three individual circles in a Venn diagram, where would the crossover be for you? What's available nearby? What's affordable? How much time do you realistically have every week or month to spend on this? Since grocery shopping in a more sustainable way is not a one-size-fits-all solution, your answers to these questions will determine the best place for you to start.

What You Can Do

Create a Reusable Grocery Shopping Kit

Having a stash of reusable materials you can reach for any time you head out to buy food is incredibly helpful for cutting down on packaging waste. Some of the most common examples include reusable grocery bags or boxes, cloth, mesh, or net produce bags, and containers or jars in all shapes, sizes, and materials—like plastic, glass, or tin. If you already have these types of reusable materials and use them regularly, then carry on.

Although packaging has less of a measurable impact than the type of food itself, that doesn't make it insignificant. This is similar to our conversation about plants first, followed by local, seasonal, and organic. It's that same solid cake foundation with the icing and cherry on top. Considering the packaging you bring into your home is key for reducing waste, avoiding excess plastics, and effectively recycling and composting, all of which we will talk about more in the coming chapters. I think packaging is also a fairly simple starting point. It's obvious and tangible, so you have a visual reminder of it. Replacing disposable packaging with reusable options on a consistent basis will cut down on your kitchen waste almost immediately—and who doesn't love some immediate results?

Putting together your own reusable packaging materials does not need to be complicated. It also doesn't need to involve spending any money. I would encourage you to take a look around your home and see what you already have that could be repurposed. The receptacles you transport food in do not need to be cute or matching either. They should just be clean and contained, meaning no holes or cracks. You likely already have some reusable grocery bags, boxes, or buckets at home. If you do not have any of these items, ask your friends and family members if they have any to spare. Chances are, someone has extras.

If you find it hard to get into the habit of actually reusing grocery bags, try storing them in a more convenient location. That could include your vehicle, at the office, in your front closet, or in the garage. For me, the most convenient place is our basement stairwell, which is lined with hooks. I walk past these materials any time I go out the back door, so I don't forget them. I also keep one reusable bag stashed in the side door of our vehicle, in case I happen to need a bag unexpectedly when I'm out and about. There's one other way you can really force the habit of not forgetting your reusable bags: If you get to the store and realize you've left the bags behind, make yourself go home and get them. This may be unpleasant, but you'll be unlikely to do it again.

Reusable cloth produce bags are meant to replace disposable plastic produce bags. Back in 2018 when I did my sustainability project, I purchased some cloth produce bags. I have to say, I love the versatility of a solid cloth produce bag. I use them to transport a number of goods beyond fruit and vegetables, too, like loose bulk foods, wine bottles, dog treats, and even bar soap. Reusable produce bags are not made only of cloth—you can find mesh and netted ones too. If you don't already own cloth produce bags, you can explore a few different options. You can sew your own out of any old materials lying around, like T-shirts, tablecloths, bedsheets, or pillowcases that you're not actively using. Check online for DIY patterns. Alternatively, you might be able to repurpose small reusable bags that you already have. For example, Paul and I bought a new set of bedsheets a couple of years ago, and each sheet came packaged in a cloth bag with a drawstring. I repurposed these bags and have been using them as cloth produce bags ever since. You can also buy brand new cloth produce bags at eco-friendly stores, health food stores, or bulk bin stores.

The one thing I'd caution here is that if you're purchasing new cloth produce bags, buy only a few to start. See if you even like using them, and get a sense of which sizes you prefer. I have both large and small bags, but I find the large ones more useful. The last thing you want to do is stock up on a bunch of new cloth produce bags, only to discover that you don't actually need or like what you bought. It's also a good idea to make sure that whatever you're sewing or buying is machine washable so that you can clean the materials properly. I wash our cloth produce bags once a month, unless they happen to get particularly dirty from use. I store them stuffed in my reusable grocery bags in the basement stairwell, which makes it easy to just grab all the materials at the same time.

You can also use other reusable containers you already own to transport loose produce or bulk foods home. Examples include glass jars, peanut butter jars, margarine containers, yogurt containers, and metal tins. I have a collection of various plastic and glass containers that I bring with me to the bulk bin store, which I use for transporting wet or dusty foods like peanut butter, garlic powder, or coconut oil; coconut oil in a cloth produce bag is just not going to end well. You may prefer certain receptacles over others if you are avoiding plastic in particular (more on plastics later!), but note that glass jars can be heavy to transport, especially when they are full of food. For this reason, I tend to use only small glass jars, mainly for things like spices and seasonings. Another option is to skip using a bag or container altogether for certain items. For example, loose bananas, onions, garlic, apples, tomatoes, squash, avocados, sweet potatoes, and zucchini don't need a bag. If you don't want these items to touch a public shopping basket or cart, just put them directly into your own reusable grocery bag or bucket. You could also lay a reusable grocery bag on the bottom of the cart and then place the loose produce on top of it, unbagged.

Once you start actively trying to reduce food packaging, you'll begin to realize that packaging is everywhere. While not all packaging is necessary, some of it is. How else would diced tomatoes get from point A to point B safely? So replacing conventional packaging with your own reusable materials won't be possible for everything. Fresh produce, bread, spices, snack foods, baking staples, and dry goods like rice, lentils, and pasta tend to be some of the easier foods to shop for package-free. Other items like frozen foods, cooking oil, meat, sauces, and condiments are a bit tricker to find sans packaging. The exception is if you have access to a zero-waste store, which we'll get to shortly. But if you can put together some of your own reusable materials and get in the habit of bringing and reusing these items regularly, it will cut down on food packaging considerably.

Building up a collection of reusable materials may take a bit of time. Even today, I still add reusable materials to my collection on an ongoing basis. You always have the option of thrifting reusable items or buying new, but there's no need to have everything organized immediately. Sometimes, just being patient can reduce wastefulness. So try grocery shopping in a more package-free way with just a few reusable materials to start. That way you'll gradually get a sense of which materials you prefer and use most often, and can expand from there.

It's become much more common for people to shop with their own reusable containers and cloth produce bags, particularly at bulk bin stores, zero-waste stores, and the farmers' market. But I have been at a conventional grocery store in the past, minding my own business with my cloth produce bags, and witnessed another person serving up some serious side-eye in my direction. This may happen to you too. It really depends on how common these types of practices are where you live. My advice? Do it anyway. If anyone asks you about this—store employees included—just explain what you're doing. You can even show them the materials if needed, which is why having clean receptacles is important. But for every person who thinks your cloth produce bags are silly, there's likely another person who sees them and thinks to themself, "What a great idea." Perhaps that person will feel inspired to begin using their own reusable materials when they shop in the future. You just never know.

Find a Bulk Bin Store Near You

Before we get into this solution, I want to clarify what I mean by bulk bin stores—because I'm going to shorten this to "bulk stores" right away here, for ease of writing. When I say "bulk," I am not talking about buying large quantities of food in prepackaged portions for a reduced price. I am talking about stores that have bins containing loose foods, where you serve yourself using either a dispenser or a good old-fashioned scoop. There are two main benefits to bulk stores for our purposes: You can bring your own reusable packaging, and you can buy only what you need, which helps reduce food waste.

Of course, you can also shop at a bulk store in a way that ignores both of these benefits. If you use the plastic baggies provided or purchase way too much of something and end up throwing it away, then you miss out on packaging and food waste reduction. So bulk stores are not inherently more sustainable simply because they sell bulk foods. Food still has to arrive at the bulk store packaged to a certain extent. Some bulk stores may be making efforts to reduce packaging on the back end though. For example, if they purchase huge quantities of a given food, there may be less packaging involved overall—versus if they had purchased several smaller packages of that same food to fill the bins. You can always ask any bulk food store you visit about the behind-the-scenes packaging situation. But the most obvious benefits here lie primarily on the consumer side of things.

To get started, see if there are any bulk stores near you. You may already be familiar with one, but if not, do a quick online search or check the Resources List. Some stores that are not specifically bulk stores may have bulk bins in addition to other packaged goods. This is more likely to be the case at health food stores, organic markets, food co-operatives, smaller independent grocers, or grocers that sell specific cultural foods. Conventional grocery stores may also have a bulk foods section, though some chain grocers removed this option during the COVID-19 pandemic and have not brought it back since.

In Canada, the most recognizable and widespread bulk store is Bulk Barn, a Canadian company that was started in Ontario in 1982. There are around three hundred Bulk Barn locations across Canada today, with stores in every province, though not in the territories. In Saskatoon there are currently two Bulk Barn locations. I was in high school when Saskatoon's first Bulk Barn opened—not too far from where I attended high school—and I remember being completely floored by its selection of candy and snack foods. After it opened, my girlfriends and I would often hit up the Bulk Barn during our school lunch hour. Unsupervised and hungry, we loaded up plastic bags with goodies galore. We'd then chow down on our selections as we sat in someone's vehicle, catching up on all sorts of pressing Grade 11 matters. Perhaps not the healthiest lunch, but certainly a memorable time.

Bulk Barn doesn't sell just candy and snack foods, though. These days, I'm much more interested in what they have going on in the aisle for dried beans and lentils. And let me tell you—they have a lot going on there. It's a plant-based, package-free paradise. But prior to working on this book, I had never bothered to shop at Bulk Barn. Once I started looking for more package-free options, though, bulk shopping became an obvious choice. So I decided to visit the nearest Bulk Barn location and see what they had.

At first, I had no intention of buying anything—I was visiting with research in mind. Armed with a notepad and pen, I walked up and down the aisles and wrote down any items I saw that I already bought on a regular basis. But my list quickly got out of hand. There were just too many foods to write down. I noted the obvious ones: pasta, quinoa, rice, lentils, beans, nuts, seeds, pretzels, popcorn, and oats. But there was much, much more. I saw all of the typical baking supplies I had at home—white sugar, all-purpose flour, cocoa powder, baking soda, chocolate chips, etc.—along with other specialty baking items, like different gluten-free flours, other varieties of sugar, shredded coconut, and dried fruit. Then there were dog treats, coffee, tea, spices, seasonings, gravy mixes, and soup mixes. Plus, there were some liquid and wet foods, like coconut oil, nut butters, tahini, and corn syrup. I was once again floored by the selection—although this time for very different reasons than my high school self had been. I resolved to incorporate a monthly trip to Bulk Barn into my grocery routine. I brought all of my own reusable packaging materials for these trips. In doing so, I cut down on our packaging waste substantially.

What's available at Bulk Barn may vary a bit, but much of it will be similar from one store to the next. One additional benefit of shopping at Bulk Barn is that every Sunday, it offers 15 percent off all regular-price purchases for customers who shop using their own reusable packaging. This program, called Sustainable Sundays, is available at every Bulk Barn location Canada-wide. Bulk Barn actually saves over one million plastic bags every year thanks to customers shopping with their own reusable grocery materials, which just goes to show that using your own reusable materials *does* add up and make a difference collectively. Of course, you can shop using your own packaging at Bulk Barn on any day of the week, but I typically head there on Sundays. If I'm going to shop with my own packaging anyway, I might as well save a bit of money in the process. Other bulk stores may have similar programs for customers using their own packaging.

It's now been a year since I incorporated bulk shopping into my grocery routine, and I have discovered a few tricks of the trade along the way. To help you navigate your own bulk store journey, I have put together the following list of tips.

- If you are new to bulk shopping or are visiting a bulk store for the first time, plan to give yourself adequate time to peruse the aisles on your initial visit. Make a list of the foods they offer that you already buy, so that you have a sense of how much reusable packaging you should bring when you shop.
- When you arrive at any bulk store, you'll need to get your containers weighed. This is called "taring." At Bulk Barn, for example, I go to the counter first thing to get my jars and containers tared. They write the weight directly onto the receptacles, typically on the lid. This weight is then subtracted later on when you pay, since most bulk stores are pay-by-weight. I don't normally bother getting my cloth produce bags weighed as they are very light, but if you have heavier bags, you may want to have those tared as well. Most bulk stores do this automatically, but if you happen upon a bulk section in a conventional grocery store, taring might not be an option. If I ever buy bulk foods at a conventional grocery store, I use my cloth produce bags rather than jars, to ensure I'm not paying for the weight of the container.
- Until you get used to bulk shopping, your eyes may deceive you. Three scoops of pasta doesn't seem like much—until you get home and realize that you've bought six jars' worth of pasta, when you needed only one. So in the beginning, it can be helpful to shop using actual jars or containers instead of bags. The more you shop in bulk, the more you'll get a sense of how much one scoop translates to physically in your storage receptacles at home.
- When you get home and put away your food, write down the date of purchase. If needed, write down what the item is as well—for example, if you've bought a few different types of flour that all look the same. Shopping in bulk means you don't have packaging with a label or best-before date to refer to, so you have to keep track of this yourself. I typically write this information directly on the jar or container I'm storing the food in, using a permanent marker, or I create a new label with a piece of masking tape. You could also keep a list with this information on the fridge or on your phone.
- Invest in a funnel if you plan to do a lot of bulk shopping. After a few attempts at transferring something like quinoa or beans from a cloth bag to a container at home, you'll see that a funnel is essential. I purchased a wide-mouth stainless steel funnel that's compatible with multiple different sizes of containers, and it's been a lifesaver.

- If you have food allergies, sensitivities, or restrictions, then shopping in bulk may not be the best option. This is not an issue for me personally with avoiding gluten, but I do not have celiac disease, so I'm not worried about potential cross-contamination. Although food at bulk stores is separated into individual bins, you have no way to guarantee that someone else didn't use the scoop meant for peanuts in the bin of sunflower seeds. If you have an allergy, this is largely up to you and your own comfort level, but it's also something to consider if you have other people in your life with allergies who often come to your home. Both my mom and sister have nut allergies, for example, so I have designated containers for nuts I buy at the bulk store. If any nuts accidentally touch one of my cloth produce bags, I wash it immediately afterwards.
- You can purchase washable markers or crayons so that you can write directly on cloth produce bags. This may even work for some jars and containers, depending on the material and the marker. When I shop in bulk, I tend to keep a list on my phone of the various codes for the food I'm buying, which works nicely as well.
- If you are interested in the nutritional information or ingredient list for a given food at a bulk store, it's usually displayed on the bin. Take a photo on your phone so you can refer to it later.

Transitioning to buying food in bulk does not need to be an overnight change—similar to how it takes time to mindfully put together your own reusable packaging materials. When I started going to Bulk Barn, I initially purchased only foods that we ate on a weekly basis and therefore ran out of quickly, like oats, lentils, and pretzels. It took several months to use up various spices and baking supplies before I started buying them in bulk. I still have a few lingering plastic bags of certain spices, for example, that I haven't quite finished up yet. Once these items are gone, I'll buy my next batch from the bulk store. But all of this takes time.

On the whole, I have found the experience of shopping in bulk both relaxing and enjoyable. I like measuring out the quantities of various foods myself. I feel more connected to what I'm buying and how much of it I am buying. But shopping this way does take more time—I will say that. I also discovered there were some trade-offs; for example, I could buy certain beans at the bulk store that were not local, or I could buy those beans locally elsewhere but in packaging. I could not consistently find certain local beans in bulk, though. Depending on the bulk shopping options near you, you may be able to find food in bulk that's local, organic, or both. If not, you will probably have to choose one or the other. I did find that plant-based eating and bulk shopping were quite compatible overall. It was easy to find plant-based staples like dried beans, lentils, and grains in bulk. I also appreciated that I could buy only what I needed. During our plant-based shift, I wanted to try certain dried lentils and beans that I had never cooked with before, so it was great that I could buy small quantities of these foods to start. This was also true of other foods: I don't really need an entire container of coconut oil or Greek seasoning under normal circumstances. A little bit is just perfect. On the flip side, if you happen to need a lot of coconut oil or Greek seasoning, you can stock up without also buying a lot of packaging. Either way, the fact that you're measuring out the food yourself really forces you to think mindfully about how much food you'll actually use.

Shop at a Zero-Waste Grocery Store

Zero-waste grocery stores—sometimes called package-free grocery stores—take bulk shopping to the next level. What you can buy at a zero-waste grocery store will vary from one store to the next. In general, though, these stores often carry many of the same items found at a conventional grocery store, just with a reduced selection. Many zero-waste grocery stores go beyond typical bulk foods like dry goods and baking supplies to include foods like cooking oils, vinegars, preserves, frozen foods, dairy, eggs, meat, tofu, and even sauces or condiments, which they may have on tap. Zero-waste grocery stores usually have household and personal care products, too, like hand soap, dish soap, or pet supplies. Most of these items are sold in a loose, bulk format so that you can shop with your own reusable packaging. Some stores may have take-back programs for certain packaged goods, like glass jars for preserves, for example. If any packaging is involved, however, it's usually materials like glass, paper, or aluminum. In other words, no plastic or single-use disposable packaging. Almost everything at zero-waste grocery stores is sold by weight, so your reusable packaging has to be tared before you shop. You get all the same bulk store benefits we just talked about, like reduced consumer packaging and the ability to buy only what you need, at a zero-waste grocery store.

Zero-waste grocery stores often implement other sustainable initiatives that go beyond consumer benefits. I have encountered zero-waste stores that are able to reduce waste and packaging throughout their supply chain, influencing their suppliers to either cut down on packaging or swap to reusable packaging options. A zero-waste store might also purchase larger quantities of food, which reduces the amount of packaging involved overall. For example, if they receive a large block of tofu in one bigger package, which they divide up and sell loose, this is less packaging overall compared with several smaller, packaged blocks of tofu. Zero-waste stores often serve as community hubs too, hosting events or workshops with a focus on sustainable living. Beyond packaging, there's also typically a focus on reducing waste more generally. In an effort to reduce food waste, a zero-waste store might turn excess food into premade meals or prepared foods, which can then be sold in the store. For example, leftover unsold fruit becomes a batch of jam, which is sold in glass jars that can be returned when empty and then reused.

Zero-waste stores have become more common in Canada in the last ten years or so, particularly in larger cities like Toronto, Montreal, Ottawa, and Vancouver. They are less common in smaller cities and rural areas. In Saskatoon, we do not have a zero-waste grocery store (as of the time of writing). We do have other sustainability-focused stores that offer household and personal care products in bulk. I refill certain home and personal care products at The Better Good in Saskatoon, for example, which has a "refillery" section for products like soap and deodorant. In the Resources List, I have noted various zero-waste stores across Canada, some of which may be located near you or have online options.

Whether or not food costs more at a zero-waste store will depend on what you're buying and the store itself. If you live near a zero-waste store, it's worth paying it a visit to see what it offers. If the prices are higher, it may be because the store is smaller, so it does not benefit from economies of scale in the same way that larger stores or grocery chains do. The more food a store buys, the less it costs per kilogram, litre, or item, so if a small zero-waste store is buying less food, its costs per item are likely higher, which in turn might mean the food costs more for the customer. This is the case for many small, independent, locally owned grocers—not just zero-waste stores. But pricing depends on so many factors, which is why checking directly with any zero-waste grocery store near you is important.

I think it's also worth highlighting that zero-waste grocery stores are going against the grain. They are trying to make grocery shopping possible in a more sustainable way by reducing packaging, reducing food waste, and often supporting local farmers or other small businesses in the process. These benefits are being realized both on the store's end *and* on the consumer's end. For that reason, zero-waste grocery stores deserve a lot of credit. At the end of the day, they're also usually small, locally owned businesses. If you happen to live near a zero-waste store and it's possible for you to support its efforts, then do so.

Buy Large Quantities to Save on Packaging

Bulk stores and zero-waste grocery stores can reduce packaging on the back end by buying large bundles of food. But you can do this too. An enormous bag of flour or rice, for example, will mean less packaging overall, compared with purchasing several smaller bags of that same item. Doing this will probably save you some money too. Sometimes larger bags of food are also more likely to be made from non-plastic materials, like paper.

However, I have to stress that this solution is a good option only if you will actually *eat the food*. I don't do this because Paul and I can't eat larger quantities fast enough. But it might be a good option if you have a big family, live with roommates, or do a lot of baking, for example. You could also buy large quantities of food and then split it up with other people, if that makes sense for you. This is sort of like taking the concept of bulk shopping and applying it to your friends and family. It may work for some liquid foods, too, like cooking oil, for example.

If this sounds up your alley, check with wholesale grocers or even bulk stores themselves, which may sell case lots of certain goods. Some conventional grocery stores also sell larger quantities of packaged foods, particularly baking staples and dry goods like rice, beans, and lentils. Another option is to contact local businesses directly for specific goods. For example, there's a bakery in Saskatoon that sells wholesale quantities of organic flour that they mill in-house, using Saskatchewan grains.

Visit Individual Local Businesses

Go to the bakery to buy your bread and buns. Head to the butcher to buy meat. Visit the small produce stand on the corner. Get your spices directly from a spice store. Find olive oil and vinegar at a specialty store—and so on. Will this take more time? Yes. It's also unlikely that you'll be able to buy every item on your grocery list by shopping this way. On the other hand, shopping this way supports local and is likely to cut down on both food waste and packaging. If small businesses don't already sell food without packaging, they are much more likely to accommodate a customer with reusable packaging materials. Just explain yourself and ask nicely. You could also make this solution more time-efficient by planning a monthly trip to the bakery, for example. Stock up on bread once a month and freeze what you buy, if you have enough freezer space to accommodate.

Subscribe to a Food-Saving Produce Box

During my research, I came across a Canadian company called Odd Bunch. Odd Bunch works with various farms, greenhouses, and distributors to collect surplus produce, along with produce that doesn't meet cosmetic grocery store standards. This produce is completely safe to eat, but there's too much of it, or it doesn't have the right aesthetic—simply put, it's odd. Think about it: All the apples at the grocery store look exactly the same, but this isn't actually how nature works, right? Odd Bunch packs the collected produce into boxes, which customers subscribe to for weekly delivery. It offers boxes in various sizes and has options for fruit boxes, vegetable boxes, or boxes with a mix. It also has a box option that's specifically for organic produce. What you get in the box varies on a weekly basis depending on what's available. This solution is similar to the concept of a Community Supported Agriculture program or local food box, although the produce in these boxes is not exclusively local.

Odd Bunch's program has numerous benefits. First, it avoids food waste. By subscribing to Odd Bunch, you help ensure that produce doesn't get thrown out for no good reason. Second, it means that farmers and distributors still get paid. If their surplus or odd-looking harvest weren't being reworked into a program like Odd Bunch, not only would that food go to waste, but they might not make any money for growing it either. Third, it saves you money. A produce box from Odd Bunch costs anywhere from 35 to 55 percent less than the same produce from the grocery store. Given that these boxes are built around what's available, you are agreeing to work with what you get. It's that same reciprocity we talked about earlier. I was going to say that all of this is a win-win, but there are definitely more than just two wins here.

Odd Bunch is available in certain provinces across Canada. If it's not available near you at the moment, it's worth checking back in the future, because it's growing rapidly. Some other, similar programs in Canada are noted in the Resources List. To see if there are any programs local to you, you could also try searching your location along with keywords like "produce box" or "food waste box."

Before we move on to the next solution, let's address the reality of grocery delivery. Having your groceries delivered seems like it would be an absolute environmental blunder, but it's really not the end of the world. Think back to how much transportation accounts for in the grand scheme of the food system's greenhouse gas emissions. It's not much, compared with the emissions caused by producing food itself. Furthermore, some studies have shown that grocery delivery can actually reduce greenhouse gas emissions from food transportation. This is especially true if delivery is done efficiently with an optimized route. If fifty people, for example, individually drive to the grocery store—or even multiple stores—this can end up being more driving and more greenhouse gas emissions overall than if those same fifty people had their groceries delivered via an optimized route. So if having your groceries delivered is the best option for you, don't fret about it. What you can do here is consider whether there's a way to have food delivered that incorporates some of the other sustainability priorities. Can you order produce from a local CSA box or a food-saving produce program, rather than from a conventional grocery store? Can you order more plant-based foods? Can you think more mindfully about how much food you actually need, to reduce waste?

However, it's fair to say that when it comes to packaging, grocery delivery typically doesn't do so hot. Cloth produce bags simply won't help you here. But the extent of the packaging will vary, depending on the source. Groceries delivered from a conventional grocery store are likely to involve more packaging. Produce delivered from a CSA box or a food-saving produce program may or may not involve the same extent of packaging. Our Instant Locavore box, for example, included a mix: Some of the produce was loose—squash, cabbage, onions, garlic—and some of it was in plastic bags, like the carrots and potatoes. Because we were getting a consistent monthly delivery, I saved some of the packaging and gave it back to the driver the following month—including any boxes, reusable grocery bags, and egg cartons. But there was plastic packaging involved for other items that couldn't be reused. Wild rice, for example, came in a plastic bag, but it was from Saskatchewan. I could have gone to the bulk store and bought wild rice using my own cloth produce bag, but that rice would not have been local. What does all of this come back to? Trade-offs. They're everywhere.

Shop More Sustainably at a Conventional Grocery Store

At a conventional grocery store, you can bring your own cloth produce bags for fresh fruits and vegetables and put certain loose produce directly into your basket or cart unbagged. You can buy plant-based foods and stay mindful about how much food you're buying to reduce food waste. Depending on the store, there may be bulk bins for dry goods, or there may be deli counters for meat, dairy, or prepared foods where you can bring your own containers. Certain stores may also have a specific section for locally sourced food. You can also shop for organic food at most grocery stores. Some grocery stores may sell enormous bags or boxes of food, which can help reduce packaging overall. Beyond these options, there are a couple of other things you can do.

If there is a section for discounted produce that's going to spoil soon, and you know that you'll be able to either eat or preserve that produce in a timely manner, then shop the discount section. These items are almost always wrapped in plastic or some other sort of packaging. But by buying and eating them, you're preventing food waste. Besides, if nobody buys and eats these items, they're still wrapped in packaging *and* become food waste anyway.

There are also apps that aim to reduce food waste by selling unwanted, surplus, or overripe and soon-to-spoil food from grocery stores at discounted prices. One example is the app Flashfood, which offers grocery deals of up to 50 percent off. It's active in many places across Canada for grocers large and small. Grocery stores on Flashfood sell everything from individual items and prepared meals to mixed boxes and bags of assorted food like produce. Most of the stuff on the app typically comes in some sort of packaging, but this is yet again another trade-off—you're reducing food waste and saving money in the process. I've noted this app and a couple of other, similar apps in the Resources List.

Bonus: Apply These Principles to Everything You Buy

You can take these sustainability considerations and apply them to anything else you buy, including both food and non-food purchases. Consider the principles of plant-based, local, seasonal (when applicable), organic, and reducing waste and packaging when buying other consumables—from alcohol to personal care products and beyond. Is the item plant-based? Where was it produced, and by whom? Is there a way to buy it with little to no packaging? Asking questions isn't just an important part of engaging with our food system—it's an important part of engaging with anything we're buying.

Takeaways

- Put together some reusable packaging materials for grocery shopping, like cloth produce bags, and containers or jars—and then keep them in reach! If you can repurpose items you already have, even better.
- Shop at a bulk bin store to reduce both packaging and food waste. Bring your own materials to transport goods home.
- If there is a zero-waste grocery store near you, try shopping there.
- Reduce the overall amount of packaging you end up with by purchasing large bundles of food (but only if you'll actually eat the food).
- Check out individual local businesses like the bakery, the butcher, a fruit stand, etc.
- Reduce food waste by subscribing to a produce-saving box program like Odd Bunch.
- Do what you can to shop more sustainably at a conventional grocery store.
- Bonus: Apply these considerations to other purchases you make.

Does Sourcing Food Sustainably Cost More?

All right, time for a little chit-chat about prices. Now that we've discussed food waste, plant-based eating, shopping for local, seasonal, and organic food, packaging considerations, and alternative methods of grocery shopping, the big question is whether all of this costs more. This is a tough question to answer, but I'm going to answer it anyway, because this question probably crossed your mind as you were reading the last few chapters. It certainly crossed my mind while I was working on this book. In order to accurately track my grocery spending and any potential changes, I kept all of our food receipts over a period of several months so that I could review them later on.

Prior to making any changes in how we ate or shopped, Paul and I already bought fresh produce regularly. But we ended up eating *more* fresh produce during this process, because of the quantity we received through the Instant Locavore and Box of Crop programs. I also purchased additional produce as needed from the farmers' market or the grocery store to fill in the gaps between box deliveries—like fresh greens and fruit, for example. Even though we were eating more produce, the amount of money we spent on fresh produce stayed the same, given the low cost of the box programs. To diversify the plants we were eating, I also added more frozen vegetables to our meals. But this was fairly insignificant to our grocery budget, since frozen produce tends to cost less than fresh.

Overall, the amount of money we spent on protein foods didn't change much, either, but within that category, there were significant changes. Any of the meat we were now buying came from local sources, which did cost more on average compared with non-local meat from the grocery store. So we spent more money per unit on the meat that we bought, but we made up that difference by spending less money on meat overall, due to our plant-based shift. The plant-based proteins we bought helped make up this difference, because they had a low price tag. This mainly included bulk and canned lentils and beans, along with tofu and some plant-based dairy products, to a lesser extent. I found that most of the plant-based proteins I bought at the bulk store were cheaper compared with purchasing them in a non-bulk format.

Many other staples I began buying in bulk cost less on average, too, compared with packaged versions of those same foods—like spices, pretzels, pasta, and baking supplies. For example, as of the time of writing, a typical 370-gram bag of salted pretzel sticks from a Saskatoon grocery store is $4 to $5. That same amount of salted pretzel sticks from Bulk Barn is $3.20. A typical prepackaged container of garlic powder at the grocery store can be anywhere from $5 to $8 for 165 grams. At Bulk Barn, 165 grams of garlic powder is $2.50. These prices don't factor in Sustainable Sundays, which would be an additional 15 percent off with your reusable gear.

In the end, I was pleasantly surprised to discover that the final dollar amount of our monthly grocery budget did not change overall. The biggest difference I noticed from my saved receipts had less to do with prices and more to do with where we were spending our grocery money. We used to spend most of our grocery dollars at conventional chain grocers, like Sobeys, Save-On-Foods, and Costco Wholesale. Now, more of our grocery dollars were being allocated to local sources, including the Wandering Market and the Saskatoon Farmers' Market. This was followed by Bulk Barn for package-free foods. The remaining portion of our grocery budget—which was now also the smallest portion—went to conventional grocery stores, primarily for plant-based products like soy milk, tofu, frozen produce, canned foods, and certain snack foods that I couldn't find in bulk.

But cost is incredibly subjective. For starters, where you live in Canada is going to determine certain differences in food prices. The other crucial factor here comes down to how you were shopping *before* you made any changes. For example, if you already eat a lot of certified organic food and then replace certified organic meat with certified organic lentils, you will probably save money. If you eat a lot of meat and cheese and then replace those foods with plant-based proteins like dried beans and lentils, again, your food budget is likely to go down. A program like Odd Bunch or eating seasonal produce when there's a surplus will likely bring the cost of fresh produce down. But if you start purchasing a bunch of frozen premade plant-based meals, buy fresh produce when you previously bought very little of it, swap non-organic food for primarily certified organic food, or stock your fridge with artisanal nut-based cheeses, then your grocery expenses are likely to increase. It's also hard to make overarching statements about the cost of plant-based versus animal-based foods, since this can still vary depending on the specifics of what you're buying and where you're buying it from. Steak or kidney beans? The beans will probably cost less. Oat yogurt or cow yogurt? The cow yogurt is likely less. But in my experience, those individual differences balanced themselves once I zoomed out and looked at our costs as a whole.

It's also worth mentioning that when we talk about cost comparisons, we are not comparing apples to apples. If organic meat costs more, that's because it's raised according to the Canadian Organic Standards with animal welfare considerations in mind. Considering animal welfare on a farm, however, requires inputs like high-quality feed and additional space for the animals, which ultimately costs the farmer more. Similarly, if local produce is more expensive, it might be because it's coming from a smaller farm that doesn't use pesticides and has lower yields. But buying local, seasonal, or organic food typically means that you're gaining quality and freshness through that transaction. That doesn't erase any potential increase in cost, but if you are paying more, it's often because you are also receiving *more*. For example, Paul and I agreed that swapping larger quantities of grocery store meat for smaller quantities of meat from local sources was a worthy exchange. The meat we were now eating tasted better than any meat I'd ever bought at a conventional grocery store.

I think it's worth letting go of any preconceived notions you may have about all of this. How much any given local, seasonal, organic, bulk, plant-based, or animal-based food costs is going to vary based on a variety of factors. For example, a Canadian study from 2022 looked at whether eating local food was more expensive in Quebec. It found that for 70 percent of the categories studied, local food cost either the same or less than non-local options. So what's the best thing you can do here? Go out and see for yourself. Visit the farmers' market, the bulk store, or the zero-waste store, or subscribe to a box program. Save any paper or email receipts, write down your purchases, and track this over time. What you find may surprise you, or it may not. But you won't really know until you try.

CHAPTER 6:

Composting

FOR AS LONG as I can remember, my parents had a backyard compost bin. It wasn't fancy—just a wooden bin constructed with space between each of the boards to allow airflow, and a lid that was attached at the back with hinges. I recall regularly being asked to take our kitchen compost pail out to the backyard bin, once it was bursting with fruit peels, eggshells, and vegetable scraps. As a grumpy preteen, I dreaded this chore. Walking to the backyard bin, I would attempt to do the entire act as quickly as possible: lift the lid, dump the contents, slam the lid shut, and then run back to the house, with the empty pail swinging. In winter it wasn't so bad, but in warmer months when the compost was doing its thing, I found the smell of decomposing food and yard scraps unbearable. And the flies that sometimes swarmed the pile? Even worse. I questioned why anyone would keep up such a nasty practice. I promised myself I never would.

Well, I was wrong. Promises you make to yourself as a preteen rarely hold up—and this one certainly didn't. Especially since it turns out composting matters a lot from an environmental perspective. If you already compost, either at home or through an organics collection program, stay with me here. In addition to the environmental side, we'll look at how you can compost more effectively, along with the logistics of how it works.

In 2018, when I started my Instagram sustainability project, I decided to set up a backyard compost as a means of reducing our household garbage. A friend mentioned she had an old compost bin she wasn't using, so Paul and I went to pick it up and then plopped it in the back corner of our yard. We started putting food scraps into the bin, and our household garbage was immediately reduced by half. We ended up downsizing our kitchen garbage pail from a forty-two-litre can we took out weekly to one eighteen-litre can per week.

But we had no real use for the finished compost. The yard of the house we were renting was basically an unfenced open space, riddled with weeds and totally exposed to the street. Starting a garden there just didn't make sense. After a while, we decided to instead sign up for the City of Saskatoon's curbside organics program. At the time, this program was a voluntary subscription service for residential households. In exchange for an annual fee, the city provided curbside collection of organics from May to November. You could put fruit and vegetable scraps, coffee grounds, eggshells, paper tea bags, food-soiled paper products, and yard waste into your green cart. Although it was collected seasonally, we continued to put materials in the cart throughout the winter, which were then picked up with the first collection each spring.

In 2023, this voluntary subscription service turned into a city-wide organics program for residential single-family households, with pickup provided year-round. The variety of items you could put into your green cart also increased. Meat, dairy, bones, and more were now allowed, which further reduced our household garbage. The City of Saskatoon estimates that 57 percent of what residents formerly tossed in the garbage now goes in the green cart, which is on par with other municipalities' waste reduction rates resulting from organics programs.

How Does Composting Work?

Let's start with a composting definition: Composting is an age-old biological process in which micro-organisms break down organic matter in an oxygen-filled environment. The end result of this decomposition is a soil-like material—the finished compost—which acts as a slow-release fertilizer, adding nutrients to the earth over time.

Remember how food scraps in landfills that are deprived of oxygen naturally produce methane, a powerful greenhouse gas that contributes to global warming? Composting is sort of like the opposite. The food scraps are given access to the oxygen they need, so they can live their best decomposing life. Composting is known as an aerobic process, which means that oxygen is involved. Food scraps in landfills exist in what is called an anaerobic environment—meaning they have no oxygen. All organic matter, including food waste, inedible food scraps, paper, and yard waste, faces an anaerobic fate if put into a landfill, producing various levels of methane over time. Therefore, reducing methane through household kitchen actions is twofold: First, prevent food waste as much as possible, and second, compost the rest.

Composting set-ups vary from those that are small-scale, like a backyard compost, to large-scale industrial facilities that process incredible amounts of organic materials using more complex technology and equipment. Regardless of the scale, the goal is similar: to successfully turn organics into a usable finished product by managing various factors along the way, including water, air, and temperature.

To gain a better understanding of how industrial composting works, I requested a tour of the Loraas Disposal North organics facility, just outside of Saskatoon. This particular Loraas facility processes the materials collected through Saskatoon's curbside organics program, as of the time of writing. The Loraas staff graciously agreed to my request, so on a bright, windy April morning, I headed out of the city on Highway 12 toward Martensville.

When I arrived, I was greeted by the supervisor of the organics facility, Kylene Goodman, who gave me a pair of oversized black rubber boots, a bright yellow safety vest, and a red hard hat to borrow for the morning. I suited up, and we hopped into a branded Loraas truck and drove off toward the compost building, which looked like an enormous white warehouse from afar. We chatted as we drove, and it was immediately clear to me that Kylene was passionate about composting. Her enthusiasm was infectious, and as we neared the building, I too was feeling increasingly excited about composting. When you think about it, the ability to save organic material from a death sentence in the landfill and turn it into something usable *is exciting.*

At the back of the warehouse was a pile of wood stacked high. This wood was from both residential and commercial sources and was destined to get mulched up and become the carbon-rich "browns" needed for an ideal compost recipe. For good compost, you need both carbon-rich material and nitrogen-rich material, which are often used at a one-to-one ratio. Carbon-rich material is commonly referred to as "browns" because it includes wood, paper, straw, sawdust, and dried yard materials like leaves or grass. Nitrogen-rich material is known as "greens" and includes food scraps and fresh yard material.

Other piles of brown and green materials sat inside the Loraas building, in a large open space known as the "tipping floor." The tipping floor has a sprinkler system in the roof that adds moisture to the piles, and a couple of different pieces of large machinery. The first machine is a depackager, which is mainly used for loads of material that come from commercial sources like grocery stores or restaurants. The depackager mechanically separates food from its packaging, and any packaging that is removed gets sent to the landfill. Household green cart materials that arrive and are piled onto the tipping floor normally don't go through the depackager because they are considered source separated, meaning that they are *supposed* to arrive containing only organic materials. This, however, is not always the case, as I found out later that morning.

The second large machine in the tipping floor area is called a mixer, where the green and brown materials are combined. After being mixed, the material is taken outside the building and loaded into a bunker. The bunkers at Loraas are 25 feet wide by 164 feet long. They look like large, rectangular trenches and are covered and lined with panels that have little holes throughout, which helps to regulate factors like airflow and heat. This particular Loraas facility had eight bunkers when I visited, with control rooms at the end of each bunker to allow for careful monitoring of the decomposing piles' water, air, and temperature levels.

Managing these factors is essentially us replicating how decomposition happens in nature. Think of it like setting up an ideal house party for the micro-organisms. You start with the one-to-one ratio, then add some air and a bit of water. Once the set-up is just right, things will start heating up and the micro-organisms can throw the decomposing event of the century. The more closely you manage these factors, the more control you have over the overall process and timeline.

Temperature, for example, can change things dramatically. When a high temperature is maintained during composting for a certain period of time, pathogens are destroyed and the overall process can be sped up. While it's harder to control temperature in a backyard compost setting, industrial facilities can manage this closely. That's why curbside organics programs that process their materials in industrial facilities can accept meat, bones, dairy, and even pet waste, because they can ensure dangerous pathogens are killed and don't make it into the finished compost. At Loraas, for example, the mixture of greens and browns stays in the bunker for four weeks initially, and during that time it has to meet the required temperature to kill off pathogens. When it hits the right temperature, a clock starts. If the temperature dips down, the clock resets.

After four weeks, the mixture shrinks significantly, reducing by about half and up to three-quarters of its original volume. The mixture is rotated at the four-week point and then stays in the bunker for an additional two weeks to further decompose. Then it's put through a trommel, which sort of looks like a clothes dryer when it's running. The trommel's purpose is to remove anything that shouldn't be there. As it spins around, screens inside determine what goes into the finished compost and what gets filtered out. After that, the compost sits in piles outdoors where it cools down, or "cures." It is then tested to ensure it checks a number of boxes for quality and safety—it can't contain bacteria like salmonella, for example. From there, the finished product can be sold to farmers, gardeners, and anyone else in the market for some compost. This entire process from start to finish takes about eight weeks.

Kylene led me down a pathway that stretched between two bunkers, and as we walked along, I saw steam rising from the compost piles—they were so hot. But I also saw something else: plastic bags, dog food bags, food cartons, plastic cups, a juice box, and more, poking out of the piles. These contaminants came from household green carts and were mixed into the piles as the actual organic material decomposed. The only thing was, the contaminants weren't decomposing.

While most contaminants will get filtered out later in the trommel, their presence in the decomposing piles is less than ideal. For starters, contaminants take up valuable space in the bunkers that could instead be used to create more actual compost. If contaminants include things like rocks, glass, or metal, this is like game over in the early stages of the composting process. These materials can damage or even wreck machinery, costing thousands of dollars in repairs. If glass happens to be in a load of material and shatters, for example, that entire load is sent to the landfill. If something like a plastic cup doesn't decompose through the composting process, but instead breaks into a bunch of tiny pieces, those plastic pieces could also make it through the trommel's screen and end up in the finished compost. Nobody wants pieces of plastic in their compost, so this can ultimately affect the facility's ability to sell the final product.

We'll look at contamination in more depth shortly, but let's just take a moment for the final product. At the end of the tour, I grabbed a handful of finished compost from one of the cooling piles. It looked like soil, and it felt crumbly and warm. It was a deep, rich, dark brown colour, comparable to cocoa powder. And it smelled like earth—beautiful, natural, nourishing earth.

Why Composting Helps Create a More Circular System

Regardless of where you live, you produce organic waste. Every household does. About 30–40 percent of the residential waste generated in Canada is organic waste, and something has to be done with it. If Saskatoon's organic waste weren't being collected through a curbside program, where would it go? Probably the landfill. When organic waste is diverted from landfills, it avoids the production of methane, as we know, but it also reduces the sheer amount of waste in landfills. The average lifetime of a landfill can be extended by twelve to sixteen years when organic waste is diverted, which means that creating future landfills can potentially be avoided, or at least delayed.

Diversion of organic waste from landfills has been on the rise in Canada over the past twenty years. In 2002, a total of 1.3 million tonnes of organic materials were diverted from landfills. In 2020, that number doubled and then some, rising to 3.1 million tonnes diverted. The number of curbside organics collection programs in Canada has also increased during this time frame. As of 2021, about 70 percent of Canada's population had access to a curbside program for food and yard waste. This rate is higher when you account for those who have access to a curbside program for yard waste only. All of this is good news, but with a caveat: More can be done.

Creating waste and then dumping it in a landfill is considered a linear system. The waste moves down the line from one point to the next and then stays at its final resting place. In Canada, there are more than three thousand municipal solid-waste landfills. Only about half of these landfills are active, but even closed landfills continue to produce methane. Today's methane is partially from yesterday's organic waste—this issue doesn't just go away when the landfill closes.

One option for dealing with landfill methane is to capture it. Landfills can be outfitted with gas management systems that essentially catch the methane before it's released into the atmosphere. The captured methane either is burned or can be used to create energy like electricity. However, roughly just 110 landfills in Canada have systems for capturing landfill gas. Even with a gas capture system, only around 60 percent of methane actually gets captured. So while gas capture can help—especially for landfills already filled with organic materials—what we really need to do is stop adding more fuel to the fire.

When organic waste is diverted, either through an organics collection program or through home composting, it decreases the overall environmental impact associated with dumping waste in landfills. There is no environmental upside to organic waste sitting in landfills forever, other than perhaps the fact that the waste is contained. Organic material sitting in landfills could actually be considered a missed opportunity, because while landfills are linear, composting is circular. Organic waste is transformed into compost, which can be used to grow things, be it flowers or food. Once those flowers and food are at the end of their life, they too can be turned into compost, and the circle keeps going.

When farmers, gardeners, and growers use finished compost, it helps take care of soil long-term. Compost strengthens overall soil structure, attracts beneficial organisms like earthworms, increases the soil's ability to hold moisture, and reduces the need for synthetic fertilizers. It also provides nutrients, which is important because plants need nutrients to grow—but there has to be both give and take in that exchange. Otherwise, growing food indefinitely on depleted soil ultimately affects the quality of our food. But when the soil receives nutrients from compost, it can then pass those nutrients along to plants—which means that compost is like a gift that keeps on giving.

What You Can Do

Use Your Curbside Organics Collection Program—and Use It Well

If you have access to an organics collection program and use it already, then give yourself a check mark. Why do you deserve a check mark? Because 17 percent of households in Canada that have access to a municipal composting or organics collection program don't use it. If you fall into this 17 percent, I encourage you to figure out why you're not using the program, and then change that.

Separating mouldy strawberries from their plastic clamshell and placing each in their respective bins might be more work than chucking the entire container in the trash, but how much more work are we talking about here? A minuscule amount, truly. Having access to an organics collection program makes it incredibly easy to avoid landfilling your organic waste. There is no way to make household composting easier than to use an organics program.

It's not just about using such a program, though. It's about using it properly. I know I'm not the only person who has ever thrown something into a green cart without being fully certain it could actually go in there, all the while hoping for the best. But just like good intentions don't equal less food waste, hopeful thoughts about composting don't equal composting.

When we put things into household municipal bins that don't belong there, it's called contamination. Contamination isn't just a problem of green carts. Putting food into your recycling bin, recycling materials into your green bin, and hazardous or dangerous items into any bin are all examples of contamination. On the more extreme end, contamination can affect the health and safety of waste management workers. It can also damage or even fully wreck equipment and machinery—and composting equipment doesn't come cheap. Like I saw at Loraas, contamination can also impact the quality of the finished compost. It's also just a waste of everybody's time if material that is truly garbage goes through a composting process, only to get filtered out and sent to the landfill in the end anyway.

Contamination also includes materials that aren't compostable at the facility where they end up, even though they might be compostable somewhere else. Municipal organics programs across Canada differ in how they process the materials they collect, because there are a few different methods that fall under the umbrella of industrial composting. The type of facility and the way the organic materials are processed essentially dictate what's acceptable in a green cart program. For example, pet waste is accepted in your green cart if you live in Toronto, Calgary, or Ottawa, but not if you live in Saskatoon, Halifax, or Whitehorse (as of the time of writing). These variations are why it's difficult for me to make a general recommendation like "Put dog poop in your green cart," because even though dog poop is technically compostable, it can go in your green cart only if the processing facility in question accepts it.

Municipalities with organics programs almost always have a search function or an extensive list on their website where you can look up the accepted materials, because they want you to use the program correctly. This information is most commonly called a "Waste Wizard" search tool and can be found on a municipality's website or app, if they have one. It's sometimes also referred to as a "Waste Explorer" or "What Goes Where" searchable database. These search tools are for more than just organics—they tell you what can go in your recycling and garbage bins too. For information on how to find this for your municipality, see the Resources List.

Regardless of the program or location, some of the most common items that get tossed into green carts but don't belong there include plastic of any kind, packaging from fruits and vegetables, grocery store produce bags, produce stickers (remove these as they're usually made of plastic), painted or treated wood, personal hygiene products like makeup wipes or toilet paper, soiled diapers, disposable coffee cups, and pet waste (unless the program specifically takes pet waste). Compostable plastics are also an issue, which I will address shortly in more detail. As a general rule, it is always best to check before putting something in your green cart if you're unsure about it.

On the other hand, across Canada in places where municipal organics programs do exist, around 30 percent of the garbage collected is organic material that should have gone in someone's green cart. While it's likely that this is partially coming from people who don't use their green cart at all, it's still worth checking to see if there are more materials you could be putting into your green cart that you don't know about.

As a last note here, I have heard people lament that kitchen compost pails and green carts are gross, so they don't like using theirs. Although my preteen self would relate to this, my question as a thirty-something is this: Are garbage cans and landfills somehow more pleasant? I'd say the answer is no. However, there are things you can do to minimize the composting gross factor. Line your kitchen pail with something; whether that's newspaper or a paper bag, or if your program accepts certain compostable bags, use what they recommend. Check what they allow for bags, though—don't guess! Even if your green cart isn't full on collection day, put it out for collection. In the past, when our green cart was only partially full, we neglected to put it out. But letting the cart sit there for weeks makes it smell truly terrible—especially in warmer months. Paul has also rinsed out our cart using the hose before. For a more thorough clean, you could use vinegar. Just avoid using a cleaner that cannot be composted itself, since residue may stay on the cart afterwards and end up on future organic materials.

Advocate for an Organics Program Near You

If no organics program exists near you, advocate for one. Talk to your local representatives about why you want such a program and what it would mean for waste diversion. If representatives don't know that residents care about having this service, it might not be top of mind.

One other solution is applicable here that I learned about when I visited Loraas. If there is enough interest within a rural or smaller community for a curbside organics program, Loraas can provide this service for a fee. They supply household green carts, and then they collect the contents. If there is a similar private compost facility operator near you, along with solid community interest, it's worth checking whether this can be arranged. Private composting facilities are a business, after all, and if there are enough organic materials to be picked up and turned into finished compost, they just might be able to help.

Choose a Home Composting Option

If the previous solutions are not available to you, then the solution is to choose your own home composting adventure. While this might sound daunting, all you have to do is manage those same factors of air, temperature, water, and the carbon-to-nitrogen ratio, and then let the micro-organisms take it from there.

Composting Outdoors

If you have access to a yard or even a small green space, you can set up a backyard compost. There are several different options for backyard composting. The most common method is using a backyard bin, which keeps the organic materials enclosed while they break down, protecting it from pests and the elements. Backyard compost bins normally sit upright and come in a variety of sizes. You can buy these at home and garden stores, or you can make them yourself. Be sure to put your bin in a decently sunny spot, as the more shade it gets, the longer the compost will take to decompose.

With a backyard compost bin, you have to turn the material manually every week or so using a shovel or garden fork, which airs out the pile. If you don't want to do this manually, you can purchase a tumbler composter, which is basically a barrel-shaped bin that is mounted on a stand. This design allows you to more easily rotate the barrel, which airs out the material inside. It's best to buy a tumbler that has two compartments, because once one side is full, you have to let it sit and decompose. With two compartments you can at least continue adding fresh scraps to the second compartment while you wait for the first to break down.

For a backyard bin, the basic formula is still the one-to-one green-to-brown ratio. Greens are kitchen waste: raw fruit and vegetable scraps, along with coffee grounds, tea leaves, rinsed eggshells, and fresh yard clippings. Browns are paper, like coffee filters and newspaper, and dried yard materials. You can shred or break these items into smaller pieces, which helps to speed up the process, and layer the greens and browns to ensure they are well mixed. Add a bit of water as you layer the materials if they are very dry, or if the materials are extremely wet, add more dry carbon-rich items. The pile should be moist—I'm sorry if you hate that word, but it is the best descriptor here.

If you are using a backyard bin or a tumbler composter, you could have finished compost in anywhere from two to twelve months. You will know it's done because there won't be any visible pieces of food left and the overall volume will have shrunk. The material will be a dark, earthy brown colour that will look, feel, and smell similar to soil. The time of year that you start your compost will also determine how long it takes. You can use a backyard set-up throughout the winter months, but the decomposing process will either slow or stop, depending on how cold it gets. Once the weather warms up, mix your pile, and the process will begin again.

Although you could technically compost meat, bones, dairy, bread, pet waste, cooking oil, and cooked food in a backyard bin, it is generally not recommended. These items can attract pests or even larger animals, depending on where you live. Additionally, because you have less control over the level of heat as materials decompose, it's difficult to monitor the temperature to ensure pathogens die off. As a result, you won't be able to put all of your kitchen waste into a backyard compost bin. If you have shifted to a plant-based diet, however, you may not have meat, bones, or dairy waste to deal with at all. Either way, if you are composting what you can, you are still diverting a significant amount of organic material from the landfill and reducing your household garbage overall.

One backyard method that does allow for composting meat, dairy, and cooked food is trench composting, which requires the least amount of equipment and effort but does need more yard space. You just dig a trench, bury your food scraps directly in the soil, and then leave them there. You do not need to turn or monitor a trench compost; you're basically giving the food scraps over to the earth. The scraps will take longer to decompose since you're doing less managing of the process, but it makes composting extremely simple. One of the people I spoke with for this chapter even referred to trench composting as a foolproof method. It can take anywhere from a few months to over a year for scraps to decompose in a trench; the timeline largely depends on the quality of the soil surrounding the materials. A trench is best set up in warmer months when the ground is easier to dig into. Just be sure to dig the trench at least forty-five centimetres deep so that pests can't get into it. Then cover it thoroughly with soil and mark it somehow, so you don't accidentally dig it up.

Along the way, any problems that arise with backyard composting are likely to come from something being off with any of the factors. If the materials are too wet, too dry, not getting enough air, or too rich in either nitrogen or carbon, this can cause issues like a funky smell or make it take a long time to decompose, for example. All of these issues are fixable though. While I have outlined the basics here, if you are new to backyard composting, see the Resources List—I have included a number of sources that can help you navigate setting up and maintaining your compost. If you already have access to an organics program but want to set up a home compost for personal use, you could certainly do that too.

Composting Indoors

If creating a backyard compost is not an option for you, there are a couple of methods that can work indoors. One is called vermicomposting, which involves keeping an indoor bin of red wiggler earthworms. The worms essentially eat through the organic material to break it down. You can vermicompost similar organic materials to those you would put in a backyard compost bin: Fruit and vegetable scraps, coffee and tea grounds, some paper, and eggshells are all okay. Meat, dairy, and cooking oil are not. If done properly, vermicomposting shouldn't smell at all. You can make your own bin or buy supplies for vermicomposting at home and garden stores. Red wiggler earthworms are the most commonly used and readily available worm for vermicomposting. This is because they reproduce and eat quickly, and because they are surface-feeder worms. That means they naturally prefer to live in the top bit of soil, rather than burrowing into it, which makes them ideally suited for a shallower vermicomposting environment.

A second indoor option is called bokashi, which is a method of processing food scraps that technically ferments the material, instead of composting it.

Food scraps—including meat and dairy—go into a sealed bin, along with something known as bokashi bran. The bran is a dehydrated mixture of sugar, rice and/or wheat bran, and a bacterial culture containing micro-organisms, known as "effective micro-organisms." Once the bin is filled, you put the lid on and then let it sit for about two weeks to ferment. As with the tumbler composter, you'll want a second bokashi bucket to add fresh scraps to while the first one ferments. You can buy or make bokashi buckets. Bokashi produces two things: a liquid known as bokashi tea, which you can dilute and use as fertilizer, and a sort of fermented pre-compost material. This fermented material then needs to be further composted to complete the process. Since fermenting food scraps does not fully decompose them, they have to be added to a backyard bin or buried in a trench compost as a final step.

Bokashi is useful if you want to process meat and dairy scraps at home, alongside a backyard compost bin filled with other food and yard waste. It is less useful if you don't have anywhere to put the fermented material to finish the composting process. One option would be to take that pre-compost material somewhere else, like a friend's backyard compost or a community garden compost, for example. If either bokashi or vermicomposting sounds like the right fit for you, see the Resources List.

Although not impossible, it can be tough to compost if you live in an apartment or have limited space. It's also not your fault if organics programs don't exist near you, or if you don't have a yard to start your own backyard compost. If none of these solutions is feasible, focus on doing what you can to reduce food waste, which will mean less organic waste overall.

Bonus: Understand Compostable Plastics—but Keep Them Out of Your Compost

We will look at both plastics and packaging in greater detail in the coming chapters, but I want to address compostable plastics here because they relate to organics programs specifically. To illustrate the current reality of compostable plastics, I'm going to tell you a hypothetical story.

Let's say I design a compostable plastic cup at home. It looks like a regular plastic cup, but it's made from plants. I test this cup in my super-cool basement science lab, and after one hundred days of me labouring away in the lab with the heat cranked way up, the cup decomposes without a trace. (In this scenario I look like Ms. Frizzle from *The Magic School Bus*, by the way, with the big hair and a colourful science-themed printed dress.) I live in a faraway kingdom where there are no rules about what can be labelled as compostable plastic, so I slap "compostable" onto this cup and sell it to the masses. People buy it, thinking to themselves, "Hey, this is great, it's compostable!" When they're done using my marvellous cup, they put it into their household green bin, confident in its compostability—the label says so, after all.

But when this cup ends up at an industrial composting facility and goes through the composting process in a typical period of several weeks, it doesn't decompose. Why? Because the conditions and timeline it took to decompose in my super-cool basement science lab don't match up with the conditions and timeline at the compost facility. The cup might be technically compostable, but my invention doesn't work in practice. Instead, the cup gets filtered out along with the rest of the contaminants through the industrial composting process. From there, the whole contaminated gang checks into the local Landfill Hotel for an indefinite staycation.

I said this situation was hypothetical, but that's mainly because I am no Ms. Frizzle. I dropped out of physics in high school because I simply could not wrap my brain around concepts like velocity and kinematics, so having any sort of super-cool basement science lab is not in the cards for me. Everything else in this story, however, is just a slightly embellished version of how compostable plastics work—at least right now, anyway. Let's break this down.

Regular plastics are derived from fossil fuels. They are cheap, durable, and effectively everywhere. Their end-of-life scenario is a problem, because although some plastics can be recycled, they can be recycled only so many times. Plastics are a major cause of pollution, and given that many plastics are single-use, their brief lifetime is mind-boggling to reconcile with their environmental impact. Don't worry—we will unpack all of this and more in the coming chapters.

Then, in walks compostable plastic, the new kid on the block with grand plans to help us tackle both our dependency on fossil fuels and the end-of-life problems associated with plastic. Compostable plastic promises that we can still enjoy the cheap and durable benefits that plastic provides. While compostable plastics do make sense in theory, their presence in municipal waste streams has made things complicated and confusing, especially for consumers. For starters, there are a few terms that get thrown around interchangeably here but have different meanings, including *bio-based*, *biodegradable*, and *compostable*.

Bio-based means the plastic is made from plants, like corn or sugar cane. However, that says nothing about whether the item is compostable or biodegradable. Whether something breaks down has more to do with its chemical structure than its ingredients. Bio-based items can be designed to be compostable or biodegradable, but they can also be designed to act like regular plastics. Some plastics can be made either partially or fully from plants and still not break down at all. If you see "bio-based" labelled by itself on an item, it tells you that the item was made either partially or fully from plants, and that's it. Full stop. In practice, this information is basically useless to you and me. Bio-based plastics that have no further labelling almost always have to go in the garbage.

Then there's *biodegradable*, which is sometimes called *degradable*. These terms mean that the item can be broken down by micro-organisms in a natural environment. If done correctly, biodegradable plastics will break down into substances that already exist in nature, like water or carbon dioxide. The problem is that biodegradable plastic typically has no specific timeline attached to it; it just means the item might break down eventually. And in this case, "eventually" could take years—or longer. If you discard a cup that's labelled "biodegradable" in a forest, that cup is still litter until it hopefully, after an unknown amount of time, breaks down. Either way, biodegradable plastics are not accepted in most curbside organics programs, because an unspecified timeline means nothing to compost being processed in a matter of weeks or months.

Finally, we have the star of this show: *compostable*. Compostable plastics are biodegradable but without the "eventually" tag. Instead, plastics labelled "compostable" are meant to break down alongside food and yard waste in an industrial composting facility under specific conditions, including a certain time frame and temperature. But that means compostable plastics won't magically turn into a natural, earthy compost wherever you leave them. You may have seen something like "compostable where facilities exist" written on some of these products before, which stresses that point. The issue is that while compostable plastics might break down when they are tested—like in a lab setting, let's say—they are often not compatible with the conditions in most industrial composting facilities. This problem is essentially a mismatch between a good idea and how things currently work.

One of the key issues here is that there are no standardized labelling requirements for biodegradable and compostable plastics in Canada. As of the time of writing, the Government of Canada is working toward developing labelling regulations that would limit use of the words *biodegradable*, *degradable*, and *compostable* on plastics, so that items could be labelled as such only if they were proven to meet certain standards. These future regulations would certainly help, because then we could all rest assured knowing that plastics labelled "compostable" were truly compostable in standard facility conditions. Compost facilities could then accept these items for processing with that guarantee.

But without standardized labelling, it's hard to tell if plastic is compostable just by looking at it when it arrives at a compost facility. It's basically up to the individual facility or organics program to determine whether they want to accept compostable plastics, because if there's no guarantee the items will break down, they risk contaminating the finished compost. Labelling also matters here because even plastics that *are* truly compostable often get filtered out alongside the phony ones. Future federal labelling regulations would help with recycling, too, because compostable and biodegradable plastics are not compatible with current recycling infrastructure. Even though they may look like other recyclable items, they are not designed to be recycled, so they too contaminate recycling streams when people toss them into their curbside recycling bins.

There are also organizations with composting standards that are external to the government. In Canada, one of the main ones is the Biodegradable Products Institute (BPI) certification. BPI is a third-party certification body for compostable plastics and packaging in North America. You may have seen its green logo on items before. BPI tests products for compostability, and if those products pass BPI's requirements, they can be labelled as certified. This certification is a voluntary process for manufacturers.

Even with BPI certification, many industrial composting facilities in Canada still don't accept these items. Again, it's up to the individual facility or program to determine what they accept. One BPI-certified item that *is* commonly accepted in green carts in Canada is compostable plastic bags that are used as kitchen compost pail liners. In Calgary, for example, BPI-certified compostable bags are accepted—but they're the *only* compostable plastic item they accept, because the facility tested these bags to confirm they would decompose through its composting process. Calgary's facility has also tested other BPI-certified plastics in the past, and those items did not break down, possibly because BPI certification requires that compostable plastics disintegrate in a maximum of eighty-four days in the lab, but Calgary's entire compost process takes sixty days from start to finish.

Similarly, Halifax's website notes that compostable plastics are not accepted because they simply break into microscopic plastic pieces that contaminate the finished compost. At Toronto's facilities, compostable plastics don't even have a chance to potentially decompose. Their system has a preprocessing stage where contaminants like plastic are removed right from the get-go—and this includes anything that looks and behaves like plastic. So compostable plastics are automatically filtered out. Toronto also has an informational video on its website that makes a valid point worth repeating: Its organics program was designed to process food waste, not packaging.

I will admit that when I started working on this section, I felt strongly opposed to compostable plastics. They seemed like a band-aid solution that did nothing to address the root cause of our global dependency on plastics. But while a widespread reduction of that dependency should be priority number one, it's just not happening. We're still making plastics, using plastics, landfilling plastics, and littering plastics. A compostable version of these products is so far one of the better solutions we have, if we're going to continue relying so heavily on plastics.

Consider takeout containers. Takeout isn't going to just disappear, so what's the best option for reducing plastic waste when you order food? Sure, you could bring your own reusable containers when picking up food. But this is already an available solution, and only a small minority of people actually do this. Reusable container take-back programs are slowly starting to appear in Canada, but in cases where these types of programs aren't available, compostable takeout options might make sense.

Compostable plastics currently make up a tiny fraction of all plastics—less than 1 percent. But if implemented well overall, they could have the potential to help create a less linear and more circular way of dealing with waste, which would mean that less plastic ends up in landfills or littering the planet. For that to happen, though, we need compostable plastics to be manufactured and tested in a way that guarantees they break down. We need federal regulations for labelling so that *compostable* and other related terminology have a defined and consistent meaning across Canada. We probably also need changes to certain infrastructure and technology at composting facilities, so that they can process a wider variety of items beyond those that are traditionally considered compostable.

Without these changes, however, don't make decisions about whether compostable plastics can go in your green bin based on what the label says. Instead, make these decisions based on what your organics program says it can or cannot accept. You can look this up on your municipality's Waste Wizard or similar search tool. Sometimes items may be labelled "home compostable," but in practice, whether these items decompose depends on individual home compost set-ups, so it's best to keep compostable plastics out of there, too. Although home composting has a longer timeline, you likely won't be able to get the compost pile hot enough to decompose plastics. You could test these items on your own, but just know you may end up picking plastic pieces out of your finished compost.

So, where are compostable, biodegradable, and bio-based plastics supposed to go? Typically in the garbage, which sucks. In the future, we will likely see changes in Canada surrounding the usage and labelling of all of this, as it's very much an evolving landscape.

There's one more takeaway here: Labels don't automatically make things more sustainable. In a world where you and I are encouraged to buy more and more stuff—including compostable plastic stuff—it's important to dig deeper beyond the claims that any labels make. Even if an item is labelled with a descriptor like "100 percent" in front of the word *compostable* or *biodegradable*, and even if these words are written in an earthy green colour, it doesn't change the situation. This is just marketing. In that case, a healthy dose of skepticism is the most reliable defence.

Takeaways

- If you have access to an organics collection program, participate in it. Check what types of materials are accepted, and keep contaminants out of your green bin.
- If there is no organics collection program near you, advocate for one or see if a private compost operator can provide this service to your community.
- Set up your own home composting system. If you have outdoor space, try a backyard bin, trench compost, or tumbler system. Inside, vermicomposting or bokashi can work.
- Bonus: Check if your organics collection program accepts compostable plastics, but usually, it's best to keep compostable plastics out of both compost and recycling bins—at least for now. This may change in the future in Canada, so it's something to keep tabs on.

CHAPTER 7:

Recycling

AS A KID IN THE EARLY 2000s, I grew up knowing about recycling—and knowing it was good for the environment. My parents had a little blue box in the kitchen where they collected certain materials like aluminum cans, which they then dropped off at the local deposit return depot. Later on, in 2013, the City of Saskatoon implemented a curbside recycling program. So for my entire adult life, I have had consistent access to a curbside recycling program. Although I have heard other people talk about how recycling isn't everything it's cracked up to be—and every now and then a news article pops up poking holes in the entire recycling system—I chalked this up to background noise. I continued recycling my household containers and packaging, dutifully doing my part. I assumed that all of the materials I put into my blue bin were, in fact, being recycled into new and wonderful things.

But then I started writing this book. I quickly discovered that recycling is much more complicated than it appears. While I'm not about to tell you that recycling is bad, I am going to tell you that it can be messy and that, in general, we are much too reliant on recycling as the ultimate solution to the escalating problem of packaging waste. In this chapter we will focus first on how recycling works and, from there, on how you can use that information to more effectively engage with the recycling services available to you. We will also look at how to shift your energy toward reducing and reusing over recycling whenever possible—and why doing so is fundamentally the better choice for the environment.

A Brief History of Recycling

Recycling is a process in which materials are collected, stripped down, and turned into new ones. Recycling therefore prevents resources from becoming waste by keeping them in use. In an ideal scenario, recycling creates a continuous circle, as new aluminum cans are created from old ones—represented by the universal recycling symbol with the three chasing arrows that loop continuously. Recycling can conserve natural resources and save energy in the process, because when recycled material is used in place of new material, it reduces the need for more raw resources to be extracted, processed, and manufactured. This is true whether we're talking about wood for paper or fossil fuels for plastic. The energy savings can be significant too. The process of recycling aluminum, for example, uses about 95 percent less energy than producing new aluminum does. Recycling can also reduce the amount of material that gets littered or landfilled by keeping materials in circulation longer.

Widespread interest in recycling in Canada took hold in the 1970s, parallel to the environmental movement of the same decade. The universal recycling symbol and the classic "Reduce, reuse, recycle" mantra were both introduced into popular discourses during this time as well. The concept of a blue box system where recyclable materials are picked up on the curb was actually created and launched in Canada, first appearing in Kitchener, ON, in 1981. The original blue boxes of the 1980s were much smaller than the typical blue carts of today, because they were meant for significantly fewer materials—mainly cans, bottles, and newspapers. Throughout the 1980s, 1990s, and beyond, blue box recycling systems and the corresponding infrastructure for processing collected materials spread across Canada. I think it's interesting that although recycling is incredibly common now, in the grand scheme of things, recycling programs in Canada are not actually that old—forty-five years at most.

What Is Mechanical Recycling?

There are different types of recycling, but the way that most household recycling is processed in Canada is known as mechanical recycling. Mechanical recycling systems can vary in practice depending on specific facilities, but they generally follow the same basic steps. Step one is the collection of materials. From there, the collected materials go to a materials recovery facility for processing.

To see mechanical recycling in action, I went on a tour of Loraas Recycle, which is the materials recovery facility where recyclables collected through Saskatoon's curbside program end up. At Loraas Recycle, materials arrive by the truckload and are dumped inside a large warehouse onto what is known as the tipping floor—just like at the Loraas organics facility. From there, the materials go through a machine that fluffs them up to break apart any clumps that are stuck together. Then the materials go to a presort station, where people are waiting to pull out anything that visibly should not be there. This includes garbage, hazardous items like propane tanks, and recyclable material like electronics, which this specific Loraas facility does not handle but can be recycled elsewhere in the city. The items that are pulled out in the presort phase will end up in the landfill if they are garbage, or in the case of the electronics, Loraas staff generously takes these to the local electronics drop-off—which is technically not their job and should have been done by the consumer.

After presorting, recyclable material moves from one machine to the next along a series of fast-paced conveyor belts. Each part of the process is designed to pick up on different cues that help sort by material type. Examples of these cues include the weight or size of the material, which is determined by equipment like magnets or sensors. For example, large cardboard is identified by specialized machinery, while everything else that is not identified as large cardboard falls through and continues on to the next machine. At another machine, a magnet yanks the metals out, and everything else moves on. This continues throughout the entire loop until everything is sorted, and then the sorted material is compacted into large, square bales. At this particular Loraas facility, about sixteen thousand kilograms of material is processed every hour.

Anything that gets to the end of the process without being properly sorted either is too small to be recycled, like tiny bits of paper or plastic, or was never meant to be there in the first place, like garbage that was missed in the presort phase. These leftover items are taken to the landfill for disposal.

Where the square bales of recyclable material get sent next depends on the material and whether a further processing facility exists nearby; the bales may be sent to a neighbouring city or to another country. Recycled material can be made into either the exact same thing, like an aluminum can becoming an aluminum can again, or something different, like plastic bottles being turned into polyester clothing or park benches. When this happens, it's called downcycling, which means that through the process of recycling, the material becomes a lower-quality item than it originally was. Downcycling also has a clear end point—it is unlikely that a polyester T-shirt or a park bench made from plastic bottles will be recycled into anything else in the future.

I did this recycling tour a couple of months after I did the organics one, and I noticed a key difference between the two facilities. Within a matter of weeks, the composting facility turns organic materials into a final product—the finished compost. But the materials recovery facility I visited was just one step in a much longer and more complex chain. The baled recyclable material is not done when it leaves Loraas Recycle; it still has to be broken down and turned into something new elsewhere.

Which Materials Recycle Well?

In my own kitchen recycling bin, the most common materials I recycle are glass jars, wine bottles, aluminum beverage cans, steel cans from canned food, paper or cardboard, and a variety of plastics—most often bottles and containers from foods like ketchup or oat yogurt. Food packaging makes up at least 90 percent of our overall household recycling, because I don't order stuff online if I can help it and I try to be minimal about what I buy in general. So aside from the odd item, our recycling is almost entirely composed of materials from the kitchen. We clean these recyclable materials to remove food residue, and then once our kitchen bin is full, we transfer the items either to our household blue bin in the back alley, or to various sorting bins in our garage for materials that have to be dropped off elsewhere, including a deposit return program for glass and aluminum cans.

Mechanical recycling works better for some of these materials than for others. Aluminum and steel, for example, are two of the most desirable recyclable materials. This is because they can both be melted down and reshaped over and over again without affecting the quality of the material. This means they can be recycled infinitely, which in turn leads to higher recycling rates. For example, aluminum beverage cans are the most commonly recycled drink receptacle in the world, with nearly 70 percent of all cans being recycled globally.

Glass is also infinitely recyclable with no impact on the overall quality. But container glass—which refers to glass jars and bottles, most often used for food and beverages—can sometimes be difficult to recycle because it's heavy to transport and breaks easily, especially if it's collected via a curbside recycling program. Broken glass is low in value and also a potential hazard at recycling facilities, so it's typically either downcycled or landfilled. Downcycled glass may become something like fibreglass insulation, for example. If you take glass directly to a deposit return drop-off, there's a much higher chance of it being either recycled or cleaned and reused—like beer and wine bottles being redistributed once they're sanitized. Glass is also easily reusable at home, especially in the kitchen for purposes like food storage.

Although paper cannot be recycled infinitely, it is considered a valuable and desirable material, given its widespread and versatile use. Regular paper can be recycled up to seven times before the paper fibres get too short to be made into anything else. Corrugated cardboard—cardboard that has those zigzag layers—can be recycled up to ten times.

Unsurprisingly, the material that fares the worst in mechanical recycling is plastic. Plastic doesn't fare just kind of badly in mechanical recycling either—it fares very badly. Between the years 1950 and 2015, out of all the plastic waste that was generated globally, only 9 percent was recycled. Furthermore, only 10 percent of that recycled 9 percent was recycled more than one time. When I first read these stats, I thought there was no way this information could be true—how on earth could this be happening? But this information comes from a study in *Science Advances* that is both reputable and widely cited.

Now, keep in mind that this dismal 9 percent applies to *all plastic waste* generated between 1950 and 2015, meaning that it includes much more than just your typical household plastic recyclables. Plenty of the plastics created since 1950 were never meant to be recycled in the first place, like furniture or certain packaging, for example. Plastic recycling didn't even start until after 1980. So that 9 percent stat does not mean that only 9 percent of all the plastics you've ever personally put into your household bin were actually recycled. The recycling rate for household plastics varies, depending on location and individual recycling programs. But even plastics that *can* potentially be recycled face a number of obstacles that determine whether they will be. We will discuss plastics more in the coming chapters, but for now the question is this: Why is it so difficult to recycle plastic?

The Challenge of Recycling Plastic

Types of Plastic—and How They Affect Recycling

The first thing to understand is that not all plastics are created equal. The easiest way to tell the difference between types of household plastics, especially those found in the kitchen, is to look for something called their resin identification code. This sounds more complicated than it is. These codes are actually just numbers, and you may already be familiar with them. If you head into your kitchen and look at various plastic bottles, containers, and packaging, you should be able to spot a little triangle on each item, with a number inside the triangle ranging from 1 to 7. On plastic bottles and containers this number is normally found on the bottom, indented directly into the plastic, whereas on flexible or soft packaging it is usually on the back or side and looks more like a printed label. These numbered triangles tell you what type of plastic the item is made from. Each number refers to a different type of plastic with different properties, including its structure, flexibility, and melting point.

For reference, the following is a breakdown of the resin identification codes. Although this information may seem tedious, it is important for understanding and navigating plastics recycling, so bear with me here. This information will come up again in future chapters.

- **Plastic #1:** This is polyethylene terephthalate (PET), which is a clear plastic that is often used in food packaging. Salad dressing bottles, pop bottles, water bottles, and clamshell packaging for berries or mixed greens are all made from plastic #1.

- **Plastic #2:** This is high-density polyethylene (HDPE), which is widely used for a variety of purposes. Food packaging examples include milk jugs and sturdier bottles or containers for foods like mustard or baking powder. If you look at a bottle made from plastic #1 beside a bottle made from plastic #2, you'll see that plastic #2 is noticeably thicker and stronger than plastic #1.
- **Plastic #3:** This is polyvinyl chloride (PVC), which has a wide range of applications including flooring, vinyl siding, credit and debit cards, and health-care uses. Certain types of food packaging like cooking oil jugs are sometimes made from plastic #3, but overall this plastic is less common for food purposes.
- **Plastic #4:** This is low-density polyethylene (LDPE), which is a soft, stretchy, and flexible plastic sometimes referred to as plastic film. Produce bags, grocery bags, plastic wrap, sandwich bags, and other bags for foods like bread, apples, or bell peppers are all plastic #4. More flexible bottles can be made out of plastic #4 as well.
- **Plastic #5:** This is polypropylene (PP), which is often used for more rigid containers for foods like yogurt, sour cream, and margarine. Some takeaway food packaging is also made from plastic #5, like the containers that cooked rotisserie chickens come in at the grocery store. I also own some sturdier reusable food storage containers with lids that are made from plastic #5.
- **Plastic #6:** This is polystyrene (PS), which is what many single-use food and beverage items are made from. This plastic is very lightweight. Examples include plastic cutlery and foam packaging like egg cartons, meat trays, and takeout containers.
- **Plastic #7:** This plastic category is known as "other," which basically means it's a catch-all for any type of plastic that does not fit into the previous six categories. This includes plastic that is mixed together. Biodegradable or compostable plastics are sometimes tossed into this category as well. Examples from my own kitchen of plastic #7 include a zip-top bag of gluten-free flour, and kitchen equipment, like a manual plastic vegetable spiralizer.

The best way to become familiar with this number system is to look at different plastics you already have in your kitchen. Or, the next time you're at the grocery store, peruse various plastic packaging and products. My goal in telling you this is not for you to be able to look at a plastic bottle and immediately identify it as polyethylene terephthalate. Instead, the goal is to be aware of the fact that "plastics" are not all identical or interchangeable. More importantly, their unique properties mean that they cannot be lumped together during recycling.

For plastics to be recycled, they first have to be separated by number at a materials recovery facility. So plastic #2 gets recycled alongside other pieces of plastic #2—and that's it. There is no equation where plastic #1 plus plastic #4 equals new and shiny plastic #5. The only equation where plastic is mixed and forms a different number is #7, the catch-all category, which is also one of the hardest plastics to recycle because it is mixed. Out of all the plastic numbers, the most common ones accepted for recycling are #1 and #2. The rest of the numbers are largely dependent on where you live and on individual recycling programs. You may find some plastic that has no number at all, and this almost always means it cannot be recycled. Common examples include the tear-away piece of plastic on the top of a sour cream or yogurt container, or the thin plastic bags that snack foods like crackers are packed in, inside a box.

The fact that plastics have to be separated by their resin identification code to be recycled also means that if plastics get mixed accidentally, they may be considered contaminated. This can result in low recycling rates. Recycling contamination is similar to organics contamination. It can include recyclable materials that are contaminated with food, like paper that is soaked with food grease, or a plastic ketchup bottle that still has globs of ketchup in it when it arrives at the facility. Both of these contamination examples would be discarded as trash at a recycling facility, because they risk contaminating other clean recyclable materials. Beyond food, recycling contamination also refers to materials that get mixed together when they shouldn't be, like different plastic numbers. It can also refer to recyclable materials that end up at a given facility but are not actually accepted at that facility. Examples of this include the electronics at Loraas that I mentioned earlier, or if someone puts glass in their blue bin, but glass isn't accepted in their blue bin. If that glass breaks, it can contaminate the materials around it. In simple terms, recycling contamination basically refers to anything that should not be there, or anything that should not be mixed together for mechanical recycling purposes.

The Economics of Recycling Plastic

Another reason plastics have a low recycling rate is that new plastic isn't expensive to make. There are also limitations to plastic's structural properties. Many plastics lose quality when they are recycled, which means they can be recycled only one or two times—if they make it that far. As a result, plastics that do get recycled are most often downcycled. This means that recycling a plastic water bottle doesn't necessarily reduce the amount of raw material being manufactured to create new plastic water bottles. Instead, if a plastic water bottle is downcycled into something else—say, a polyester shirt—it only delays the eventual disposal of the plastic, rather than keeping the plastic material in existence in an ideal and ongoing recycling loop.

It's important to remember that recycling is not just about breaking things down—it's about turning them into something new. Whether the material gets made into something new is determined by factors like existing infrastructure, contamination rates, and the material's quality. Finally, there needs to be a market for the recycled material. Although recycling may have been born from environmental concerns, in reality it is driven largely by market ones. There is simply no reason for a facility to sort and bale material that nobody wants to buy. Recycling facilities are businesses, after all, and recyclable material is bought and sold according to market value, the same way that new material is bought and sold. It costs money to run a recycling facility, so the price to process, sort, and transport recyclable material can't outweigh the profit. That's why aluminum and steel fare better in mechanical recycling—they don't lose quality when recycled, they are highly compatible with mechanical recycling, and there are people who want to buy the recycled material and turn it into something new on a regular basis. But if it's difficult to recycle plastic #7, and nobody wants to buy a bale of it anyway, then it's unlikely to be recycled.

The recycling market is often reflected in what local or provincial programs do or don't accept. In Saskatoon, for example, plastic film and bags made from plastic #4 were removed from the municipal curbside collection program in 2018, because the companies that process Saskatoon's curbside recycling couldn't find a consistent market for these materials. This included plastic grocery bags, sandwich bags, and other plastic bags for foods like bread and produce. Then, in late 2024, these materials—along with other flexible, soft plastics—were added to a different provincial program called SK Recycles, which began accepting the materials via drop-off at depot locations throughout the province. These fluctuations demonstrate that recycling is not static; a number of factors are at play. This also means that something I can currently recycle nearby may become unrecyclable near me in the future—or vice versa.

The Challenges of Composite Plastics

I'm about to make this even more complicated—hang in there. Around the mid-2000s, the types of materials used for packaging began to change, becoming increasingly complex. The main culprit here is composite packaging, which refers to various materials that have been mixed together to become a single package. Common examples of composite kitchen packaging include coffee bags that are plastic on the outside with aluminum foil on the inside, butcher paper that has a thin layer of plastic on one side, and soft plastic juice pouches that have hard plastic nozzles, which are made from different types of plastic. Composite materials have grown to dominate packaging, and plenty of food packaging now incorporates two or more types of material, one of which is usually plastic. Composites are not always obvious either. Chip bags, for example, look like they're made of a single material, but they're actually made of three different materials jammed together—paper, plastic, and foil, which are laminated together to form the bag.

When different types of materials are smushed together to form one single package, in order for them to be recycled they need to be separated first. In other words, the coffee bag needs to be split into its aluminum and plastic components. But mechanical recycling was not designed to rip apart aluminum from plastic—it was designed to sort aluminum from plastic. Same with a soft plastic juice pouch with a hard plastic nozzle. Let's say this particular juice pouch makes it all the way to the sorting phase of mechanical recycling. But if the soft plastic part is #4 and the hard plastic part is #2, the machine might not be able to tell if it should go with the #4 plastics or with the #2 plastics. In the end, that juice pouch is unlikely to be sorted and instead will get filtered out and landfilled.

You may be wondering: If composites are largely incompatible with most mechanical recycling infrastructure, why not design new infrastructure or create a machine that could recycle the entire package as one? One answer to that question is that recycling infrastructure is not cheap to build or maintain. When I was at Loraas Recycle, I asked how much it would cost to build a new facility with updated equipment—around $30 million. So that's certainly one barrier. Another answer here goes back to the fact that in order for a mixed aluminum and plastic bag to be recycled as one package, there needs to be someone who wants to buy a bale of that mixed aluminum and plastic material and turn it into something else. If a market for that mixed material does not exist, that bag is not going to get recycled. Composite materials are typically low quality since they are by nature a mixed material, which exacerbates all of this.

It's worth noting that I did come across some benefits of composites. They can be durable, long-lasting, and lightweight, which makes them ideal for shipping long distances. Composites are also effective at prolonging the shelf life of foods. This is true of most food and beverage packaging, which is necessary to a certain extent for ensuring food safety and avoiding cross-contamination. Packaging can also help prevent food waste, which is a good thing since food waste has a massive environmental impact of its own. For example, think of cucumbers wrapped in plastic. This seems silly—why can't cucumbers just be left unwrapped? But wrapping cucumbers in plastic can extend the shelf life of a cucumber by up to two weeks, which is significant from a food waste perspective. So, guess what? This is another example of a trade-off. Do we leave cucumbers unwrapped to avoid plastic, or do we wrap them in plastic and extend their shelf life to prevent food waste? Both are important considerations. On the other hand, three-packs of cucumbers—which are often wrapped individually in plastic, and then grouped together in another layer of plastic—do not need all that packaging. Although the first layer of plastic may be helpful for extending the shelf life, the second layer is likely unnecessary.

I think packaging can be both beneficial and problematic; both can be true. The issue is that as packaging materials continue to evolve and increase in volume, mechanical recycling cannot keep up. Perhaps recycling would work better overall if we cut out all composites and certain plastics, stripping it back to the materials of the 1980s. But this is looking at the past with rose-coloured glasses. Ultimately, I don't think eliminating plastic and composite packaging is on the horizon. Either way, the world cannot recycle its way out of the growing mountain of packaging waste. Recycling may be able to handle some materials, but it is not currently handling all of them. Nor is it going to in the future, unless changes are made to recycling infrastructure, packaging designs, the materials used, the sheer amount of packaging being produced—or, most likely, all of the above.

Understanding Recycling Labels

I want to mention one thing here regarding the chasing arrows recycling symbol. This symbol is in the public domain, meaning that anyone can use it for free. So in theory, I could concoct some packaging and then add the recycling symbol to it, like my example in the previous chapter about creating compostable plastics in my super-cool basement science lab. I could then test this packaging for recyclability. If it were possible to recycle it, that would make it technically recyclable, right? But if this packaging ends up in, let's say, Halifax, where it can't be recycled, well, this isn't really my problem. It's the consumer's problem, because they see the recycling symbol on the package, assume it's recyclable, and toss it into their household bin. From there, it's the materials recovery facility's problem, because if that packaging isn't actually recyclable in Halifax, it can contaminate the recycling stream. Other versions of similar labelling on packaging may include phrases like "100 percent recyclable," "recyclable where facilities exist," or some other variation of this wording.

As a result, the Government of Canada is working toward establishing labelling rules to limit the use of the chasing arrows recycling symbol on plastic products and packaging. This would mean that the symbol could appear on plastics only if 80 percent of the recycling facilities in Canada accepted those items, *and* if those facilities had a consistent market in North America for them. These labelling rules would hopefully improve the overall recyclability of plastics in Canada, in addition to making things less confusing for you and me. They are similar to the compostable plastics labelling rules that the federal government is also working toward—as discussed in the previous chapter—and are something to watch for in the coming years.

While it's completely understandable to conclude that something is recyclable near you if you see the recycling symbol on it, this isn't always the case. We will look more closely at how to determine if something is actually recyclable near you shortly. The main thing to know is that even if something has the recycling symbol on it, this does not guarantee it can be recycled. When in doubt, check your local Waste Wizard.

Our Obsession with Recycling

This chapter has been hefty so far and I've given you a lot of difficult information, but not everything is terrible. Remember that mechanical recycling works very well for some materials, like aluminum and steel, and that there are environmental benefits that stem from that.

However, I decided to do a deep dive into the behind-the-scenes of recycling firstly because recycling is not necessarily as straightforward as it seems, and secondly because we place a lot of emphasis on recycling, both as individuals and collectively in Canada. We tend to put recycling on a pedestal as one of the most important things we can personally do for the environment. If you care about the environment, you recycle. Full stop. But is this justified? A 2022 report from the Intergovernmental Panel on Climate Change provides hierarchical lists of household actions that can reduce greenhouse gas emissions. "Recycle" appears on one of these lists—but at the bottom, in last place. Switching to more efficient appliances, owning a smaller car, and producing your own food, for example, all rank higher than "recycle" does on that list.

My point is not that I hate recycling. I have diligently recycled for most of my life and will continue to recycle, because otherwise my recyclable materials will be either burned or landfilled, both of which have environmental implications of their own (which we will discuss in the coming chapter). My point is that although recycling is important, it's not the be-all and end-all. If you're a superstar household recycler, you can still keep that up, but on an individual and collective scale we need that superstar energy to be directed elsewhere too—like into reducing and reusing.

What You Can Do

Go on a Recycling Tour

Some materials recovery facilities and other recycling facilities offer tours, typically for groups of school-aged children. But depending on the facility, they may also offer tours for adults. To determine if this is an option, first look up what type of recycling facilities exist in your area. If you can't find any information about possible tours on the facility's website, it's worth calling to ask, because it's possible that they allow tours but aren't actively advertising it.

On a tour, you'll see how materials are sorted and baled, what contamination looks like in practice, and why the facility in question can or cannot accept certain items. But the most important part is that you'll leave the tour with a much better understanding of all the things I've talked about in this chapter, especially if you ask questions along the way.

Follow the Waste Hierarchy: Reduce, Reuse, Then Recycle

The saying "Reduce, reuse, recycle" was not just invented to be a catchy slogan—it's a waste hierarchy. It's also commonly known as the 3R's. The highest priority is reducing consumption and overall waste, followed by reusing whenever we can and, lastly, and only if the first two are not possible, recycling.

We have to use resources, products, and packaging to some degree, and the waste hierarchy lays out how to do that with the least environmental impact. However, this hierarchy is not reflected in the way that most of our cities, businesses, and industries normally operate. Nor is it reflected in the way that most of us operate at home. Imagine what might happen if we gave as much thought and attention to reducing and reusing as we do to recycling, on both an individual and a collective scale.

The first part of the waste hierarchy is *reduce*, which means stopping waste at the source. In a broader sense, this applies to the way that products and packaging are designed and manufactured; for example, is it possible for that three-pack of cucumbers to be encased in less packaging? While you probably don't have any control over how cucumbers are packaged, the concept of *reduce* can still be applied on a smaller scale. In your own kitchen, reducing refers to changing your actions to prevent waste, and it's really about doing more with less. Reducing is not flashy or consumerist; it's practical, functional, and sensible. Reducing might mean you stop purchasing disposable kitchen items that typically can't be recycled, like plastic wrap or paper napkins, or you change how you grocery shop, so that you buy groceries with less packaging, like we discussed in the "Grocery Shopping" chapter. When you do this, you reduce the amount of packaging you are bringing into your home, which in turn reduces the amount of recyclables and waste you have overall. Other concepts we have already looked at like reducing food waste and low-waste cooking fit into reducing as well.

Reuse, like *reduce*, is also practical. On a wider scale it can be implemented in concepts like reusable container take-back programs. For example: You buy something in a reusable container—say, preserves in a glass jar from the farmers' market—and then the vendor accepts the glass jar back once it's empty. Then, the glass jar gets reused, over and over again. This example is technically both reusing *and* reducing in action, because when you reuse, you often inherently reduce. Similarly, in your own kitchen, *reuse* means repeatedly using items and supplies for their original purpose for as long as possible—like a cast iron pan that you use and take care of for decades. Both reducing and reusing also mean that you actively choose to not purchase any other new and trendy pans that catch your eye.

Reuse can also mean that you use something for a purpose different from its intended one. I'll give you an example of this from my own kitchen. When I started buying more food at Bulk Barn and transporting it home in reusable cloth produce bags and containers, I had nothing to put my loose pasta or pumpkin seeds in once I brought these foods home. Rather than going out and buying a bunch of new glass storage jars, over a period of several months, Paul and I saved glass jars from food. This included larger jars from foods like pickles, and smaller ones from foods like jam. Paul deserves a shout-out here for cleaning and painstakingly removing all the sticky labels from these jars. Once they were clean, I turned the jars into pantry containers for all the bulk food I was now buying that needed a home. Paul also thrifted a number of vintage glass jars that we started using for food storage. All of these jars are different shapes and sizes; they are not a matching set. But the point is not to have a matching set of jars—the point is to reuse glass jars for the next several decades. If I weren't actively thinking about implementing the waste hierarchy and needed some glass storage jars in any other scenario, I probably would have gone out and bought a bunch of new ones, while recycling all the jars that came through my kitchen—without even realizing the irony of this.

Why are reducing and reusing better than recycling? Recycling can conserve natural resources, save energy, and reduce the amount of waste sent to the landfill—all of this is still true. But guess what can do all of those things even better than recycling can? Reducing and reusing. If you reduce, you create less waste or no waste in the first place; if you reuse, you keep items and therefore resources in circulation longer. Recycling is not the same as reusing, because in order to reuse recyclable materials, they have to be broken down and turned into something new first. While recycling can require less energy than making a new product, it still involves processing, manufacturing, and transporting goods. In the case of downcycling, this is also just delaying disposal, not preventing it.

Following the waste hierarchy is really about changing your priorities. If up until this point you've prioritized recycling at home over reducing and reusing, then flip this around. For example, let's say you grab an iced coffee in a disposable plastic cup, but you're not concerned about using a disposable item because the cup is recyclable. Or you order a package of ten reusable straws online that come in a recyclable cardboard box, rather than buying them in person from a local shop, where you've seen them before being sold in a package-free format. You don't actually need ten reusable straws, and eight of them will probably sit unused in your cupboard, but it's easier to buy them online, and the box is recyclable anyway. In these two examples, recycling is given priority over reducing. This is a default response for most of us, and it's a deeply ingrained one. Prioritizing reducing and reusing instead might go something like this: You make coffee at home, bring your own reusable mug to grab coffee, or drink your coffee at the coffee shop in a ceramic cup. Or: You go to the store and buy the two straws you actually need, and bring a small bag to transport them home. Know that you will probably have to actively think about responding this way until reducing and reusing become your new default. Like I said, responding this way is not flashy—and it's not groundbreaking either. This is just straight-up practical, which I dare say is an undervalued quality in today's world.

In the coming chapters, we will discuss this waste hierarchy along with other corresponding strategies for reducing and reusing in greater detail. What I hope to have demonstrated to you so far though is why it is important to follow "Reduce, reuse, recycle" *in that order*. Reducing and reusing conserves resources, saves energy, and reduces waste more than recycling ever will.

Even when you implement this waste hierarchy at home, you are realistically still going to recycle, and that's fine. This is similar to what we've seen in previous chapters: Reducing food waste is the goal, but composting is necessary for the rest. Same here—this is not about eradicating recycling. Reducing and reusing are the goal, but when that's not possible, recycling is necessary for the rest.

Use the Recycling Services Available to You—and Use Them Well

Many municipalities in Canada with recycling programs still end up with recyclable materials in their garbage streams. In Saskatoon, about 17 percent of the garbage collected from single-family homes could have been recycled, either via the city's curbside collection program or at a drop-off depot, including glass, paper, and certain plastics. This is not just a Saskatoon problem. Many other cities or provinces—depending on who tracks this information—have similar rates of potentially recyclable material that ends up in the garbage.

If you participate in the recycling programs available to you, your recyclable materials at least have a chance of being recycled. But if you throw these materials in the garbage, then they are garbage. In short, even if the system isn't perfect, it's still better to engage with it than not.

Recycling programs work similarly to organics programs in that each program accepts different materials based on a variety of factors, like infrastructure or viable markets. It's not the chasing arrows recycling symbol that determines whether or not something is recyclable in a given program—it's the program itself. You can look up what is recyclable on your municipal Waste Wizard or similar search tool; see the Resources List. Often the same search tool is used for organics and recycling if both programs exist in one place. I have the City of Saskatoon's Waste Wizard app on my phone, for example, which makes it easy to quickly search items wherever I am. If no such search tool exists for your program or area, there will most likely be an extensive list available online that details accepted materials. Many recycling programs also have some sort of online guide with specific tips and further information about how to best use the program. If anything is unclear, you can always contact the program facilitator directly.

Some provinces, like British Columbia, have more cohesive systems where the same materials are generally accepted for recycling province-wide. In other provinces and territories this is determined by each municipality or community's individual program. Because this varies across Canada, it's important to check which materials are accepted, rather than making assumptions. Case in point: You can recycle black plastic in Calgary, Vancouver, Whitehorse, Halifax, and Ottawa. You cannot recycle black plastic in Toronto, Winnipeg, or Saskatoon (as of the time of writing). Black plastic may not be accepted because it is difficult for sorting machines to detect, given that it's often the same colour as the conveyor belt, so it just gets filtered out at the end of the sorting process. Black plastic can also be made of mixed plastics that are just dyed black, rendering it low quality, so there is a limited market for it. This means that if black plastic is not accepted in a given recycling program but ends up there, it's contamination. And not contaminating your recyclable material is one thing you can do that absolutely makes a difference.

I didn't really understand how much of an issue recycling contamination was until I did the tour of Loraas Recycle. I was completely floored by the sheer volume of garbage that the workers—*humans*, mind you, not machines—had to sort through. Within less than five minutes I saw all of the following gliding past on a conveyor belt: three dirty diapers (which are apparently a common contaminant), a container of salsa with dry salsa encrusted on the outside, a flattened burger (literally, the bun, patty, and cheese all squished together), plastic film covered in what I think was some sort of orange food residue, mouldy mushrooms in a brown container, and a plastic bag filled with dirty cat food containers. Needless to say, this was disgusting. None of it should have been there. Some of this is also problematic for the health and safety of workers, who were all wearing protective gear as a preventive measure. But this was not an abnormal day—I even asked, just to be sure. What I saw was a typical amount of garbage that people toss into their recycling bins. There could be any number of reasons why this contamination happens; regardless, it's entirely avoidable. All of this garbage will get sent to the landfill. But the fact that it goes through the recycling stream to get to the landfill means that it likely contaminates other materials along the way. If a dirty diaper, for example, comes into contact with clean recyclable material in the truck, on the tipping floor, or on the conveyor belt, it can take down other perfectly recyclable material with it in the process.

This is also why it's recommended that you clean and dry your recyclables. They don't need to be squeaky clean, but they need to be free of food or other residue. That burger patty and diaper were never going to be recycled, clean or not, but the salsa container and the cat food tins could have had a chance. But the reality is that nobody is cleaning crusty salsa or smeared cat food off of containers at a materials recovery facility. It's not a cleaning facility. It would require too much time and money for a facility to bother cleaning dirty recyclable items—it's typically just not worth it. Instead, that's our job, as the ones participating in the recycling program.

I'm going to hammer these points one more time here, because what you do or don't put into a recycling bin *does matter* and *can affect* the functioning and success of recycling's end result. Let's do this pop quiz–style:

Q: What happens if I put something like black plastic into my recycling bin, knowing it can't be recycled in my specific program, but hoping that it might be anyway?

A: It goes to the landfill and doesn't get recycled. This is also known as wishcycling, which means you put something into your bin that can't be recycled but hope that it will be regardless. Although wishcycling is rooted in good intentions, it's ultimately not helpful.

Q: What happens if I put a plastic mayonnaise container that still has large, visible blobs of mayonnaise into my recycling bin?

A: It's not being cleaned, it goes to the landfill, and it doesn't get recycled. It also might get mayonnaise on other items in the process, effectively ruining them as well.

Q: What happens if I put a mixed garbage bag of trash and recyclables into my recycling bin?

A: You guessed it—the whole bag is going to the landfill and doesn't get recycled. There is nobody on the other end who is going to unbag, clean, and separate these items, even if there are recyclable materials in the bag.

For ease of use, the following list sums up various ways to best utilize recycling services, including some points we've already discussed in greater detail throughout this chapter and in previous ones.

- If I have to buy something in packaging and have the choice between some sort of unrecyclable packaging and some other material that *is* recyclable in Saskatoon, I'll pick the second option. If you want to take this a step further, you could also choose packaging options that have higher recycling rates. For example, if you are buying pop, choose aluminum cans over plastic bottles.
- Get familiar with what materials are recyclable near you. Look this information up for your specific program, whether it's run by your municipality or your province/territory. It is also worth checking this information periodically, as it can change. Especially check

plastic—just because something has a plastic number on it does not mean it can be recycled where you live.

- If you are travelling to a new city and are unfamiliar with its waste management guidelines, check its website or app before you throw something into a public recycling bin. Don't assume what's recyclable in Vancouver is also recyclable in Ottawa, and vice versa.
- Do not put food, hygiene products, unrecyclable materials, or other garbage into your household recycling bin. Do not take these contaminants to a drop-off centre either.
- Do not put compostable or biodegradable plastics into your recycling bin. These items cannot be recycled and are considered contaminants.
- If something is smaller than a credit card, it is generally too small to be properly sorted by recycling machinery and therefore cannot be recycled.
- Paper that is soiled with food—like a grease-soaked pizza box—cannot be recycled. There is just no way to clean this, and it contaminates other paper around it. However, food-soiled paper materials can usually be composted. Check with your individual organics program to confirm. You can also put food-soiled paper in a home compost, provided it's not soiled with food that shouldn't go in a home compost, like meat.
- Clean and dry your recyclables. If you are already doing a load of dishes by hand, add your recyclables and then let them air-dry. To save water, you could use a spoon or spatula to first scrape out any hard-to-get food, prior to washing. Adding a bit of water to a container, closing it with the lid, and then shaking it vigorously can also help remove residue without excessive rinsing.
- If you have the option to drop off recyclable glass at a depot, rather than putting it into your household bin, do that. This increases the chance of the glass being recycled or reused and decreases the chance of it breaking.
- It is sometimes possible to separate mixed materials yourself, which might make them partially recyclable. For example, a paper bread bag or a paper pasta box with a little plastic window is considered a mixed material. Remove the plastic and then you can recycle the paper portion; the plastic window is garbage.

If there are no recycling programs near you, focus on reducing and reusing as much as possible. However, I realize this is possible only to a certain extent, as not everything can be bought without packaging or in reusable packaging. There is also a limit to the number of glass jars you can stockpile and reasonably use before you have a glass jar problem on your hands. Where you live in Canada will determine what you can buy and also what you can recycle, so all you can do is your best within the options available to you. If advocating for a recycling program or a more comprehensive recycling program is an option, you could also do that—like advocating for an organics program, as discussed in the previous chapter.

Do Your Homework for Hard-to-Recycle Items

What should you do if your coffee maker breaks? Where can you take a frying pan that you can no longer use that isn't in good enough condition to donate? Can you put a broken spatula in your household recycling bin? What about seasonal or holiday items?

These one-offs are typically questions that go beyond most curbside collection programs and deposit return programs. In Saskatchewan, the best source to consult is the Saskatchewan Waste Reduction Council, a non-profit that has an online database for various materials and how to dispose of them province-wide. I can search items by community and by material type, and the combinations are endless. Bottle cap, bread maker, blender, barbecue, and more are on the list—and that's barely even scratching the surface of the B's! In addition to recycling options, the database provides repair or "pass it on" options for some items. This is honestly an amazing resource. Even if I search for some specific item and no recycling options come up, at least I know that for sure.

Whether or not you can recycle barbecues, blenders, and bread makers again depends on where you live. Some other provinces have resources similar to the Saskatchewan Waste Reduction Council's database; I've noted this information in the Resources List. If no such database exists where you live, you can try searching for this information online more generally, or try contacting any household recycling programs in your area to see if they can point you in the right direction. The most common options for where these types of items can go are facilities for specific materials, like small appliance and electronic recycling drop-offs. We will look at appliance recycling in particular in more depth in the "Appliances" chapter (page 273).

One thing that is not a good idea is to put a blender or bread maker in your curbside collection bin, while crossing your fingers that it will be recycled. It is not possible to recycle a small appliance, for example, through a typical household mechanical recycling process. Certain items can also be hazardous and cause further problems, like wrecking equipment or starting fires. When I was at Loraas Recycle I saw those pesky electronics I've already mentioned, but I also saw a vacuum and a tangle of electrical cords being removed from the conveyor belt during the presort phase. A vacuum is not going to make it through the mechanical recycling process alongside food and household packaging materials. It's just not—no matter how many times you cross your fingers.

Not everything is recyclable in the first place, and not everything that *is* recyclable is going to be recyclable near you, but I do think it's worth checking before you throw something in the garbage. Part of buying and owning stuff involves responsibly dealing with it when it dies or is no longer of use. Just for the sake of it, let's go back to the waste hierarchy one last time in this chapter: If you reduce the amount of stuff you buy, you have less stuff to deal with overall in the end. If you reuse the stuff that you do buy for as long as possible, you won't have to deal with that stuff's end of life as quickly—you prolong its life. And if all else fails—that's where recycling comes in.

Takeaways

- Go on a recycling tour to better understand mechanical recycling.
- Put the waste hierarchy into practice by following the 3R's in their true order: reduce, reuse, and then recycle.
- Follow the guidelines for your specific recycling program. Just like with organics programs, take the time to look up which materials are accepted for recycling. Then, put only accepted materials into your bin, and keep contaminants out.
- When you have a one-off item—like a blender or barbecue, for example—check if the item is recyclable near you by utilizing local resources or databases.

CHAPTER 8:

Garbage

GARBAGE AND SUSTAINABILITY don't really belong in the same sentence. Garbage is just not climate friendly, and there's no secret method to make it so. But since we all produce garbage in our kitchens to a certain degree, we still gotta talk trash.

Defining Waste

Okay, I wasn't totally honest with you. There is one thing you can do to make your garbage more sustainable: produce less garbage in the first place. To do that, you need to change what you bring into your kitchen and challenge how you think about waste.

Waste is defined as anything that gets discarded because it's unwanted or unusable. But to a certain extent this is subjective, because *you* have the power to determine if something is unwanted or unusable. As a simple example, let's say you buy a plastic jar of peanut butter. Once the peanut butter is gone, you could save the jar for other uses—like for storing bulk food. You might be able to recycle the jar, depending on where you live and the type of plastic it's made from. Or you could throw it away. That peanut butter jar is either a reusable or recyclable item, or it's waste, but it's largely up to you.

Take a moment here to think about all the items you bring into your kitchen regularly that have to be discarded because they are not recyclable or reusable to begin with. Food packaging is a particularly bad culprit: plastic from blocks of cheese, foam trays from meat packaging, netted bags from citrus fruits, granola bar wrappers, fast-food wrappers, snack baggies—the list goes on. Sometimes these items are accepted for recycling. But if not, these materials and more get tossed into kitchen trash cans across Canada. The materials are then transferred to residential garbage bins or carts, and then whisked away to the landfill by the garbage collection service. Problem solved.

But has it always been like this? I am certain that my great-great-grandparents didn't have kitchen trash cans filled with granola bar wrappers and netted fruit bags. While working on this chapter, I decided to research the history of garbage and ended up falling down a bit of a rabbit hole. But learning about the history of garbage helped me to understand that how we view and deal with waste is not static—it has changed over time, which means it can change in the future.

A Brief History of Garbage

During the Industrial Revolution, the amount of waste produced globally increased dramatically, and it has been trending upward ever since. As a snapshot of this upward trend, between 2002 and 2022, the amount of solid waste generated in Canada increased by 19 percent to equal a total of 36.5 million tonnes in 2022. That's the equivalent of 36.5 billion kilograms, for reference. This amount includes both residential household waste and non-residential waste, like materials from construction or industry.

Increases in waste generation can be attributed to factors like population growth, improvements in living standards, and, unsurprisingly, escalating consumerism. Ordering mass-produced stuff online was not an option in the year 1850. Historically speaking, there was much more focus on reusing, repairing, and repurposing everything, largely out of necessity. When something tore, it was mended; when something broke, it was fixed. Leftovers were not chucked out in favour of ordering pizza, prepackaged snacks in individual wrappers did not exist, and nobody bought yet another water bottle when they owned five already.

Even if previous generations produced less waste than we do today, there have always been issues with what to do with waste. In the past, garbage has found a home in gutters, on the street, in bodies of water, or wherever it was convenient to dump it. The modern landfill as we know it—which is called a sanitary landfill—appeared in the 1910s. In the decades that followed, the sanitary landfill became widely regarded as the best method for garbage disposal, and more and more were built. Today, landfilling is the number one solid-waste disposal method in the world.

The Grim Reality of Landfills

How do landfills work? I must admit I rarely think about my garbage after it gets picked up by the collection service. The landfill seems like a vague place with a massive hole in the ground where garbage is sent to disappear. But sanitary landfills are more like well-managed, engineered holes, designed to minimize the landfill's environmental impact over time. Sanitary landfills have a thick bottom lining—often a dense clay layer with a plastic liner on top of that—to prevent waste from making contact with the surrounding area. When loads of garbage arrive at the landfill, they are pressed down and covered by soil (often by a bulldozer), which helps to control pests, prevent windblown litter, and reduce the smell. Compacting garbage in between layers of soil means that more garbage can fit into the landfill long-term. It also helps the garbage stabilize and decompose—but only to a certain extent. How much the waste actually breaks down depends on what it is, along with the specific conditions of a given landfill. But it should be noted that garbage in landfills does not magically vanish. The purpose of a landfill is not to naturally decompose waste—it's to contain and manage it.

We've already talked about the creation of methane gas from organic materials sitting in landfills, but other gases like carbon dioxide, nitrogen dioxide, and sulphur dioxide can also be generated as waste decomposes. Carbon dioxide is a greenhouse gas, as we know, and sulphur and nitrogen dioxide both cause air pollution. Not all landfills have gas capture systems, and even in landfills that do, some gas is missed and released into the atmosphere.

Then there's leachate, which is sometimes referred to as garbage juice. Leachate is the result of moisture in landfills, caused by both precipitation and the dumped garbage itself, which naturally contains various levels of moisture. As this moisture filters and flows downward through the compacted waste, it picks up a variety of contaminants along the way, which are often toxic. I dare you to search "leachate" on the internet, and you'll see that garbage juice is a fair description for this dark-coloured liquid. It looks gross. If you think about the different types of trash that are put into a landfill—mouldy food, pet poop, used hygiene products, and more—and then imagine liquid running through all of that, it's easy to understand how leachate is a problem.

Sanitary landfills are designed to manage and reduce the impact of leachate. But if a landfill is not well managed, or if there are tears in the original lining, then leachate can leak into the surrounding area. This can lead to contamination of water and soil, which can then create problems for the plants, animals, and humans that live wherever the toxins end up. Overall, the less controlled a landfill is, the more it pollutes the air, water, and land, and the more it affects the health of both living things and the environment.

Most of the garbage collected in Canada winds up in landfills, while a small quantity of it is incinerated—which is just a fancy word for burning garbage in a controlled setting. Incineration has its own problems, like toxic ash that results from burning waste. Landfills and incineration are not cheap waste management practices either. Local governments in Canada collectively spend billions of dollars on waste management every year, and although landfills are enormous, they don't last forever. The average lifespan of a landfill is about thirty-five years, so eventually new ones have to be built.

A couple of the people I spoke with for this book made comments about landfills that have stuck with me and are worth repeating here. One person said landfills are not really a disposal method but more of a storage method. Another person referred to a landfill as a tomb, because the garbage is buried. If I think about garbage being dumped in a landfill versus being dumped in a river, I have a much stronger negative reaction to trash flowing down a body of water. Garbage in bodies of water is obviously not good. But is a garbage tomb any better? In a landfill's best-case scenario, the waste is contained and managed long-term. Still, we are literally cutting the Earth open and filling that space with all sorts of unwanted trash. Whether in a body of water or a landfill, we're giving our garbage over to the Earth to deal with and then washing our hands of it—meanwhile continuing to produce more and more waste.

Linear Versus Circular Systems

This entire system of dealing with waste is linear. It's also sometimes referred to as a "take-make-use-waste" system, because resources are extracted, items are manufactured and used, and then they are disposed of—all moving in one direction toward the landfill. All of this has also been described as a "throwaway economy," which is equally fitting. The continual extraction of materials to make new products, only to throw them away, not only generates waste but also puts a strain on natural resources. Since 1970, the amount of resources extracted globally has tripled and then some. Any time we produce something new, it comes with an environmental price tag, which is often hidden or ignored. Examples of this price tag include water usage, greenhouse gas emissions, the destruction of nature, biodiversity loss, and the end-of-life impacts once items are discarded.

Alternatively, a circular system—also known as a circular economy—approaches waste in a way that sharply contrasts with a linear system. In a circular economy, resources are used for as long as possible, and landfilling is considered a last resort, not a given. This means that items are designed and manufactured with longevity in mind. Then, at the end of an item's life, its design allows it to be easily repaired or turned into something else. If you think about this visually, a circle keeps looping around on itself forever. At no point does the circle stop so that you can drop stuff off at the landfill. Instead, items that might otherwise be tossed are brought back around—like composting food waste, for example.

Landfilling and incineration are end-of-life waste management strategies, but a circular economy is different because there's little to no final waste to manage if implemented properly. Because a circular economy brings constant overproduction to a halt, it requires full-scale, across-the-board reimagining of the way we produce anything and everything. This, of course, makes it difficult. Transitioning to a circular economy on a global or even national scale would require monumental change and investment at every level, including government and industry. But it also requires another thing: changes in collective consumer behaviour. Compared with the other factors, this is the one element you actually have direct control over.

The Zero-Waste Hierarchy

You've probably seen someone on social media or in the news touting a mason jar that contains all their household trash for any given year. The idea of sending very little garbage to the landfill is one characteristic of the circular economy that has been popularized by the zero-waste movement. Remember when I said that researching the history of garbage showed me that our perceptions surrounding waste can and have changed over time? The zero-waste movement is proof of that. If it can become trendy and admirable to create less garbage, then why can't these concepts be implemented more broadly?

Although *zero-waste* might seem self-explanatory, one definition I particularly like comes from Bea Johnson, a zero-waste activist and the author of *Zero Waste Home: The Ultimate Guide to Simplifying Your Life by Reducing Your Waste*. In her book she describes zero-waste as "a philosophy based on a set of practices aimed at avoiding as much waste as possible." I am generally not a fan of all-or-nothing approaches, so I appreciate that the goal here is to reduce waste *as much as possible*. Our household produces much more than a mason jar worth of trash every year, but that doesn't mean I should give up.

In practice, Johnson recommends a zero-waste hierarchy of five R's: refuse, reduce, reuse, recycle, and rot—meaning compost. Her list adds two R's to the typical "reduce, reuse, recycle" hierarchy that we just discussed in the "Recycling" chapter. There is a visual of Johnson's hierarchy on page 163 to illustrate this, reprinted with permission from her book. *Refuse*, like *reduce*, involves avoiding the creation of waste in the first place. *Refuse* means saying no to things you don't want or need. This could mean refusing leftovers you know you won't eat from a family gathering, politely declining a branded mug that's being handed out at a conference, or resisting the urge to buy the latest trendy item. *Reduce* is about changing your actions to prevent waste, like implementing low-waste cooking habits or buying groceries without packaging. *Reuse* applies to how you actually use what you allow in your home—like my mix-and-match glass jars getting a second life as pantry receptacles for bulk foods. *Recycle* and *rot* apply to end-of-life scenarios. Although recycling and composting can help with circularity, they are noted as fourth and fifth in Johnson's hierarchy, below the other R's. Landfilling is not even included in the hierarchy, because in a zero-waste model, throwing things in the garbage should be avoided at all costs.

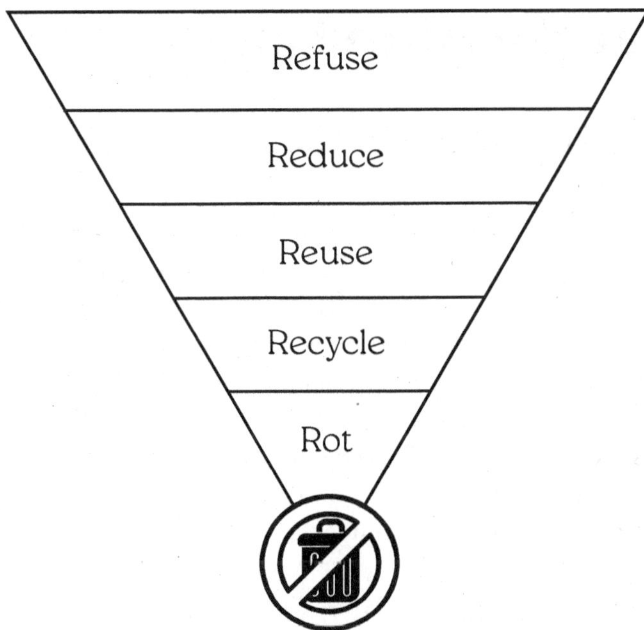

I have done other reading on low-waste and zero-waste living (see the Resources List for book and blog recommendations), and a number of other R's pop up in waste reduction discourses, including repair, repurpose, rethink, refill, recover, resell, regift, rent, refurbish, redo, remanufacture, and redesign. All of these words are really just different ways of providing solutions for waste reduction. Taken together, they also demonstrate that when you remove landfilling as an option, you have to get creative. While it's true that throwing things in the garbage is more convenient and requires less effort than something like repairing or repurposing, you have to decide how much convenience means to you. I can't answer that question for you.

Reducing your waste might be hard at first because it means you are going against the established linear system. When you refuse, reduce, and reuse at home, it's sort of like creating your own miniature circular economy. If we had a full circular economy in Canada, being circular in your own home would be a lot easier. Instead, you are essentially forcing a line into a circle, and I'll be the first to admit that can sometimes be difficult. Either way, being more circular at home requires that you approach waste with both mindfulness and intention—which also happens to be a great place to start.

What You Can Do

Replace *Garbage* with *Landfill* in Your Vocabulary

When I attended the University of Saskatchewan, I saw *landfill* written on a public garbage can for the first time. It made me think twice before chucking anything into the campus landfill bins. Replacing *garbage* with *landfill* in your own vocabulary means you are consistently describing trash as more than just trash—you're describing where it ends up. Thinking this way creates a direct link between my kitchen garbage and the landfill, which makes it harder to reconcile throwing things out absent-mindedly or just because it's easy. You could even make a label that says "landfill" and tack it onto your garbage can as a reminder.

Take Stock: Do a Kitchen Garbage Inventory

If you don't know what you're throwing away, you can't change it. I am not suggesting you go poking through a full bag of kitchen garbage, because let's face it, kitchen garbage bins can be nasty. Instead, write things down on a list as you throw them out. Do this for a week or even a month to get a sense of what a typical trash load looks like for your household.

In Canada, the average amount of solid waste disposed per person from residential sources is about 275 kilograms every year. Multiply that number by however many people are in your household and you'll see that this adds up quickly—and that's just for one year. If you want to be more precise with your own inventory, you could also weigh your garbage before and after making any changes. And although we're focusing on the kitchen here, an inventory can easily be applied to your entire home if you want to track and reduce waste more generally.

Make Less Garbage

The good news is that by this point in the book, you're probably doing this already. Much of what we've discussed in previous chapters has actually been about making less garbage all along.

In general, a simple approach to take is to first reduce, then divert. Prioritize reducing the sheer amount of stuff you bring into your kitchen that will eventually become waste—like using cloth produce bags to replace certain packaging, or buying only the amount of food you actually need, for example. Then, divert waste as much as possible, through reusing, composting, recycling, and any of the other creative R's, like repairing or reselling. Stop and think before you trash something to ensure you're using the landfill only as a last resort.

Consider Your Garbage Bag

You may be wondering: Is there a way to make your garbage bag more sustainable? The short answer to this question is: No, not really.

The plastic garbage bag was actually invented by Canadians in the 1950s and was widely adopted for popular use in the 1960s. Before that, it was common to wrap waste in newspaper or to just put it loose into your bin and then—get this—steam-clean your trash can so it didn't become disgusting. Plastic garbage bags were understandably embraced by the average person because they kept odours and mess contained and eliminated steam-cleaning.

What's interesting and perhaps not widely known is that in some places in Canada, it's not a requirement to bag the garbage you put into your household garbage cart. I contacted ten Canadian cities to ask about this, starting with Saskatoon, where, as in Halifax, Vancouver, and Winnipeg, garbage has to be bagged. Reasons for this include preventing loose waste from spilling out during garbage collection and ensuring the health and safety of collection staff. But in Ottawa, Toronto, Whitehorse, Victoria, Calgary, and Edmonton, you do not have to bag most household garbage, with a few exceptions as determined by individual municipalities. Examples of these exceptions include sawdust, ash, pet poop, and sharp objects, which all typically have to be bagged no matter where you live. But this means that most general kitchen waste that cannot be composted or recycled is fine to go in your household garbage cart unbagged, if you live in a city that doesn't require bagging.

So, the first option is to check whether your waste has to be bagged, as per your municipality or collection service. You can also buy reusable garbage bags that are machine washable. That way, you can still have a lining for your kitchen trash can and then just dump the contents loose into your household garbage cart. If you are composting organic waste, you likely won't have much wet garbage anyway, which makes a reusable bag more appealing. I have noted a couple of reusable options in the Resources List.

If your garbage has to be bagged, there aren't really any "better" bag options. Compostable plastic bags, for example, are meant to break down in an industrial facility under set composting conditions, just like other compostable plastics. Since compostable plastic bags won't magically turn into compost in a landfill, they're not much different from normal plastic bags. The one benefit is that compostable plastic bags are more likely to be made from plant-based ingredients, like corn, instead of conventional fossil fuel–based plastic. But similarly to how other organic matter like food waste behaves in a landfill, compostable bags made from plants will produce methane as they break down over time.

Rather than purchasing plastic garbage bags, you could reuse plastic bags you already have, especially if they are not recyclable. Depending on how big your garbage can is, some examples include bread bags, dog food bags, or produce bags. If these bags can't be recycled near you and are destined for the landfill anyway, you may as well give them one extra reuse before they become waste.

At the end of the day, I think it's more important to generate less garbage than to use any sort of special bag. Even in an ideal scenario in which someone invented an amazing garbage bag that easily broke down in a landfill, an enormous load of trash in a slightly better bag is never going to be preferable to less trash produced overall. When it comes to your kitchen garbage, priority number one is reducing the volume of waste. If you can reduce your waste drastically, you might not even need a bag at all—perhaps a mason jar will do.

Takeaways

- Start using the word *landfill* instead of *garbage* to consistently describe where waste ends up.
- Do an inventory of your kitchen garbage to get a sense of what you're throwing away and how much of it there is.
- Implement the solutions we've discussed in previous chapters to make less garbage overall. Consider strategies to reduce waste first, then divert it.
- Check if you are required to use a garbage bag for local collection. You could also explore a reusable bag option, or repurpose other bags you already have.

My Experience Making Less Garbage—and the Limits of Individual Action

I believe that individual action is important—I really do. But garbage is one topic where I think it's quite plain to see the limits of individual action. Now that we've talked extensively about waste reduction in numerous chapters, I'm going to bring it all together and illustrate this reality by telling you about my own waste-reducing experience.

Prior to writing this book, I had already been composting through Saskatoon's curbside organics collection program, reducing food waste, and cooking low-waste at home. I had been buying produce at the grocery store for years using my own cloth produce bags. I also didn't bother bagging certain foods when I felt it wasn't necessary—bananas, for example. Anyone who knows me will also tell you that I am brutally honest—admittedly, sometimes rather harsh—about refusing stuff I do not want, or regifting and reselling stuff that I've received unsolicited. Even doing all of that, we were generating one eighteen-litre trash can of kitchen garbage every seven to ten days.

Then I began to implement the solutions outlined throughout this chapter and in previous ones. In undertaking our plant-based shift and changing how I source food, I cut down on packaging and began using my own jars, containers, and cloth produce bags for a variety of other foods. I also reduced the amount of disposable kitchen items we used, completely eliminating products like aluminum foil, which I'll discuss more fully in the coming chapter on disposables and reusables. I then began to implement some of the other creative R's more consistently, repairing and repurposing various items as needed. These changes had a measurable impact on our volume of kitchen waste, reducing our trash by at least 50 percent and sometimes more, depending on the week.

However, I eventually got to a point where I felt like I had exhausted my waste-reducing options.

A few different challenges emerged, the first of which is cost. On the one hand, I find that buying bulk dry or wet goods like spices, beans, or peanut butter is typically no more expensive than buying these items prepackaged. In many cases, it can actually be cheaper. But on the other hand, buying produce loose can sometimes be more expensive than buying it prebagged. A few common examples are apples, oranges, and bell peppers. If I need a large number of bell peppers, but buying them loose costs twice what a prebagged version of the same quantity costs, I will skip my cloth produce bags and buy the peppers prebagged. Paying double to use my own cloth produce bags is both ridiculous and penalizing.

Another challenge is that both the meat we received in the Instant Locavore box and the meat I now buy from the Saskatoon Farmers' Market are frozen and prepackaged in plastic, so buying meat with my own packaging isn't an option. And meat isn't the only problem. Tofu comes wrapped in plastic too—I cannot find loose tofu anywhere in Saskatoon. My current freezer space is another limitation. We go through a lot of frozen fruit and vegetables, which I buy in plastic bags because that's the only way to buy them here. I don't have a freezer large enough to purchase, wash, and freeze enough fruit or vegetables in season for later use. Buying a larger freezer doesn't seem like a better option, given that we don't have space for it.

In Saskatoon, I can recycle a wide range of materials through our curbside collection program or at drop-off depots—as in many other places in Canada. But I have been trying to implement the waste hierarchy in its true order by focusing on refusing, reducing, and reusing. The system, however, prioritizes recycling. While it's great that I can recycle a lot here—for example, plastic bags from frozen fruits and vegetables—what would be even better is if I could buy frozen fruits and vegetables in a way that did not require recycling in the first place.

All of this is to say that after implementing a number of waste-reducing strategies, there's still some trash left in my trash can. The trash that's left is extremely lightweight. It's almost entirely made up of certain composite and plastic packaging that is unrecyclable in Saskatoon. This is primarily from food that I cannot buy here without packaging or in different recyclable or compostable packaging.

Reducing waste is hard. It's clear to me that my attempts to force a linear system into a neat circle will work only to a certain extent. As we've seen in other chapters, where you live determines a lot of this. If you live in a city larger than Saskatoon, with access to a zero-waste store or a massive year-round farmers' market, you will probably have an easier time. But if you live somewhere smaller than Saskatoon, your experience is likely to be more difficult. What you are able to compost or recycle will be largely determined by the waste management options in your area, again making all of this more or less challenging.

I have reduced our waste considerably, and there's merit in that—don't get me wrong. Even if I work within the confines of what's available to me, waste reduction still adds up in a significant way. For example, if every week I buy even 10 items without packaging and instead bring my own cloth produce bags or reusable containers for these goods, that's 10 pieces of packaging I have avoided that week. In one month this is 40 pieces of packaging; in one year it's 520 pieces. If I continue doing this for a full thirty years, that is 15,600 pieces of packaging avoided, just from changing how I shop for 10 items each week. If a group of one hundred people do this exact same thing for thirty years, that's just over 1.5 million pieces of packaging avoided. While one person avoiding 10 pieces of packaging per week doesn't sound like much, when it's added up collectively and cumulatively, it's easy to see that it does equal a lot.

Still, I am bringing these various challenges up because I don't want to sugar-coat anything as I send you on your way to reduce waste in your own kitchen. You probably recall that in earlier chapters, we discussed how the environmental impacts of packaging are less significant than the impacts from the production of food itself. While this is true, I still felt frustrated that I couldn't take my waste reduction further. I tried not to stress about this too much, but I was spending all my time and energy on researching and writing this book. If anyone should have been able to hold up a mason jar's worth of trash for the year, it should have been me.

Unfortunately, this is where the limits of individual action in certain contexts become glaringly clear. I have done what I can to prioritize the waste hierarchy in order, but I need wider, full-scale changes to be made in Canada and beyond to be able to refuse and reduce more myself. In other words, the system needs to catch up and prioritize the waste hierarchy in order too. While I can avoid 520 pieces of packaging over the course of this year alone, with more widespread change, it's possible that I could double or triple that number. And I am going to be vocal and honest about that, to my friends, to family, and also to elected officials, because not doing so only makes broader changes less likely.

So if you come to my house, I won't hide the fact that I have tofu in plastic packaging in the fridge or plastic bags of frozen green beans in the freezer. What I will do is hand you a homemade plant-based treat—I have become rather good at making these—and gladly explain the rest.

CHAPTER 9:

Disposables and Reusables

In this chapter in particular, I talk about avoiding disposable or single-use items, including those made from plastic. If you need to use a single-use disposable item like a plastic straw or water bottle, for example, for health, safety, medical, and/or accessibility reasons, please do so. Ideally, these priorities would always be intertwined with more-sustainable options, not separate from them, but until that is actually possible in our society, health, safety, accessibility, and well-being must come first.

THE DOMINANT LINE of thinking in lifestyle sustainability is that things that are reusable are inherently superior to things that are disposable. This fits with common sense. Since disposable items are often single-use, they have very short lifetimes before they are thrown away. Common kitchen examples include plastic wrap, aluminum foil, paper towel, plastic zip-top bags, paper napkins, and wax paper. Many disposable items are not compostable or recyclable, so they end up in landfills as waste after what can sometimes be mere minutes of use. As a result, sustainability tips in media sources often tout a number of attractive reusable items you can buy to replace disposables in your home, like brightly coloured beeswax wrap or sleek stainless steel straws. Admittedly, in the past, I have written articles detailing these types of simple sustainable swaps myself.

But I wanted to know what research says about whether or not reusable kitchen products are truly the environmentally superior choice. Back in 2018 when I did my sustainability project, I assumed they *were* superior without doing any homework, and I replaced various disposable items in my kitchen with trendy reusable options. So before I even started writing *Building a Sustainable Kitchen*, I had not purchased or used a variety of disposable kitchen items, like plastic wrap, paper napkins, and wax paper, for years. Additionally, I had previously tried out various reusable alternatives, like cloth napkins, stainless steel straws, silicone bags, beeswax wrap, and silicone bowl lids. I still have and use most of these reusable items today. However, even with all that, when I started working on this book, there were still a couple of disposable items I used regularly, because I had found it hard to let go of them over the years—particularly aluminum foil and parchment paper. If I was going to replace these items now, I wanted to ensure I was doing right by the environment.

Are Reusable Items Always More Sustainable?

During my research for this chapter, I came across a number of studies that compared common disposable items with their reusable counterparts using life-cycle assessments. A life-cycle assessment is a research tool that measures the environmental impact something will have over the course of its entire life, from when it's made to its end-of-life options.

First up were reusable bags versus single-use plastic ones. A study from the United Nations Environment Programme combined the results of several different life-cycle assessments that compared single-use plastic bags with bags made from materials like cotton or sturdier plastic. One of the key conclusions was that the number of times a bag is used has a clear impact on its overall environmental toll. For example, a paper bag needs to be used four to eight times to have less of an environmental impact than one single-use plastic bag, while a reusable cotton bag needs to be used at least 50 and up to 150 times to have less of an impact. The range for cotton accounts for different types; conventional cotton is on the lower end, while organic cotton requires up to 150 uses. A thicker and more durable plastic bag that was made to be reusable needs to be used 10–20 times to have the same impact as one single-use plastic bag.

Why is this? Most reusable bags are made from heavier and more durable materials than the average single-use plastic bag, since they are designed to last longer. Although single-use plastic bags suffer from low recycling rates and often end up being littered or landfilled, they are cheap and easy to make. Durable materials are much more resource intensive to source and manufacture. Think of the physical difference between a paper coffee cup and a stainless steel coffee tumbler, or between a disposable pan made from aluminum foil and a good old reusable aluminum baking pan. The difference in durability and quality between these materials is evident.

In another study from 2018 that compared reusable plastic and glass food storage containers, the results showed that glass containers can have up to 64 percent more of an environmental impact than plastic ones. To match the environmental impact of a plastic container, a glass container's lifespan needs to be anywhere from 1.3 to 3.5 times longer. On the high end of that, if a plastic food container is used 50 times, that would mean a glass container needs to be used 175 times to have an equal environmental impact.

Another study, from 2021, considered various single-use and reusable items, including straws made from different materials. The straws were compared in a few categories, like energy use and water consumption. The goal was to see how many times you would have to use a reusable version for it to pay back its environmental impacts and become equal to the impacts of a single-use one. The results followed a pattern comparable to the one seen in the other studies noted. For example, in order to match the energy use of a single-use plastic straw, a metal straw would need to be used 37 times, a silicone straw 16 times, and a glass one 20 times. Similarly, to equal the water consumption of a single-use plastic straw, you'd have to use a metal straw 93 times, a silicone straw 34 times, and a glass straw 12 times.

While the material and the manufacturing process contribute to an item's overall environmental impact, another factor noted in the latter two studies was dishwashing, which requires water and energy. Various washing techniques have different impacts (we will talk more about dishwashing in "Water" starting on page 245). However, even if more-durable reusable items need to be washed regularly, they are likely to pay back their impacts eventually if you continue to use them repeatedly for extended periods of time. If you used the same metal straw nearly every day for one year, for example, it would surpass 93 uses and more than pay back its water consumption impacts within that year-long time frame.

If we consider all of these studies together, here's what they mean: If I took a reusable water bottle, used it once, and threw it in the landfill, and then took a single-use plastic water bottle, used it once, and also threw it in the landfill, at that point the reusable water bottle is no better than the single-use plastic one simply because it's a reusable item. If both water bottles have an equally brief lifetime and are treated the same at their end of life, the reusable bottle will actually have a larger environmental impact because of the materials and process required to make it. And so the environmental impact of reusable items depends on just that—*actually reusing them*. We're inclined to interpret a single-use plastic water bottle as much worse for the environment than a reusable one, even in a silly example like this one here. But reusable items in and of themselves are not an automatically superior environmental choice, just because they could be reused in theory. If we *use* reusable items repeatedly for as long as possible, though, then they *can become* the superior environmental choice.

I want to be clear: This does not mean the better choice is to keep buying and throwing out disposable items. Rather, it means that what makes a reusable item sustainable is not the item itself, but *our behaviour*.

Let's be real about this behaviour bit: How many water bottles do you own? Paul and I each have a water bottle that we use daily, and then we also have a couple of other, older water bottles stashed in the cupboard, which we use every now and then. What about this: Have you ever purchased a new water bottle that you didn't need, for the sake of keeping up with the latest and greatest water bottle trend? What about kitchen cupboards filled with enough food storage containers to supply a small army? What about hall closets stuffed with reusable tote bags?

This last question is especially relevant in the context of Canada's single-use plastics ban, which included plastic grocery checkout bags as one of the six prohibited single-use plastic items. Since the ban was implemented in 2022, grocery bags are now commonly made from paper or some sort of reusable fabric. But if I happen to take home a paper bag from the grocery store, I typically do not use it again. I might use it one additional time before composting or recycling it, but I am certainly not using it the four to eight times required for it to have an environmental impact on par with one single-use plastic bag. News articles from Canadian media sources have also reported that since the ban, reusable bags from grocery stores are piling up in customers' homes with nowhere to go and nothing to do. There is a limit to the number of reusable bags one person can reasonably use at any given time, and many reusable bags that are discarded end up in landfills because they typically can't be recycled or composted.

Here's the thing, though—we're meant to own a few reusable bags that we *bring to the store*. And then we're supposed to repeat that, over and over again, with those same bags. Getting a new reusable bag every time we go to the store is just replacing one single-use material like plastic with another, more durable single-use material that is more intensive to produce. This completely misses the point of reducing and reusing. Furthermore, if you end up with more reusable items than you actually need—bags or otherwise—it becomes difficult to truly pay back the environmental impact of those items through reuse. So while there are millions of good intentions behind reusables, if we treat well-made, durable items as single-use or disposable, or if we stockpile reusable items without ever actually using them to their fullest potential, it has no positive impact on the environment.

The Zero-Waste Hierarchy: Zooming In on *Refuse* and *Reduce*

All of this serves to reinforce the importance of the waste hierarchy: refuse, reduce, reuse, recycle, and rot (or compost). Reusing is better than recycling and composting, but *it's still not first on the list.*

Refuse and *reduce* mean saying no to yet another reusable grocery bag or water bottle. They also mean that the best purchase is not a green purchase or a sustainable purchase—it's little to no purchase at all. So the most sustainable water bottle you can use is the one you already have at home. The most sustainable grocery bag is the one hanging in your hall closet. The most sustainable coffee tumbler is the one that's sitting in your kitchen cupboard.

If this seems boring, that's because it is. Reusing a water bottle or bag you already own isn't sexy, fun, or exciting, because it was never meant to be any of those things. Don't get me wrong—I do not find reducing and reusing to be restrictive or joyless in the slightest. It's about understanding that *less is actually more*, and then finding solutions that work within that framework. This is that same undercurrent of practicality we talked about in the "Recycling" chapter coming up again, but this time with a touch of minimalism too.

I'll be honest with you here. When I bought my trendy reusable kitchen items back in 2018, it *was* fun and exciting. I remember feeling like I was really onto something. I went into a gorgeous sustainability store where they sell beautiful, well-made, and natural-looking goods. I was overwhelmed with the temptation to feel like I could change the world, so I bought several items. Although these items were far from cheap, I waltzed home feeling like I had just made a significant difference to the future of the planet. If you have ever shopped for home goods at a sustainable or eco-friendly store, you'll know exactly what I'm talking about. I have nothing against these types of stores—they are a gold mine if you do need to buy some sort of unconventional or hard-to-find sustainable item. Plus, eight years later I still have and use some of the reusable items I bought, so they've likely paid back their environmental impact by now.

The problem lies in buying stuff you don't need or won't use, regardless of what type of store that stuff comes from. It's all too easy to justify buying stuff in the name of sustainability, but buying more items for the sake of reducing waste is counterintuitive. In 2018, I wanted to do *something* that made a difference, but it was easier for me to buy stuff branded as sustainable than to tackle other actions, like eating more plant-based, for example. Eating a plant-based diet is far more impactful than buying a new reusable tote bag. But at that point in my life, I hadn't done enough homework to even realize this. In addition to wanting to make a real environmental impact, I'm telling you this so that you can avoid making these same purchasing assumptions, because popular reusable items often come with a decent price tag. While this might even out over time from all the disposable items you're not buying and therefore saving money on, it doesn't eliminate the upfront cost. My goal is for you to replace disposables in your kitchen in a way that's affordable. So the game plan here is to refuse and reduce as much as possible and to buy reusable items only when and if absolutely necessary.

What You Can Do

Refuse: Use Up What You Already Have—and Then See What Happens

Finish using up any disposable kitchen items you already own. At this point, it's worth wandering over to your kitchen to make a list of the various disposable items you have, so that you know what you're working with. Depending on what you have and how much of it there is, using up your disposables may take a while, and that's okay. This isn't a quick weekend project—it's a journey.

Once you have finished using up a disposable item, don't replace it. If you have a habit of using plastic wrap, you're going to be tempted to reach for it if you have a roll in your kitchen cupboard. But if you don't have any, you can't fall back on it. This may seem daunting, but it's worth doing. If you cannot imagine functioning in your kitchen without plastic wrap, wax paper, or some other disposable item, let's try a quick thought experiment to prove that you *can* address that reliance.

Pick a disposable item you feel strongly about—something you use in the kitchen regularly, if not daily. Let's say it's aluminum foil. One day, your roll of aluminum foil runs out and you head to the grocery store to buy more. But when you get there, there's no aluminum foil on the shelves. In fact, you notice there aren't even any disposable aluminum pans on the shelves either. "Weird," you think to yourself. You ask the store clerk if they have any in the back, but the clerk informs you that aluminum foil has been discontinued globally. You'll never be able to buy it again. You check the news on your phone, and sure enough, several articles pop up confirming that aluminum foil no longer exists. One headline reads: "The Era of Aluminum Foil in the Kitchen is Officially Over." People are even selling scraps of aluminum foil on eBay to the highest bidder, and those scraps are going for exorbitant prices.

What would you do in this scenario? The specifics don't really matter; what does matter is that you would absolutely figure it out. You're a smart and capable human who does not need aluminum foil to get by. You'd move on, and in ten years, you'd look back and wonder why you were so reliant on aluminum foil in the first place, because nowadays you're doing just fine without it. End of story.

I picked aluminum foil as my example because it's one of the items I was still using when I started working on this chapter. So, I went through this process with it. I finished up my last roll, and then I did not replace it. Guess what happened? As predicted, I figured it out. I had been using aluminum foil mainly to cover baking dishes or pans in the oven, and instead I started using cookware I already owned with corresponding lids. This included a ceramic Dutch oven, a small enamel roaster and lid, and a glass casserole dish with a lid, the last of which I had completely forgotten about—it was stashed in the back of a cupboard. I had also been using aluminum foil to wrap potatoes when baking them in the oven, but once I didn't have any foil, I took to the internet. This is where it gets crazy: I read online that you can bake whole potatoes in the oven uncovered, no aluminum foil necessary. At first, I thought this was fake news. If this was true, then why on earth had I been relying on aluminum foil to bake potatoes for so long? At that point I didn't have another option, since I never replaced my roll of foil, so I decided to try it. Lo and behold—it worked! Baking the potatoes without foil took a similar amount of time as baking them with foil, so no problems there. And the end result? The potatoes were crispy on the outside, soft on the inside. Perfection.

This experience was a game-changer for me. What else could I simply use up and not replace? Could I use kitchenware I already had, in place of other disposable or reusable products, with no impact on the end result? It turned out the answer was yes. Cut something in half—a lemon, a watermelon—and put it upside down on a plate in the fridge for short-term storage. Cover other dishes like bowls with an upside-down plate, or with any cookware lid that happens to fit. Grease and flour a baking pan to avoid using any parchment paper at all. The list goes on. Although this realization may have been game-changing for me, none of these suggestions is revolutionary in the slightest. I am sure my great-great-grandmothers are rolling their eyes at me from beyond even as I type this. ("Cover food with an upside down plate? Duh, honey.") The key point is that many of the disposable *and* trendy reusable items I had assumed were necessary in my kitchen weren't all that necessary after all—and this realization was a catalyst for change.

Implement the Zero-Waste Hierarchy in Your Kitchen

In this section, I am going to walk through common kitchen disposables and offer alternative solutions that correspond to the waste hierarchy. We've already covered Refuse, and to help out with the nitty-gritty, I've added Replace, which I define below. The idea is to follow the categories *in order*. If the Reduce and Replace option is not possible for you, then move on to the Reuse option, and then finally to Recycle and Compost. Some of the solutions provided for various disposables overlap, but this just means that certain solutions can serve as a sort of two-for-one deal in the kitchen. This is especially helpful when we're talking about more-durable, long-lasting items—the more frequently you use something, the sooner it will pay back its environmental impacts, which in turn makes that item more sustainable over time.

The Waste Hierarchy Categories

Reduce and Replace: Suggestions provided in this category will aim to reduce the need for a disposable *or* brand new reusable item altogether. This category also provides options for replacing a disposable item with different common kitchen items you probably already have, like using a baking dish with a lid in place of foil on a pan. This is about being innovative and resourceful with the things you already own; in this category you are not buying anything. What you have in your kitchen may go beyond the ideas I've noted, which is completely fine. Feel free to get creative.

Reuse: This category will refer to reusable options that can be bought in place of disposable ones. You may purchase these items new or second-hand, like at a thrift store or through an online marketplace. Just be sure to thoroughly clean and/or wash anything you thrift. If you purchase something from this category, like a silicone bag, I strongly recommend starting with one or two at most. Then, try the item out at home. If you like that silicone bag, and you can see yourself using it regularly for years on end, then perhaps you buy a few more. What you want to avoid here is buying more reusables than you can possibly use, especially if you don't actually like them after you try them out. Consider this category like an audition phase, and ask yourself if you want to cast that silicone bag for a long-term, leading role. If not, if you bought only one or two bags, at least you can gift or sell them easily—rather than being stuck with a drawer full of fifteen bags and a gnawing sense of buyer's remorse.

Recycle and Compost: If the options noted in the previous two categories don't work for you, then choose a disposable item that is compostable or recyclable. This will vary based on where you live and what your recycling or organics program accepts. As we've discussed, if you can compost or recycle a disposable item at the end of its life, it is better than the item going to the landfill, but keep in mind that composting and recycling don't erase the environmental impacts that come from producing items in the first place. Reducing and reusing are always going to be preferable to composting or recycling, which is why this category is last.

Learning to Think Zero Waste

Use the waste hierarchy categories to assess any disposable items in your kitchen. You can also use the following guiding questions if you are evaluating a disposable or reusable item and trying to determine the best path forward:

- What is this item made from?
- Is the material durable, and how long will it reasonably last?
- Could I see myself using this item for five years? A decade? Longer?
- Do I already own anything else that could be used instead?
- Is this item going to be easy to wash or clean?
- What can I do with this item at the end of its life? Is it compostable or recyclable?
- Would it be possible to repair this if it broke or ripped?
- Does the company sell replacement parts for this product, should that be necessary?
- Is this item multi-functional, or is it too specific?
- Is there anything that already annoys or bothers me about this item that will make it less likely I will reuse it repeatedly over time?

This waste hierarchy evaluation process may relate to certain food products as well, like cooking spray that comes in disposable aerosol cans, for example. Once my last can of spray olive oil ran out, I implemented the practices outlined in this chapter. I did not replace it with another can and instead just used regular olive oil in its place. But after a while, I realized there were certain things I needed the aerosol can for, like crisping falafel in the air fryer, or lightly dusting beets or carrots with oil prior to roasting them in the oven. So I purchased a reusable spray oil bottle made from glass that I can easily refill, and I'm very happy with this switch. No more aerosol cans, but I still get the functionality of the spray oil, in a reusable format. If I take care of this reusable spray bottle well, it should last me a very long time.

In the Resources List, I have indicated where you can look for the various reusable items listed throughout the rest of this chapter. If you do decide to purchase new reusable kitchen items, be sure to follow the information and guidelines provided, especially if the material is unfamiliar to you. Check to confirm it's okay before freezing, heating, microwaving, cooking, or dishwashing with any reusable product. Proper care and maintenance go a long way in maximizing the lifetime of reusable goods. Silicone is a good example. Ensure you purchase silicone products that are food grade and made with 100 percent silicone. These types of products are going to be pricier, since they are higher quality. If you come across silicone products that have a very low price tag, it is probably too good to be true. The product in question may not be made entirely of food-grade silicone or could contain some sort of filler material. Also know that if you are baking and cooking with silicone, it's not recommended to heat it above 425°F (218°C).

If you have implemented several strategies that reduce your kitchen disposables but just cannot shake the habit of one or two specific items, know that this process is still worth doing. If 80 percent of the time you reduce and reuse, and 20 percent of the time you use wax paper and aluminum foil pans, it *does* still make a difference. Remember the discussion about how reducing 10 pieces of packaging per week can turn into 15,600 pieces of packaging avoided over thirty years? Doing something 80 percent of the time is still better than not doing it at all.

Aluminum Foil and Pans

Reduce and Replace: Try avoiding foil altogether for certain foods. For example, bake potatoes uncovered in a pan in the oven, grill corn in its husk, or put cookies directly onto baking sheets. Use cookware you already own that has a lid, like a Dutch oven, rather than covering a pan or dish with foil. If you are taking something out of the oven and want to keep it warm, cover it with a clean plate or a lid. If you use aluminum foil to wrap up food in the fridge, instead put that food directly into food storage containers you already own. Rather than using a disposable aluminum pan, pie plate, or baking dish, use the regular cookware you already have. Even if you're going to a potluck or you are giving someone a casserole, use your regular cookware and then just clean it when you get it back. If you often prepare and freeze meals like lasagnas, for example, you can freeze regular aluminum pans or glass baking dishes, if you happen to own several already and can spare a couple for freezing purposes.

Reuse: If you do not own a Dutch oven, aluminum baking pan, or dishes and pans that have corresponding lids, you could invest in any of these items. Purchase something that is versatile and will work well with the foods you cook most often. Alternatively, you may be able to purchase an oven-safe lid separately for cookware you already own, especially if your cookware is from popular brands. If you want a reusable option for lining baking pans or dishes, you can buy silicone baking mats that are non-stick. You can also purchase oven-safe silicone baking lids that are stretchy and fit different-sized cookware, like a casserole dish. If you often use disposable aluminum products for grilling food on the barbecue, you may want to purchase a reusable grill basket, wok, or skewers.

Recycle and Compost: Aluminum foil and pans can sometimes be recycled, but this depends on specific recycling programs. For disposable aluminum to be recycled, it has to be clean. If you cannot clean the foil or pan because food is stuck to it, then it has to go in the garbage; otherwise it can contaminate the recycling stream. Some programs may ask you to crumple clean foil into a ball before recycling. A disposable option that can be used in place of foil for grilling is cedar wraps or planks. In many cities these items are accepted in organics programs. You may even be able to get more than one use out of a cedar plank. I do think aluminum foil is not easily replaced in some scenarios—like if you are grilling very delicate vegetables over an open flame, or if you are going camping and won't have reusable items on you. In these one-offs, foil is likely the best option.

Dinnerware (plates, cups, utensils, etc.)

Reduce and Replace: Whenever you're at home, use the dishes, cups, and utensils you already have. Disposable versions of dishes, cups, and utensils are often used in relation to gatherings, holidays, and events. If you are hosting a very large event and you don't own enough reusable dinnerware to accommodate everyone, you can ask friends and family to BYOD—bring your own dinnerware—or you could borrow additional dinnerware from someone else for the day.

Reuse: If you need more dinnerware for any reason, look for second-hand options. It's generally easy to find second-hand dinnerware that's both aesthetically pleasing and in good condition. If you frequently host events or gatherings and you don't want to continually use your regular dinnerware on these occasions, you could source a second-hand set of party dinnerware that you reuse whenever you have people over. If you need a utensil set for work or meals on the go, you can purchase travel cutlery sets that are reusable. You can also put together your own travel cutlery set from utensils you already own, or thrift some instead. A good example of this is camping: Paul and I do a lot of camping, so we have a separate set of designated camping dishes and cookware that we have mostly thrifted. This way we don't have to pack our regular dinnerware, but we also avoid disposables while on the road.

Recycle and Compost: Plastic plates and cups are sometimes accepted in recycling programs. This varies greatly depending on the program and on what type of plastic the item is from #1 to #7. If plastic plates and cups can be recycled near you, they need to be clean—just like aluminum foil. Plastic cutlery, however, is typically not accepted for recycling, but you can check with your recycling program to be sure. Plates and cutlery that are made entirely from paper or bamboo are typically accepted in most organics programs. They can also be home composted if they are not soiled with food that cannot go in a home compost, like dairy. Be cautious, however, because paper plates with some sort of coating may not be made entirely of paper. You want to look for wording that says "100 percent paper" or something similar. If a package of paper plates is labelled "compostable" or "biodegradable" but doesn't actually say it's made entirely of paper, it might mean that the plate has a compostable plastic coating, which would make it not compostable in most organics programs or home composts. True paper plates are normally plain brown or white, and they are less resistant to liquids and grease. If you pour cooking oil on a paper plate, for example, it should absorb some of the oil. If it doesn't, it's probably coated.

Drink Receptacles (water bottles, coffee tumblers, cold drink cups, etc.)

Reduce and Replace: Use any water bottle, coffee tumbler, or cold drink cup you already have for as long as possible. If you own multiple drink receptacles but struggle with actually reusing them, store them in strategic locations. A coffee tumbler stashed in your uppermost kitchen cupboard simply does not help you when you are on the go. Instead, keep these items at work, in the car, in a stroller, in your backpack or purse, etc.

Reuse: If you do not own a reusable water bottle, coffee tumbler, or similar drink receptacle and feel that you would benefit from having one, purchase a product that is durable and easy to wash, and that you can see yourself using for several years. You may be able to find something second-hand, or you can also ask your friends and family members if they have any to spare.

Recycle and Compost: Disposable plastic water bottles are often accepted for recycling. If you have a more durable water bottle or coffee tumbler that has reached its end of life and is broken or damaged, try to find a recycling option for it. Refer to the Resources List for where to find information about recycling these types of items. We will talk about recycling disposable hot beverage cups specifically in greater detail in the "Coffee and Tea" chapter.

Paper Baking Products (parchment paper/rounds, paper muffin liners)

Reduce and Replace: To avoid using paper baking products, grease or spray baking pans or muffin tins with cooking oil prior to use. For cake and loaf pans in particular, grease them before use and then dust them with a light layer of flour. When your cake or loaf is done, run a butter knife around the edges and turn it upside down, and it should slide out easily.

Reuse: The silicone baking mats I mentioned earlier also work here in place of parchment. These normally come in rectangular and square shapes, but you may be able to find them in circles or other specific pan shapes too. Be sure to measure your pans to ensure they are compatible with any silicone baking mats you plan to purchase. I have never personally tried silicone baking mats, but if you do a lot of baking at home, they may be useful. If you make muffins or cupcakes regularly, you can also buy reusable silicone muffin cups.

Recycle and Compost: Muffin liners that are made entirely of paper are often accepted in organics programs and can also be home composted. Parchment paper and rounds are sometimes accepted in organics programs, but it depends on the program—check with yours. For the highest chance of compostability, look for brown parchment paper that is unbleached.

Paper Napkins

Reduce and Replace: If you already own any sort of cloth napkin, this is ideal. Or, if you have fancy cloth napkins that you rarely use, why not make these your regular napkins? If you know how to sew—or if you know someone who does—you can make your own cloth napkins. If you have any fabric lying around, repurpose it into napkins rather than buying new material. You can even do this with other material like old T-shirts, curtains, a tablecloth, or any other fabric item you're not actively using. Cotton or linen are typically best for napkins, but either way make sure the fabric is machine washable so you can clean them as needed. It's also worth considering how often you actually use napkins. I eat plenty of meals without using a napkin and use one only if we're having hand-held food like tacos or fries. This applies to scenarios out of the house too. For example, if you pick up takeout and they offer you a wad of paper napkins, don't take them if you know you won't use them.

Reuse: You can buy reusable cloth napkins that are machine washable. I have some that we have been using for years, and let me tell you, this is one trendy reusable item that I absolutely love. Given how long cloth napkins can last, I think they're worth the money. I don't wash our cloth napkins after every use either; if a napkin isn't dirty, we hang it on our oven handle alongside our dishtowels and use it a second or even third time before washing. I also like that cloth napkins are easy to repair. If they rip or get a massive stain that won't come out, I can sew it up or add a patch. If you don't want to buy new cloth napkins or sew them yourself, you might be able to thrift some. Before you invest in any new cloth napkins, though, try using a clean dishcloth or dishtowel as a napkin first, to see if you even like it.

Recycle and Compost: Used paper napkins are not recyclable, since they are food-soiled and therefore contaminated. They are compostable, though, if they are soiled only with food or water. If they are soiled with something else, like cleaning products, then they are garbage.

Paper Towel

Reduce and Replace: Paper towel can easily be replaced with several other items, including rags, dishtowels, and dishcloths. If you use paper towel to dry produce after washing it, a clean dishtowel or even a clean cloth napkin works just as well. If you are wiping up something, depending on what it is, you may want a rag, but if it's a minor spill, a dishcloth or dishtowel should do the trick. If you don't have any rags, you can cut some out of old clothes, towels, bedsheets, tablecloths, or anything else that is made from fabric you're not actively using. If you normally use paper towel for something messy like food grease, you may want to have a couple of rags that are designated for this purpose only.

Reuse: If you don't have reusable cloths or rags, or if you don't have anything to make them out of, try to thrift some. This is another item you could ask friends and family about; they may have spare dishcloths or rags galore. Swedish dishcloths are commonly advertised as a reusable paper towel option, because they are extremely absorbent and dry quickly. You can also buy reusable paper towel rolls, which are made out of cloth fabric that clings together easily so you still get the functionality of a "roll." This is one trendy item I bought in the past, but after using it at home, I found it redundant. The cloth paper towels did the exact same thing my regular dishcloths, rags, and dishtowels already do. I ended up disassembling the roll of cloth paper towels and now just use them separately as additional dishcloths. But if you like having an actual roll on the counter that is easy to grab, this may be a good option.

Recycle and Compost: Used paper towels, like napkins, are not recyclable, but they are compostable if they are soiled with food or water only. Otherwise, put them in the garbage.

Just a note here that applies to both paper towels and napkins: You may be wondering if cloth replacements for paper towels and napkins are really the better choice, given the water required to wash them repeatedly. The answer is yes. While using a washing machine does require water, it also requires water to make paper towels and napkins. For example, estimates suggest it takes anywhere from 9.5 to 19 litres of water to make one roll of paper towel. It also requires a significant amount of paper towel to wipe something up in the kitchen. You can easily blow through a couple of rolls of paper towel in one week alone if you use them daily. Either way, water is required, whether you're using reusable cloth items or paper products. If you go the cloth route, just be mindful of how often you wash things. Wait until you have a full load before doing laundry, and if things don't actually need to be washed, continue to use them until they are dirty. I do one load of all of our dirty dish-related cloths, towels, napkins, and rags every seven to ten days, but if I can stretch this even longer, I will.

Paper towel is something that people sometimes have a hard time letting go of—and I can understand this sentiment. We use rags, dishcloths, and dishtowels for almost everything, but I keep a roll of unbleached paper towel under the kitchen sink for one specific reason. I put one sheet of paper towel alongside certain produce in the fridge if it looks like that produce is going to go bad faster than expected. Greens are a common example—the paper towel soaks up excess moisture, which helps the greens stay fresh longer. Then I compost the paper towel after use. I find that cloth towels just don't work as well for this purpose. This is also a bit of a trade-off—food waste versus using a disposable item. You may feel the same about paper towels for other reasons. Cleaning up puke or dealing with bacon grease are two other uses I've heard people keep paper towels on hand for—both completely fair. Of course, try to reduce as much as possible, but if you have a backup roll of paper towel in your kitchen for specific and limited reasons, there are certainly worse things you could be doing.

Plastic Wrap or Cling Wrap

Reduce and Replace: Rather than covering plates or bowls with plastic wrap, transfer and store food in storage containers you already own. You can also use glass jars with lids to store food. If you have bowls that came with lids, use the lids in place of plastic wrap. If you are letting dough rise, cover the bowl with a lid, a plate, or a clean, damp dishtowel. If you are storing certain foods short-term in the fridge, like an undressed salad, for example, cover it with a lid or a plate. Some produce can also be put face down on a plate—half of a watermelon, tomato, onion, lemon, etc. If you normally pack a lunch in plastic wrap, store your lunch in reusable food storage containers instead.

Reuse: There are a number of reusable alternatives to plastic wrap on the market. One is beeswax wrap, which is typically made from cotton cloth coated with beeswax, tree resin, and oil like jojoba. The coating makes it mildly sticky and malleable. You can use beeswax wrap to cover bowls and plates, wrap produce or sandwiches, and so on. It has a limited lifetime of about one year, or three hundred uses. You can also make your own beeswax wrap at home. I have not personally done this, but a quick internet search will bring up many DIY recipes. If you have a set of glass or stainless steel bowls that did not come with lids, see if you can buy lids that go with them, which may be possible if the bowls are from popular brands. Other options include silicone stretch lids or silicone food savers/huggers. Silicone stretch lids act like plastic wrap or a lid, but they're stretchier than actual lids and come in a variety of sizes. They are often sold in sets; measure your bowls or dishes to ensure you buy silicone stretch lids that actually fit. Silicone food huggers or savers are similar; they come in a variety of sizes and you can put them directly onto the cut side of a zucchini, tomato, avocado, etc.

Recycle and Compost: Plastic wrap is sometimes recyclable, sometimes not. Some cities may have a drop-off recycling depot for it; check with your individual recycling program. If not, it goes in the garbage. It's worth mentioning here that other materials that often replace plastic wrap have end-of-life concerns as well. Silicone is not compostable, and although it's technically recyclable, it's not accepted in many household recycling programs in Canada. Beeswax wrap is also not recyclable, but it may be compostable in a home compost or accepted in some organics programs. You would need to check with your individual organics program or, if home composting, confirm the ingredients used in the specific wrap. Alternatively, you can cut old beeswax wrap into smaller pieces and then use it as fire starter.

Plastic Zip-Top Bags

Reduce and Replace: Many of the suggestions noted for plastic wrap also apply to plastic zip-top bags. The swap that is probably the most similar in functionality is food storage containers or glass jars of all shapes and sizes, to match the various sizes that plastic zip-top bags come in. Plastic zip-top bags are commonly used for freezing food, but you can freeze food in other food storage containers you already have, including glass jars. I initially found the thought of freezing glass a bit concerning—my imagination was feeding me all sorts of terrible scenarios involving soup and frozen broken glass. But I tried it anyway, and so far I have not had any issues. The only thing is that it's important to make sure you leave a few centimetres of empty space in the jar, since food expands when it freezes. This is especially important if you're freezing something with a lot of liquid. Make sure the food is fully cooled as well; I usually let food cool completely in the fridge prior to freezing it in glass. If you don't want to freeze glass but you still want to avoid plastic, you can freeze other materials like silicone and stainless steel.

Reuse: The reusable option that is most comparable to plastic zip-top bags is reusable and resealable silicone food storage bags, which come in a variety of sizes. One of the most common brands for these bags is Stasher, which offers bags that are dishwasher, freezer, oven, and microwave safe. I have four of these bags and I really like them, but they are not cheap. Two Stasher sandwich-sized bags plus two Stasher snack-sized bags cost me $68 with tax. So while I find these four silicone bags incredibly useful, I do not plan to purchase more. You can also buy snack pouches or sandwich bags that are made from fabric and have a zipper or snap top. Or you can make your own cloth snack bags for foods that are not wet, like crackers or pretzels. Make sure to buy or make something that is easily washable so that you can clean it properly. If you already have a large collection of plastic zip-top bags and you wash and reuse them repeatedly, this is also a form of reuse. Try to do this only until the bags you already have reach their end of life. Once that happens, replace them with more-durable, long-lasting options, rather than buying more. I am currently in this situation—we have a stash of stockpiled zip-top bags that we have accumulated over the years. I haven't bought any new zip-top bags in a long time, but I continue to reuse the ones I already have and will do so until they are no longer usable. At that point, I'll replace them with a different option. I'll also talk more about this in the "Plastics" chapter (page 193).

Recycle and Compost: Plastic zip-top bags are sometimes recyclable, but again this depends on the recycling program. Some may be accepted at a drop-off depot. I have also noticed that a compostable plastic version of zip-top bags is now being sold at some grocery stores. These have to be given the same considerations as all other compostable plastic. You'd have to check whether your individual organics program accepts these bags in the first place. Another bag option is plain brown paper bags, which are both home compostable and accepted in organics programs. Paper bags may be useful in certain cases, like for packing dry snack foods.

Straws

Reduce and Replace: If you are content to go without straws, then do that. This applies to your own kitchen, but also to dining-out scenarios. If you don't actually want a straw, then say so at cafés, restaurants, and elsewhere, regardless of whether the straw is made from plastic or paper.

Reuse: You can buy reusable straws made out of glass, stainless steel, bamboo, silicone, and sturdier plastic. These types of straws come in different widths. We have a few stainless steel straws that are thinner and great for cold beverages, and then we also have a few that are much wider, which are ideal for smoothies. If you purchase reusable straws, it's worth buying a straw cleaning brush, too, so that you can properly clean your straws after use.

Recycle and Compost: Plastic straws are typically not accepted for recycling and have to go in the garbage. Paper straws made entirely of paper are accepted in most organics programs or can be home composted.

Wax Paper

Reduce and Replace: As with aluminum foil and parchment paper, see if you can go without wax paper. If you like to put a sheet of wax paper down on the counter or kitchen table to prevent messes—when decorating cupcakes, for example—use a cutting board or clean dishtowel instead. If you use wax paper to wrap or cover food, instead use any of the other options previously mentioned for food storage, like bowl lids or storage containers you already own. If you put wax paper between layers of baked goods when freezing them in a container, instead let the baked goods cool completely first, which will help prevent sticking. If you are freezing something very sticky, though, like iced sugar cookies, you can first freeze the cookies on baking sheets and then layer them in the container after that initial freeze, once the icing is firm.

Reuse: Depending on what you use wax paper for, the best reusable options are silicone baking mats, beeswax wrap, or any of the other food storage methods noted already.

Recycle and Compost: Wax paper is typically not compostable or recyclable and instead goes in the garbage. If you need to choose between using wax paper, aluminum foil, or parchment paper, pick the option that is compostable or recyclable near you, which is most likely going to be parchment or aluminum, respectively.

Takeaways

- Use up any disposable items you already have in your kitchen. Then, don't replace them and see what happens. Get creative—you may find you don't need certain items anyway!
- Apply the three-step waste hierarchy process for kitchen disposables. Prioritize reducing and replacing, followed by reusing and, lastly, recycling and composting. Use the list of guiding questions to help make an assessment.

Share What You Have

What should you do if you already own an overwhelming number of kitchen items? Maybe you have kitchen cupboards overflowing with baking pans, kitchen gadgets, dinnerware, water bottles, coffee tumblers, and more, all of which have simply accumulated over time. Or perhaps you have a collection of reusable glass straws and beeswax wraps that seemed like a good idea when you bought them but that never actually get used. Either way, the default reaction is to purge your cupboards and drop any unwanted items off at the closest donation centre. But before you do that, take a deep breath.

It will take time and effort to sort through and responsibly handle an excessive number of reusable kitchen items, but I do think it's worth it. If you take a box of reusable dinnerware, water bottles, and coffee tumblers to a shelter that actually needs them, for example, those items are much more likely to get a second life than if you drop them off at a general donation centre or thrift store, which might already be at peak capacity.

Kitchen items may be needed at non-profits, shelters, food banks, or similar organizations. You can also look online for groups that take donations but don't operate out of a physical building—like Facebook groups dedicated to helping recently arrived Canadians settle into their new city. Call any local organizations or groups in your area and inquire about whether they need the items you have to offer. Be sure the items you are offering are in good working condition and are not damaged or broken. An especially good time to tackle this is around the holidays, when organizations may be looking for certain goods anyway. Many organizations have changing donation requirements based on storage space or seasonal needs, so it's worth checking periodically. There are also organizations that will take donated goods off your hands and then do the background work for you, typically for a fee. In Saskatoon, for example, a program called Reroute does just that. These types of services often have direct connections with other local organizations, so if you want to give your reusables a second life but don't have time to do the research yourself, check if a similar program exists near you.

Another option is to ask friends and family members if they need any of the extra items you have. If you explain what you are doing and offer these items freely, people may be inclined to take you up on it. Alternatively, you could implement any of the other creative R's we've talked about, like reselling or repurposing. You can also check if there is a Library of Things nearby that may be interested in certain items. A Library of Things works similarly to a regular book library but instead lends out household objects like tools, equipment, small appliances, and more. A quick internet search will tell you if there is one in your area. Or look for online groups where people give away items for free, which is often called "freecycling" or "buy nothing." You won't get any money out of this, but at least the items will go to someone who wants them. People in these types of groups may also be interested in broken items or certain pieces of household goods, like a coffee tumbler that's missing a lid. It's worth offering these types of items to see if there are any takers; just be up front about the condition. If none of these options work, see if your items can be recycled. For more information on recycling options and what to do with stuff you don't need, see the Resources List.

CHAPTER 10:

Plastics

YOU ALREADY KNOW my kitchen isn't plastic-free, since I told you in previous chapters that I still buy certain foods in plastic packaging. Plastics have come up in a number of other chapters as well—we've talked extensively about packaging, disposable items, compostable plastics, and the challenges of recycling. Plastics don't exactly have a shining environmental reputation, and I am certain you're already aware of some of the other problems associated with them, like the impact of plastic pollution on marine ecosystems, for example.

I had so far enjoyed doing the research for this book. Although it had been dense at times, it had also been interesting, engaging, and in some cases inspiring. But I want *Building a Sustainable Kitchen* to be as relatable and honest as possible, so I'm going to be completely frank with you here: Researching plastics completely knocked me off my feet. Never have I felt so genuinely overwhelmed by the sheer amount of information I was wading through, or by the complexity of a global problem as a whole. It's like everybody knows plastics aren't great for the environment, and although we have plenty of proof to back that up, plastics are still being produced, used, and discarded, with no obvious or immediate end in sight.

I don't have any novel solutions to offer here that will solve the world's plastics problem—other people with much more expertise are working on that already. What I can tell you is that if you're looking for personal action in the plastics realm, the one thing you can do is avoid plastic as much as possible in your own kitchen and, beyond that, in other areas of your life as well.

There are several good reasons for doing this. But I think most of those reasons relate back to one simple fact that we often either forget or ignore: The building blocks of conventional plastics are fossil fuels—most often crude oil or natural gas, although coal can be used as well—and chemicals, many of which are petrochemicals, meaning they are derived from oil and gas. Producing plastic is responsible for an estimated 4–8 percent of the world's total oil consumption, and making new plastic also results in greenhouse gas emissions.

I knew plastics were derived from fossil fuels prior to doing this research, but I simply accepted this reality as justified and unavoidable—perhaps because plastics are everywhere. Unless you are actively trying to avoid them, most of us buy food wrapped in plastic, we wear clothes made from plastic, we eat and drink out of plastic receptacles, we buy toys for our kids and pets that are plastic, we sit in plastic chairs, we have plastic decor in our homes—it's never-ending. Plastics have permeated almost every imaginable aspect of our lives. Once my brain reconciled plastic's ubiquity with the information about what plastics are derived from, something clicked. Why, exactly, was I so comfortable with the fact that food and beverages *I was going to consume* had come into contact with materials made from fossil fuels? How had I accepted that some of the clothing I wear and some of the toys that our beloved dog, Rue, puts in her mouth are made of plastic? These questions were the root of why I was so overwhelmed. I felt like I had been a complacent bystander in a world filled with plastic everything, and this made me both irritated and angry—at the global plastic problem more generally, but also at myself.

This chapter is not any sort of complete guide to the global plastics problem—there is simply too much information for me to come close to that in one chapter alone. A number of topics concerning plastics that I won't touch on here are still incredibly important, but less pertinent to the kitchen, so see the Resources List if you would like further information on plastics more broadly. The information I did choose to include in this chapter is that which I have identified as the most relevant tidbits for helping you understand food- and kitchen-related plastics better. My overall goal is that you will be able to use that information to make decisions about how much plastic you want in your life. Lastly, we'll talk about how to move away from relying on plastic in the kitchen. Detaching yourself from plastic is not only good for the environment—as we will see, it's good for you too.

What Even Is Plastic? When Was It Created?

Plastic is a polymer, which means that it's made from large molecules that are created from chains of smaller molecules, all of which are bonded together. Polymers occur naturally—rubber and silk are both examples of natural polymers—but plastic is a synthetic, human-invented polymer. The creation of plastic polymers can be credited to a few different chemists and inventors, some of whom discovered it by accident. These discoveries happened in the latter half of the 1800s and into the 1900s. Early plastics were not widely used for mainstream purposes, however, and have since evolved into the plastics we know and use today.

The year 1950 is widely considered to be the beginning of more widespread, global production of plastics. This isn't really that long ago—not even a hundred years. In the decades that followed, a number of common kitchen- and food-related plastics hit the scene. Saran wrap—now also known as plastic wrap or cling wrap—was first sold for household use in the early 1950s. Resealable plastic bags with an integrated zip-top were invented in the 1960s, and by the early 1970s, they had become a staple in North American households. Plastic grocery bags, same thing: invented in the 1960s, and by the end of the 1980s, they were the grocery store go-to. It makes sense that many people embraced these new plastic products, just as people embraced plastic garbage bags. For example, Saran wrap was initially advertised as a sort of magic food-saving material. In many ways, this was and still is true; it keeps food fresh, and it's clear, lightweight, water resistant, smell-proof, and, of course, cheap.

Because plastics have such a low price tag *and* such a wide range of applications, over time they increasingly replaced other materials. In the food packaging world, for example, plastics took over many of the roles formerly occupied by glass and metal. Eventually, single-use and disposable plastics became the norm. Although the growth and dominance of plastics have created an enormous environmental problem, to plastic's credit, it's also basically unmatched by any other human-made material. One source

I read noted cement and steel as two examples of comparable widely used materials, but these two materials are more limited to certain applications. In contrast, plastic's versatility is truly remarkable, whether we're talking about its many food and kitchen uses or its role in other areas, like health care, clothing, furniture, electronics, construction, and more.

All of this relates back to what I said in the "Recycling" chapter about how packaging can be both beneficial and problematic—the same is true for plastics as a whole. Many of the qualities that make plastic so appealing, convenient, and versatile are also the qualities that make it so damn hard to deal with. It's great that plastic is lightweight, but this makes it easy for litter to get blown around in the wind. Plastic's durability is certainly a strength, but it makes it almost impossible for it to break down naturally. The fact that plastic is cheap makes it an obvious choice for single-use disposable purposes, but then again, this has led to an escalating single-use disposables problem. And it's this very paradox that makes it so hard for us to kick plastic to the curb. We have become heavily reliant on plastic, so even if we know it's environmentally terrible for a number of reasons, it's hard to eliminate it altogether.

What Happens to Plastic Once It Becomes Waste?

Let's go back to that 9 percent stat from the "Recycling" chapter: Out of all the plastic waste generated globally between 1950 and 2015, only 9 percent was recycled. What happened to the other 91 percent?

Some of it was incinerated—12 percent, which is a *full 3 percent more* than the amount that was recycled. The rest of the plastic waste, which is more than three-quarters of it, ended up in either landfills or the environment. More plastics were created during this time frame that are still in use, but they are not included in this calculation, since they are not yet waste. Plastics still in use are likely to be more-durable materials that were meant to have longer lifetimes, like plastic for building and construction purposes, for example. The largest use of plastics is packaging, however, which also has the shortest lifetime. In fact, most plastic packaging becomes waste within the same year that it's made. This is especially true for single-use plastics, which essentially become waste as soon as they're done being used.

Plastic waste is typically destined for one of three things: incineration, recycling, or disposal, either in a landfill or the environment. Incineration seems initially tempting because it physically reduces the sheer volume of plastic. But when plastics are burned, they release a toxic mix of substances into the air. Depending on the incinerator, these substances may be controlled and managed, but if they're not, it is problematic for the health and safety of both humans and the environment. Option two, recycling, is one we've already discussed extensively. Even when plastics are recycled or downcycled, it doesn't mean those plastics stay in circulation forever. Plastic cannot be recycled infinitely, and of the 9 percent of plastics that were recycled between 1950 and 2015, remember that only 10 percent was recycled more than one time. So although recycling plastic may temporarily prolong its life, it really only stalls disposal.

What about plastic in landfills and the environment? The vast majority of fossil fuel–based plastics are not biodegradable, and when they are disposed of in a landfill or the environment, they do not break down in any sort of quick or beneficial way. Instead, plastic slowly weakens and fragments into smaller pieces over time. This happens faster if the plastic is exposed to physical elements like sunlight and wind, which causes more wear and tear. Plastic that ends up on a sunny beach will therefore fragment much faster than plastic that ends up in a well-managed sanitary landfill or in a cool, dark place. To be clear, plastic fragmenting into smaller pieces is nothing like how organics can be broken down and become compost. Although plastic fragments can become tinier and tinier as time goes on, they do not actually disappear. These tiny pieces of plastic are known as microplastics, which you've probably heard of. Microplastics are particles that measure five millimetres or less in diameter—five millimetres is about the size of a pencil eraser. There are also particles called nanoplastics, which are a subcategory of microplastics that are one micrometre or smaller. For reference, one micrometre is one-millionth of a metre, so these plastic particles are incredibly tiny. You can't even see nanoplastics with the human eye, which makes them even more challenging to address.

You've probably heard various timelines thrown around regarding how long it takes certain plastic items to break down. In my research I came across sources saying that some plastic will degrade in hundreds of years, and others saying it can take up to one thousand years. It's important to remember that we don't actually have any real-life examples of what happens to plastic at the four-hundred-year mark—plastic just hasn't been around that long. Even if we could list off exact timelines for various plastic products, I don't know how much it matters for everyday purposes. If I use a disposable plastic cup and then throw it in the garbage, is that action justified if it breaks down in two hundred years versus seven hundred years? While two hundred years sounds much better than seven hundred years, it's still a very long time. Either way, that cup is going to outlive me, and I probably used it for thirty minutes or less. Even if plastic takes only a couple of hundred years to break down, then it's highly likely that the very first rolls of household plastic wrap ever used, back in the 1950s, are still out there today, lingering somewhere on Earth and only partially broken down even now.

But whether plastics are full-sized, partially fragmented, or microscopic, when they end up in the environment, it's a problem. This is where further reading will help if you're interested in specific topics, like plastic pollution in the ocean, for example. The overarching thing to know is that a colossal amount of plastic is already accumulating in natural environments around the world. Some of the most common single-use plastics that end up on beaches and coastal environments are food-related ones, including plastic straws, food wrappers, grocery bags, and beverage bottles and caps. Canada is not excluded from this—about ten thousand tonnes (over twenty-two million pounds) of plastic ends up in the Great Lakes alone every single year, and this plastic comes from both Canada and the United States. The six items listed in Canada's single-use plastics ban—including plastic grocery bags, cutlery, and straws—were specifically chosen for the ban because they are hard to recycle and frequently wind up in natural environments as a result.

Plastic in natural environments affects the living things in those environments—plants, fish, birds, mammals, etc.—and these impacts are heinous. Marine species, for example, may see plastic and think it's food, which over time can cause a buildup of plastic in their stomachs. Or they may become tangled and stuck in plastic. Both scenarios can have severe health implications and even lead to death. There is no end to the horrible effects that plastics have on living things and ecosystems, and plastic has even been discovered in the unlikeliest locations—including the polar ice in Antarctica and the Arctic.

But it's easy to hear this type of information and then just carry on with your life. Plastic in the Arctic feels like a distant problem—what can you personally do about it anyway? Most of us use plastic every day without giving it a second thought.

Although plastic in the Arctic might appear to be a distant problem, I have to question that assumption, because everything is connected. Humans will not be immune to the consequences of the global plastic problem, no matter where that plastic ends up. How could we possibly slip away unscathed from such a complex mess of our own creation? We won't. In fact, we're already being affected.

Microplastics, Chemicals, and Us

On an annual basis, it's estimated that the human intake of microplastics is between 39,000 and 52,000 particles per person. *On an annual basis.* Microplastics can enter the human body in various ways. Particles may enter through your skin, or you can inhale microplastics at an estimated rate of 26–130 particles per day. You can also ingest them, which can happen through the food chain—say, if you eat some fish that already has microplastic particles in it. But fish and seafood are not the only types of food that can contain microplastics. For example, it's been shown that a spoonful of sugar can contain 1 microplastic particle, a spoonful of honey can contain up to 13 particles, and a spoonful of table salt can contain up to 14 particles. Drinking water can contain microplastics, too, including both tap and bottled water. Bottled water is likely to have significantly more microplastics than tap water, because microplastics can enter food and beverages through plastic packaging itself. The extent of this transfer can vary, depending on factors like the type of food, the packaging in question, and the temperature. All of this is particularly concerning when we remember that the building blocks of conventional plastics are fossil fuels—not exactly a healthy and wholesome foundation.

Then there are chemicals. Chemicals added to plastics include flame retardants, stabilizers, colourants, plasticizers, and more, all of which are meant to change and enhance the plastic. Plasticizers make the material soft and pliable, for example. There are over 13,000 chemicals that are related to plastics and their production overall, and over 3,200 of these chemicals have been identified as potentially concerning because of various hazardous properties, including but not limited to endocrine disruption, carcinogenicity, and mutagenicity. In a specific food context, over 1,000 chemicals have been shown to transfer into food from plastic food-contact materials, which includes packaging, along with other items meant for food-related purposes, like kitchen utensils. While many chemicals are intentionally added to plastics, there can be unintentional chemicals in plastics as well. For example, when older plastics are recycled, it can cause chemicals that were banned in the past to enter new plastics, or it can also cause various chemicals to react together and form new substances in the recycling process. The chemicals in plastics can be released at any point, including while they're in use or at the end of their life, when they're floating in the ocean or sitting in a landfill.

I'm not telling you this to scare you. Although I would personally say that all of this *is* a bit scary, I'm telling you so that you *know*. I've often taken for granted that plastics are generally fine, because they're everywhere. But just because plastics are everywhere doesn't mean there aren't any risks associated with them. It's worth noting that the bulk of the information in the previous two paragraphs comes from reports published by the United Nations Environment Programme. This information is available online to anyone. Although these reports are lengthy, they are thorough and illuminating. If you want to read them yourself, see the bibliography (page 310).

Although it's not feasible for you to screen every single thing you eat or touch for microplastics and leaching chemicals, what you can do is avoid obvious sources of plastic as much as possible in your own life. The kitchen is an absolute hot spot, where microplastics and leaching chemicals can occur not only from food packaging but from kitchen tools and equipment too. This can happen through actions that cause friction and abrasion, like chopping or cutting. For example, studies have shown that plastic cutting boards release microplastics into food when used. Overall, the amount of microplastics released depends on factors like how the food is being cut, what type of plastic it is, and how old the cutting board is. Most plastic cutting boards usually become indented over time with all sorts of knife marks from where the plastic has been slowly worn away. You have to wonder, where did that plastic go? Other actions where abrasion can occur include mixing, stirring, or scraping, like using plastic mixing bowls with a whisk, for example.

Heating plastics is also a problem, because high temperatures can affect the integrity of the plastic, which can cause it to fragment and release microplastics and/or chemicals into food. This is why it's often not recommended to cook or microwave food directly in anything plastic. It's also partially why cookware with a non-stick plastic coating tends to get flagged as potentially concerning. Non-stick plastic coating is technically called polytetrafluoroethylene, or PTFE for short, and is most often used for pots, frying pans, or small appliances like rice cookers. Non-stick plastic coatings can release both microplastic particles and chemicals, particularly at very high temperatures and if the coating becomes altered in some way, for example, if it's scratched or cracked.

Whether or not microplastics or chemicals are being released into food from plastic kitchen tools or equipment can depend on a number of factors, including the temperature, how the item is being used, and the age and type of plastic in question. Plastic cookware and kitchen tools that are older and have more obvious signs of wear and tear, like scratches or staining, are likely to be more of an issue than newer items. But I think it's safe to assume that some level of leaching or fragmentation happens whenever you use anything made from plastic in the kitchen. If microplastics and chemicals can enter food simply from that food being wrapped in plastic packaging, then why would mixing, heating, or cutting with plastic be A-okay? One study I looked at from 2024 estimated that if meals are prepared at home using plastic cookware on a daily basis, it may result in approximately 2,400 to 4,960 microplastic particles entering home-cooked food every year—and possibly even more than that, since nanoplastics were not included in the study.

Why Avoid Plastics?

I wasn't initially planning to address information about human interactions with microplastics and chemicals in this chapter. This book is about sustainability and the environmental impacts of our actions in the kitchen, so I had mentally categorized human impacts as related, but separate. That was silly of me, because I quickly realized that all of this is interconnected. Whether we're talking about the microplastics we ingest, a plastic bag that gets stuck on a marine mammal, or plastic food packaging that cannot be recycled, it's all part of the same global problem. We can't solve the problem of microplastics in our food if we don't fix packaging issues, we can't solve packaging issues if we don't fix end-of-life waste management options, and so on. Don't get me wrong here—choosing to avoid plastic in your own kitchen is not going to single-handedly turn the plastic problem around. To tackle the global plastic problem, we need massive, system-wide change on a number of fronts, including how much new plastic is being produced and how existing and future plastic waste is managed. But that doesn't make avoiding plastic in the kitchen or other areas of your life any less important.

First, avoiding plastics helps protect you to a certain extent from long-term, ongoing exposure. You can't eliminate exposure entirely since you have little control over whether you inhale airborne microplastics while doing errands, but at least you can control how much plastic you let into your own home. It may seem as though plastics are the automatic and obvious choice for kitchen and household goods, but they don't have to be. To a certain degree, you get to decide whether you buy and use plastics.

Second, avoiding or even reducing plastic usage cuts down on the amount of plastic waste you are producing, whether that plastic is recyclable or not. The world already has a tremendous amount of plastic sitting in landfills and polluting the environment—we don't need more of it. Given the challenges of recycling plastics, there isn't a best-case scenario for disposal either. Plastics in well-managed sanitary landfills are at least locked away from the environment in a sense, but the best disposal of plastics is no disposal at all—meaning that reduction is once again the gold standard.

The third and final reason avoiding plastics matters is that when you make the effort, it will make you both more aware of and vigilant against plastic's omnipresence and the host of global problems that stem from it. These global problems affect the environment and living things, including you and me. And we absolutely need more people to be talking about and working on this issue. In doing this research, I realized just how desensitized I had become to plastic. But part of plastic's dominance relies on us using it. What would happen if a quarter of Canada's population—which would be about ten million people—said no to plastic in their kitchens and beyond? I suspect plastic dominance in Canada would start to shift in some capacity—how could it not? But if we collectively ignore all of this instead, then we are simply bystanders in what is increasingly being referred to as the Plastic Age. Here's the ultimate question: Is this seriously how we want to be defined in history?

What You Can Do

Take Stock: Do a Plastics Inventory in Your Kitchen

Doing a plastics inventory means going through your entire kitchen to assess the plastics that you already have. How you do this inventory is your call. You can write items down, take photos, pull everything out of the cupboards, lay it on your kitchen table—whatever you want. Items to address include any single-use and disposable products, like plastic wrap or plastic bags, along with plastic cookware, tools, and equipment, like cooking utensils, cutting boards, mixing bowls, non-stick pots and pans, ice cube trays, dishware, food storage containers, and so on. Think about non-obvious sources of plastic, too, like dishtowels and dishcloths, which may be made from polyester, for example (we will talk more about dish supplies in "Cleaning" starting on page 255). If you have plastic kitchen items in other areas of your home, like plastic party plates in a storage room, for example, you can include those items in the inventory too.

I'm going to walk you through my own plastics inventory, but I first want to address the reality of this process. Chucking out plastics is great for the sake of avoiding them, but it's not great from a waste perspective. So keep in mind that the point of this inventory is not to throw out a bunch of plastic stuff. The point is to become aware of what you already own, and to identify certain items that are more concerning than others. For example, a non-stick frying pan with a scratched coating or an ancient plastic food storage container that's discoloured could be considered a red flag. But what you consider concerning is entirely up to you. Which plastics are you comfortable continuing to use in the kitchen, and which ones are you not comfortable with? My response to that question likely won't be the same as yours, because this is an individual experience.

For my own inventory, I decided to sort plastics into one of two piles: "keep" or "to deal with." We'll call that second pile TDW for short. I had never made any sort of active effort to avoid plastics in the past, but once I started my inventory I realized I had naturally gravitated toward other materials. All of our dinnerware, serving dishes, bakeware, mixing bowls, measuring cups, and most of our kitchen tools and utensils were made from ceramic, glass, enamel, stainless steel, or wood. There were some plastic items I automatically identified as "keep" because they were longer-lasting pieces of kitchen equipment, including our Vitamix blender, a vegetable spiralizer, lids for various glass and stainless steel bowls, and one frying pan with a non-stick coating that was in perfect shape. I also kept certain kitchen tools that had plastic only on their handles. I did not make any effort to eliminate our microwave, coffee maker, and toaster—all of which have plastic on certain exterior parts—or our dishcloths and dishtowels, because I wasn't sure what they were made from. We have had most of these cloths and towels for years, and I couldn't tell whether they were partially or fully made from synthetic materials.

Several things ended up in my TDW pile though. The first was a microwaveable egg poacher that was indented on the back with a triangle indicating it was plastic #5. This particular egg poacher was a go-to for me back in university when I sometimes ate eggs as a cheap and easy meal, but I never used it anymore. Plus, the fact that using it meant heating up plastic in the microwave now made me shudder. Then there were three very old plastic cooking utensils, all of which were made out of black plastic and had seen better days—the plastic was faded and scratched. Two of the utensils were flippers and one was a pasta fork. I also put in the TDW pile two plastic cutting boards, both of which were old and excessively scratched, and a whole pile of plastic food storage containers and lids in various shapes and sizes.

The next two items were the worst of all. I'm cringing as I write this, just thinking about them. One was a medium-sized blue pot I had purchased from a department store several years prior that had numerous visible nicks in the non-stick coating. I knew it had these nicks, but until I was actually doing my inventory, I hadn't given it much thought. I used this blue pot at least once a week, if not more. We own other pots made entirely from stainless steel, but I had always reached for my cute blue pot any time I was cooking. Now, however, it was clear to me that the dented non-stick coating wasn't so cute after all. As bad as this pot was, it was nothing compared with the next item, which left me panic-stricken. The offender was a small frying pan that had visible chunks missing from its non-stick coating, which was both scratched and frayed. I could have picked at the coating and peeled off small sections of it if I wanted to—which I didn't. Paul had owned this particular frying pan for years prior to us living together, so it had to have been at least a decade old. We didn't use it on a regular basis anymore, but I knew I had used it at least once in the past year. As I put this frying pan in my TDW pile, I felt sick to my stomach. We had likely eaten the missing chunks of non-stick coating; if not, we had probably washed them down the drain. There was no way to know. But the fact that I saw, used, and ignored this frying pan in its deteriorated state for so long demonstrated just how indifferent I had become to plastics over time.

My instinct at this point was to toss all the TDW items into our household garbage bin in the back alley, and then never, ever think about them again. Instead, I forced myself to pause the inventory. I put everything on the kitchen table and then walked away from it for the day. I spent the entire evening ruminating about non-stick coating as I cooked dinner, did laundry, and attended a yoga class, but I didn't touch the pile or throw anything in the garbage, so I considered this a win.

The following afternoon, I picked up where I left off and went through the rest of the cupboards. I didn't have many disposable plastic kitchen items at the time of the inventory, since I had been working on reducing disposables for a while already. If you implemented the strategies in the previous chapter on disposables and reusables, you may also find this is the case. But I still had some plastic zip-top bags—the ones we had been collecting and reusing for years. I also had some plastic cutlery in the basement storage room, from previous party planning efforts. The last thing I added to the TDW pile was a host of assorted plastic margarine and yogurt containers, which I had also been collecting and using for years, mainly to freeze meals like stews and soups. With that, the first part of the inventory was complete.

The next step was actually dealing with the TDW pile. I felt conflicted about most of the items, because although I didn't want to continue using them, I also didn't want to just throw them away or purchase a bunch of new alternatives. As a result, I decided to keep the plastic food storage containers, the margarine and yogurt containers, and the zip-top bags, mainly because these were items I still used regularly and didn't heat up. I had slowly been collecting and using glass jars for food storage purposes, but this was an ongoing effort, and I didn't yet have enough jars to replace all of these various plastic containers and bags. Since I was acquiring glass jars mainly by either thrifting or repurposing them once they were empty—like from pickles or pasta sauce—this process was going to take a while. I also kept the plastic cutting boards from the TDW pile, with the intention of using them only for foods that would stain a wood board, like red beets. I already owned two other wood cutting boards, which I rarely used for no good reason other than habit. The plastic cutting boards could also be used for other purposes, like larger pot and pan holders, if I was hosting an event. I also left the plastic cutlery in my party bin—if that cutlery was going to end up in the landfill one day, I might as well use it once first. I downgraded one of the black plastic flippers to our camping supplies bin, since we didn't have a flipper in there. If we used it only a handful of times every summer, I was okay with that.

I decided I would fully get rid of the rest of the items, which included the egg poacher, the blue pot, the frying pan, and the remaining two cooking utensils. Most of these items were in questionable condition, or using them involved heating plastic. In some cases—like the frying pan—both were true, which was a double strike.

I first checked if any of these items were recyclable by searching for them on both the City of Saskatoon's Waste Wizard and the Saskatchewan Waste Reduction Council's database. Pots and pans made of metal were listed as accepted at the city's material recovery centre and at scrap metal recyclers, but my items were not made entirely of metal—if they were, I wouldn't be in this situation. The utensils were not recyclable either, and when I tried searching various versions of "plastic egg poacher," unsurprisingly, nothing came up. However, given that the egg poacher was labelled as plastic #5, I decided to email Loraas Recycle in Saskatoon to ask if they accepted any household plastic goods for recycling that were labelled #1 to #7. An email back confirmed that, yes, Loraas could accept the egg poacher since it was plastic #5. So I put it into my household recycling bin. Out of all the plastic items I was eliminating, the egg poacher was the only one with a plastic number on it, and the only one that could be recycled.

Another obvious option would have been to donate these plastic items, but I didn't want to do that. If I was uncomfortable using them, why should I pass them along to someone else? That didn't seem right. Besides, given their condition, a donation centre might send my plastic items to the landfill anyway. Still, I was reluctant to throw these remaining items in the garbage. I wanted to reduce waste, not create more of it. So I let the items sit on the kitchen table for a few days in purgatory, as I debated their fate. After a week, I gave in. I put the frying pan, blue pot, and two plastic utensils in our household garbage cart. There was no other option for their end of life, but there was also no point in keeping them in the cupboard, since I wasn't going to use them anymore.

With that, my plastics inventory was complete. It took me about five hours in total to do, including the time I spent researching where the TDW plastics could potentially go. Set aside a decent chunk of time for your own inventory, so that you're not in a rush and can take a break if needed. After you've gone through your plastics and have narrowed it down to the items you want to eliminate, check to see if anything can be recycled near you. For recycling resources, refer to the options we've already discussed in the "Recycling" chapter (page 135). If it is unclear whether or not an item can be recycled, you could contact the facility directly. If you have gently used items, you could consider donating or reselling them, but this is highly dependent on what they are and their condition. Certain items could alternatively be repurposed for non-food uses. For example, once I stockpile enough glass jars to replace my margarine and yogurt container collection, we will repurpose these plastic containers for organizing things like nails and screws in the garage.

As you embark on this inventory, remember to be kind and gentle with yourself. This process can be especially overwhelming if you have a lot of plastic in your kitchen. Certain types of plastics are also going to be easier to eliminate quickly than others. For example, replacing plastic wrap with any of the options discussed in the previous chapter is much more straightforward, than deciding what to do about a plastic food processor or a drawer filled with plastic food storage containers. It's important to acknowledge that having a lot of plastic in your kitchen or home is honestly not your fault—owning plastic products and items is the default. Once I was done my inventory, I resolved to not purchase any more plastic kitchen tools, equipment, or disposable items going forward. That much, at least, was up to me—and it's up to you, too.

Reduce and Avoid Plastics Moving Forward

For this chapter, I spoke to a number of people who either avoid plastic or live nearly plastic-free, and all of them said that detaching themselves from plastic took months or even years. If you have been buying and using plastics for your entire life up until now, it's fair to say that reducing plastics is not going to be an overnight process. Instead, it's going to be ongoing, because you are repeatedly going to be faced with decisions involving plastic products, packaging, and more.

The first step here is to continually reduce plastic packaging, along with any disposable and single-use plastics you still have. We have already discussed various reduction strategies in previous chapters, including "Grocery Shopping" (page 95), "Recycling" (page 135), and "Disposables and Reusables" (page 171). All of those strategies taken together will help reduce the amount of plastics you bring into your kitchen on a regular basis.

Although I find reducing single-use and disposable plastics fairly simple, food packaging is an ongoing issue. As mentioned previously, even after changing how I grocery shop and implementing various waste-reducing strategies, I still buy certain foods in plastic. I cannot find these foods anywhere without packaging, or without plastic packaging specifically—frozen fruits and vegetables, for example. But this is yet another trade-off. This time it's between plastic avoidance, waste reduction, and plant-based foods. In certain cases, one goal cannot be accomplished without sacrificing the other. You are probably going to encounter similar trade-offs as you navigate a life with less plastic. How you choose to prioritize in those scenarios is up to you. Regardless, I think these challenges just speak to how pervasive plastics really are.

The other ongoing task here involves the plastic kitchen tools and equipment you kept after the inventory. The best-case scenario is to use those items until their end of life, responsibly deal with them if possible when that time comes, and try out other non-plastic solutions in the meantime. Additionally, when you do need to purchase kitchen tools and equipment, say no to buying more plastic whenever possible. You'll have to address this less frequently than avoiding disposables or packaging, but doing so speaks to a wider conversation about the types of items we choose to spend our money on. I'll give you an example from my own kitchen regarding one of the items I decided to keep.

After the inventory, I kept the one frying pan we had with a fully intact non-stick coating. But in addition, I already owned a cast iron pan that I rarely used, mainly because cast iron can be intimidating. Given my newfound plastic avoidance, I now felt motivated to become a cast iron person. So I seasoned my cast iron pan and moved it from its former location in a bottom cupboard to a prime spot front and centre. That way it would be easier to grab. I then gave it the ultimate test: Thanksgiving dinner. I was pleasantly surprised by how well it worked. I sautéed green beans, caramelized candied nuts, and cooked leeks and bacon, one after the other with ease. I actually felt a bit foolish—I should have been using this cast iron pan more often, rather than ignoring it for years. Even with my cast iron pan plan set in motion, I decided to still hold on to the other non-stick frying pan we had, just to have a backup for situations where I need more than one frying pan at a time. But I am going to use that pan only sparingly and until its coating shows any signs of wear and tear. Maybe by the time that happens, I'll have turned into a cast iron wizard in the kitchen—fingers crossed—and if I do need a second pan, I'll find a second-hand cast iron one.

If you do need to replace certain items that you eliminated through your inventory, or if you plan to replace plastic items in the future once they reach their end of life, choose quality products made from non-plastic materials like stainless steel, glass, ceramic, cast iron, wood, or enamel. You could also look for second-hand options first, either at a thrift store or through an online marketplace. Non-plastic materials are much more likely to last longer—there is a massive difference in the lifetime of items made from cast iron versus plastic, for example. Purchasing items that are made from one single material, like stainless steel, will also make it easier to potentially repair or recycle them in the future, if needed.

One other thing I'll mention is that since I do not currently have children, owning non-breakable dinnerware is not on my radar. But if you do have kids and already own a collection of plastic bowls, cups, plates, and more, you can include these items in your inventory and then make a call as to whether or not you want to replace them, depending on their condition. Again, some items may be more problematic than others—for example, a scratched plastic plate that's several years old is probably more concerning than a stainless steel spoon that simply has a plastic handle. It is possible to purchase dinnerware for kids made out of non-plastic material, like wood, stainless steel, and enamel, but these products may be more expensive than their plastic counterparts. At the same time, dinnerware made from non-plastic material is likely to last longer, so you could continue to use these dishes as regular dinnerware once you're done with them in a kid-friendly capacity. Certain materials like enamel are also easier to find second-hand.

You can go further and implement a plastics inventory throughout your entire home if you want. Although my priority has been to reduce plastics for food and kitchen purposes, throughout this process I have also become much more aware of other sources of plastics in our home, especially those that we come into contact with on a daily basis. For example, I replaced my plastic bottle of hand soap in the bathroom with a bar of soap, and I now look at what type of material fabric items are made from before purchasing, whether new or second-hand. But I am less concerned with items that we don't interact with directly or regularly—for example, we have plastic bins in our basement and front closet for storage. Although I'm not going to buy any more plastic items going forward, I'm also not going to throw away these storage bins. Again, this is a trade-off between reducing waste and avoiding plastics—which appears to be an unending showdown.

Although my kitchen isn't plastic-free right now, it does contain less plastic than it did when I started this book. I also feel hopeful that in the future, I will get to a point where it has even less. It's not impossible to live without plastic—people have done it and authored books or blogs about the process, some of which you can find in the Resources List.

As I worked on reducing and avoiding plastics, I went from angry and overwhelmed to slightly less angry and slightly less overwhelmed. What initially felt unmanageable became manageable, as I moved through the information and the plastics in my kitchen. Somewhere along the line I realized that all I could do here was my best. If I continued fixating on how much non-stick coating I had potentially eaten in the last few years, I would only make myself ill. Instead, I decided to focus on what I could do and be up front about the parts that I found difficult. What I said earlier in the "Garbage" chapter about my waste reduction experience also applies to my plastic experience: If we're not vocal and honest about what is challenging in all of this, it will only make broader changes less likely.

So yes, this is hard. And yes, plastic is everywhere. When combined, those two facts equal a truly rotten hand. But guess what I'm going to say here? It's worth reducing and avoiding plastics anyway.

Takeaways

- Set aside some time to do a plastics inventory in your kitchen. Go through all the plastics you have, and then assess what you want to keep or get rid of. If possible, find a solution for each item's end of life, like recycling.
- Stay vigilant! Reduce and avoid plastics as much as possible on an ongoing basis. In practice this might look different for certain goods—like disposable single-use items versus long-lasting kitchen equipment, for example.

CHAPTER 11:

Coffee and Tea

I STARTED DRINKING COFFEE while working at a summer camp in high school. Every morning, all the cool camp counsellors would gather around the coffee station in the cafeteria, joking with each other and yawning excessively as they waited for the coffee to brew. I wanted to be cool, so I joined in. At first, I choked my coffee down with an ungodly amount of white sugar, but over time I came to truly enjoy the taste of coffee on its own. These days, I prefer my coffee with soy milk, and I drink at least two cups daily, sometimes three. I can't remember when I first started drinking tea, but Paul and I often have tea at home in the evenings to unwind—green tea with soy milk for me, peppermint with a spoonful of sugar for him.

Aside from water, coffee is the single food item that I consistently consume every day, and I'm not the only one. The world drinks three billion cups of coffee daily. While that's a lot of coffee, tea is the real winner here—it's the second most consumed beverage in the world, after water. Coffee and tea's place in the beverage hierarchy seems unlikely to change any time soon, which is why I decided to give them their own chapter.

But there is one other reason I singled out coffee and tea. While they are both enormous global commodities, each with its own environmental footprint, they are also both examples of crops that are already being affected by a changing climate. On a personal level, I wanted to know if I could engage with coffee and tea in a more sustainable way. It's all too easy for me to head to the grocery store, grab a random package of coffee or tea off the shelf, and give the matter no further thought. But I now had dedicated time and space to contemplate it, and I wanted to do my due diligence. Could I make even a small difference by buying, preparing, and consuming coffee and tea differently?

The Environmental Impacts of Coffee

We already know that plant-based foods have less of an environmental impact than animal-based ones, but there are some exceptions, and coffee is one of them. If we look at the greenhouse gas emissions generated per kilogram of various foods, coffee ranks higher than poultry, pork, or farmed prawns, but still lower than beef, lamb, or cheese (see the chart on page 45). In studies that have looked at the environmental footprint of coffee's overall life cycle—from when it is produced through consumption and its end of life—two key phases stand out as having the largest environmental impact: on-farm production and consumer preparation. This reinforces what we already know: The production of food is often the main driver of its environmental impact, rather than transport or packaging. That's not to say that shopping local and reducing packaging aren't important for other reasons, but if you live in Canada, the reality is that the coffee in your morning cup has likely travelled a far distance to get to you, and was packaged to some extent for that journey.

More than fifty countries produce coffee, with over twelve million coffee farms around the world. Some of these are large farming operations, but the vast majority are small-scale farms run by people who depend directly on their coffee crops to make a living. After the farm, coffee's supply chain includes processing, roasting, and packaging, prior to consumption. There is a divide, though, between where coffee is grown and who drinks the majority of it. Coffee consumption is broadly linked to disposable income and population growth. The United States is the top coffee consumer, clocking in at about twenty-seven million bags of coffee annually. Canada is also in the top ten, at about four million bags per year. A couple of coffee-producing countries, like Brazil and Indonesia, are in the top ten of consuming countries, but most do not have high consumption rates.

On the production end, some of the factors that can contribute to the environmental impact of coffee include water and energy use, how both waste water and organic waste from the process are managed, and the use of synthetic fertilizers and pesticides. The use of synthetic products is a bit of a catch-22. Climate change is already making it difficult for coffee to thrive, because as weather conditions change, predictable growing cycles are disrupted. This might mean altered rain patterns or excessively hot and dry conditions. While coffee plants can sustain some heat stress temporarily, they cannot sustain ever-increasing temperatures long-term. Weather changes also make conditions more favourable for pests and diseases—for example, coffee leaf rust, which is a fungus that gets worse when the weather becomes hot and humid. All of this directly affects coffee yields, which directly affects farmers. To counter this, farmers who can afford to may apply more fertilizers or pesticides to ensure their crop is successful, but this helps only on a short-term basis and increases the environmental impact.

The situation could become pretty dire. Most coffee grown globally comes from two species, robusta and arabica. Some estimates suggest that, owing to increasing climate change, about half of the global land currently used for growing robusta and arabica will become unsuitable for coffee production by 2050. Just think about that for a moment: *half of the land*. In certain areas, land used for coffee production could potentially become entirely unsuitable. While climate change will make some land unsuitable for coffee production, other land could *become* suitable. This land is likely to be at higher altitudes—up a mountain, for example. If it's profitable for farmers to plant crops higher up, they may do so, but if it's a forested area, moving crops up there could result in deforestation and biodiversity loss.

There are some solutions here, one of which is to breed more climate-resilient varieties of coffee. Organizations like World Coffee Research, a non-profit created by the global coffee industry, are already working to develop new hybrid coffee varieties that will be more tolerant of weather changes and diseases, while still producing high yields. Another solution is modifying growing practices. A good example is growing coffee in the shade, which protects coffee plants from direct sunlight and rising temperatures. Coffee grown in the shade more closely resembles a forest, so it provides habitat for wildlife like birds, increases pollination, and helps with natural pest control. But shade-grown coffee typically has lower yields, which is why full sun is often the preferred growing method. Coffee plants also take a few years to mature, so any changes made aren't going to turn things around overnight.

The Environmental Impacts of Tea

On average, the carbon footprint of coffee can be up to ten times larger than that of tea. This is because of differences in how each crop is processed, and because it requires fewer tea leaves to produce a finished kilogram of tea than it does coffee berries to produce a finished kilogram of coffee. Some of tea's main environmental impact drivers come from the use of synthetic pesticides and fertilizers and energy used during processing. As with coffee, consumer preparation also plays a part.

Around the world, about thirteen million people work in tea production, nine million of whom are small-scale farmers. More than fifty countries produce tea, but unlike with coffee, many tea-producing countries also have high consumption rates. But like coffee, tea faces climate change challenges. Tea needs consistent rainfall and temperature levels, and climate change means that typical weather patterns are becoming increasingly unpredictable. Extended periods without rain alongside higher temperatures put tea bushes under stress. Then, when the rain does come, it's often too much all at once, which can wash away soil and cause landslides. Changing weather can also mean frost and hail in locations that don't usually get that kind of precipitation. Extreme weather puts both yields and the quality of the tea leaves at risk, which then affects the amount of money farmers can get for their crop. Suitable land for tea production is also predicted to decrease by up to 26 percent by 2050, with rates of decrease varying by location.

Growing climate-hardy varieties of tea is one possible solution, but it can take years before a tea plant produces anything, which makes research slow. Other solutions include planting shade trees, which helps shield tea crops from the heat, or protecting the soil by using compost or cover crops. One solution that can help make both coffee and tea farmers more resilient in the face of climate change is diversifying the crops they plant. This therefore diversifies their income, so they are less reliant on tea or coffee alone. However, for any of these solutions to be broadly implemented, farmers need access to funding and resources.

A Sustainable Morning Cuppa

While a reduced global demand for coffee and tea does not seem to be on the horizon, current consumption levels are incompatible with the challenges imposed by a changing climate. At the same time, the answer is not for everyone to just stop drinking coffee and tea. Doing so would have a disastrous impact on those who depend on these crops for their livelihoods—and it wouldn't solve the problems affecting crops anyway. On top of all of this, we have the environmental toll of disposable coffee culture, which I will address shortly.

The solutions in this chapter are not going to single-handedly solve the challenges that tea and coffee face. No amount of buying different types of coffee and tea is going to reduce extreme weather events, for example; global action needs to be taken to address climate change and reduce greenhouse gas emissions. And while coffee and tea are two examples of crops already being affected by a changing climate, they are not the only ones. So, the solutions are meant more to help you become conscious of the ways in which you consume. Drinking a cup of coffee or tea is a seemingly minor part of my daily routine, but I now think about what I've learned here every single time I pour myself a cup. I can't ignore it. Awareness alone doesn't solve problems, but at least it's a starting point—because there's no way to take further action if you don't even know what the problem is.

Before we get into the solutions, I want to pass along some questions that have been on my mind ever since I started working on this chapter. How much is your daily caffeine fix worth to you? Is it worth the initial inconvenience of changing your habits? Is it worth paying more for coffee and tea that come with certain environmental guarantees? Is it worth thousands of disposable cups sitting in a landfill, from a lifetime of beverages on the go? And if sometime in the future you cannot drink coffee or tea the same way you currently drink it, because the impacts of climate change have become too great, what, exactly, will that mean to you?

What You Can Do

Buy Coffee and Tea That Are More Sustainable

When I began researching this section, I thought there was going to be a straightforward answer to what type of coffee and tea I should be buying. Instead, I stumbled into the wildly complex and confusing land that is sustainable consumerism. I'm going to walk you through what I did to navigate the terrain, and then—heads up—I'm going to give you some homework. That way, you too can come to your own understanding of what more-sustainable consumerism means in practice.

Certifications: A Helpful (but Imperfect) Starting Point

Hoping to find a gold star of environmental certifications, I started by researching certifications for coffee and tea. You have likely heard of some of these before: Smithsonian Bird Friendly, Fairtrade International, Rainforest Alliance, Canada Organic, USDA Organic, etc. Certifications felt like an obvious place to start because buying any sort of certified coffee or tea means that you as a consumer know it was produced according to the certification's standards—whatever those standards may be. For farmers or producers to get certified by any given certification body, they have to undergo a voluntary third-party assessment, which they usually have to pay for themselves. The cost of certification can make it less accessible for small farmers—a common criticism of certifications in general—but it does equip you as a consumer with information.

I read about a number of certifications, each with their own priorities. Fairtrade, for example, is well known for setting a minimum product price. Regardless of what's going on in the global market for coffee or tea, certified farmers will get paid the set minimum price for their crop, which provides a level of financial security. Although Fairtrade does have environmental information included in its standards, it seemed to me that more focus is placed on the social and economic aspects. These aspects are important, but they weren't my main criteria here.

Through a process of elimination, I decided that Smithsonian Bird Friendly had the strictest environmental standards. These standards were developed by scientists at the Smithsonian Migratory Bird Center in Washington, DC, and require that all coffee be shade grown. This is good for coffee in the face of climate change, and it's good for birds, too, as it provides habitat and fosters biodiversity. Plus, all Smithsonian Bird Friendly coffee has to be certified organic. In contrast, about 43 percent of Fairtrade tea and 63 percent of Fairtrade coffee are certified organic, but it's not a requirement. It's just a certification crossover, depending on the individual farm or producer's practices.

As I read, I found that people online had differing opinions about certifications. But without certifications, it can be difficult to verify if your coffee or tea was grown in a way that was better or worse for the environment. Therefore, in many ways, certifications are essentially filling a gap in the system. The more rigorous a certification is, the better it is at filling this gap. However, more rigorous certifications are typically more expensive for both the farmer and the consumer, which can make them less accessible. So I don't think it's fair to say that certifications are a be-all and end-all solution, or that they aren't any good at all. They are merely one tool in the tool box, and they happen to be one of the more useful tools at present.

Direct Trade

In addition to certifications, I came across the concept of direct trade, which is not a certification but means that companies are doing the due diligence themselves. Companies practising direct trade should be able to tell you where their coffee or tea comes from, because they have a long-term relationship with the farmers and may have even visited the farms as well. In an ideal scenario, direct trade results in transparency and traceability, along with increased financial stability for the farmer. But there's no standard definition of the term, so the only way to know if companies' direct trade claims are legitimate is to do some sleuthing on their website, call them to ask questions, and then just trust that what they're saying is true. Like farmers in the "Local, Seasonal, Organic" chapter, some coffee and tea producers may be implementing organic practices without a certification. A coffee or tea company might have information on its website about sustainable growing practices or initiatives but not bear any specific logos. This is where research comes in.

Accessing Certified Brands

Once I had settled on Smithsonian Bird Friendly coffee (they certify only coffee and cocoa), I went to their website, where they have a handy tool for finding certified coffee near you. To my dismay, there was no certified coffee near me. The closest option was in Winnipeg, MB, or online ordering.

I generally avoid ordering stuff online as much as possible, so I didn't want to get into the habit of having coffee shipped to my doorstep. Instead, I decided to venture into the real world and look around to see if any Smithsonian Bird Friendly coffee was sold near me after all. Plus, a shopping trip was in order anyway because I needed to look for tea. I decided that the option I liked best for tea was Canada Organic, or an equivalent organic seal.

I identified five locally owned shops specializing in organic or natural foods in Saskatoon that I thought would be my best chance. While none of them had Smithsonian Bird Friendly coffee, I did see some other certifications to add to my growing list, like Frog Friendly Coffee, which I noted to look up later. Given my options locally, I shifted gears to searching for just organic, which is more widely available. At Steep Hill Food Co-operative, a local and organic non-profit food co-op in Saskatoon, I found a brand called Level Ground based out of Victoria, BC. Level Ground's coffee displayed logos for both Canada Organic and Fairtrade, while their loose-leaf tea had neither of these logos but said "direct fair trade" on the label. I purchased a package of both and resolved to do some more digging at home.

When I got home, I searched for Level Ground online. I found that they buy their coffee and tea from small-scale farmers. I also discovered that thanks to recycling and composting practices, they have kept their waste out of the landfill for over two decades. I decided to give them a call as well, just to be sure. The person who answered the phone told me that one of the owners had visited certain farms in the past, and that the loose-leaf tea came from growers that did in fact practise organic farming but just weren't certified. The fact that there was a human on the other end of the phone line who had immediate answers to my questions was reassuring. Although it wasn't Smithsonian Bird Friendly certified, Level Ground checked a lot of boxes for me: I could buy their products at a local shop in Saskatoon, direct trade was involved in the business model, the coffee and tea were organically grown, the company was Canadian, and they had other low-waste initiatives. The one downside was that while the tea came in a recyclable box, the coffee came in a bag I could not recycle in Saskatoon. The coffee and tea were also more expensive, as expected.

The Reality of Cost

We have to talk about the price here. There is no way to buy more-sustainable coffee or tea that is also cheap. Before taxes, I can buy a 900-gram package of big-brand coffee for $15 to $30 from the grocery store, depending on whether it's on sale. That same amount of coffee from Level Ground costs about $45, in the form of three 300-gram bags at $14.99 each. Same with the tea: $6.99 for 70 grams, versus big-brand tea at $10 to $12 for 160 grams.

The higher monetary cost of these products makes them less accessible. It also makes purchasing more-sustainable coffee and tea a privilege. It absolutely sucks that sometimes sustainable purchasing requires a certain level of disposable income. It really shouldn't be like that. This isn't just a problem with coffee and tea either. Higher price tags can also be a factor when buying other sustainable home goods. So if buying more-sustainable coffee and tea is not an option for you, then you might prioritize other solutions in this chapter that are more accessible instead.

How to Find More-Sustainable Coffee and Tea Near You

If purchasing more-sustainable coffee and tea is something you can pursue, then it's your turn to do the research. Here's your homework: Commit to spending a minimum of one hour of your time reading about all the different certifications and sustainable coffee and tea options online. Pour yourself a mug and dive in. If an hour feels unmanageable all at once, do ten-minute chunks of time when you'd otherwise be scrolling on your phone anyway. There are sources noted in the Resources List, and if you simply search "coffee certifications" or "how to buy sustainable tea," you'll find more than enough information to fill an hour of reading. You can also search any coffee and tea brands you already buy and see if information about sustainability pops up. If you can't find information about a brand's sustainability policies, this probably isn't a good sign. If the company were doing something sustainable, it's highly likely it would be advertising it.

Once you feel armed with a base amount of knowledge, visit various stores near you that you think might have what you're looking for. Coffee shops and cafés that also sell tea leaves or coffee beans are a good place to check. Take photos of packaging, write down brand names, and then look at their websites or call to ask questions later. Take notes as you go along. Repeat all of this until you feel confident in your purchases. You can also take into consideration how the coffee or tea is being sold. If you can find more-sustainable coffee or tea that's sold locally in a loose format, and can bring your own jars or cloth produce bags to transport it home, this is ideal.

While I could have provided you with an exhaustive list of all the options out there, I am assigning you this homework for two reasons. First, there are many different coffee and tea brands, all at a variety of price points, and what you are able to purchase will also depend on where you live—making all of this individual-specific. Capturing every single option out there is simply beyond the capacity of this chapter. Second, when you do this research yourself, you are practising what it means to be a more engaged consumer, which is a skill you can apply to anything else you buy. As in the "Local, Seasonal, Organic" chapter, asking questions is a key part of making your kitchen more sustainable. Regardless of whether you can consistently purchase more-sustainable coffee and tea, engaging in this conversation is both useful and important.

Take Stock: Clean Up Your Home Coffee and Tea Routine

The way you prepare your coffee and tea at home can affect both the overall environmental footprint and the amount of waste generated. Before we get into the details, I want to be clear on something: Do not immediately go out and buy a number of more-sustainable coffee and tea accessories and supplies. Use what you already have, and when supplies run out or accessories break, make changes if necessary. But there is no point in chucking out a perfectly usable plastic coffee maker. If you take anything from this solution, let it be this: Move through your at-home routine creating as little waste as possible, and use the accessories and supplies you already own for as long as you can.

Impacts from Preparation Methods

Coffee preparation methods that use less energy during brewing have a lower impact. Overall, coffee makers and machines tend to use more energy than simply boiling water. Therefore, a French press and pour-over are two brewing methods with lower impacts, because they only require heating water. Instant coffee actually has an even lower impact, because not only does it just require boiling water, but it also uses less coffee to make one cup. Tea fits in here as well because standard preparation only involves boiling water.

From there, we have coffee makers and machines, but these are not created equal. Drip filter coffee makers are typically less energy intensive than fully automatic coffee machines or coffee pod and capsule machines. But if you leave any coffee maker or machine with a "keep warm" or "standby" feature on for an extended period of time, it uses more energy.

Raise your hand if you have owned a few shitty coffee makers in your life—I'm certainly raising mine over here. If I buy a cheap coffee maker for less than $50, I won't be surprised if it breaks after a couple of years. It's highly unlikely that I'll be able to fix it, and even if repairs are possible, they'll probably cost either the same or more than a new shitty coffee maker. I could buy a more expensive coffee maker in the hope that it lasts longer, but the more expensive the coffee maker, the more automatic and energy intensive it usually gets. There's also not necessarily any guarantee that it's made to last anyway. (We'll talk more about the logistics of appliance repair and end-of-life options in the "Appliances" chapter starting on page 273.) Coffee and tea accessories that are manual, like a French press, pour-over, tea press, or stovetop kettle, aren't going to just quit working the same way many small appliances tend to. I have had the same French press and stovetop kettle for nearly a decade, but I have owned three different drip coffee makers in that same amount of time. So if you're looking for a new at-home coffee set-up now or in the future, consider a pour-over or French press; they tend to be more reliable.

Other habits can also increase overall impact, like boiling extra water or making too much coffee and then dumping it out. Wasting brewed coffee is a particular problem of drip filter machines, especially in group or office settings. If I ever make too much coffee, I store the leftovers in mason jars in the fridge for future iced coffee. And regardless of how you brew it, if you put cow dairy products in your coffee, it increases the impact. In some cases the impact of the cow dairy can outweigh that of the coffee. For example, if an espresso is compared with a cow dairy latte—which is an espresso with steamed milk—both drinks use a similar amount of coffee, but the added milk in the latte makes the carbon footprint jump to nearly five times more than that of the plain espresso. So if you like dairy in your coffee and tea, consider switching to a plant-based alternative.

Waste from Brewing

Different brewing methods create different amounts and types of waste. On the low end are preparation methods that require no brewing supplies, like the superstar French press. When you're done with your coffee or tea press, you can simply compost the grounds or leaves. On the high end are preparation methods that require supplies that are not reusable, compostable, or recyclable and therefore end up in the landfill.

I'll let tea go first here. The least wasteful option is loose-leaf tea, which you can steep in a reusable press, tea ball, or infuser and then compost the tea leaves when you're done. Next is a paper tea bag, which is compostable in both home composts and organics programs. The most wasteful options are tea bags made out of plastic, like nylon ones. Plastic tea bags are noticeably different from paper ones—they have a silky, almost luxurious feel. Plastic tea bags are not recyclable or compostable in most curbside collection programs. If you use one, the best option is to cut it open, compost the tea leaves, and put the plastic tea bag in the garbage. Plastic-based tea bags are not just bad news from a waste perspective though. Steeping a plastic tea bag in hot water for five minutes has been shown to release about eleven billion microplastic particles *plus* three billion nanoplastic particles into one cup of tea. So you are literally drinking peppermint-flavoured microscopic plastic pieces. Yum? I don't think so. I don't need to tell you again why this is bad.

Coffee grounds and paper coffee filters are also compostable in home composts and through organics programs. If you don't want to use paper filters, sometimes pour-overs and coffee makers come with a reusable coffee filter, or they might be compatible with one you can purchase separately. Reusable coffee filters are most often made from stainless steel or plastic, but you can also buy reusable cloth cotton filters—like from the popular brand CoffeeSock. Cloth filters last about a year, have to be rinsed after use, and then typically need to be boiled every couple of months to remove any buildup.

Then there are coffee pods or capsules, which get a lot of waste-related flak. And rightly so: On a global scale, twenty billion coffee pods get dumped in landfills every year. Pod machines do benefit from the fact that brewed beverages are less likely to get wasted, since they make only a single serving at a time. But they create a lot of other waste, since you need a new pod every time you make a cup.

A study commissioned by the City of Toronto found that about four in ten residents own and use a pod machine for coffee or tea, with each user consuming an average of seven pods per week. While half of respondents said they throw their used pods in the garbage, 38 percent said they put their used pods in their municipal recycling or organics bin. Overall, the study found there was a lot of confusion about where pods are supposed to be discarded. In Toronto, all pods—whether made of plastic or aluminum or labelled compostable—go in the garbage (as of the time of writing). This is not exclusive to Toronto either. I checked waste-sorting options for eight major Canadian cities, and all of them noted "garbage" as the waste disposal method for all types of pods, with the notable exception of Vancouver, where plastic pods are recyclable.

One challenge with recycling pods is that because they are so small and lightweight, mechanical recycling equipment often sorts them incorrectly. As a result, they can contaminate other types of recyclables, like paper. Another issue is that the popular Keurig K-Cup is made with plastic #5, which is not always accepted in recycling programs in Canada. Some companies have their own recycling programs, like Nespresso, which makes its pods out of aluminum. Nespresso's aluminum pods are not recyclable in most curbside programs, but the company has a take-back program. If you own and use a pod machine, you can double-check your city's Waste Wizard or similar search tool to find out where you are supposed to put used pods. And if you don't want the extra waste, you can buy reusable pods, which are often made from stainless steel and work similarly to reusable coffee filters.

Think back to what we learned in the "Disposables and Reusables" chapter, though: Reusable items need to actually be reused over and over again to become an environmentally superior choice. Buying a cloth filter or a reusable pod when you're in the mood for sustainability but then stashing these items in your cupboard to collect dust doesn't help. If you genuinely need to replace your coffee or tea supplies and choose to go the reusable route, buy items you will actually use. Then, reuse them for as long as possible.

A note on real-life sustainability here: Paul is the one who makes our coffee most mornings while I hit snooze on my fifteen consecutive alarms (not my best habit), and he cannot be persuaded to switch to a reusable filter. He'll eat more plant-based, but rinsing coffee filters first thing in the morning? No, thank you. This is simply not a hill I'm prepared to die on. As you embark on making your own kitchen more sustainable, if you live with other people, you will likely have to pick your battles too. So, we use unbleached paper filters, which we compost alongside the grounds. And then I hold him to his word and make lentils for dinner.

Deliberately Reject Disposable Coffee Culture

Why is it so hard to get into the habit of bringing a reusable coffee cup everywhere you go? My guess is that you already own at least one of these, if not one for every person in your household. I just went and looked in my kitchen cupboard and we own six different reusable coffee cups. *Six.* For two people.

At various points in my life I have been more or less hooked on disposable coffee culture, the worst of which was in university. There were numerous options on campus for grabbing a coffee, and I savoured taking a little break in the afternoons from writing history papers to treat myself to a soy latte. It took me five years to complete my bachelor's degree, and I bought a coffee in a disposable cup nearly every day I was on campus. I don't even want to think about how much money that adds up to, but I calculated how many cups that would have been over ten university terms: about eight hundred disposable cups. Thousands of other students on campus did the same.

When millions of people grab beverages in disposable cups, all around the world, day after day, drink after drink, it adds up. Globally, five hundred billion single-use disposable beverage cups are used every year. Such cups are within the top ten items that litter beaches worldwide. The number of single-use disposable beverage cups used globally is also projected to increase, as food and beverage trends perpetually lean toward all things convenience.

Let's take a moment to talk about recycling disposable hot beverage cups in particular. These cups look like they are simply made out of paper, but that's not true. If they were, warm beverages would soak through the cup and onto your hands. To prevent this, the cups have a thin plastic lining known as polycoat. Wax linings were used in the past, but they have largely been replaced by plastic. Some takeout boxes and fountain pop cups are similar. Before the paper in any of these items can be mechanically recycled, it needs to be separated from the polycoat lining. This process typically involves shredding the cups and then submerging them in water in a hydropulper, which agitates the material so that the polycoat lifts away from the paper. But if the facility where your household recycling gets sent for processing doesn't have this infrastructure, it can't recycle polycoated items. Even if a facility has this infrastructure, it may choose not to accept these items anyway. Why? One reason is that polycoat can get stuck easily and jam machinery, which results in additional cleaning. Another reason is that it's not in demand. Recycled paper cup material can be made into paper products like napkins and egg cartons, but there's basically no market for the leftover polycoat. It's considered waste from the recycling process and discarded.

As of the time of writing, Calgary, Toronto, and Vancouver all accept disposable hot beverage cups in their curbside recycling programs. But in Halifax, Saskatoon, Winnipeg, or Edmonton, for example, they go in the garbage. While I'm really harping on cups here, they're not the only problem—waste is also created from lids, straws, stir sticks, cup sleeves, and little packets of cream and sugar, most of which cannot be recycled or composted. The lids in particular often get lost in the shuffle, as some recycling programs in Canada don't accept them because they are too light and small to be sorted correctly, similarly to coffee pods.

What's the answer here? We have to follow the waste hierarchy. Now that I work from home, I find the temptation to buy coffee on the go has greatly lessened; still, when I started working on this book, I decided that I would not use any more disposable coffee cups. I had been here before with my initial sustainability project in 2018, but I gave up during the COVID-19 pandemic. I once again roped Paul into this renewed disposable cup avoidance too. He already takes coffee to work in a reusable mug every morning, but he's since stashed a collapsible silicone cup—arguably the more useful of our six reusables—into his backpack, just in case.

How has our disposable cup avoidance gone? I find it's easier when you know in advance that you're getting a coffee. If we're travelling somewhere, we bring our cups because we like getting coffee on the road. If I meet a friend for a walk and coffee, I pack a reusable cup. But unplanned scenarios can be tricky. One day I was out walking and passed a local coffee shop on Broadway Avenue. I caught the scent of aromatic, earthy coffee grounds—simply delicious. But I didn't have my reusable cup with me. My internal dialogue flip-flopped between "Make an exception" and "Keep going, you know the rule." In the end, I gritted my teeth and kept walking, annoyed with myself for not having a cup on me at all times. This approach was effective, though, because the next time I walked somewhere I made sure to bring a cup.

All of this points to why I chose to title this solution "Deliberately Reject," rather than "Try to Avoid" or "Be Mindful of" disposable coffee culture. Deliberately rejecting means that you have to be both steadfast and intentional. If it seems like grabbing a beverage in a disposable cup is an autopilot action for you, recognize that you do have a choice in the matter. The decision is entirely up to you.

This brings us back to the six reusable cups biding their time in my cupboard. As we learned two chapters ago, actually reusing these cups is key. But how many times do you need to use a reusable cup for it to have an environmental impact similar to or better than that of a single-use one?

Anywhere from 10 to 670 times, depending on factors like end-of-life options and the material the cup is made from. Let's say you have a stainless steel coffee tumbler and you use it five days a week for three years. You would have used that tumbler 780 times, which is well over the high end of 670 uses. If you continue to use that tumbler for more than three years, and take good care of it, in the long run that tumbler will more than outlive its environmental impact. Every single time you reuse it, you save the Earth from the burden of another disposable cup.

Therefore, the best solution is to use the reusable cups you probably already own. If you don't own a reusable cup already, then mindfully choose one that you could see yourself using for the next five years or more. Look for a cup you genuinely like that's high-quality and versatile for different types of beverages. Then stop buying new reusable cups and choose to not use any more disposable ones. Put your reusable cup in your purse, in your backpack, in the car, at work—wherever the problem spots are for you. If you already own multiple reusable cups, you could disperse them to a number of places so that you always have one handy. Then reuse, reuse, and reuse again, until reusing becomes a habit, and then becomes a normal part of your routine. You could even keep a tally for every time you use a reusable cup and effectively say no to a disposable one. It can be both satisfying and motivating to see how this adds up.

While this is all very simple in theory, our disposable coffee culture means the responsibility rests on you to go against the grain. Paul and I can likely get by for the rest of our lives with the six cups we already have, but the choice is ours. However, the weight of this problem is currently placed on us, the consumers. If coffee chains, for example, took disposable cups away, we would have no choice but to bring our own cups or actually sit down and drink our coffee from a ceramic mug the old-fashioned way. This should be a twofold responsibility—we as consumers need to change our behaviour, but we also need system-wide changes from those who are handing out disposable cups left and right. Because we can't have it both ways—we can't continue grabbing coffee and tea in disposable cups but then look despairingly at cups littering a beach and see no connection. The two are intertwined.

Takeaways

- Do some research to locate more-sustainable coffee and tea near you. Certifications can be a helpful starting point, or you can look for other options like direct trade.
- Consider your at-home coffee and tea routine, including brewing supplies and waste from the process. Can you prioritize longevity and reduce waste along the way?
- Use any reusable coffee cups or tumblers you already own, and choose to deliberately reject disposable coffee culture.

CHAPTER 12:

Gardening

I COME FROM A FAMILY of avid gardeners. My parents and grandparents have always kept large vegetable gardens, in addition to having bountiful fruit trees and blossoming flower beds in their front and back yards. Despite that, prior to working on this book I had never had a garden of my own, partly because of our living situation as renters, and also because I already regularly received fresh produce from both my parents' and grandparents' gardens during the growing season. But the timeline for *Building a Sustainable Kitchen* happened to coincide with the year Paul and I bought and moved into our first house, so when spring rolled around and I was faced with a thawing yard of my own for the first time, it felt like the universe was giving me a gentle nudge to plant a garden.

There are many different ways to garden, from backyard and community gardens to those on balconies, boulevards, and windowsills. About 60 percent of Canadian households grow vegetables, fruit, herbs, or flowers for personal use, most of which is done in yards across the country. Gardening can contribute to overall food stability and security and can provide access to fresh, nutritious, and seasonal produce at an affordable price. Planting and tending a garden can also do wonders for mental health and well-being. Additionally, gardening can help us connect with nature, build an appreciation for food and how it's grown, and create a sense of community, particularly if gardens are shared. I also value the fact that gardening demands slowing down. There is simply no fast-tracking nature, and I think that's a good thing, since you can fast-track nearly anything and everything these days.

Even knowing all of these benefits, I decided I would still conduct my research for this chapter like any other. I scoured the internet for information and spoke to a number of gardening, yard, and plant experts. What I found surprised me. Gardening seems obviously sustainable. You're growing your own food, you're outside, and everything is fresh, natural, and, well, green. But I soon discovered that there were certain practices that can make gardening more or less environmentally friendly. In other words, a garden is not automatically sustainable just because it's a garden.

As a result, this chapter does not explain how to start a garden in general. There are plenty of resources on that topic already. What you'll find here is mainly aimed at gardening with the environment in mind. Whether you garden already or not, there's one key thing to remember as we go along here: Sustainable gardening is rooted in the idea that you leave the environment better than you found it.

Building My Sustainable Garden

Later on in this chapter, I'm going to use my experiences in my yard to illustrate some of the principles of sustainable gardening, so I'm going to share the beginnings of my own garden here with you.

Our new yard didn't have a garden bed, and there was no obvious place to put one. The backyard wasn't very large: a third was taken up by a wood deck, and the rest was covered with patchy, uneven grass. There was a narrow flower bed along the left side, but it was home to an ancient elm tree with an elaborate root system, and I wasn't keen to disturb the old soul. Our front yard had only about 150 square feet (14 square metres) of green space—and an equally patchy grass problem—with one flower bed right up against the house's exterior. Nevertheless, I was undeterred. I felt inspired by something I had once heard a gardening expert say: View every inch of your green space as a potential opportunity. So, nothing was off limits.

That spring, some irises were starting to poke through in the front flower bed, and I planned to dig them out because irises are toxic to dogs, including our Rue. But as I thought about digging those irises out, I realized that I could just as easily turn the front flower bed into a front garden box. Why not? It was my yard, after all. So I consulted a professional—in this case, Paul, who is well versed in the household fix-it department. I do not possess any talents in that area, other than a gift for providing unsolicited commentary while other people work.

That weekend, Paul started working on a box that measured 3 metres long by 0.75 metres wide, so it would have a decent amount of space for a few different vegetables. My sister-in-law offered us a couple of smaller free-standing garden boxes she no longer needed, and I found various pots for herbs on Facebook Marketplace. All together, this felt like a manageable amount for a first-time gardener. I didn't want to end up hating gardening or feeling overwhelmed. If all went well, there would be many more growing seasons in the future to experiment and expand.

Paul and I paid a visit to the Loraas organics facility just outside Saskatoon—the same place I went for my composting tour—to purchase topsoil and compost, which they sell by weight. We hauled it all home with a lot of sweat and sore muscles. Next, I needed to figure out what I wanted to plant. I settled on West Coast Seeds, a seed company based in British Columbia. It's Canadian, and as a first-time gardener, I felt reassured by their website, which has a thorough breakdown of each type of seed, its growing conditions, maturation period, and more. West Coast had some organic seeds, too. Buying certified organic seeds is an inexpensive way to eat organic produce, especially given how many plants you can grow from a single package of seeds. I spent hours on their website, comparing seeds and filtering results with categories like "easy to grow" and "good for containers." I decided to track everything in a garden journal, so I took notes as I went along. After much deliberation, I purchased Scarlet Nantes carrots, Dukat dill, peppermint, Cimmaron lettuce, lacinato kale, a tricolour blend of bush beans, two varieties of onions, and a blend of radishes—all foods we already eat.

When my seeds arrived in the mail a couple of weeks later, I realized I may have gone a bit overboard. After I planted the garden in early June, I still had plenty of seeds left over, so I set the extras aside for next year. It didn't take long for a few early shoots to appear. The radishes were ready first—a mix of bright and muted pinks, with generous leafy green tops. Although radishes are a small and humble root vegetable, for a first-time gardener, this felt like a massive win.

What You Can Do

Start a Garden

If you have the space, start your own garden! Make use of any green space available to you, whether that's a backyard, front yard, side of the house, or balcony. I referred to numerous how-to resources in setting up my own garden; I've noted these in the Resources List.

If none of these options are available to you, see if there are any community gardens nearby that you could join. If not, see if you could start one. Community gardens have to be initiated and organized by someone—maybe that someone is you. If you have friends or family who have yard space they are not actively using, you could also ask them if they'd be open to letting you plant a garden there. If you offer to share the fruits of your labour, perhaps they'll agree.

Another option is boulevard gardening, which is allowed in some cities in Canada. A boulevard is the grassy space between the road and the sidewalk, but in some cities, other spaces like traffic circles may also be eligible. Boulevards are typically public spaces owned by the municipality, but some cities allow gardening on them, including Victoria, Saskatoon, Vancouver, Halifax, and Edmonton. However, even though you might be using the space for a garden, the boulevard is still accessible to the public. This can be annoying if other people wander by and snag your prized zucchinis, but at the same time, it's also a good use of otherwise empty space. To check if boulevard gardening is allowed in your city and what the planting regulations are—for example, if gardens have to be registered—you can do an online search or contact your municipal government.

If it's not possible for you to have any sort of garden, supporting other gardeners during their busy time is the next best thing. Take advantage of your local farmers' market or subscribe to a Community Supported Agriculture program near you during the growing season. There's no better way to eat fresh, local produce than to buy it when there's a seasonal surplus.

Take Care of the Soil

It's easy to forget or ignore the fact that soil is alive, filled with bacteria, fungi, and insects. The health of any given plant is linked to the health of the soil itself, which is why spending a bit of time tending to your garden soil is key. Ideal soil will hold water and nutrients well, while allowing for decent airflow so that organisms can move through it with ease. The soil should be crumbly; if you squeeze a handful of it together, it should clump loosely.

The soil in our front and back yards did not initially exhibit any of these ideal soil qualities. It was dry, cracked, and hard as a rock in certain places. It seemed to be lacking in both nutrients and moisture. So, I turned to compost. One of the simplest and best ways to improve soil health is to add finished compost to it. If you grow food or flowers in the same soil repeatedly, over time the soil's nutrients become depleted. When you add compost, you're essentially feeding the soil, helping to create better soil structure, which in turn helps plants grow. In a forest setting, for example, this happens naturally as plants die and decompose, giving nutrients to the earth. In a more controlled setting like a backyard garden, we have to do this manually.

If you're adding compost to your garden and yard, you'll want to do it once or twice a year, typically in the spring and/or fall. Less is more, though, because too many nutrients can be a problem. You'll need only a thin layer—about 1.5–2.5 centimetres, depending on whether you're adding it once or twice annually. If you add it on top of the soil, you can just leave it to integrate slowly on its own, or you can instead lightly incorporate it by hand or with a garden hand cultivator. If you use compost, you probably won't need any other sort of fertilizer. While fertilizers provide an immediate release of nutrients, compost is more of a long-term process, because it releases nutrients slowly and improves soil health over time.

If you are looking for compost locally, check with your municipality. Sometimes municipalities have free or for-purchase compost options, especially if they run a year-round organics program or even a seasonal program for yard waste. You can also check with garden centres or organics facilities, like we did at Loraas. You could also make your own compost, of course, as discussed previously in the "Composting" chapter.

Another way to take care of the soil is by using mulch, which reduces the amount of water that evaporates and keeps the soil's temperature even. If soil is left uncovered, the sun can bake it and dry it out. Compost helps manage this, so if you use compost you don't necessarily need mulch, but mulch can be used alongside compost for additional benefit. Try to avoid dyed mulch, which comes in colours like black or bright red, and instead opt for natural materials like undyed wood chips, leaves, pine cones, grass clippings, or straw. A natural mulch will slowly decompose over time, adding nutrients to the soil, so you'll have to add more after this happens.

Mulch needs to be only a few inches thick and can be applied around plants. Just be careful that the mulch is not directly touching the stems of the plants, as this can sometimes cause disease—so leave a little space between the stem and the mulch. One of the main reasons I was sold on mulch is that it can actually lower yard maintenance. By retaining moisture, you'll need to water less. Natural mulch also offers habitat for insects like ladybugs and spiders, which can lead to fewer pests in your yard.

Say No to Synthetic Pesticides and Fertilizers

I was determined to do things as naturally as possible and keep our garden and yard chemical-free. This resolution was put to the test immediately. In the spring, Paul and I noticed there was an ant problem in the backyard. Ants were building their kingdoms around and underneath a number of stepping stones. I consulted *The Prairie Gardener's Go-To for Pests and Diseases*—which is a fantastic book; see the Resources List—and it noted that ants can indicate dry soil. Ants don't like soil with a lot of moisture, which checked out, given the dry soil problem that plagued our yard. So we took more compost and spread a thin layer around the areas affected by ants. A couple of months later, once the compost had worked its magic, the ant problem was gone. This seemed almost too good to be true—was there anything compost *couldn't* do?

Although synthetic pesticides and fertilizers may work wonders, they can be damaging to the environment and living things. Synthetic pesticides include insecticides, fungicides, herbicides, and others, all of which are meant to be toxic. Even if they're meant to kill one specific pest or plant, they don't discriminate and can harm plants, soil organisms, insects, birds, and even larger animals, depending on the circumstances. These impacts can be either direct or indirect. A direct impact, for example, would be if a given species' eggs are exposed to the product, while an indirect impact might mean that their habitat or food source is altered in some way from pesticide use.

Synthetic fertilizers, on the other hand, contain nutrients like nitrogen and phosphorus. When these nutrients run off from farms, gardens, and yards, they can make their way into the surrounding environment, where they build up and pollute soil or water. Excess nutrients in bodies of water can cause an overgrowth of algae, which can then lead to lower oxygen levels in the water, affecting fish and other organisms over time. This process is known as nutrient pollution or eutrophication. Fertilizer use in agriculture is one of the main causes of eutrophication, but smaller-scale use in gardens and yards can also contribute to the problem. Again, the impacts from synthetic fertilizers may be direct or indirect.

Everything in nature is connected, so even if you can't personally see any impacts from a product you use, it doesn't mean those impacts don't exist. Additionally, low-risk products do not mean there's no risk at all. So if you want to forge a sustainable path for your garden and yard, the best practice is to avoid anything synthetic entirely. Natural methods typically require more time and effort than picking up a chemical spray bottle from a garden centre. This is similar to using compost—it's a long-term strategy that requires time to pan out. But if the point is to leave the environment better than you found it, synthetic products don't really fit with that goal.

One last note here: Organic products are sometimes marketed and sold as a less toxic pesticide option, but it's important to remember that these products are still meant to be toxic. They don't discriminate, even if they are made with different or non-synthetic ingredients. So tread cautiously. If you have a severe problem in your garden or yard that won't go away, an organic pesticide may be necessary as a last resort. But be sure to do some research or talk to a garden expert about a product's ingredients before you apply anything, so you understand the potential impacts.

Harvest Rainwater

Harvesting rainwater reduces the amount of potable water you'd otherwise need for watering your yard and garden. This process involves redirecting your downspouts so that water flows straight into a rain barrel, which is a large container that typically holds about 50 gallons (190 litres) of water. The barrel can't be just any random container; it needs to be a food-grade one. Most rain barrels also come with an attached spigot so that you can access the water easily, along with an overflow hose to direct excess water to a designated area. You can buy rain barrels new or used, or if you're feeling ambitious, you can make them yourself.

As I was plotting my first garden, I happened to come across a local wildlife rehabilitation organization that was selling rain barrels as part of a fundraiser—a double nudge from the universe. These barrels were used, and they were cheaper than new ones, so we decided to order two for a total of $180. Paul did the dirty work: He put one rain barrel each in the front and back, redirected the downspouts on our house and garage so that water flowed into the barrels, and set up an overflow system so that any excess water went toward the ancient elm in the back and toward the green space in the front.

Shortly after he completed this set-up, there was a solid overnight rainfall that continued into the morning. Just like that, both barrels were filled to the brim. As the weeks went on, Paul and I became obsessed with the rain barrels. We checked them daily, discussed their remaining contents, and predicted when it might rain next. If it rained during the workday, I texted Paul to update him on the status of the water in each barrel. The joy and intrigue these barrels brought us was both unexpected and unrivalled; we were thrilled with how practical and functional they were. We actively discussed where we might be able to put additional rain barrels the following year. I even found myself wondering if we could somehow treat the water we collected, so that we could drink it in case of an emergency.

The rain barrels were a great solution for saving water and reducing the utility costs associated with seasonal watering. Household water usage generally increases during the growing season, with the sheer number of people using additional water for their gardens and yards. In Saskatoon, water usage during the growing season doubles compared with the rest of the year. Collecting your own rainwater can help conserve water by reducing this demand, especially during dry periods. That summer, there were a few extended dry periods when we had to rely on potable water, but for the most part, the rainwater carried us through. This was reflected in our utility bill, which changed very little during the summer months.

Although harvesting rainwater has a number of benefits, it does require an upfront cost and some work. If you are interested in setting up rain barrels, check with your municipality to see if they have any regulations or support programs. They may also have a rebate for rain barrels—we received a $40 rebate with proof of purchase. At the end of the growing season, be sure to drain and dry your rain barrels so that they don't freeze and crack once it gets cold. You could store them in a garage or shed, or cover them with a tarp for the winter. Depending on your set-up, you may also have to redirect or extend your downspouts during the fall and winter, to accommodate the fact that you're not collecting precipitation in a container.

If you don't have a yard or space for a barrel, then this isn't a realistic solution, but there are a couple of other things you can do to conserve water. Watering earlier in the day can help, because less water will evaporate and more will be absorbed, especially on hot summer days. Other options include using mulch, which helps the soil retain moisture, or choosing drought-hardy native plants if you are planting anything new, which we will discuss in more detail shortly.

Don't Buy a Bunch of New Garden Stuff

We've already looked at how manufacturing new items requires resources; at how more-durable reusable items need more resources to make than their less-durable counterparts; and at how paying back the environmental impacts associated with producing material goods depends on whether we reuse those goods repeatedly over long periods of time. All of this still applies in the case of yard and gardening tools, gadgets, and supplies, even if you're using those items to grow your own food.

In a study from *Nature Cities* that compared the carbon footprint of low-tech urban agricultural sites—which included community gardens, urban farms, and backyard gardens—with that of conventional agriculture, the authors found that the biggest factor that can cause urban agricultural sites to have a large footprint was gardening infrastructure, and the length of time that infrastructure is used. Raised garden beds can have an environmental impact that's four times larger per serving if the bed is used for only five years, than if it's used for twenty years. Other examples of infrastructure noted were sheds and composting set-ups. The longer you use these things, the lower the overall footprint becomes. To a lesser extent, this logic would apply to other gardening supplies and tools as well—which aligns with what we already know about reusable items. Other factors noted in this study that can affect the overall footprint included whether rainwater is used as a resource and if compost is used in place of synthetic fertilizers.

Knowing the impact of buying new gardening supplies, Paul and I were in a bit of a predicament. As first-time homeowners and gardeners, we did not already own everything we needed. So I first asked family members who are long-time gardeners if they had anything extra they didn't need. From this one inquiry alone, I received a pair of gardening gloves, a weed puller, a three-prong garden cultivator, and tomato caging. Although I didn't plant tomatoes that year, I took the caging anyway because I intended to plant tomatoes in the future. Next, I searched for second-hand options; as mentioned already, I found some pots on Facebook Marketplace. But we could not find a decent-sized second-hand watering can. We needed one that could hold a lot of water, so that watering with the rainwater would be an efficient process. After searching for a while with no luck, we bought a new, large, metal watering can, which was durable and worked well for our needs.

If you're looking for gardening tools and supplies, and you have gardeners in your life, chances are they have extra supplies on hand. You can also see if you can borrow certain items that you don't need at all times—like a pitchfork, for example—from friends and family, or from a local Library of Things. If you are doing more intense landscaping, you may be able to rent specialized tools and equipment from a garden or home centre. If you are building something for your yard, like a shed or garden box, see if you can use scrap wood or source reclaimed materials. If you do need to buy something, first check second-hand sources like thrift stores or online marketplaces. If you can't find what you need second-hand, choose a new item that's durable and that you know you will use long-term. On the other hand, if you happen to have a lot of gardening and yard tools already that you don't actually need, see if friends and family want them, or try reselling them. And if you have garden tools, supplies, and infrastructure that you *are* using, continue to use these things for as long as possible to maximize their lifetime and minimize their environmental impact.

Consider End-of-Season Practices

There are a number of things you can do at the end of the growing season that contribute to overall sustainability. Perhaps the most obvious one is the age-old practice of preserving food by canning, dehydrating, freezing, or cold storing it, which helps make the most of fresh, seasonal produce by extending its lifetime into the colder months. This is beneficial on a number of fronts: You can eat seasonal produce when it's not in season, you become more self-sufficient with your food supply, you save money on produce over the winter, and you reduce food waste. Whether you can do this depends on how much surplus you end up with and having the storage space for it. Our garden did not produce enough to bother preserving any of it, so we just ate it all fresh. Although I do have grand plans to become a master canner in the future, for now, check the Resources List for information on preservation. If you have an excessive garden surplus that you cannot possibly eat or preserve in time, be sure to offer it to others so that it doesn't go to waste. There are online groups dedicated to this type of thing, particularly on Facebook. Try searching phrases like "garden swap" or "harvest swap," along with your location, to see if this option exists.

Another sustainable practice is composting, which we looked at in the "Composting" chapter already. Anything that comes from your garden or yard that you're not eating or leaving as is should be composted through an organics program or your own home compost, rather than being thrown in the garbage. If organic yard materials end up in a landfill, they will produce methane—just as food waste does. You may also be able to use certain leftover yard and garden materials in other ways. Leaves, for example, are a common yard material that gets bagged in plastic and then landfilled come fall, but if you rake your leaves and add them to the top of your garden bed or box, they will act as a natural mulch over the winter. As the leaves decompose, they also add extra nutrients to the soil. Otherwise, compost your leaves.

Although gardening seems simple enough, in practice it involves a bit of trial and error—and I made a few errors. While garden journals are fairly common practice, I think keeping track is important for overall sustainability. If I write down what worked, what didn't, and everything in between, I can make my garden and yard as efficient and productive as possible long-term. I'd also like to point out that gardening takes time. Although I planted and harvested our garden, Paul took care of all the in-between bits like the watering and weeding. Prior to starting the garden, we had agreed that the garden would be my thing, but I was enthusiastic to a fault in my pursuit of a green thumb and failed to appreciate that gardening is an active, ongoing task. Luckily, Paul was there to pick up the slack. As a first-time gardener, this learning curve is natural, but a note for my garden journal is to plant only that which I can realistically tend in the future. These types of details are easy to change, but I know I might not remember them unless I write them down. Thanks to the journal, my next garden will be that much better.

Bonus: Rewild Your Green Space Using Native Plants

As I was doing my gardening research, I stumbled upon the practice of rewilding. If you've ever seen a house with an unruly-looking front yard featuring all sorts of shrubs, grasses, and flowers surrounded by rocks or wood mulch, this is exactly what I'm talking about. Although these types of yards are a far cry from the typical manicured lawn, they are often intentionally planned to incorporate native plants and help biodiversity thrive.

Native plant refers to any plant that grows naturally in a given region and has been there for a long time. Native plants include grasses, flowers, shrubs, and trees that adapt to a given region's growing conditions, like the soil, temperature, and precipitation levels. Once established, they typically require less water than their non-native counterparts, which makes them hardier to dry periods and drought. Native plants are also more resistant to pests and diseases. Because they have evolved in specific places over time, their existence supports insects, birds, and small animals that are also native to the region, by providing food and shelter that those organisms are familiar with. The cherry on top is that native plants are low maintenance. This makes perfect sense, because if I put plants that are native to Saskatchewan in my yard, those plants already know how to thrive in Saskatchewan—they don't need my interference.

A classic lush, green lawn is, by comparison, high maintenance and requires a lot of water and regular mowing. Kentucky bluegrass is an extremely common lawn option used widely across Canada—it's what we typically think of as regular green grass—but it's not actually native to Canada. Kentucky bluegrass is pollinated by the wind—not by the birds and the bees—so it provides little, if any, value to native pollinators. But it is aesthetically pleasing and doesn't crumple under foot traffic, which helps explain why it's everywhere. The worst offenders, however, are artificial lawns. Not only are artificial lawns lacking in any benefit for biodiversity, but they're normally made of plastic, which can fragment and cause microplastics to enter the soil over time.

Why does any of this matter to the kitchen? Let's go back to the "What We Eat" chapter, when we talked about biodiversity loss and the fact that approximately one million species are facing extinction. There are many reasons for biodiversity loss; our food system and climate change are two of them. As a more specific example, I'll talk about pollinators, since they relate to food, gardens, and yards.

Bees are the most common pollinators, but moths, wasps, flies, butterflies, and some birds, beetles, and bats are pollinators too. Pollinators transfer pollen from one plant to another, effectively fertilizing the plants so that they grow and produce. Over 75 percent of food crops rely on this process, including many fruits and vegetables. Some estimates suggest that one out of every three bites of food we take is owing to pollinators, which goes to show how important they are. But, like many species, pollinators are declining in population and diversity levels. Some of the reasons for this include the use of pesticides, an inadequate food supply, and the loss of natural habitats, which can happen if habitats are turned into farmland or urban areas, or if severe weather events result in drastic changes to a given ecosystem.

Rewilding your green space with native plants may seem trivial, but it's not. You have the power to turn your green space into a habitat that *does* support local biodiversity like pollinators—even if all you have to offer is a small yard. Rewilding is all about planting for the birds, bees, and everything in between. In doing so, you provide food, shelter, and even a rest stop as insects, birds, and animals make their way to other, larger habitats, like parks, grasslands, or forests. It's kind of like setting up a complimentary bed and breakfast for all the local critters.

As I researched rewilding and the benefits of native plants, I realized that I couldn't just walk away knowing this information without addressing our yard's dismal patchy grass—which was Kentucky bluegrass, *of course*. There was no way around it—the bees needed my yard!

Rewilding isn't the type of thing you just throw together haphazardly; it requires some thought and planning. Luckily, planning and overthinking are two of my specialties, so I set aside some time and dived into the research. I utilized a number of resources, including the Canadian Wildlife Federation's Native Plant Encyclopedia, the Plant Selector tool from Birds Canada, and the Find Your Roots tool from Pollinator Partnership Canada, all of which are databases that are searchable by location and plant type. I filtered my searches to show results for local perennials, shrubs, and grasses, which were the types of plants I wanted. Once I had a solid list of plants—some native to Saskatchewan and some to the Prairies more generally—I began to narrow it down. When looking for native plants, it's a good idea to search for those that are native to your province, territory, or region first to maximize the biodiversity benefits; plants that are native to Canada generally might not be overly helpful because of how large Canada is.

I checked all my possible plant options against two additional criteria: whether they were non-toxic to dogs, and whether I could buy them somewhere nearby. In the end, my final selections included a few different larger plants and shrubs, like shrubby cinquefoil and a Thiessen saskatoon berry bush, and a number of flowers, like aster, fireweed, blanket flower, common sunflower, and bergamot.

Before adding our new plants, we had to deal with the Kentucky bluegrass. In addition to the shrubs and flowers, we decided to pursue an alternative lawn option. Common alternative lawn choices include clover, yarrow, and creeping thyme, which are all beneficial to pollinators. It's a good idea to check what types of alternative lawns do best near you, because if you can find a native plant that doubles as an alternative lawn, then that's ideal. I chose to go with a type of clover that's both dog friendly and a pollinator favourite. We decided to leave most of the grass in the back and seeded the clover in between the spots of patchy grass, to achieve more of a clover-Kentucky mix. But in the small front yard, we removed the patchy grass to provide adequate space for both the new native plants and clover to thrive.

You can rent equipment like sod cutters to remove grass, but why bother doing that when you can just remove it by hand yourself? This is what I told myself before we started. On a sunny afternoon in May, Paul and I painstakingly removed all of the front grass by hand, using an axe and a shovel. I quickly came to regret that decision—the level of enjoyment for this task was straight-up zero. If you are rewilding a larger area, it would absolutely be worth it to rent the damn equipment. Your muscles will thank you later.

Once the front had been cleared and the clover and shrubs planted, we added some habitat elements—rocks, stepping stones, and wood mulch. We left an old decaying tree stump in the front too. We had initially planned to remove the stump when we bought the house, but it now fit with our rewilding agenda. I had to wait until fall to plant most of the flowers, because they required stratification; some northern native plant seeds require an extended cold period to activate their germination process. I would simply have to wait until the following spring and summer to see my full vision realized. But the clover popped up right away, and the tiny green shoots were so sweet and dainty, they reminded me of a fairy garden.

If rewilding is something you're interested in, all the sources I used and more are in the Resources List. The key to rewilding is using a variety of plants in all sorts of shapes, sizes, and colours. The more plant diversity you have, the more species will benefit. A large yard is not a prerequisite for rewilding, though. Ours is proof of that. It's also worth noting that native plants don't necessarily cost more than non-native ones. A tree or shrub is going to be more expensive than seeds, but the flower and clover seeds we bought were not any pricier than the vegetable and herb seeds I bought for the garden.

If you already have a yard filled with non-native plants that are not invasive, this is not necessarily a problem—those plants may just be less beneficial to native insects, birds, or animals. But even if local bees are better suited to native plants, it doesn't mean they can't derive benefit from non-native ones. At the end of the day, ripping out non-native perennials or cutting down non-native trees that are doing just fine is not necessary. If you have the option to plant something new in the future, though, prioritize native plants.

If you do choose to rewild, especially the front, you may get negative comments from other people. Do it anyway. There aren't really any good reasons why we put perfect green lawns on a pedestal, but there are plenty of good reasons why we *should* put rewilded lawns on a pedestal. So if a neighbour gives your rewilded green space some serious side-eye, kindly explain to them what you're doing and why it matters. As for me, I've decided to view any negative comments as compliments. I sincerely can't wait for the years to come when our rewilded green space takes on a truly unruly state—bring it on. I could tell things were already moving in the right direction when a family member stopped by one day, took a long look at our front yard, and then turned to me and said: "This looks . . . nice?" Success, indeed.

Takeaways

- Start your own garden using any available green space, or see if there's an opportunity nearby for community or boulevard gardening.
- Tend to the health of the soil by using compost or mulch.
- Keep it natural! Avoid synthetic pesticides and fertilizers in your garden and yard, and research natural alternatives.
- If it's an option available to you, install a rain barrel to harvest rainwater and cut down on seasonal water use.
- Continue to use the garden infrastructure, supplies, and tools you already have for as long as possible. If you need something new, rent it, borrow it, or find it second-hand.
- At the end of the growing season, implement end-of-season practices. For example, preserve or freeze any surplus, share your harvest with others, or make notes in a garden journal.
- Bonus: Go the extra mile and rewild your green space. Do some research and source native plants near you that will help support biodiversity.

CHAPTER 13:

Water

IT'S EASY TO TAKE WATER FOR GRANTED. Household taps give the impression that there's an unlimited supply of water, but that simply isn't true. Less than 1 percent of the Earth's water is accessible fresh water that humans can actually use. All of the other water on Earth is either salt water or frozen, inaccessible, or both. Whenever there's an increase in water demand—from population growth or climate change, for example—additional fresh water doesn't miraculously appear to meet the need. That 1 percent number stays the same. When freshwater supply is incompatible with the amount of water needed in any given area, it is known as water scarcity.

If you ever have to go without water in your home for a few days or more, it's immediately evident that daily life without water is downright difficult. The rental house that Paul and I lived in previously was located in an older area of the city, which was constantly plagued by road and sewer maintenance issues. As a result, our water was regularly shut off with little notice. Whenever that happened, we had to buy bottled water, cooking became a challenge, showers had to wait, and dishes and laundry piled up. It was inconvenient, but even more so because we had unrestricted access to water under normal circumstances. When that access was cut off even temporarily, we were reminded rather quickly that water is an essential resource, and a finite one too.

Water Use in Canada

In Canada, about 55 percent of the drinking water that's produced is used for residential purposes, at a rate of about 223 litres per person each day. If this seems like a lot of water for one person to use on a daily basis, that's because it is. When compared with other countries for individual water consumption, Canada comes in second place, after the United States. And yet, even with a high individual water consumption rate, not everyone in Canada has equal access to potable water, which is especially true for Indigenous and remote communities.

The vast majority of Canada's potable water—nearly 90 percent of it—is taken from freshwater sources like rivers and lakes. Although some of this water is later redistributed to the bodies of water it came from, the process of removing and recirculating fresh water can affect both the quality and quantity of the water in those locations. When water flows freely from your tap, it's easy to forget that it was initially drawn from the environment. But the crossover between water and the environment is becoming increasingly difficult to ignore. Climate change and water are intricately linked, evidenced by severe events like droughts, floods, and wildfires, all of which involve either too much water or not enough. Global warming also causes bodies of water to become warmer, which can affect how ecosystems function. All of this trickles down—quite literally—and can affect things like agriculture and infrastructure, for example, or lead to increasing water scarcity.

How does this relate to water usage in your kitchen? For the average household, the kitchen is one of four key areas that use water, alongside the laundry room, the bathroom, and outdoors, which applies more seasonally in Canada. When household water usage is reduced through practical solutions aimed at conserving it, this can decrease the amount of fresh water that needs to be withdrawn, treated, and redistributed again afterwards. This is especially true if water conservation practices are adopted more broadly on a collective scale.

The first step to conserving water at home is to become more mindful about how you use it. You probably saw this coming, since mindfulness is a recurring theme throughout this book. To put it simply, water is a precious resource and deserves to be viewed and treated as such. From there, we can apply the waste hierarchy to water use, focusing in particular on reducing and reusing to conserve and repurpose water at home. In the average household, the kitchen is responsible for about 15 percent of all indoor water usage, while the bathroom is responsible for about 50 percent. That's not to say that the kitchen isn't important. But it means that if you apply mindfulness and the waste hierarchy to other areas of your home, you can increase the amount of water you are able to conserve. We've just discussed more-sustainable options for outdoor water usage in the "Gardening" chapter, but in the coming solutions, some of the water conservation tips can be applied beyond the kitchen too—like in the bathroom, for example.

Take a moment to think about where you use the most water in the kitchen. What are the big spenders? That's the best place to start.

What You Can Do

Waste Less Water When You Cook

You can reduce water usage and corresponding water waste when cooking or preparing food at home in a number of ways. The key thing to keep in mind is that the water you get from the tap can often be used more than once. There are ways to cook and prepare food that reuse or repurpose water, which will reduce the amount of water that you use overall. I've put together the following list of tips, but you can also just start by observing your own habits the next time you prepare a meal. Take note of how much water you're using and where it ends up. See if you can come up with any creative solutions for reducing, reusing, or repurposing that water.

- If you are washing fruits and vegetables, rather than letting the water run, put some water into a bowl or basin and then just soak or rinse your produce in there. This is useful if you're cleaning a bunch of produce at one time, but if you're washing a single apple, it may be less practical. Once you're done with that water, use it for plants or your garden rather than dumping it out.
- If you are taking food out of the freezer to thaw, plan to take it out in advance and let it thaw slowly in the fridge, rather than running it under water.
- Try making one-pot meals, rather than cooking a number of ingredients separately and then combining them. For example, any time I

make soups or stews, I use only one pot and cook everything together in the liquid directly. Cooking everything in one pot also naturally thickens dishes, especially if you're working with starchy foods like potatoes, pasta, or lentils. One-pot meals also equal fewer dirty dishes, which is always a bonus.

- Roast or steam your vegetables rather than boiling them. You could also boil something in a pot underneath as you steam something else on top, which is like a two-for-one cooking technique that saves water in the process.
- Measure your cooking water. In the first few years I lived on my own, I used to cook vegetables, rice, and pasta with way too much water. I always overestimated how much water was needed. Then I ended up dumping water out as the food cooked, to prevent the pot from overflowing. If you're unsure how much water you need to cook something, a quick internet search should tell you what you need to know.
- If you make too much coffee, tea, or other water-based beverage, you can cool it down and then save it in the fridge for other purposes, like iced tea and iced coffee. I also sometimes use leftover brewed coffee as a replacement for other liquids in certain baking recipes. Anything chocolate-based that calls for milk or water typically works well with coffee in its place.
- If you have cooking or rinsing water left over from foods like pasta, grains, beans, legumes, or vegetables, you can cool this water, save it in the fridge, and then use it for the base of a soup, stew, sauce, gravy, or other similar dish. If you're not going to use the leftover water fast enough, you could freeze it once it's cooled. Vegetable cooking water, for example, is basically a simplified vegetable stock, so it's incredibly versatile. I also upcycle certain types of cooking water. For example, if I ever boil beets, I save and cool the beet water and then use it to make beet lemonade. The reserved cooking water is extremely flavourful, and by adding lemon juice and white sugar, you have an easy, delicious, and colourful drink.
- Leftover water from cooking certain foods, like vegetables or pasta, for example, can also be used to water your outdoor garden. Note that the water should have only vegetable matter in it—meaning no salt, oil, spices, or anything else—and it should be cooled completely. You do not want to be pouring hot, salty water with chunks of food onto your plants! A little bit of food residue from vegetables or smaller pasta

particles is okay, as it will just get broken down into nutrients once it's in the soil. But this is for outdoor plants only. I consulted a few garden and plant experts, and the consensus was that using cooking water for indoor plants can upset the soil's balance and cause issues like mould, because there is so much less soil.

Put Thought into Your Drinking Water

We've already looked at disposable and reusable options for drinking receptacles in previous chapters. But if you are drinking tap water at home, you can still reduce water waste. Most people—myself included—don't want to drink tap water that's warm or hot, but running the water until it's cold results in water going down the drain. Instead, cool your drinking water with ice cubes, or keep a pitcher of water in the fridge that you refill on an ongoing basis. I also do this with Rue's water bowl, adding ice cubes to cool it down in the summer. Similarly, if you are running the tap as you wait for the water to get hot, catch that running water and use it for something else—cooking, watering plants, refilling a water jug, etc.

Some people also filter their tap water. Depending on where you live and the quality of the drinking water, a filter may be necessary. If you prefer the taste of bottled water over tap water but want to kick your bottled water habit, you may also want to invest in a filter. There are filter systems that mount directly onto a kitchen faucet, or you can use a stand-alone water pitcher with a filter. The one thing to consider is end-of-life options for filters. Most curbside recycling programs in Canada do not accept filters, and as a result, they often end up in the landfill. Check with your municipality's Waste Wizard or similar search tool, along with other local recycling databases, to see if any specific types of filters can be recycled near you (see the Resources List). Some filter companies may have take-back options. For example, certain London Drugs locations in Canada accept Brita filters and related products through their in-store recycling program, but only if those products were purchased at London Drugs.

Check Your Kitchen Sink and Tap

As I was working on this chapter, we hit the one-year mark of living in our current house. During that entire year, the kitchen tap had a near-constant drip. When we moved in, Paul and I talked about fixing the drip, but then we got busy—and we got used to the sound of the drip. But then, as I was doing my research on water, I came across a jaw-dropping piece of information: If you have a leak that releases one drop of water every second, it can add up to ten thousand litres of water in one year alone. This information stopped me in my tracks—had we seriously sent ten thousand litres of water down the drain in the past year, simply because we hadn't made it a priority to fix the leak? What a complete waste! This information propelled me into immediate action. That coming weekend was Thanksgiving, and my in-laws were visiting from out of town. Paul's stepdad, Rick, is experienced in all things home repair, so almost as soon as he arrived, I asked him to please address the leak at some point during the course of the weekend—the sooner, the better.

I assumed that fixing the leak would be simple, but our home is a 1918 build and nothing is ever simple about fixing it, so I should have known better. What started as taking a quick look at the kitchen tap turned into several hours of investigation with no resolution. Rick's final assessment was that if we wanted to fix the leak, we needed a new tap. During this process, he also noticed that the basket on the right side of our sink was leaking water—something that neither Paul nor I had observed before. In the end, Rick replaced the tap and the sink basket, effectively fixing both. I was happy the leaks were resolved, but I wished we had addressed this earlier. We could have saved a lot of water in that year.

Once you've checked for leaks in the kitchen, you can then check other areas of your home as well. Leaks may not always be obvious. Semi-regularly, take an in-depth look at all of your taps and appliances, listening closely to see if you can hear any water dripping. You can also do a more calculated check if you have a water meter in your home, which measures how much water your household uses. This is often recommended as an overnight test: You record the reading on the water meter before you go to bed and then check it again in the morning. If no water was used overnight but there is a change in the reading, this may indicate a leak. Check the Resources List for more information, and if you don't want to check and fix any potential leaks yourself—or if you don't have a home repair expert for a father-in-law—you could hire a professional to do this, of course.

Another thing you can address is the kitchen tap itself. One way to save water is to install a low-flow tap or faucet, which controls how much water travels through the faucet when it's in use. A typical faucet's flow rate is about 8.3 litres of water every minute. The flow rate for a low-flow faucet is about 5.7 litres a minute, but can be even less depending on the tap. This lower rate of water flow is thanks in part to something called an aerator, which basically combines air with water as it flows, resulting in increased water savings without a decrease in the water pressure. Most taps come with an aerator these days, but you can check your tap to see if it has one already. If your tap doesn't have an aerator, you can buy these separately. You can also clean the aerator, which will eliminate any buildup that has collected there over time, helping it work more efficiently. Another benefit of low-flow taps is that they save money from reduced water usage.

In the kitchen, a low-flow tap will save water only during specific tasks. If you're putting water into a pot for cooking purposes, for example, you're going to use a set volume of water—the flow rate makes no difference. A lower flow rate is just going to mean it takes longer to fill the pot. But if you're running the water while rinsing dishes or washing your hands, that's where the lower flow rate can help, since it reduces the amount of water flowing overall. You can take this solution to the next level by implementing it in the bathroom, where most water use happens.

The last consideration here applies to kitchen sinks that have a built-in garbage disposal unit, also known as a garburator. Garburators grind up food waste and then wash it down the drain, but they use a lot of water in the process. Their use can also put unnecessary strain on municipal waste-water treatment systems from all the additional food waste that's sent swirling down the drain and beyond. As a result, garburators are restricted or banned in some Canadian municipalities. If you have one in your home already and can get by without using it, it will reduce your water usage. The other thing to consider is that once your food waste disappears down the drain, it's not necessarily going to be composted. Where it ends up depends on the municipality. Composting food waste is always going to be a better option than having that waste end up elsewhere—like in the landfill, for example. So if you have a home compost or make use of an organics program, add the dregs from your kitchen sink to your compost pile. Paul and I have stainless steel drain catchers in our kitchen sink that make it very easy to collect any food scraps and then dispose of them in our compost bin.

Consider Your Dishwashing Habits

Whether you are washing dishes by hand or using a machine dishwasher, certain practices can either increase or decrease the amount of water and energy being used. I'll start with hand washing because Paul and I don't have a machine dishwasher, so we wash all of our dishes by hand.

There are three main methods that people use to manually hand wash dishes. The first is scrubbing and rinsing the dishes while the tap runs the entire time, or at least most of the time. This method is called the running-tap method. The second method uses two basins or sinks, one that you fill with hot, soapy water for washing, and one that has plain cold water for rinsing. In this method, the tap is not running at all, other than when you're initially filling up the basins. Guess what this method is called? The water-bath or two-basin method, rather fittingly. The third method involves a combination of the first two—for example, if you use one sink filled with soapy water for washing but then do your rinsing as the water runs.

Unsurprisingly, the running-tap method uses more water than the other two. Since the water is running almost constantly, this method also uses more energy to heat up the water. Now it's time for a confession: Both Paul and I typically hand wash dishes using the running-tap method. I know—not good. I think we developed this habit because not only have we never had a machine dishwasher, but the first house we lived in together had only a one-basin sink. I also usually wash a couple of dishes here and there throughout the day while I'm working at home, to avoid a massive pileup of dirty dishes later on. I always assumed that filling up the sink would be more wasteful if I was washing only a small number of dishes. But in reality, I'm probably not wasting any less water from running the tap the entire time, even if it is just for a few dishes.

The recommended best practice for manual dishwashing that has the lowest impact overall is therefore method number two—the two-basin method. But in studies that have looked at dishwashing behaviour, the two-basin method is the one that people use the least. It's much more common for people to hand wash dishes by either running the water the whole time or using a combination method where the water is running part of the time. For this reason, the two-basin method is not considered typical washing behaviour—it's considered the ideal. Washing dishes manually using *typical* behaviour, in a period of one year at a rate of four loads every week, uses approximately 12,950 litres of water and results in greenhouse gas emissions totalling 562 kilograms of carbon dioxide equivalent. You can bring these numbers down by adopting the two-basin method: Wash in one basin with hot, soapy water, rinse in a second basin of cool water, air-dry the dishes, and, throughout the process, don't let the tap run.

A machine dishwasher is less susceptible to fluctuations in human behaviour. Typical machine dishwashing behaviour is categorized as selecting the "normal" cycle and rinsing the dishes before putting them into the dishwasher, even though prerinsing is usually not necessary. If this typical machine dishwashing behaviour is applied to that same scenario of four loads of dishes every week, then in one year this equals 6,170 litres of water and emissions totalling 209 kilograms of carbon dioxide equivalent. This is less than half of the water and half of the emissions that result from typical manual dishwashing behaviour. The overall impacts from a machine dishwasher can be further reduced if you run the dishwasher only when it's completely full, select the "normal" cycle rather than more intensive and time-consuming settings, and avoid prerinsing the dishes. Just scrape your dishes instead, putting any food waste into the compost. Not using the "heated dry" setting on your dishwasher—or a similar setting, if it has one—will also decrease the amount of energy the machine uses.

What's better overall, manual dishwashing or using a machine dishwasher? All of this is highly dependent on individual behaviour, but in a scenario where typical washing behaviours are followed and compared, machine dishwashing wins for both water usage and emissions. However, if you hand wash your dishes using the ideal two-basin method, then manual dishwashing becomes much more competitive. In fact, ideal two-basin dishwashing can actually have an equal or even lower impact than machine dishwashing in some cases. Regardless of how you wash your dishes though, the key point is that there's probably a way to do it more sustainably. If you hand wash, don't let the water run. If you machine wash, don't prerinse. And so on.

It's worth noting here that hand washing dishes is not associated with manufacturing and end-of-life concerns to the same extent that machine dishwashing is. Hand washing mainly requires reusable supplies like dishcloths, scrub brushes, and a dish drying rack. But machine dishwashers require more extensive resources to make. Once a dishwasher stops working and can no longer be fixed, where that dishwasher ends up largely depends on the recycling options available nearby. In the "Appliances" chapter, we will talk more about end-of-life options. We'll also talk about what to look for if you're shopping for a new machine dishwasher in that chapter—there are energy-efficient options you can consider when buying. In the next chapter on cleaning, we'll take a look at hand dishwashing supplies as well.

At this point, you may be wondering if I have adopted the two-basin method in my own kitchen. The answer is both yes and no. I have switched from the full running-tap method to the combination method—filling the sink with water to wash, but rinsing with cold running water. Our kitchen sink is one of those two-basin ones where the second basin on the right side is a little baby sink. I am certain that whoever invented that sink size never hand washed a single dish during their lifetime. The baby sink barely fits a regular-sized dinner plate, making basin rinsing impossible for bigger items like pots, pans, and larger dishware. We intend to replace the entire kitchen sink eventually, along with installing a machine dishwasher in the future. Although we both dislike doing the dishes, Paul hates this chore more than I do. Over the years, he has brought up installing a dishwasher frequently. I have largely ignored these comments, brushing them off with a healthy dose of "Sure, love, great idea." But now that I know machine dishwashers are more than just a time-saving luxury—especially if we cannot practise the two-basin method to the fullest extent—I just might be convinced.

Takeaways

- Observe your own water habits in the kitchen. Find ways to reduce, reuse, or repurpose water to cut down on water waste when cooking and preparing food.
- Find alternatives to running your tap for temperature control, and if you use water filters, check if any specific filters can be recycled near you at their end of life.
- Address any leaks in your kitchen, consider installing a low-flow tap, and if you have a garburator, see if you can make do without using it.
- Find a way to make your dishwashing habits more sustainable by implementing best practices for either manual hand washing or using a machine dishwasher.

CHAPTER 14:

Cleaning

TAKE A LOOK AT THE BOTTLES of any conventional cleaning products you already use to keep your kitchen looking spic and span. No, seriously—go take a look. Whether it's dish soap, stove cleaner, or an all-purpose spray, there's a solid chance you won't be able to recognize or pronounce most or all of the ingredients listed. That's if the ingredients are even listed—which they might not be. If ingredients are not disclosed on the packaging directly, you can sometimes find this information on the company's website. Even then, I find that ingredient lists for cleaning or dish products are rarely useful at face value. When confronted with a long list of ingredient names, I almost always have to research what exactly those ingredients are or do. How is the average person supposed to know this otherwise?

But we interact with cleaning and dish products and their residues regularly, if not daily. The ingredients they're made from can have both health and environmental concerns associated with them. We also don't give these products much consideration on a day-to-day basis. Conventional cleaning and dish products are the norm—just like plastics, for example. We grab these products from the grocery store, use them at home to clean various surfaces, and we barely give it a second thought. So what I really want you to do here is give all of this a good, long second thought—and then some.

This chapter is laid out in a similar fashion to the solution on how to buy more-sustainable coffee and tea in the "Coffee and Tea" chapter (page 216).

Because there is so much variety when it comes to cleaning products, dish soaps, and their respective ingredients, it's once again difficult for me to make sweeping statements like "Your dish soap is toxic to aquatic life," or "That cleaner is linked to asthma." Maybe it is, maybe it isn't. The specific impacts depend on the particular products you're using. So, we're going to take an investigative approach here. If you did the homework in the "Coffee and Tea" chapter, then you've already played the sustainable detective game once before. The first step is to check the products you already have to see what the major concerns are. From there, two options emerge as alternatives. You can navigate the world of "green" cleaning products and dish soaps. Or you can take the do-it-yourself route and dive into basic staples like vinegar, baking soda, and lemon. To bring it all together, we will touch on cleaning and dishwashing supplies as well.

At this point, I am confident you will be able to implement many of the other solutions we've already talked about throughout this book. For example, you can apply considerations about packaging, asking questions, and shopping local to this chapter. Although we're going to focus on kitchen products specifically, you can also take the following solutions and apply them to the rest of the cleaning products you use throughout your home—bathroom cleaners, laundry detergent, and more. Regardless of what you're buying or using, navigating more-sustainable options as a consumer is always worth practising. The more you do it, the better you get at it. At the end of the day, when we evaluate any given cleaning or dish product, we have to remember that everything is connected. Generally speaking, what's good for the environment also tends to be good for you and me—and vice versa.

What You Can Do

Take Stock: Do an Inventory of Your Kitchen Cleaning and Dish Products

I don't actually use that many cleaning products on a regular basis. This mainly has to do with the fact that I despise cleaning. So I keep things as simple as possible. I frequently clean with vinegar and baking soda, which are natural options we'll touch on shortly. Otherwise, there were three conventional products in my inventory: a dish soap we had been using for years, a cleaner for the top of the stove that I used semi-regularly, and an adhesive remover, which Paul typically used in a kitchen context to remove sticky labels from glass jars, which we then repurposed for food storage.

Once you've identified the products in your inventory, the next step is checking them for any potential environmental and health concerns. The easiest option is to use a third-party source that evaluates the health and environmental safety of products. One of the most widely known in North America is the Environmental Working Group—EWG—which rates both individual ingredients and entire products on a scale from A (the best) to F (the worst). They also have a certification program where products can become EWG Verified, meaning the product has met their standards. Being EWG Verified is the best option; it comes before the A rating. EWG's verification standards consider a number of criteria, such as ingredient disclosure and whether the product contains certain ingredients they have deemed concerning. EWG doesn't do this just for cleaning products; their searchable databases include a range of home and personal care products, including laundry detergent, sunscreen, cosmetics, and more. Other, similar sources you can also use are noted in the Resources List.

Another option is to simply look up ingredients yourself online. Search for articles about specific ingredients or products from reputable sources like health, academic, or environmental associations and organizations. You could also simply search a brand, product, or ingredient along with keywords like "sustainable," "environment," or "health." If fifteen separate organizations have a bone to pick with some specific ingredient or product, this isn't a great sign. Going this route can also be helpful if you're seeking additional information beyond what's listed in a given database.

All right—back to the three products in my inventory. I checked the bottles of these three products for an ingredient list, but none of them had one. So I took to the internet. I found the dish soap's ingredients on the company website, which included a list of numerous components. I recognized only two: water and sodium chloride, which is salt. As expected, ingredients like "C9-11 Pareth-8" and "phenoxyethanol" meant absolutely nothing to me. Then I searched for the dish soap on EWG, where I found that it had a D rating overall. A further breakdown of the ingredients and their individual ratings showed that C9-11 Pareth-8 itself had a D, for example, and was a concern for acute aquatic toxicity, along with human health concerns related to issues like skin irritation and allergies.

Although this wasn't a great start to my inventory, the stovetop cleaner fared much worse. While I did find a short ingredient list online after some digging, on EWG I saw the product's ingredient disclosure was noted as "poor." Overall, the stove cleaner had an F rating. The situation for the adhesive remover was similar: poor ingredient disclosure, F rating overall. I could have told you myself that the adhesive remover wasn't going to do so hot in the ratings department, though. It had warnings on the front of the bottle that included the flame hazard symbol, for flammable, and the skull and crossbones, for poison/toxic.

Since I was already knee-deep in the EWG database, I figured I would also look up some other cleaning products I had bought in the past. One product I searched for was an all-purpose spray that is commonly found in "green" cleaning aisles. But on EWG, this cleaner had a D rating, and several ingredients that did not sound green in the slightest. When I'd bought this spray in the past, I figured it was a good choice, given that it was sitting pretty on the shelf surrounded by other "green" cleaning options. In hindsight, I'm not sure why I assumed its location on the shelf meant anything.

Once you have gone through the items in your inventory, what you do next is up to you. This is similar to our conversation about plastics. We don't want to be throwing things out simply for the sake of it—doing so is incompatible with waste reduction. But you have to decide what you are comfortable continuing to use. Personally, there were all sorts of red flags for me with the three products I checked. First, there was the fact that I wasn't entirely certain about the ingredients in the stovetop cleaner and the adhesive remover. While ingredient disclosure is one thing, I seriously doubted that the ingredients themselves were wholesome anyway—both products smelled like chemicals. After browsing various sections on EWG's website and doing some other reading online, I concluded that I did not want any of these three products coming into contact with surfaces where we would be eating, preparing, or storing food on a long-term basis. I decided that I would use up the rest of the dish soap, though, since the bottle wasn't full and we needed something to do dishes with for the time being. In the meantime, I'd look for a different dish soap option. But it was time to say goodbye to the stovetop cleaner and adhesive remover.

However, these types of products cannot just be dumped down the drain. Any products—cleaning or otherwise—that are labelled with the hazard symbols and/or wording like "warning," "toxic," or "poisonous" have to be taken to a drop-off location for household hazardous waste. This service is typically provided by municipalities. Some cities have specific days that hazardous waste can be dropped off. You can look up products on your municipality's Waste Wizard or similar search tool, which will often tell you whether or not the product is considered hazardous waste in the first place. If you are unsure about anything, contact them directly, rather than making assumptions. Household hazardous waste is labelled as such because it contains ingredients that can result in illness or death for humans. These products can also have dire consequences for the environment, affecting not only plants and animals but the soil and water as well. That's why you can't pour them down the drain, dump them in the toilet, empty the contents on the ground, or toss them into your household garbage, recycling, or organics bins.

Common examples of products people use in the kitchen that are considered household hazardous waste include bleach, disinfectants, oven cleaners, and drain cleaners. Some all-purpose cleaners also make the hazardous list, along with cleaners containing certain ingredients, like ammonia. The irony in all of this is that cleaning products are meant to keep things clean, and by extension, we often assume that clean also means safe, or even healthy. However, doing your own inventory and checking various products and their ingredients will illustrate that this isn't always the case. Having to drop off an all-purpose cleaner or an oven cleaner at a hazardous waste disposal location serves to reinforce this point.

Although most common dish soaps wouldn't be considered household hazardous waste, it's important to keep in mind what I said earlier—everything is connected. Anything we put down our kitchen drain makes its way to the waste-water treatment system. Once waste water is treated, much of the water is redistributed to the waterways it came from, like rivers and lakes. The treated water has to meet certain criteria, but that water will inevitably become someone else's drinking water again at some point down the line, as the cycle repeats itself. Less harsh ingredients are better for us and the environment, and they also reduce the strain on the waste-water system, which is always helpful.

Opt for Greener Cleaners

Let me be the first to welcome you here to the baffling and complex land that is more-sustainable cleaning. I started my research for this section by going to a few different pharmacies and grocery stores to peruse their aisles of cleaning products. Navigating any cleaning aisle can be overwhelming, to say the least. Neat and tidy bottles line the shelves, row after row. All the bottles are competing for your attention, with bright labels highlighting various claims about grease-cutting ability, scrubbing potential, and more. Most cleaning aisles now have an obvious section for the "green" cleaners too. These cleaners are also competing for your attention, with words like *natural* and *plant-based* prominently displayed on their labels. The rise of these types of "green" products demonstrates that consumers care about having greener options, and companies know that. But how are you supposed to know which "green" cleaner is best?

Unfortunately, there's no exact way to know which one is best unless you do your own research. You may have noticed that I've been putting "green" in quotation marks in this chapter. That's because most of the "green" terminology that's commonly found on cleaning and dish-related products—words like *green*, *natural*, *eco*, *non-toxic*, *environmentally friendly*, *sustainable*, and *plant-based*—does not have any sort of standard definition in Canada, as of the time of writing. In reality, this terminology may mean very little—if anything at all.

We have seen this terminology and labelling issue before in other chapters. It's come up in a food sense with terms like *sustainably raised*, and in the realm of compostable plastics, for example. This concept actually has a name: greenwashing. Greenwashing is essentially a marketing tactic where environmentally friendly wording, colours, and/or imagery are used to sell something to consumers. The consumers in question are often people like you and me who want to purchase products that are better for the environment. But greenwashing terminology is often intentionally vague and loosely applied, meant to create an illusion of sustainability. On the whole, it's a misleading practice. This is especially true if there is no further information provided, either on the package or online. And as with compostable plastics, greenwashing makes it harder to identify the genuinely eco-friendly products in the mix. The bottom line is that much sustainable terminology can be used in either an authentic *or* greenwashed way. In the Resources List, I have included some sources for help on understanding greenwashing more broadly.

What are you supposed to do here? It's tough to navigate all of this based solely on a store's cleaning aisle set-up or on claims slapped onto product packaging. The way I approach this is by automatically assuming claims are false until proven otherwise. I treat both conventional and "green" products exactly the same. Once I've looked up the product or the individual ingredient myself—using the same tools and strategies from when we took our inventory—I can make an assessment as to whether or not there is anything "natural" or "green" about it.

You can also look for logos on products that indicate various certifications. This is the same concept as certified organic, or any of the other certifications we talked about in the "Coffee and Tea" chapter. In this case, various third-party certifications apply to cleaning and dish products, including EWG. Other examples are EcoLogo and Green Seal. If you see a certification logo on a bottle of something, you can check what that logo means and what its certification standards are.

One other thing that may hold some legitimacy here is if a company or brand lists specific numbers or facts, either on its packaging or online. Greenwashing tends to be vague, so concrete information that involves numerical values or percentages has a higher likelihood of being true. But even then, take these claims with a grain of salt. When I was doing my cleaning aisle perusal, for example, I noticed labels with more specific descriptions like "98 percent plant-based." Although 98 percent of that product may in fact be plant-based, you have to wonder—what's up with the other 2 percent? And how are they defining plant-based anyway? If you really want to go the extra mile, you could also contact companies directly to ask questions.

A last option here is to find a product that is being made and sold locally near you. If you buy a homemade cleaner from a small business at the farmers' market or an artisan fair, for example, it's highly likely that the person making it will be able to tell you about the ingredients they used. Local products are probably not going to be listed in any large database, and they may not be certified by a third party either, but you could still try searching for their ingredients individually in a database. Being able to talk to someone directly about a product they've created—and are also typically using themselves—definitely helps create more transparency.

If you think all of this seems like a ridiculous amount of work, I'd have to agree with you. This is exactly why I find more-sustainable cleaning both baffling and complex—and unnecessarily so. Finding cleaners that are genuinely safe for us and the environment should not be this difficult or time-consuming. It's for this very reason that people often bypass dabbling in "green" cleaning altogether and instead skip straight to working with ingredients they already have at home. Cue the vinegar, lemon, and baking soda.

Try Cleaning with Household Ingredients

I tend to lean toward cleaning with natural ingredients like vinegar over "green" cleaning products. I use vinegar as a glass cleaner, all-purpose spray, and kitchen floor cleaner. I use baking soda to whiten surfaces or to get rid of grime and dirt. But I have been doing the exact same thing with these two ingredients for years. So when I began working on this chapter, I decided to widen the scope. I tried using vinegar and baking soda for other cleaning jobs, and I started working with additional ingredients too, like lemon. What I have learned from this process, however, is that the world of natural cleaning is vast and varied. I'm going to give you a brief overview of some of the most common natural cleaning ingredients, but if you are keen on cleaning your kitchen—or your entire home—with vinegar, baking soda, lemon, and other natural products, then I highly recommend consulting other resources. Unless you have a background in chemistry or a strong understanding of how various ingredients work together, consulting other resources is going to save you a lot of time and trial and error.

Natural ingredients like vinegar, lemon, and baking soda are popular cleaning options for many valid reasons. For starters, these ingredients are simple. You can basically swap a cluttered cupboard of cleaning products—try saying that five times fast—for a few ingredients that you probably already have on hand. These three ingredients are also edible, which means no lengthy internet searches to suss out whether your cleaning products are a safe choice for your family and home. They're also not susceptible to greenwashing. A lemon is obviously natural and plant-based and does not need to be advertised as such to make a sale. Additionally, these items are inexpensive. You may even be able to find vinegar or baking soda in bulk format for a reduced price. Or, depending on where you live, these items might be available at a refill, zero-waste, or bulk foods store where you can bring your own packaging. Of course, you can also buy lemons loose with your own packaging at most grocery stores. Overall, there are a lot of positives here already, and we haven't even started talking about cleaning.

Vinegar is one of the most popular natural cleaning ingredients. It's made from water and acetic acid, which is created through fermentation. Regular white vinegar is typically 5 percent acetic acid. You can purchase stronger vinegars, though. Pickling vinegar, for example, is 7 percent acetic acid. There is also cleaning vinegar, which is usually 10–12 percent acetic acid. I normally just use regular white vinegar at 5 percent acetic acid for cleaning at home, but you may prefer stronger concentrations. Most of the time when you clean with vinegar, you'll be diluting it. I dilute regular white vinegar with water at a one-to-one ratio, but I've seen other dilution recommendations too. I put my half-and-half solution in a glass spray bottle, label and date it—which is so important with DIY cleaning solutions—and then use it to clean our countertops, backsplash, windows, microwave, fridge, kitchen table, and more. Truly, it's an all-purpose solution. Various concentrations of vinegar can also be used to remove wall markings, clean a coffee machine, remove buildup in a kettle, and remove adhesive from surfaces like glass jars. Which, by the way, I started doing to replace our adhesive remover after my inventory. If you take a clean cloth, douse it in undiluted vinegar, and then lay it over the adhesive for about fifteen minutes, you can then more easily scrape or scrub the sticky gunk off.

Lemon is also an acid, so its usage is similar to that of vinegar. If you don't love the smell of vinegar, lemon can be a good alternative in certain cases. I hadn't used lemon much prior to working on this book, but when I did my research and interviews for this chapter, I discovered I had been missing out. For example, you can use lemon to clean your microwave. Quarter a lemon, and then microwave it for one or two minutes. Once the microwave stops running, leave the door closed for about five minutes. The acid from the lemon, combined with the heat, will help to loosen any nasty bits stuck on the inside of the microwave. After it sits for five minutes, you'll be able to easily wipe the crud away with a cloth. You could do this exact same thing with vinegar, too, just by microwaving a bowl of it. You can also deodorize cutting boards with lemon. After you've cut something like an onion, for example, take a lemon, cut it in half, and rub it all over the board. Then let it sit for a few minutes, rinse with water, and you're good to go.

Unlike vinegar and lemon, baking soda is not an acid—it's a base. Baking soda can be used to remove grease, odours, and dirt, or to whiten surfaces. For example, you can sprinkle baking soda in the sink, spray a bit of water on top, scrub the sink clean with the paste, and then give it a final rinse. I often make a mushy paste of baking soda directly on a cloth, just by wetting the cloth, sprinkling baking soda on one side, and then folding the cloth together to mash it up. I then use this to get scuffs, marks, and grime off of various surfaces, like the floor or kitchen table. Baking soda, vinegar, and lemon can also be used in combination. For example, you can infuse vinegar with leftover lemon rinds, which gives a classic all-purpose vinegar spray both an extra cleaning boost and a lovely scent.

Once you start dabbling in the world of natural cleaning, you'll quickly come across many other ingredients, including apple cider vinegar, salt, washing soda, essential oils, and olive oil. The range of ingredients and their various applications is why I strongly recommend consulting other resources if you go down this path. In the Resources List, I have noted several blogs and books that get into the nitty-gritty of natural cleaning.

Consulting other resources that have already done the work is not only helpful for saving time, but also important for safety and proper care of your home. For example, it's not recommended to use vinegar on cast iron, waxed wood, or natural stone like granite or marble, because it can etch surfaces. Vinegar is also not recommended for use in machine dishwashers or washing machines, as it can damage various parts of the machine. Any time you are mixing ingredients together, you'll also want to tread cautiously. I don't just mean for the sake of avoiding a chemical reaction, though that is possible. Certain ingredients can simply cancel each other out—like mixing an acid with a base—which decreases the effectiveness. I have also found that other resources are incredibly helpful in one-off situations, including beyond the kitchen. For example, a wine stain on your couch is not a great opportunity for trial and error. Unless you know what you're doing, you could potentially make the stain worse. Doing a small test patch on a given surface when working with natural ingredients for the first time can help avoid unintended issues as well.

You also don't have to pick one or the other when it comes to natural or "green" options. I lean more to the natural side of things in the kitchen, but I use other, "green" products in the bathroom. I also feel like I've only just begun to grasp how natural ingredients work together and what they can do. Learning about this takes time. Natural cleaning is more of a long-term journey, where you slowly make changes and build up your knowledge base. One of the simplest ways to go about this is to find alternatives on an ongoing basis, rather than trying to do everything all at once. After you use up a given product, take to the internet or consult a book to find a new, more sustainable solution. That might involve natural ingredients, or it might involve researching "green" cleaning options near you. The choice is yours.

Evaluate Your Dish Soap

If you go the natural cleaning route, you will likely encounter recipes for making your own dish soap. There is also one particular soap that features prominently in sustainable cleaning circles: castile soap. It is often praised for being a "true soap," given that it does not contain animal-based, synthetic, or harsh ingredients. Most castile soap is made from a combination of a few different vegetable oils, like coconut, jojoba, olive, sunflower, or hemp. Therefore, its ingredients are natural, non-toxic, and plant-based, making it a genuinely green product—no quotation marks here. The gentle ingredients also make castile soap incredibly versatile for both home and body purposes. It can be used for laundry, hand washing dishes, and cleaning various surfaces like the stove or windows. You can also use castile soap to clean cast iron, since it's so mild. It can be combined with baking soda to give it an extra scrubbing boost, among other DIY recipes. If that weren't enough, castile soap can also be used to wash your hair, your pet, fruits and vegetables, and more. This alone makes it stand out. You can buy bar and liquid castile soap, both of which are typically sold in a concentrated format. This is another reason why castile soap is so popular: the liquid soap has to be diluted with water at home, which means less packaging is involved overall.

I was aware of castile soap prior to conducting my cleaning inventory, but I had never purchased it before. Once I discovered my conventional dish soap's D rating, however, I began looking for other options. So I purchased a bottle of Dr. Bronner's liquid castile soap in citrus scent from a local shop. Dr. Bronner's is one of the leading brands of castile soap—if not *the* leading brand—and its history dates back to 1858. The ingredients are listed on both the packaging and the company's website. The soap boasts eighteen different uses. While I initially intended to use it to hand wash dishes, I appreciated how multi-purpose it was. One of its listed uses is toothpaste, for example. I couldn't see myself using the soap as toothpaste, but I did intend to try it as hand soap and for Rue's next bath. To confirm that all was truly well, I checked Dr. Bronner's liquid citrus soap in the EWG database and was pleased to see that it had received an A rating and had a number of third-party certifications as well.

At home, I diluted the soap according to the instructions and then tried cleaning with it in the kitchen. It worked very well on the counter, floor, and stovetop. Then I tried using it to hand wash our dishes. But as I was washing, I noticed something—there weren't many suds. I wondered if I had diluted it incorrectly, so I made a second batch. But the amount of suds did not change. Then I found out something interesting: The vegetable oils in castile soap tend to produce less durable suds than a dish soap made from synthetic ingredients, for example. Either way, suds are not necessarily an indicator of cleanliness. Some synthetic products have ingredients added to them to help make suds, but this has more to do with making things sudsy and less to do with making things clean. How very interesting—the more you know!

A great place to start your own search for dish soap is by visiting any bulk, health, zero-waste, refill, or natural stores near you. See what they have and then do your own research to confirm that the product is a good option. You may be able to find local brands of castile soap or other dish soap at farmers' markets or refill stores. There are also non-liquid concentrated options, which cut down on shipping volume and require less packaging. Solid dish soap blocks—basically concentrated bars of dish soap—are becoming increasingly popular, for example. If you need detergent for a machine dishwasher, apply the exact same investigative process we've discussed throughout. You can sometimes find machine dishwasher tablets or powder in a refill format as well. The one thing to note is that it's not recommended to use castile soap in a machine dishwasher—it's not made for that purpose. Be mindful that dish soap and dishwasher detergent can also be greenwashed, so be sure to do your own research.

Will you be paying more for greener dish products? Yes and no. When you go to a refill store—where you pay by weight to fill your own containers—the dish soap often costs more than the price of conventional dish soap at the grocery store. But this is because you're not buying a refill version of conventional dish soap. The natural ingredients in something like castile soap, for example, are typically high quality and therefore cost more. The other thing to keep in mind is that these products are usually sold in a concentrated format, which makes them seem more expensive up front. Just because I was curious, I did a calculation to compare the cost. My bottle of concentrated liquid castile soap was $27 for 946 millilitres. The dilution ratio for hand dishwashing is one part soap to ten parts water, which means that my 946-millilitre bottle of concentrated castile soap equals 9.46 litres of soap once it's diluted. Conventional dish soap from the grocery store is about $3 to $5 for 946 millilitres. If I wanted to buy 9.46 litres of conventional dish soap, then I'd be paying $30 to $50 overall. So while castile soap may cost more up front, in the end the price is similar or less for an equal amount of soap.

Of course, all of this depends on what you're buying and where you're buying it from. "Green" dish soaps and cleaners sometimes cost more than conventional products, but baking soda and vinegar are much cheaper than either option. At the same time, in some cases more-sustainable products do cost more, as we've seen in previous chapters. Is this fair? No. But that's the current reality for some goods—food, cleaning, or otherwise. My advice in these types of scenarios is the same: Just do what you can, within the window of what's affordable and available to you.

Evaluate Your Cleaning and Dishwashing Supplies

My cleaning supplies include homemade rags cut from old towels and clothes, a broom, a small hand-held vacuum, and a spray mop with reusable pads that are machine washable. That's it. I've had these same materials for years and reuse them over and over again until something like a rag is in absolute tatters. On the dish front, we have also been using the same dishcloths and dishtowels for years. When these dish materials are no longer looking their best, I downgrade them to rags. All of this gets a check mark—it's the waste hierarchy in action. However, one particular dish item that we had also been using for years would not be getting any sort of check mark here: a disposable and refillable plastic dish wand.

Why was this dish wand a problem? It constantly leaked dish soap. The plastic handle portion was not durable in the slightest, so it often cracked and had to be replaced. The sponge portion of the wand disintegrated quickly with use. At the end of its life, the whole thing was destined for the landfill, only to be replaced by another wand, which would eventually head to the landfill too. It was a vicious cycle, and I knew it. Yet I did nothing about it over the years. Why? Because another problem with the dish wand was Paul. He had been using these plastic dish wands his entire adult life, and Paul is like the poster child for product loyalty—for better or for worse. So I knew that finding a replacement for the dish wand was going to be a challenge. But while the dish wand was a hill Paul was willing to die on, it was also a hill I was willing to climb. I just had to come at it from the right angle.

I gave him a gentle but straightforward two-week warning: "Good morning, you look great today! And by the way, our dish wand set-up will be changing soon, as per the book I'm writing." Although he replied with a frown and some grumbling, I was undeterred. I took to the internet to research reusable options for dish wands. I wanted something that would still provide the functionality he liked but was less flimsy and disposable. However, there were not a lot of options. I had been envisioning a refillable stainless steel dish wand with a compostable and replaceable brush head, made from something like coconut fibre. This apparently did not exist. (If you happen to be looking for a new business venture, please take this idea and run with it. I'll happily be a customer.) The best option I could find was a reusable, sturdy-looking plastic refillable dish wand that had a replaceable brush head. I wasn't thrilled by this option because it did nothing to get us away from plastic or avoid eventual landfill disposal. The main benefit was the reusability, which simply meant it would last longer than the other ones we had previously owned. Although that was only marginally better in my books, I bought it anyway since it was the best thing I could find.

But this dish wand was an immediate flop. Paul had a long list of flaws: "The bristles are way too hard" (this was true); "the bristles are already getting bent out of shape" (true, after only a few days of use); "it's spraying water all over the counter and backsplash" (also true—using it made a big mess); "it doesn't hold very much soap" (once again, unfortunately true). After a week or so with no improvement in the dish wand's functionality, I decided to take a different approach. I was happy I had purchased only one of these wands, at least. The brush itself was suitable for other cleaning purposes, so I downgraded it to my cleaning bin alongside the rags.

The next day, Paul and I went out together to browse dish supplies at The Better Good, our local refill and sustainable goods store. Many of the store options I mentioned earlier that sell more-sustainable dish soap and cleaning products—like refilleries, bulk stores, and natural stores—also sell more-sustainable dish supplies and accessories. The Better Good had a few different dish brushes that were made from natural materials. So we looked at the options. We held them in our hands. We felt the bristles. And then Paul surprised me. "This one," he said decisively. He was holding a dish brush that had a wooden handle. The brush portion was a combination of wood and bristles of Tampico fibre, which is a natural plant fibre made from agave. The brush had a little metal part that held the two pieces together, which meant that the brush portion was replaceable. Aside from the metal part, the whole thing was compostable. We bought one for $9 and then headed home.

It was clear almost immediately that this dish brush was the winning ticket. The bristles were durable yet gentle. Significantly less water was being sprayed in the process. As the weeks went on, the brush held up. I was relieved, to say the least, and I rested my case. As for Paul, he came down from the refillable plastic dish wand hill—it wasn't worth it, in the end.

If you have cleaning and dish supplies you already use, continue using them. There's no need to do anything different or buy anything new. You only need to consider any of this if you actually have something to replace—like a plastic dish wand that breaks regularly, for example. If you need new or different cleaning and dish supplies, first and foremost, consider the waste hierarchy, and refer to the following list of tips.

- You can make your own cleaning cloths and rags from any old towels, dishcloths, clothing, or other fabric you already own that you aren't actively using. Rags are a simple replacement for disposable materials like paper towels, and since they're machine washable, you can wash and reuse them on an ongoing basis. Once rags reach the end of their life, if they're made entirely of a natural material like cotton, you might be able to compost them depending on your organics program or home composting set-up. If there's a textile recycler nearby, you can also check if they will accept them. Otherwise, they have to go in the garbage; so try to get as much life as possible out of any given materials prior to disposal.
- Some of the most common more-sustainable dish supplies on the market are wood dish brushes with plant fibre bristles, wooden pot scrapers, scrub pads made from walnut shells, natural loofah sponges, and scour pads or brushes made from coconut fibre. These items are compostable at their end of life. Just double-check with your organics program first to confirm, or you could try putting them in a home compost. Either way, be sure you are buying something that is *entirely* made of natural materials. For example, I have seen scrub pads that are made from walnut and plastic combined. This combination would make them not compostable, unless you're able to rip the walnut and plastic pieces apart. If you don't live near a store that carries any of these items, the next best option would be to purchase online from a small business. Although I am always in favour of buying second-hand, cleaning and dish supplies are one case where it's unlikely to be possible or sanitary.

- If you use gloves for cleaning or hand washing dishes, you can buy reusable gloves that are also machine washable, which will have a longer lifetime than disposable, single-use plastic gloves.
- Just like with bulk foods, a funnel will come in handy if you are buying dish soap in a refillable format with your own packaging. A funnel is also useful if you're measuring out and making your own cleaning products with vinegar, baking soda, castile soap, etc.
- If you need new dishcloths or towels, look for ones made from non-plastic materials like cotton or linen. Swedish dishcloths, for example, are highly absorbent and made from cotton and wood cellulose, which makes them compostable. In contrast, cloths and dishtowels made from plastic materials, like microfibre cloths, typically have to go in the garbage when they reach their end of life. Given that cleaning is a mechanical action, the repeated contact between plastic dish materials and dishes themselves can also cause microplastics to shed. When replacing these types of items, consider the plastics inventory and subsequent recommendations on page 203.

You can apply many of these same considerations to how you clean the rest of your home. If you can't find a dish or cleaning option that's compostable or even recyclable, then prioritize longevity and reusability. Take dusting, for example. If you often buy disposable dusting cloths or pads, the next time you run out, replace them with rags, or even an old-fashioned feather duster. If you get several years out of one feather duster, you're reducing waste and reusing materials for as long as possible. The list of questions in the "Disposables and Reusables" chapter (page 180) is also a good reference point for evaluating any given cleaning and dish-related item before you make a purchase.

Earlier in this chapter, I told you that I hate cleaning. This is still true. I did not discover a newfound love of cleaning through this process. There are many things I'd rather be doing than scrubbing my kitchen floor, and I doubt that will ever change. But in approaching cleaning with a more sustainable framework, I found I hated it just a tiny bit less. Natural cleaning can actually be quite interesting. I like learning about different ingredients and how they can be used together. I can toss vinegar on a salad, pickle vegetables with it, and also use it to clean my floor and windows. That doesn't make cleaning the floor or windows more fun, but it certainly is kind of neat.

Takeaways

- Do an inventory of your cleaning and dish-related products to check for potential health and environmental concerns, using a database like EWG, for example. Be sure to responsibly dispose of any products you get rid of at the end of the process.
- Choose greener cleaners, but do your homework and check any "green" products through a database like EWG to confirm before purchasing. Be mindful of greenwashing!
- Clean with natural household ingredients like vinegar, lemon, and baking soda. Consult other resources to get a sense of how these ingredients work on their own and when combined.
- From castile soap to dish blocks to refillable options, see if you can source a more sustainable dish soap or dishwasher detergent.
- Implement the waste hierarchy for your cleaning and dish-washing supplies. Use the items you already have for as long as possible. If and when you need to replace them, consider longevity, material type, end-of-life options, and so on.

CHAPTER 15:

Appliances

THIS CHAPTER IS GOING TO COVER three main topics. First, we'll look at appliances and household energy use. Second, what to look for when buying an appliance. Last, we'll talk about how to prolong or deal with an appliance when it reaches its end of life. Before we get into any of that, though, we need to talk about energy more generally, and how it relates to the kitchen.

Appliances and Energy Consumption

From large appliances like the refrigerator and oven to small ones like a microwave and coffee maker, appliances are responsible for around 14 percent of energy consumption in the average Canadian home. Other household energy consumption comes from heating water, at 17 percent, and heating the house, which makes up the largest share at nearly 65 percent.

Whether we're heating our home or using the oven, household energy consumption is often linked to fossil fuels. Think back to what I said in the introduction: When we burn fossil fuels like gas, coal, or oil, greenhouse gases are emitted into the atmosphere. Burning fossil fuels is the number one source of human-caused greenhouse gas emissions, and one of the main reasons we burn fossil fuels is to create electricity and heat. When you think about this on a collective scale—millions of people heating their homes, using an oven, and more on a daily basis—it means a lot of fossil fuel. So, what's the solution? Voila! Enter renewable energy. If we want to reduce global greenhouse gas emissions and get to net zero, we have to move away from fossil fuels and transition to renewable sources of energy instead.

Renewable Energy

What is renewable energy? It comes from harnessing an abundant natural resource that can easily be replenished over and over. Examples include the sun, wind, and water. Since the sun continues to shine, we can harness that energy repeatedly—meaning it's easily renewed. In comparison, fossil fuels like oil and gas are considered non-renewable. Fossil fuels are not easily replenished, unless you have millions of years to wait around for more to materialize. There's also the fact that fossil fuels produce greenhouse gas emissions when burned, which we know is a problem. Since renewables don't have this same emissions issue, they're often described as "clean" sources of energy.

The broader transition to renewable energy goes way beyond the kitchen. It encompasses transportation, industry, and how we heat and cool our homes and buildings. It's also a discussion that's a bit beyond the scope of this book, but I'm bringing it up because it's important. I've noted some sources for further reading on this topic in the Resources List. If we bring this larger discussion back into a kitchen context, it becomes a conversation about appliances, how much energy we use, and where that energy comes from. Here's why: If the source of any given appliance's energy is *not* renewable, it means fossil fuels and greenhouse gas emissions are involved. In the kitchen, this primarily applies to where we get our electricity from for both small and large appliances, but it's also a consideration if you have a gas stove.

As it stands, Canada is a bit of a mixed bag when it comes to renewable versus non-renewable energy. Some provinces, like British Columbia, Manitoba, and Quebec, are much further along than others. Nova Scotia, Alberta, and Saskatchewan lag behind. There are a couple of online sources that break down where each province and territory is at with renewables; I've noted this in the Resources List. In Saskatchewan, I was unsurprised to learn that only 14 percent of electricity comes from renewables—mainly hydroelectricity—while the rest comes from fossil fuels. In this case, it would be safe to assume that most of my kitchen electricity use is probably coming from non-renewable sources. Next door in Manitoba, however, basically all of their electricity comes from renewables—almost entirely hydroelectricity.

If you're in a situation like mine, what are the options? One is to vote and advocate for the broader transition to renewable energy. Another option is to contact your utility provider and ask about the source of your home's energy. If it's non-renewable, ask if they have any sort of program where customers can choose to pay for renewables specifically. I called our utility providers in Saskatoon to see if I could opt for strictly renewables, but the answer was no (as of the time of writing). Depending on where you live in Canada, programs like this may or may not be available to you. At the very least, calling to inquire indicates that customers care about this issue.

Another option is to change the source of your energy yourself. For example, if you have the means and ability to install solar panels on your home, then great. Paul and I are keen to install solar at some point in the future. But while the cost of renewable technology has dropped drastically over time, doing this on your own can still be an upfront investment. That's why I'm not offering "install solar panels" as an official solution in this chapter. If solar is something you want to pursue, many other resources can help; I've noted a couple in the Resources List as a starting point.

If none of these options are viable—and even if they are—one of the best things you can do is reduce the amount of energy you're using. This is the option I'm going to focus on in this chapter, because it's something that you and I have more control over in an everyday sense. You can reduce the amount of energy you use in two key ways. The first is to use the appliances you already own more efficiently. The second is to prioritize buying an energy-efficient appliance whenever you happen to need a new one. Energy efficiency means that the appliance does the exact same thing as any other appliance, but it uses less energy in the process. In the solutions we will dive into the specifics of these two options for more efficient energy use.

I've given you all of this background information to help explain how the kitchen, energy use, and greenhouse gases are connected. Understanding this relationship is important. When I've used my oven in the past, for example, I did not necessarily make this connection. But knowing it now, I'm much more mindful about how I use my appliances. This is also a great example of how the kitchen can be a portal, connecting us on a daily basis to larger issues—even something as big as the broader transition to renewables.

You may be wondering whether you need to bother with any of this if the source of your home's energy is partially or fully renewable. The answer is yes. If everyone in Canada bought super-inefficient appliances or proceeded to use their appliances in the least efficient way possible, it would result in an unnecessary drain of energy. The link between household energy use, emissions, and climate change is much more obvious when fossil fuels are involved. But at the end of the day, we want to use the energy we generate efficiently and effectively, and avoid wasting it—regardless of whether it comes from a renewable or non-renewable source.

What You Can Do

Use the Appliances You Already Have More Efficiently

Many of us inherit our kitchen appliances in some capacity, either through renting or buying a house. The appliances in my kitchen are the ones that came with our house when we bought it. They're fairly old, so I doubt they're any sort of energy-efficient wonders. But whether or not your kitchen appliances are specifically energy-efficient ones, there are ways you can use—or not use—them more efficiently. I've put together the following list of tips, divided by appliance type. Reading through these tips makes clear that both knowledge and mindfulness go a long way in reducing household energy use.

Large Appliances

- If you happen to have a convection setting on your oven, use it as much as possible. Convection uses a fan to move hot air around in the oven continuously, which speeds up the cooking process. Meaning: Your oven won't be on as long to get the job done.
- Any time you use the oven, try to maximize the space. If I want to bake something, for example, I'll often wait until I know I'll be using the oven for a meal, or vice versa. That way I can bake banana bread and roast vegetables at the same time, which reduces the overall amount of time my oven is in use.
- This is fairly straightforward but worth noting: The more you open your oven or fridge door, the more hot or cold air escapes. The

appliance then has to work overtime to reach the proper temperature once you've closed the door.

- Before you preheat your oven, pause and ask yourself if preheating in that scenario is necessary. I preheat the oven only when baking, because most baking recipes call for an exact time at a certain temperature. Otherwise, I simply turn the oven on when I put the food in. I basically use the preheating time as cooking time. Since you'll be checking your food for doneness anyway, ten or so minutes of preheating time won't make much of a difference for most foods.
- In situations where you *are* preheating the oven, consider how far in advance it needs to be turned on. Preheating before you actually start a recipe is typically not necessary, especially if the oven will sit warmed up and unused for twenty minutes, for example. Only preheat once you're certain you'll be putting food in shortly.
- Choose pots and pans that are the same size as the element you're using, which will make cooking more efficient. Using lids on pots and pans also helps speed up the cooking process since the heat is contained. As with the oven, the more often you remove the lid, the more heat will escape.
- If you have a second fridge or freezer—or both—in your home, it's worth considering whether you actually need these appliances. If you use and fill the second fridge or freezer regularly, then it can be a practical choice. We have a small chest-style freezer in the basement that I use all the time; it's incredibly helpful for preventing food waste and preparing frozen meals. But if you don't actually use your backup appliances, or if you use them only occasionally and could easily consolidate their contents, then the amount of energy and money required to keep a second fridge or freezer running may not be worth it. Second fridges or freezers typically tend to be older models, too, which means they're less likely to be energy efficient.
- To ensure your fridge or freezer is closing properly, check the seal. This is very easy: Take a piece of paper, close the fridge or freezer door on it, and then try to pull the paper out. If you can remove or even shift the paper, then your seals may need to be replaced. If your fridge or freezer is not closing properly, it's essentially the same issue as regularly opening the door. The appliance is losing cold air constantly and has to work harder to make up the difference.

- Ensure your fridge and freezer are set at the proper temperatures, which helps with efficiency. Your appliances likely have a setting that notes optimal temperature, but for reference, the sweet spot is typically −18°C for the freezer and between 1.7° and 3.3°C for the fridge. You can also buy thermometers made for fridges and freezers. We have one in our fridge that clips on, which makes it easy to check the temperature.
- For tips on using dishwashers more efficiently, refer to page 253 in the "Water" chapter.

Small Appliances

- If you have a choice between using the microwave and turning on the oven, pick the microwave. Microwaves can use significantly less energy than ovens to get the same job done—up to 80 percent less, actually. Of course, the microwave doesn't work for everything. But for reheating leftovers or preparing certain foods, it is a good option.
- Beyond the microwave, most other small appliances also use less energy than the oven does. If you think about this logically, the oven is a much larger space, so it uses more energy to heat and maintain a certain temperature. Small appliances like a toaster oven, air fryer, or pressure cooker use less energy and can cut down on cooking time. Using small appliances instead of the oven is also particularly helpful in warmer months, if you want to avoid heating up your home—which also avoids having to cool it down by cranking up the air conditioning.
- For information on coffee makers and machines specifically, refer to page 220 in the "Coffee and Tea" chapter.

Check for Phantom Power

Another consideration for small appliances in particular is whether or not they use phantom power. Many household appliances and electronics continue to use energy even when they're turned off or on standby mode. Anything in your home that stays plugged in all the time could potentially be drawing phantom power. It's estimated that phantom power can be responsible for up to 10 percent of household electricity use—and the subsequent bill. This is a lot, especially if you're under the impression that "off" means "none." Phantom power tends to be more of an issue for appliances and electronics that are on the complex side, with programmable settings or an electronic control panel.

You can check whether or not your appliances and electronics are using phantom power with something called a watt meter. This little device plugs into a wall socket on one side, and then you can plug something else, like a small appliance, into it on the other side. The watt meter then takes various energy-related measurements. You can use it to check for phantom power use and for other purposes, too, like to figure out how much energy an appliance uses over time and how much it costs, for example. Although you can buy watt meters, many places lend them out. I was able to borrow one from the Saskatchewan Environmental Society in Saskatoon. Many public libraries across Canada lend out watt meters, which are also sometimes called energy meters or power meters. You could also check with your local Library of Things or any relevant environmental organizations. You'll probably get some instructions to go along with the watt meter when you borrow it, but there are many online guides that break down how to use them. I've noted a couple in the Resources List.

We always leave two small appliances plugged in on our kitchen counter: the microwave and the base for our Vitamix blender. Our drip coffee maker also permanently sits on the counter, but we unplug it daily when we're done with it. I decided to check all three of these appliances for phantom power using the watt meter, but I was surprised to find that none of them registered phantom power use. However, all three of these appliances are fairly simple and do not have any fancy settings or panels. I had fun checking them though—perhaps too much fun—so I took the watt meter on a little tour of the rest of our house. The TV was, in fact, a phantom power culprit. The most basic way to solve any cases of phantom power is to simply unplug the device in question after use. Another option is to use a power bar, which can be switched off when you're not using the device but doesn't require unplugging anything regularly.

If you implement any of the actions outlined in this solution or the previous one, it's worth tracking your utility bills to measure potential differences. See what your energy usage and related costs were before and after making changes. Saving money is a great side benefit to being more mindful about energy use—you can't go wrong with that.

Buy Large Appliances That Are Energy Efficient

This solution comes up only if you need to replace something. I'm not suggesting you replace all your large appliances right now just for the sake of saving energy. But doing so would be another example of a trade-off. Energy efficiency, or waste? For example, a machine dishwasher manufactured in 2019 is, on average, 60 percent more energy efficient than one made twenty years prior. Replacing an old machine dishwasher therefore might lower energy use, which reduces greenhouse gas emissions. On the other hand, it might create unnecessary waste. Although most people—myself included—would be inclined to continue using an appliance until it officially dies, this is still an interesting trade-off to think about. It also demonstrates the importance of buying energy-efficient models when you do need to replace something. If we're going to implement the waste hierarchy in order and hold on to things until they die, using less energy along the way is key. So shopping for an appliance is certainly one area where doing your own research and asking questions can go a long way. This is especially true for large appliances, given their longer lifetimes.

EnerGuide

If you go shopping for a large appliance in Canada, you'll likely notice the EnerGuide label. EnerGuide is the Government of Canada's rating system for evaluating energy consumption of various products. EnerGuide exists for more than just appliances—it also rates equipment for heating or cooling, for example. For our purposes, though, the EnerGuide label is required on large appliances sold in Canada like freezers, fridges, and machine dishwashers, along with electric ranges, cooktops, and ovens. When you look at an EnerGuide label for any appliance, you can quickly see how it compares with other, similar models for energy efficiency. EnerGuide ranks products based on a scale of least to most energy used per year. If you're comparing two different fridges, for example, referring to their EnerGuide labels is an easy way to pick the one that uses less energy.

Energy Star

In addition to EnerGuide, some appliances may also bear the Energy Star label. Energy Star was created in 1992 and is run through the United States Environmental Protection Agency, but it's since been implemented by other countries and has become an internationally recognized standard. So if you're looking for energy-efficient large appliances in Canada, you'll be looking for Energy Star ones. To be considered for Energy Star certification, a product has to voluntarily meet or surpass certain standards for energy efficiency. Once tested and certified, the product can bear the Energy Star logo. This is similar to other certifications we've talked about in earlier chapters. Except in this case, Energy Star is *the* certification—in contrast, there are numerous certifications you could choose from when picking out coffee or tea, for example.

In Canada, over eighty different types of products are eligible to become Energy Star certified, including freezers, fridges, and machine dishwashers. Within Energy Star certification, there is also a "Most Efficient" designation, which is like the A-list for energy efficiency. Energy Star appliances also work just as well—if not better—than conventional ones. So while you're saving energy, you're certainly not sacrificing anything else in the process.

How much of a difference do Energy Star appliances make? An Energy Star dishwasher uses about 12 percent less energy than one that isn't certified. Similarly, an Energy Star fridge uses approximately 9 percent less energy than a conventional fridge. When you consider how often a dishwasher gets used, or the fact that a fridge is constantly running, this does make a difference in reducing both energy use and greenhouse gas emissions over time. Depending on the type of appliance you're looking for, some models may have combined water and energy saving options too. While Energy Star dishwashers save energy, they also use about 30 percent less water than non-certified dishwashers, for example.

You can't find an Energy Star version of everything, though. Certain products can be excluded from certification if the energy efficiency of different models is essentially the same across the board. This is largely because for certain products, current technology has simply maxed out efficiency improvements. Examples of exclusions include stand-alone ovens and microwaves, as of the time of writing. There's also no Energy Star equivalent for smaller residential kitchen appliances, unfortunately. (There are other considerations when purchasing small appliances, which we'll talk about in the next solution.) Energy Star does certify plenty of other products outside the kitchen, however. It's worth exploring the options if you need to buy household goods like a computer, lighting, windows, or a clothes washer or dryer, for example.

In some cases, an energy-efficient version of an appliance may cost more than its less-efficient counterpart. But if you pay more up front, remember that you'll be saving money over time from reduced energy costs. Even still, this can be a hindrance when buying a new appliance—particularly if you weren't expecting to buy one. As a result, some places in Canada have rebate programs for buying energy-efficient options. I've noted where to find this information in the Resources List, along with helpful sources on both EnerGuide and Energy Star.

Ovens and Cooktops

There are some other general energy-efficiency considerations you can take into account when shopping for a large appliance. When picking out an oven, choose an electric one over a gas one. If the source of your home's energy is not currently renewable, it will ideally become renewable at some point down the line with the broader energy transition. If you buy an electric oven, you set yourself up for that transition. If you buy a gas one, you're committing to gas. When looking for an electric oven, you can also choose one that's convection.

Similarly, if cooktop types were sorted into a hierarchy from least to most energy efficient, gas would be at the bottom, followed by electric, and then induction in first place. Gas cooktops tend to lose heat while in use, making them about 30 percent efficient. Electric cooktops—with coils or a flat top—are more efficient at transferring heat; they're about 75–80 percent efficient. Induction does even better, at 85 percent efficiency. To make induction possible, though, you need cookware that's magnetic and ferrous-based. This is because induction uses electromagnetic energy to heat compatible cookware internally. It's sort of like the induction cooktop and compatible cookware become one in the process. This leads to a much more direct heating process, compared with gas or electric. As a result, induction also cuts down on cooking time. You can check your current cookware to see if it would be compatible by placing a magnet on the bottom of a pot or pan. If it sticks, it should be compatible with induction. Cast iron, for example, is compatible. Otherwise, buying additional cookware can be one disadvantage of induction.

Fridges and Freezers

If you're buying a new fridge or freezer, there are a couple of simple energy-saving options to consider. If fridge styles were put into a hierarchy for least energy used, those with a built-in freezer on top would come in first place. Next are fridges with the built-in freezer on the bottom and then, last, those that have a side-by-side design. Similarly, stand-alone freezers that are chest-style are more energy efficient than those that stand upright. All of this largely has to do with how the design affects the amount of cold air that can potentially be lost when the appliance's doors are opened. Additionally, fridges with water and ice dispensers tend to use more energy than those without.

Buy Small Appliances and Kitchen Gear Sparingly and Thoughtfully

As with large appliances—and everything else in this book, really—it's only necessary to consider buying small appliances and kitchen gear when you need to replace something. When it comes to small appliances and kitchen gear, though, buying things we don't need or won't use is pretty easy to do. It's easy to justify filling your kitchen cupboards with various small appliances or kitchen tools that were on sale, whereas it's hard to justify buying a fridge you don't need for those same reasons. In fact, in 2000, the average Canadian household had eighteen appliances. By 2019, that number had increased to twenty-five appliances. While these numbers aren't referring to kitchen appliances only, seven additional appliances per household is still a lot on a collective scale. I can think of more than a few small-appliance trends that have gained widespread popularity in the last five years alone, and I'm sure you can too. Seven additional appliances per household means more resources are needed to manufacture these products, and more energy is required to operate them. Then, once these appliances inevitably die, they all need to be either recycled or disposed of properly as well.

But if you've bought a new small appliance in the last five years because it was trendy, don't fret. The important thing is what you do with it. I don't think it's necessary to be a full-on minimalist to be sustainable. If you regularly cook, bake, and preserve food at home, then you need a certain amount of supplies to make that happen. But whether you use more or less kitchen equipment to get the job done, the guiding principle is still the same: Try to buy only what you genuinely need and will use. For some people, this may equate to more stuff than for others. What we really want to avoid here is buying new small appliances or kitchen gear regularly, using these things once or twice, stashing them away, and then donating them at some point down the line. At the end of the day, the goal is to actually use the things we own repeatedly, and for as long as possible.

If you are tempted to buy something new, or if you have something that breaks and cannot be repaired, then first pause and make a mindful assessment. Wait a few weeks before buying or replacing the item, and see if you can get by without it in the meantime. Can you use something else that you already own in its place? In the case of a replacement item, take a moment to consider if you even liked the original item. Did it serve its intended purpose? Was it easy to use and clean? If not, do some research and shop around. Another thing that's important for both small appliances and kitchen gear is versatility. Versatility checks the box for reuse and then some, because if something has multiple purposes, you'll use it much more frequently. It also means that if you have to replace the item in the future, you'll be looking to replace one item that does several things, rather than eventually replacing several items that do one thing each. I'll give you an example of this from my own kitchen.

Back in 2021, within the span of one week, my blender and food processor both quit working. These were cheap models I had owned for only a couple of years, and the cost to repair either of them would not have been worth it. But I used both of these small appliances on a near-daily basis for smoothies, chopping vegetables, blending salad dressings, making hummus, and more. I was sick of buying new models frequently, though—this wasn't the first time one of these small appliances had died on me after a short period of time. Although I took my past broken blenders to a small-appliance recycling drop-off, it still felt like a waste. So I decided I would see if I could find a better solution. While doing some browsing online, I came across the almighty Vitamix. I had always wanted a Vitamix but had dismissed the possibility in the past because of the price point. But since I was now in need of *both* a blender and a food processor, the price of the Vitamix was comparable. I did some further research on Vitamix models to confirm that the appliance could be used for both blending and food processing needs. Indeed, it could—and with that, I was sold. The model I bought also came with a seven-year warranty, which is simply unheard of for most small appliances.

Buying this Vitamix blender was easily the best kitchen-related purchase I've ever made. I still have it and use it almost daily. Functionally, I use it as a blender, food processor, coffee grinder, vegetable chopper, juice maker, and electric mixer. It can also be used for more unique purposes like grinding flour, making non-dairy milk, and blending nut butters. Over the years I have purchased a few attachments for the Vitamix as well, which has further expanded its versatility. Needless to say, I have certainly gotten more than my money's worth out of it. Meanwhile, I have avoided buying or replacing a number of other small appliances and kitchen tools—and my warranty hasn't even expired yet. My experience with the Vitamix is a gold-standard example of what I now look for when it comes to small appliances: It's multi-purpose, long-lasting, high-quality, and easy to use and clean.

Although this chapter is meant to be about appliances specifically, many of these same considerations can also be applied to kitchen gear, which is why I've tacked it onto this solution. I'll give you a kitchen gear example here, too, just so you can see what I mean. Let's talk about the equally almighty cast iron pan. My cast iron pan can be used on the stove and in the oven. It can also be used for both cooking and baking purposes. I can take the pan camping and use it over a fire if needed. Although my cast iron pan doesn't have a warranty, with proper care, it should last for *the rest of my life*. Damn—talk about a gold-standard example. Finding versatile small appliances and kitchen gear is kind of like taking a minimalist approach, but without paring down capability at all. If one item can do five things, you can still accomplish a lot—just with less.

Much of what I just said brings together many other concepts we've talked about in previous chapters. But I've also put together the following list of additional suggestions, which you can consider whenever you do need to purchase something.

- If you are buying a small appliance, choose a product that's simple in both design and settings. This can potentially help with longevity, being able to repair it if needed, and avoiding phantom power use. Many household small appliances now have electronic components in them; whether or not this is necessary is a question worth asking. In general, the simpler something is, the less that can go wrong.
- Check the warranty for any given product—or check if there is even a warranty in the first place. Reading warranties may be boring, but doing so can tell you a lot. It's also good to know whether repairing an item will potentially affect your warranty, or if the company even offers options should the appliance need a fix. Similarly, see if the company sells replacement parts. If some small part of your food processor or coffee maker happens to break, can you buy a replacement piece? Or are you going to have to bite the bullet and purchase the entire appliance again?
- Buy second-hand if possible. Check online marketplaces or thrift in person. Buying second-hand in this context is typically easier for basic small appliances or kitchen gear made out of materials like cast iron or stainless steel. If you need a random replacement part for

something and cannot get it from the company, check second-hand sources. You never know what someone else might be getting rid of.

- If you need a one-off item for a specific occasion, don't automatically buy it. See if family or friends have one you could borrow. Check with your local Library of Things or any other lending or rental service, if applicable. You could also create a group chat with people you trust for sharing kitchen tools and appliances. Sharing, borrowing, and renting are all part of implementing the waste hierarchy and creating a more circular economy. We don't all need to own one of everything.
- Consider the materials items are made out of and how that will contribute to durability and longevity. Items made out of cast iron, stainless steel, glass, wood, and ceramics are likely to last longer and hold up with continued use. This is also a consideration if you are avoiding plastics, since many small appliances and kitchen tools tend to have plastic components.
- If you are looking for high-quality items, check with restaurant or commercial suppliers. These types of suppliers often have durable cookware and kitchen gear made from long-lasting materials. While you might pay more, you'll gain longevity in exchange.
- Check if any given business or company has information available online regarding sustainability. This isn't something I paid much attention to in the past for small appliances and kitchen gear, but it is something I'll be looking for going forward.
- Read online reviews. See what other people are saying about how a product worked or changed over time, the quality of the design and materials, and what the customer service was like in situations where something went wrong. Online reviews are a gold mine of helpful information you wouldn't otherwise be able to find. Even if you're buying something in person, you can still do prior online research.
- The list of questions in "Disposables and Reusables" on page 180 may also be helpful here.

Repair Your Appliances

Before we get into end-of-life options for appliances, we're going to talk about prolonging an item's lifetime—in other words, repairing. This is one of the creative R's from the waste hierarchy that we briefly touched on in the "Garbage" chapter. If something can be repaired, it delays or even avoids eventual recycling or disposal. Since repairing keeps items in use longer, it helps us get away from a linear system and instead prioritizes one that's circular. Repairing also means that the amount of new stuff being sourced and manufactured can be reduced, which in turn reduces the overall environmental toll.

But where are you supposed to repair something? Can you even repair it anyway? First of all, the question of *if* something can even be repaired depends on what it is. How something is made, what the warranty dictates, how old it is, or how complicated the design or various components are can all affect whether small and large appliances alike are repairable. Some appliances may not be worth repairing, which really just means that the cost of repairing them either equals or exceeds the cost of buying a new one. This is obviously ridiculous—and I'm sure you have been in this situation before too.

As a result, repair is often not the default response. Just the other day, Paul and I were discussing how our microwave takes far too long to heat up a plate of food. It's inching toward eight minutes or more to reheat leftovers—something's clearly wrong. But despite the fact that I'm literally writing a book about sustainability in the kitchen, our conversation about the microwave completely skipped repair. We went straight to talking about buying a new one. I had to intentionally pause and reframe my thought process. Somehow, it's become ingrained in my mind that "This isn't working properly" automatically coincides with "Let's get a new one." If repair isn't the default response, it means circularity isn't the default either. So in reality, step number one here is taking a moment to consider repair as a valid and worthwhile endeavour.

From there, you have a few options. You could attempt to fix something yourself, depending on the complexity, or see if you can hire someone locally to do it for you. Large-appliance repair services are more common than small-appliance ones, but this will vary based on where you live. The other option is to see if there is a Repair Café near you. The concept of a Repair Café is simple: Volunteers with relevant skills are there to help you repair various household goods for free—including clothing, appliances, bikes, toys, furniture, and more. The Repair Café model was first developed in Amsterdam in 2009, but it's since expanded to many other places around the world. In Canada, there are numerous Repair Café locations across the country. The Repair Café website has a map that outlines locations; I've noted this information in the Resources List. Most Repair Cafés already have tools and supplies on hand for making the repairs possible as well. Since you bring your items to the Repair Café, this solution is less realistic for large appliances. But for small appliances, kitchen gear, and plenty of other household goods, Repair Cafés can be a wonderful way to extend product lifetime. You'll probably learn some basic fix-it skills in the process, too, which could come in handy later on. If something can't be fixed at the Repair Café, the volunteers may be able to provide resources on where you can go for additional assistance.

The Repair Café website also has a number of online do-it-yourself repair guides for various household items. As far as our microwave repair goes, this is as far as we've gotten. I sent Paul a few links to microwave repair guides from the Repair Café website. After browsing the guides, Paul identified a couple of potential causes for the seemingly excessive warming time. Should our at-home repairs fail—more accurately, Paul's at-home repairs, if I'm being honest—we will try taking it to Saskatoon's Repair Café. As a backup, I also found a repair service in Saskatoon that fixes small appliances. But when I called to inquire about microwave repairs, guess what the person on the other end of the line said? They said although they could try fixing it, microwave repairs typically aren't worth it. Yes—I am audibly sighing over here.

While you can always attempt to repair something, if it can't be fixed for reasons beyond your control, just know that this is not your fault. Not everything was made with repairability in mind. Meaning: Systems need to catch up. To achieve full circularity and prolong the lifetime of household items, products need to be designed and manufactured in a way that takes repair into account. Repair also needs to be a more consistent option across the board for household goods—not the exception. In Canada there has been some progress on this. In 2024, the federal government initiated a consultation process for developing a right to repair policy. Right to repair can mean a lot of things in practice, depending on the scope and implementation. But in general, this type of policy would ultimately make it easier for you and me to have our household appliances and electronics fixed when needed. Right to repair in Canada is still very much evolving—just like the compostable plastics labelling regulations we talked about earlier. I've noted some sources in the Resources List for further reading on right to repair in Canada, if it interests you. Until these types of changes are made, though, just do what you can to repair things whenever possible. And if repair is not possible, that's where other end-of-life options come into play.

Implement the Waste Hierarchy for End of Life

The end-of-life options for appliances and kitchen gear are similar to those for anything else that has reached the end of its useful life. If you have an appliance or kitchen item that still works well but you simply do not need it, you could donate it, resell it, regift it, give it away for free, offer it to a local Library of Things, or pass it along to a friend or family member who wants it. Even something like a working fridge or freezer may be useful to certain organizations near you. It's worth doing the homework to check, because all of these actions help to delay recycling or disposal by keeping useful items in circulation longer.

If you have kitchen gear or appliances that are no longer usable and can't be repaired, the next option is to try to recycle them. We've talked about recycling kitchen gear in particular in a couple of different chapters already, but the main point is that you typically can't put kitchen gear into your household recycling bin, even if it's made from materials like aluminum or plastic that are accepted in your curbside program. The only exception to this that I have come across was that egg poacher labelled as plastic #5, from my plastics inventory. If you happen to have all-plastic gear that has a #1 to #7 on it, you could contact your household recycling collection service to see whether they accept the item. Otherwise, kitchen gear often has to be dropped off at various depots that specifically accept and can properly handle the items in question.

Similarly, appliances do not belong in household recycling bins—although you'd have a hard time putting a fridge in your blue bin anyway. But this does happen with small appliances. Remember those electronics and the vacuum I saw being pulled off the conveyor belt when I did that recycling tour at Loraas Recycle? Those items did not belong at Loraas, that's for sure. Putting a small household appliance in your blue bin for pickup is just not going to result in any meaningful benefit. For starters, most appliances are made from multiple materials. The materials recovery facilities where household recyclables go are not set up to tear apart the various pieces of something like a vacuum or coffee maker. A mix of metal, plastic, glass, electronic components, and more means these types of items need to be handled separately from household recyclables like food packaging.

But if you put something like a coffee maker in your blue bin, what happens? The best-case scenario is that it gets pulled off the conveyor belt at the materials recovery facility before it can cause potential problems.

Perhaps the facility in question will then take that coffee maker to a small-appliance recycling depot, where it should have been dropped off in the first place. In a worst-case scenario, however, the discarded coffee maker ends up contaminating other recyclable materials, becoming a safety hazard to workers, damaging recycling equipment, or breaking into further pieces—which can be particularly problematic if glass is involved—and ultimately ends up going to the landfill. This is why it's so important to take the time to figure out where that coffee maker is supposed to go.

At this point in the book, there should be no surprises about the fact that recycling options for large and small appliances vary by province and territory. Large appliances may be recycled at drop-off depots or via pickup, or there may be designated recycling or transfer stations at the local landfill. You may also be able to take an appliance directly to a scrap metal dealer, depending on what it is. It's possible that you might have to pay a small recycling fee, particularly for appliances like fridges and freezers that contain refrigerant, which has to be safely removed prior to recycling. Some companies will take old appliances away when they come to deliver a new one. In that case, it's worth asking where they're taking it. The drop-off depots for small and large appliance recycling may also be located at the same place. Small appliances may be listed alongside household electronics for recycling, while sometimes they are noted separately. Small appliances typically have to be dropped off somewhere, though; pickup is not a common option. Some companies or stores may offer take-back programs for small appliances. London Drugs, for example, takes back small appliances for recycling if they were purchased at one of its stores.

Your municipality's Waste Wizard or similar search tool is a good place to start your search for where to recycle an appliance. I have outlined some other sources in the Resources List where you can find information on recycling small and large appliances by location. You may have to do a bit of internet sleuthing or make a couple of phone calls to find out what your options are, especially if the item you're trying to recycle is less common. This might also be the case if you live in a rural or remote area. If no recycling options exist near you, you could locate the closest available option and hang on to the item until a later date. If you know you'll be travelling to a nearby city in the future where there is a recycling drop-off, then plan for that. Paul and I keep a bin in the garage for one-off recyclable items, for example. We stockpile these things, and then we drop them off once a year or so.

Either way, doing what you can to keep your appliances out of the landfill is key. This is particularly true for small appliances. Since large appliances are so big, they're less likely to end up in landfills in Canada. Large appliances simply take up too much valuable landfill space, and they're much more obvious sitting in a pile of junk than a small coffee maker might be. But if recycling options are available, there's no reason appliances of any size should end up in the landfill—whether their presence is obvious or not. Appliances contain valuable materials that can be salvaged through recycling, like various metals, for example. Some leftover materials like bits of plastic, rubber, and foam may end up being sent to the landfill at the end of the recycling process. Even then, this is always going to be better than sending an entire coffee maker to the landfill, where it will continue to exist as a coffee maker for who knows how long. So if you happen to have an appliance—or any other household item for that matter—that's at its end of life, the best-case scenario is to deal with it as responsibly as you can.

Of course, the even-better-case scenario is avoiding end of life whenever feasible. Ultimately, the most sustainable appliances or kitchen tools are the ones you already own and reuse for as long as possible. If you don't buy something, then you don't have to store, maintain, repair, and eventually recycle or dispose of it either. Therefore, when implementing the waste hierarchy, priority number one will always be to refuse and reduce. Is this true even when something is on sale, or when a new small appliance makes a dramatic debut? Yup—it sure is.

Takeaways

- Become more mindful about how you use the small and large appliances you already own; use them more efficiently whenever possible.
- Borrow a watt meter to check if any appliances or electronics are drawing phantom power.
- When you do need to buy a new large appliance, consider both EnerGuide and Energy Star options. You can also take into account the various efficiencies of different cooktop types, or fridge and freezer styles, for example.
- Be mindful when you are buying small appliances and kitchen gear. Consider whether the item is versatile, if you actually

need it, how often you'll use it, if you could instead borrow it, and so on.
- Visit a Repair Café near you, or use an online guide for a DIY repair, to postpone an item's end of life.
- When an appliance has reached its true end of life, find a solution for responsibly dealing with it. Check with local resources to see what recycling options are available nearby.

WHAT'S NEXT?

Building Sustainability Beyond the Kitchen

IT'S A SATURDAY IN FEBRUARY 2025. Outside, the prairie air is bitingly cold, and the wind has a mind of its own, blowing snow around with impressive force. There will be snow shovelling to do later, that's for sure. But inside, I'm standing at the kitchen counter chopping vegetables for tonight's dinner: bean soup. The vegetables are almost entirely from our Box of Crop, the local food program we've continued subscribing to. Carrots, parsnips, onions, garlic, and green cabbage all sourced in Saskatchewan will form the soup's base. Earlier in the day, I also prepared a homemade stock from vegetable scraps and a chicken carcass—from a farmers' market chicken we enjoyed a few weeks earlier—that I had been saving in the freezer. The stock smelled heavenly as it cooked, warming the house with the sort of coziness that comes from anticipating a hearty, homemade meal on a cold day. While it simmered, I dug out my sewing machine from the basement. I proceeded to repair a few pieces of my and Paul's clothing that had torn over the past months—a dress, a sweater, and a pair of corduroy pants. One of our bath towels and a few of Rue's dog toys were in the mending pile too, much to Rue's dismay.

All of this seems rather ordinary to me now, but if you had witnessed me making soup on a Saturday in February a year or two prior, many details would have been different. The protein in the soup would not have been plant-based. The vegetables would not have been local. I probably would have made homemade stock, but not from frozen vegetable scraps. The chicken carcass would have been from a major grocer. Other minor details have changed too. For example, there are fewer plastics in my kitchen now. I had extra stock after making the soup, which I poured into repurposed glass jars to freeze. The spices I seasoned the soup with were all purchased in bulk using my own reusable packaging. They're now housed in mismatched jars in our spice cupboard—labelled and dated, of course.

After we ate dinner, Paul washed the dishes using the wood brush and natural soap that have become our dish staples. Tomorrow, I intend to spend some time planning our dinners for the upcoming week, taking food waste, packaging, plant-based eating, and more into account. I'm also about midway through a month of making it a priority to "eat what we already have." This is a little food waste reduction project I wanted to focus on before spring, to work with any food that has been shuffled from one of my food waste inventory lists to the next. Bread crumbs, frozen apples, raisins, canned salmon, dried kidney beans, and frozen pumpkin purée are my priority for our meals and snacks in the coming weeks. Apples and raisins are a classic combination, but is there a way I could combine kidney beans and bread crumbs? I'm still figuring that one out, but I'll get there.

Sustainability in an Unsustainable Culture

Needless to say, a lot has changed over the past year and a bit in our household—in both large and small ways. But do you know what the biggest difference has been? Me. Way back in the introduction, I expressed the sentiment that sustainability was for everyone. At the time, I believed it. But now that I'm at the end of writing this book, *I know it*. If I take a good look at that snowy Saturday in February, I can appreciate that on one hand, it may seem like an ordinary day. But on the other hand, there's a lot of time, mindfulness, and intention there—all of which now permeate my daily decisions. I have slowly but surely cultivated a foundation in our kitchen for the everyday to *become* more sustainable. There's magic in that, because it means you and I have the power to make even a small dent in the metaphorical climate change boulder—and that's the ultimate goal here, right?

In the introduction, I also told you the kitchen was a portal that could help connect us to wider issues of climate change. We've seen that concept play out throughout this book repeatedly. Addressing sustainability in your own kitchen can turn into greater action. This can include something as simple as mending your clothes on a Saturday afternoon, or it can include bigger actions, like getting involved in local climate change advocacy, or choosing to drive less and use public transit more. All of these actions stem from the awareness that emerges throughout the process of transforming the kitchen. So I want to take a moment to go over some of the consistent, overarching themes from *Building a Sustainable Kitchen*, because tackling food waste, plant-based eating, or reducing garbage are not the end of the story. While food and kitchens are an excellent starting point, they're not the finish line. I hope you'll carry these takeaways with you, once you've finished these pages and continue with your journey.

The Most Sustainable Actions Are Not Always What They Seem

Consider the following question: What are some examples of sustainable actions you could take at home in the kitchen? If you had to answer this question before and after reading this book, your answer would probably change. Common "before" answers may include recycling, shopping local, avoiding plastics, and buying reusable kitchen gear like stainless steel straws. Much of this falls back on a black-and-white picture of what is sustainable: Recycling is good. Plastic is bad. Reusables are good. Garbage is bad. Glass jars are good. Grocery delivery is bad. Local is good. Anything compostable is also good. Wait—what about compostable plastics? Are those good or bad?

Your examples of sustainable actions after reading *Building a Sustainable Kitchen* would probably highlight less popular, obvious, or visible choices, like reducing food waste, choosing plant-based foods, using what you already own, or reducing water and energy use. This just goes to show that what is popular is not always correct, and asking questions and doing your own research can be essential. Although broad conclusions can be drawn about sustainability in the kitchen—like how reducing food waste can curb methane emissions from landfills—all of the topics we looked at in this book are complex in their own way. I've said it before, but I'll say it again: Nuance is involved throughout.

While applying clear-cut labels makes it easier to categorize actions, doing so fails to capture the subtleties involved. For example, a layer of plastic on cucumbers can prevent food waste by extending the shelf life of those cucumbers by up to two weeks, compared with leaving them unwrapped. What about a tray of local meats on a reusable platter at an event? This appears to be the better choice than a fruit spread on a disposable plastic tray. Even if the entire fruit tray is eaten and nothing goes to waste, the leftover plastic is often viewed as a big, red X.

However, you and I both know by now that when it comes to sustainability, looks can be deceiving.

Throughout *Building a Sustainable Kitchen* I have tried to demonstrate that engaging with sustainability requires more than just buying some stainless steel straws, giving yourself a point in the "good" category, and calling it a day. There is so much going on with our food systems, our agricultural systems, our waste management systems, and how these systems intersect with the environment. I don't hate stainless steel straws—we own some and use them on an almost daily basis! But in reality, sustainability is rarely about buying more things. When you do genuinely need to make a purchase, you can likely find a way to make that purchase more sustainable. Otherwise, sustainability is about doing more with less, and making use of the things you already own for as long as possible.

Furthermore, to be truly engaged in this discourse, we need to go beyond straws. And I think teasing apart those black-and-white assumptions to get at the grey bits is really where you start to see true engagement. Thinking critically is essential to assessing what type of future we want to create. One-size-fits-all solutions and black-and-white thinking don't work in all scenarios and for all people, and if the future is going to be sustainable for everyone—as it should be—then we have to go beyond this type of thinking.

So just do your best to always aim for what is truly sustainable, even if it goes against the grain. If other people have questions about what you're doing, then kindly explain. You don't know until you know—and neither do they.

Individuals Can Make Sustainable Choices, but Systems Need to Catch Up

When I started this book, I did not expect to be playing a never-ending game of "Sustainable This or That?" But trade-offs have come up repeatedly. Reduce plastics or eat plant-based? Be more energy efficient or create less waste? Cut down on packaging or curb food waste? On and on it goes. Trade-offs are such a glaring symptom of why we need system-wide changes. Although individuals can do a lot to make more-sustainable choices, systems need to do more. Once we have broader system changes in place, individuals will be able to up their game in turn. Eventually, with both individual and system changes happening at the same time, these types of trade-offs will ideally start to dissipate.

Another symptom pointing to the need for system-wide changes is the fact that where you live determines much of what you're able to do. Where you can buy food, whether you can buy food without packaging, whether you can compost or recycle certain items, whether your home runs on renewable or non-renewable energy, and much more are all dictated to a certain extent by your location. This came up in numerous chapters. What that means is that individual and household sustainability is easier to achieve for some people than it is for others. No, this is definitely not fair. System-wide changes are therefore necessary to make sustainable options less dependent on where you live.

How do we tackle this one, though? Once you've done what you can in an individual context, you advocate for more. If we want to see system changes, we have to push for them. We'll talk about some ways to approach this shortly.

Sustainability Is an Ongoing Choice

If it's easier to do nothing and pick the less sustainable option, that's partly because the system was designed that way. If systems were designed to be sustainable, we wouldn't be having this conversation. Instead, engaging with all of this is an ongoing decision. You're going to have to repeatedly choose sustainability. Any time you're confronted with a trade-off, for example, you'll have to engage with these decisions again.

But on that note, I'd like to remind you that this is not about perfection. Let me ask you this: Would it have more impact in the long run if fifty people did everything in this book perfectly for one year, or if five thousand people did half of the things in this book, but for the rest of their lives? The second option, of course. And know that I'm not striving for perfection over here either. I have made numerous changes in my life as a result of writing this book, but there are still actions I'm working on, like reducing plastic food packaging and washing dishes water-efficiently. Additionally, I focus on eating plant-based as the main grocery priority. From there, I do what I can to maximize the impact by buying food that's local, seasonal, organic, or all of the above—but accomplishing all of these things at the same time isn't always feasible.

None of this means I should stop trying—not in the slightest. This is a journey. The definition of a journey is "travelling from one place to another." In this context, we're travelling from the unsustainable toward the sustainable. It won't be immediate and at times it won't be easy. But thankfully, perfection is not a prerequisite for travelling that road.

What Is the Most Impactful Action You Can Take from This Book?

When I was about halfway through working on *Building a Sustainable Kitchen*, I attended an event where someone asked me this question. I avoided answering it directly by saying that everything was important. I genuinely believed that was true at the time. I still believe that sentiment is true in some ways—particularly when actions are considered on a collective and cumulative scale. But as I neared the end of writing this book, I realized that some actions have more impact than others. I've also realized that while I had the luxury of treating this project like a part-time job for more than a year, other people don't have time for that. So I surrender. I will answer this question honestly, based on both my own observations and what research says.

The single most impactful thing you can do is shifting to a plant-based diet. The second is reducing food waste. The third is implementing the waste hierarchy *in order*, which permeates a number of areas. That last one is admittedly a bit of a cop-out on my part—it's borderline saying that everything is important. But let me explain.

If we look at Project Drawdown's work on climate solutions, the importance of both food and individual action is clear. On their list of the twenty most impactful climate actions an individual or household could adopt—you can find the full list in the Resources List—many of the actions you'd expect to see are included, like solar, public transit, and electric cars. But the number one action on their list is plant-rich diets. And guess what number two is? Reducing food waste, which happens to be a close second. These two actions top the list because they have an incredible capacity to reduce greenhouse gas emissions over time. Therefore, adopting these two actions can reduce your carbon footprint. On a collective scale, these two actions can help the world get to net zero and beyond.

Why does food have such significance? Although burning fossil fuels is the main source of human-caused greenhouse gas emissions, remember that the food system itself is responsible for about a quarter of all human-caused emissions. While we absolutely need to address fossil fuel emissions, we cannot ignore food system emissions either. The science makes clear that if we *do* ignore food system emissions, we will not meet our target of 1.5°C—or even 2°C—of warming, maximum. Emissions from every sector have to be addressed, including those from food.

Reducing food system emissions will involve system-level changes to how food is produced—things like fertilizer use and crop yields—but it also includes widespread, global efforts to shift to plant-based diets and reduce food waste. A clear line can be drawn from both what we eat and the food we waste to reducing greenhouse gas emissions. There is no way around this fact. Eating plant-based foods and reducing food waste have appeared repeatedly throughout *Building a Sustainable Kitchen*. This was not a coincidence—I did not write the book that way just for fun. These topics came up frequently because they're impossible to avoid. I don't think there's even a way for me to overstress the importance of these two actions—they're paramount.

But another thing also came up again and again throughout the chapters: implementing the waste hierarchy *in order*. This third action is key to adopting sustainability not only in the kitchen but in other areas of your life. Implementing the waste hierarchy in order means prioritizing refuse, reduce, reuse, recycle, and then compost. It also means considering the other creative R's on an as-needed basis: repair, rent, resell, refill, repurpose, etc. In practice, this means refusing what you do not need. It means reducing food waste, and composting the rest. It means reducing plastics and packaging, and recycling the rest. It means reducing energy and water consumption. It means reducing the amount of stuff you buy, and reusing what you have for as long as possible. All the while, it means treating the landfill as a last resort.

Following the waste hierarchy in the wrong order is a massively missed opportunity for addressing environmental issues. It also ironically wastes valuable energy, time, and resources. Furthermore, implementing the waste hierarchy starts with a mindset shift. You have to actively decide to follow it in the correct order, until doing so becomes your default response. Once you do that, the hierarchy will then permeate not only how you approach your kitchen, but how you approach everything else. And trust me when I say that everything else would certainly benefit from that. If you take a good look around, you'll notice that the waste hierarchy is implemented backwards here, there, and everywhere. If we collectively did a one-eighty on this, the positive impact on the environment would be tremendous.

Eating plant-based, reducing food waste, and following the waste hierarchy in order also tie in to the three takeaways about becoming sustainable in an unsustainable culture. For example, if you focus on eating plant-based and reducing food waste, it's possible that next to nothing about the way your kitchen looks will change—these actions may not be obvious or visible—but you *will* be making a difference. Similarly, implementing the waste hierarchy in order is about going against the grain. How these three actions look in practice will also vary depending on where you live and the options available. Additionally, they require very little to get started. You don't need an elaborate set-up, and you don't have to buy anything new.

Which brings us to a final takeaway about sustainability: It's not flashy or fancy. If I make a plant-based stew for dinner, featuring random food from my fridge and freezer to prevent food waste, then my dinner is a sustainable choice. On the whole, though, this action is fairly basic and mundane. Nobody is even going to know about it, except for Paul. But guess what? That's fine. Sustainability was never meant to be flashy or fancy. Perhaps this is why actions that are truly sustainable are not always the popular ones. Sustainability is like a set of unremarkable but necessary gears that grind behind the scenes, making our world work both now *and* into the future. It's like a clock that ticks dutifully in the background. But clocks and gears are not fancy or flashy. They're solid, reliable, and well designed. If a clock's working fine, you also stop noticing the tick after a while. You take it for granted. Until it stops working, that is. That's when you notice—and when you realize how much you relied on the sound.

What More Can You Do?

Once a sustainable kitchen is part of your routine, taking this book beyond the kitchen is a great next step. There are many concepts discussed throughout *Building a Sustainable Kitchen* that can be applied to the rest of your home. From there, these concepts can be applied outside the home in other realms and spaces.

But once you've tackled all that, what's left? It's time to push for system-wide changes. If this seems a bit scary, remember what I said in the introduction: Sustainability is for *you*. I also told you this was not an exclusive club and that there are no prerequisites for becoming informed and engaged. That sentiment still applies, whether we're talking about our kitchen or beyond. To help you get started on the beyond bits, I've compiled the following list of suggestions, and you're more than welcome to add your own too.

- Read books about sustainability and climate change. The more you read, the better informed you'll be. There are many excellent resources out there that explain what is happening to our planet, along with sources that detail how we can address and solve these challenges. I've included a general list of books for further reading in the Resources List. If you don't know what to read first, just start with any topics you feel particularly drawn to.
- Go outside and spend time in nature. It's important to remind yourself why the Earth is astonishing on a regular basis. The more often nature takes your breath away, the more connected you'll feel to the trees, the flowers, and even the bugs. This is a good thing for many reasons, including the fact that it can serve as motivation and inspiration to keep going.
- Vote. First, just vote in general. If you can vote, then you absolutely should. Second, vote for the people and policies that are going to do the best job at addressing the system-wide changes we need. If you and I cannot personally make these types of changes on our own in an everyday sense, then we have to support those who can.
- Get involved on a local level. Climate change feels like a massive, global problem, but there are things to address locally that tie in to the bigger picture. Across Canada, there are wonderful environmental groups, non-profits, organizations, and more that are doing solid groundwork. If no group exists near you, you could look for something to join remotely, or even start one yourself.
- Attend relevant events near you. Anything from free public lectures to documentary screenings to information sessions or workshops can be a great way to learn more, find out what's happening at a local level, and meet other like-minded people. You could also consider online options for these types of opportunities.

- If you are feeling overwhelmed about climate change, don't ignore these feelings. Climate anxiety is a very real thing. There are resources that can help, including therapists who specialize in climate anxiety. In general, I find the news can sometimes be overwhelming, but I don't experience those same feelings with other sources like books, so I turn to them more often than the news. I've noted some sources in the Resources List that may help.
- Implement other actions that reduce greenhouse gas emissions on an individual level, if those actions are affordable and accessible to you. To get where you need to go, walk, bike, or take public transit. If you need to purchase a vehicle, buy a hybrid or electric one if possible. If you can avoid or reduce air travel, do so. If it's an option, switch to renewable sources of energy, not just in your kitchen but for your entire home and beyond—like if you have a business or cottage, for example.
- Talk to other people about what you are doing and what you have learned. If you felt like this book was useful and informative, lend it to someone else. Tell other people in your life about any changes you're making. You could even encourage them to share in that process. At the end of the day, we need to be talking about climate change and sharing solutions—doing so is a solution in itself. Although it can be tempting to skip the hard stuff, not talking about climate change won't make it go away.

Other actions you could take also depend a bit on who you are and what your skill set is. Addressing climate change will require people from all backgrounds and walks of life—scientists, teachers, builders, creatives, engineers, journalists, academics, politicians, business owners, urban planners, health-care professionals, industry leaders, and more. But since I'm not an engineer or urban planner, I don't expect to be solving climate problems in those realms. It makes more sense if I lean into the things I do best, applying my own skill set to the climate change boulder. For the past year and a bit, that meant writing this book.

What does it mean for me next? I am actively figuring that out. You can also make a similar assessment for yourself. Consider the things you're good at and where your interests lie. Is there a space where those elements overlap? Figure out what that is for you, and there's your climate action. That's how you approach the boulder—that's how you make your dent.

The Future Is In Our Hands

As I wrote *Building a Sustainable Kitchen,* I had a small but mighty group of friends and family members reading over the chapters. I named this group my Feedback Crew. One of the people in the Feedback Crew, Aimee, who has been a friend since elementary school, sent me back the "Plastics" chapter one day with a comment that made me pause. She noted that this book was a form of activism. Although I gave her comment some thought, I ultimately rejected the notion. Activism? Me? Nah, no thanks.

But while I didn't see this book as activism then, I do see it that way now. I have taken a position on something I care about that will make the future better, and I am urging you to join me in that. In its most basic form, that's what activism is. I now feel bolder and braver in Aimee's assessment than ever before, mainly because the future I am hoping to make better isn't all that far away.

What stands between where we are now and surpassing 1.5°C or 2°C of warming? Humans. It's us. If I'm concerned about how the future looks should we surpass these numbers, then why am I waiting for someone else to tackle it? I'm a human too. What's more, I am merely a visitor on this big, beautiful Earth. I'm passing through in what will be a trivial blink of an eye, compared with the timelines Mother Earth is working with. Why should my actions cause her harm in the process? What right do any of us have to contribute to her demise?

None. There are no excuses or explanations for continuing to exacerbate human-caused climate change that are genuinely valid. The time for excuses and explanations has long been over. Especially because we know what we need to do to make the future work—to turn the unsustainable into the sustainable. In other words: We *do* have solutions. If you start reading more broadly on climate change, you'll quickly discover that other people have created possible road maps. We know how to address climate change with more than just gritted teeth and a big old sigh. We have research, science, technology, tools, and more. What we don't have is time.

So Aimee was right. This is activism. I accept that—no, I *embrace* that. I will rise to the challenge and ask the questions I know I'm not the only one thinking. How can we just allow this to happen? How can we be okay with watching our beautiful, extraordinary home slip away? I will not be a bystander in either creating or demanding answers to these questions anymore. I cannot sit back and pretend that everything is fine. I won't accept climate change as the end of the story.

And if you're reading these words, then I'm certain of this: You won't accept climate change as the end of the story either.

ACKNOWLEDGEMENTS

Thank you to TouchWood Editions, my literal dream publisher. I could not ask for a more supportive, collaborative, and personable team to work with!

To Tori Elliott: We both know that the manuscript I handed in to you was much different and longer than what I initially pitched. But you didn't say a word. Instead, you saw the potential in this book and just went with it. Thank you for that. And thank you for all the behind-the-scenes magic I know you pulled to make this book come to life.

To Nara Monteiro: If I was meant to have an editorial soul mate for this book, then it was you. Never have I felt so intuitively seen and understood throughout an editorial process. You just *got* this book in a way I could have only hoped my editor would. Then, you jumped head first with me straight into the editorial muck, and gave this book the scaffolding and clean-up it needed. We came out on the other side with a version of the text that was sharper than anything I could have imagined. Thank you for everything, and especially for your care and kindness along the way.

Thank you to Meg Yamamoto for copyediting with such keen attention to detail, to Emily Latimer for fact-checking this book so rigorously, and to Kate Kennedy for such careful proofreading. You were all incredibly thorough in your work—which I appreciate more than I can say.

Thank you to Alex Hennig for such a gorgeous interior and to Sara Oliveira for the beautiful cover illustration. The design of the book is truly perfect—inside and out. And a special thank you to Carolina Ortiz for all your marketing prowess in the promotion of this book. It has been an absolute joy working with you so far, and I look forward to everything that's yet to come.

To Elizabeth May: Thank you for the truly wonderful Foreword. I was over the moon when you agreed to write it, I was over the moon when I read it for the first time, and honestly, I'm still over the moon about the whole thing. I can't think of a better way or a better person to open *Building a Sustainable Kitchen*! Thank you for taking the time to read this book, and for your incredibly kind and inspiring words. It is a profound honour to have you be a part of this publication.

Thank you to everyone who took the time to speak with me for this book (see the full list of interviewees on page 335). These eighty plus conversations were instrumental. Not only did they fill in some of the gaps in my research, but they also helped me clarify and make sense of a number of ideas and concepts. Many of the people listed also answered follow-up emails, sent along helpful sources, or even had a second call to further clarify certain things. I cannot even begin to describe how crucial all of this was to the process. My sincere thanks to all of you for freely sharing your time, knowledge, and expertise.

A special thanks in particular to Sharon Howland for chatting with me multiple times, reviewing various sections of the text, and answering numerous emails about waste management. A special thank you to Kylene Goodman at Loraas Organics, and Dale Schmidt at Loraas Recycle, for the insightful and informative tours of the Saskatoon Loraas facilities. These tours were incredibly helpful to my research and writing process. Thank you as well to Angie Bugg for reviewing certain paragraphs in the "Appliances" chapter and for loaning me the watt meter. And a very special thank you to Dr. Karen Smith at the University of Toronto Scarborough for your careful review of the introduction. I am so grateful that you took the time to work with me to ensure that all the key science bits were just as they should be.

Thank you to my incredible Feedback Crew! You were all amazing: Aimee Carreiro, Ashlyn George, Aunya Zurevinski, Ellen Fitzgerald, Jazlyn Hansen, Keighlagh Donovan, Luke Hansen, Michelle MacGowan, Stephanie Mah, and Zac Carreiro. Thank you for volunteering your time to read over the chapters as I wrote them. Your thoughtful comments helped me identify what was working, what could be improved, and everything in between. I so appreciate all your time, effort, and support.

A special thanks to my Mom, Sandy Zurevinski, for reviewing the "Food Waste" and "Low-Waste Cooking" chapters, and for your long-standing insight on all things cooking and food safety. A special thanks to Shannon Josdal for your flexibility and understanding as I juggled writing and work. And a special thanks as well to Amy Jo Ehman, for writing a grant letter in the early stages of this process.

Books do not happen without supportive friends and family—of that I am certain. Thank you to everyone in my circle for showing interest and excitement about this book, and for understanding when I had zero availability to do anything other than research and write. In particular, thanks to my gals Ellen and Steph, to all my in-laws (grandparents, parents, and siblings-in-law included), to my grandparents, to my sister, and to my parents, for all your ongoing love and support.

And last, but absolutely not least, thank you to my number ones: Paul and Rue. Rue, you will never know how wonderful you are, but you truly make every day better. Plus, the fact that you come running whenever I open a can of chickpeas is just too perfect and too cute. Paul, thank you for embarking on this journey with me to make our kitchen more sustainable. When I first told you about this idea, you didn't even bat an eye—despite the fact that this was obviously going to impact you directly. Instead, you ate more plants, you installed the rain barrels, you gave up the plastic dish wand, and more. (Not to mention also initially editing the whole book—thanks for being my built-in lifelong editor!) A million thanks for walking this road with me and for being an incredible partner. All my love to you and our precious Rue.

RESOURCES LIST

For more information, helpful sources, and further reading, view the *Building a Sustainable Kitchen* Resources List at the following link:

https://www.naomihansen.ca/buildingasustainablekitchen/resourceslist

BIBLIOGRAPHY

Abeego. "Variety Square." Reusable Beeswax Food Wrap. Accessed January 5, 2024. https://abeego.com/products/variety-beeswax-food-wrap. [Chapter 9]

Accuardi, Zak, Susan Miller Davis, Karthik Mukkavilli, Jon Schroeder, and Chad Frischmann. "Plant-Rich Diets." Drawdown Climate Solutions Library. Project Drawdown. Accessed November 7, 2024. https://drawdown.org/solutions/plant-rich-diets. [Chapter 3]

Always Plumbing & Heating Ltd. Davis, Glenn. "What Are Low-Flow Faucets: Top Things You Need to Know." January 3, 2024. https://alwaysplumbing.ca/plumbing/what-are-low-flow-faucets-top-things-you-need-to-know/. [Chapter 13]

American Iron and Steel Institute. "Sustainability in Steel Recycling." Accessed August 21, 2024. https://www.steel.org/wp-content/uploads/2025/01/Steel-Sustains-in-Recyclability-Fact-Sheet-Updated-Jan-10-2025.pdf. [Chapter 7]

American Society for the Prevention of Cruelty to Animals. "Toxic and Non-Toxic Plant List – Dogs." Accessed May 11, 2024. https://www.aspca.org/pet-care/animal-poison-control/dogs-plant-list. [Chapter 12]

Antler, Susan. "The Secret to Successful Living – Healthy Soil!" Compost Council of Canada. Accessed June 3, 2025. https://www.compost.org/healthysoilpr/. [Chapter 12]

Anusha Siddiquia, Shahida, Nur Alim Bahmid, Sayed Hashim Mahmood Salman, et al. "Chapter Eight – Migration of microplastics from plastic packaging into foods and its potential threats on human health." *Advances in Food and Nutrition Research* 103 (2023): 313–359. https://doi.org/10.1016/bs.afnr.2022.07.002. [Chapter 10]

Association of Municipalities Ontario. "Ontario Baseline Waste & Recycling Report 2023." September 7, 2023. https://www.amo.on.ca/policy/land-use-planning-resources-and-climate-change/amos-baseline-waste-and-recycling-report-and. [Chapter 7]

Baker, B. P., C. M. Benbrook, E. Groth III, and K. Lutz Benbrook. "Pesticide residues in conventional, integrated pest management (IPM)-grown and organic foods: insights from three US data sets." *Food Additives & Contaminants* 19, no. 5 (2002): 427–446. https://doi.org/10.1080/02652030110113799. [Chapter 4]

Barles, Sabine. "History of Waste Management and the Social and Cultural Representations of Waste." In *The Basic Environmental History,* edited by Mauro Agnoletti and Simone Neri Serneri, 199–226. Springer International Publishing Switzerland, 2014. DOI: 10.1007/978-3-319-09180-8. [Chapter 8]

BC Hydro. "Refrigerators and freezers." Accessed January 16, 2025. https://www.bchydro.com/powersmart/residential/tips-technologies/fridges-freezers.html. [Chapter 15]

BC Hydro. "Small cooking appliances." Accessed January 16, 2025. https://www.bchydro.com/powersmart/residential/tips-technologies/small-cooking-appliances.html. [Chapter 15]

BC Hydro. "Stovetops and ovens." Accessed January 16, 2025. https://www.bchydro.com/powersmart/residential/tips-technologies/stoves-ovens.html. [Chapter 15]

Beitzen-Heineke, Elisa F., Nazmiye Balta-Ozkan, and Hendrik Reefke. "The prospects of zero-packaging grocery stores to improve the social and environmental impacts of the food supply chain." *Journal of Cleaner Production* 140, no. 3 (2017): 1528–1541. https://doi.org/10.1016/j.jclepro.2016.09.227. [Chapter 5]

Bellis, Mary. "The Inventor of Saran Wrap." ThoughtCo. Last modified April 29, 2025. https://www.thoughtco.com/history-of-pvdc-4070927. [Chapter 10]

Biodegradable Products Institute (BPI). "Commercial Compostability Certification." Compostability Certification. Accessed April 4, 2024. https://bpiworld.org/compostability-certification. [Chapter 6]

Biodegradable Products Institute (BPI). "How Composting Works." Composting. Accessed April 16, 2024. https://bpiworld.org/composting. [Chapter 6]

Biodegradable Products Institute (BPI). "Value Of Certification." Accessed April 16, 2024. https://bpiworld.org/why-bpi. [Chapter 6]

Birds Canada. "Explore Birds Canada." Accessed June 7, 2025. https://www.birdscanada.org/. [Chapter 12]

Birds Canada. "Planning Your Garden." Accessed May 3, 2024. https://birdgardens.ca/planning-your-garden/. [Chapter 12]

Birds Canada. "Plant Selector." (Search tool). Accessed May 1, 2024. https://birdgardens.ca/plant-selector/. [Chapter 12]

Bisinella, Valentina, Paola Federica Albizzati, Thomas Fruergaard Astrup, and Anders Damgaard, eds. "Life Cycle Assessment of grocery carrier bags." The Danish Environmental Protection Agency. *Environmental Project* no. 1985. February 2018. https://www2.mst.dk/Udgiv/publications/2018/02/978-87-93614-73-4.pdf. [Chapter 9]

Boehm, Sophie and Clea Schumer. "10 Big Findings from the 2023 IPCC Report on Climate Change." World Resources Institute. March 20, 2023. https://www.wri.org/insights/2023-ipcc-ar6-synthesis-report-climate-change-findings. [Introduction]

Bokashi Living. "How Does It Work?" Accessed April 15, 2024. https://bokashiliving.com/how-does-it-work/. [Chapter 6]

Bokashi Living. "What is Bokashi Bran?" Accessed April 11, 2025. https://bokashiliving.com/what-is-bokashi-bran/. [Chapter 6]

Bokashi Living. "What is Bokashi Bran?" Bokashi Composting Questions, Bokashi Community. Accessed April 11, 2025. https://bokashiliving.com/question/what-is-bokashi-bran/. [Chapter 6]

Bozzola, M., S. Charles, T. Ferretti, et al. *The Coffee Guide, Fourth Edition.* Geneva, Switzerland: International Trade Centre, 2021. https://www.intracen.org/resources/publications/the-coffee-guide-fourth-edition. [Chapter 11]

Breewood, Helen, and Tara Garnett. "Meat, metrics and mindsets: Exploring debates on the role of livestock and alternatives in diets and farming." TABLE, University of Oxford, Swedish University of Agricultural Sciences and Wageningen University and Research. March 23, 2023. https://doi.org/10.56661/2caf9b92. [Chapter 3]

British Columbia Ministry of Agriculture. "About Pesticides: Types, Names and Formulations." April 2017. https://www2.gov.bc.ca/assets/gov/farming-natural-resources-and-industry/agriculture-and-seafood/animal-and-crops/plant-health/about-pesticides.pdf. [Chapter 12]

Brommer, Eva, Britta Stratmann, and Dietlinde Quack. "Environmental impacts of different methods of coffee preparation." *International Journal of Consumer Studies* 35, no. 2 (2011): 212–220. https://doi.org/10.1111/j.1470-6431.2010.00971.x. [Chapter 11]

Brooks, Amy L., Shunli Wang, and Jenna R. Jambeck. "The Chinese import ban and its impact on global plastic waste trade." *Science Advances* 4, no. 6 (2018). DOI: 10.1126/sciadv.aat0131. [Chapter 7]

Brune, Sara, Whitney Knollenberg, Carla Barbieri, and Kathryn Stevenson. "Towards a unified definition of local food." *Journal of Rural Studies* 103 (2023). https://doi.org/10.1016/j.jrurstud.2023.103135. [Chapter 4]

BulkBarn. "Reusable Container Program." Accessed April 9, 2025. https://www.bulkbarn.ca/en/Reusable-Container-Program. [Chapter 5]

Bunn, Christian, Peter Läderach, Oriana Ovalle Rivera, and Dieter Kirschke. "A bitter cup: climate change profile of global production of Arabica and Robusta coffee." *Climatic Change* 129 (2015): 89–101. DOI: 10.1007/s10584-014-1306-x. [Chapter 11]

Canaan Group. "Shipping Food: A comprehensive guide to exporting and importing food in Canada." Accessed March 31, 2025. https://www.canaangroup.ca/shipping-food-in-canada/. [Chapter 4]

Canada Export Data. Basel Action Network. "2023 Annual Summary." Accessed July 25, 2024. https://www.ban.org/plastic-waste-project-hub/trade-data/canada-export-data-annual-summary. [Chapter 7]

Canada Organic Trade Association. "2021 Organic Quick Facts Data." 2021. https://canada-organic.myshopify.com/collections/2019-quick-fact-sheets/products/2021-organic-quick-facts. [Chapter 4]

Canada Organic Trade Association. "2024 Organic Quick Facts Data." 2024. https://canada-organic.myshopify.com/collections/2019-quick-fact-sheets/products/2024-organic-quick-facts-data/. [Chapter 4]

Canada Organic Trade Association. "Organic Standards." Accessed November 13, 2024. https://canada-organic.ca/en/what-we-do/organic-101/organic-standards. [Chapter 4]

Canada Organic Trade Association. "What is Organic?" Accessed November 13, 2024. https://canada-organic.ca/en/what-we-do/organic-101/what-organic. [Chapter 4]

Canada Safety Training Centre. "WHMIS Pictograms 2025: Your Guide to Hazard Communication." Accessed June 12, 2025. https://www.canadasafetytraining.com/Safety_Blog/whmis-pictograms-guide.aspx. [Chapter 14]

Canadian Food Focus. "What's in Season." Accessed April 2, 2025. https://canadianfoodfocus.org/whats-in-season/. [Chapter 4]

Canadian Organic Growers. "Is Organic More Expensive? A Winter 2024 Canadian Case Study." Accessed November 13, 2024. https://cog.ca/hub/is-organic-more-expensive-a-winter-2024-canadian-case-study/. [Chapter 5]

Canadian Organic Growers. "We Put Nature First: What is Organics." Accessed November 13, 2024. https://cog.ca/about-organics/. [Chapter 4]

Canadian Renewable Energy Association. "Energy Transition." Accessed February 15, 2025. https://renewablesassociation.ca/energy-transition/. [Chapter 15]

Canadian Wildlife Federation. "Gardening for Wildlife." Accessed May 2, 2024. https://cwf-fcf.org/en/explore/gardening-for-wildlife/. [Chapter 12]

Canadian Wildlife Federation. "Native Plant Encyclopedia." (Search tool). Accessed May 4, 2024. https://cwf-fcf.org/en/resources/encyclopedias/native-plant-encyclopedia/. [Chapter 12]

Canadian Wildlife Federation. "Neonics 101: Get the low down on the pesticide wreaking havoc on our pollinators." Accessed May 2, 2024. https://cwf-fcf.org/en/news/articles/neonics-101.html. [Chapter 12]

Carlsson Kanyama, Annika, Björn Hedin, and Cecilia Katzeff. "Differences in Environmental Impact between Plant-Based Alternatives to Dairy and Dairy Products: A Systematic Literature Review." *Sustainability* 13, no. 22 (2021). https://doi.org/10.3390/su132212599. [Chapter 3]

Carrington, Damian. "After bronze and iron, welcome to the plastic age, say scientists." *The Guardian.* September 4, 2019. https://www.theguardian.com/environment/2019/sep/04/plastic-pollution-fossil-record. [Chapter 10]

CBC News Calgary. "Where does all that garburator waste end up?" April 15, 2018. https://www.cbc.ca/news/canada/calgary/garburator-waste-calgary-1.4611658. [Chapter 13]

CBC News Saskatchewan. "Plastic bags no longer accepted into Saskatoon recycling bins." April 1, 2018. https://www.cbc.ca/news/canada/saskatchewan/plastic-bags-no-longer-accepted-into-saskatoon-recycling-bins-1.4601775. [Chapter 7]

CBC News Saskatchewan. "Saskatoon recycling carts roll out on Jan. 2." November 6, 2012. https://www.cbc.ca/news/canada/saskatchewan/saskatoon-recycling-carts-roll-out-on-jan-2-1.1232822. [Chapter 7]

Chang-Yen Phillips, Chris. "Canadians invented the garbage bag. Can we solve the mess they made?" *CBC News.* March 16, 2017. https://www.cbc.ca/2017/canadians-invented-the-garbage-bag-can-we-solve-the-mess-they-made-1.4024908. [Chapter 8]

Charlebois, Sylvain, and Janet Music. "COVID-19 Beef Consumption: New survey suggests one Canadian in four thought about cutting beef from their diets in the last 12 months." Agri-Food Analytics Lab, Faculty of Agriculture, Dalhousie University. May 13, 2021. https://www.dal.ca/sites/agri-food/research/covid-19-beef-consumption.html. [Chapter 3]

Charlebois, Sylvain, and Janet Music. "Local food: A new report suggests local foods are important to Canadians but not considered more nutritious, affordable or safer." Agri-Food Analytics Lab, Faculty of Agriculture, Dalhousie University. June 28, 2022. https://www.dal.ca/sites/agri-food/research/local-food.html. [Chapter 5]

Charlebois, Sylvain, Erica Finch, and Janet Music. "Household Organic Food Waste – COVID-19." Agri-Food Analytics Lab, Faculty of Agriculture, Dalhousie University. September 1, 2020. https://www.dal.ca/sites/agri-food/research/household-organic-food-waste---covid-19.html. [Chapter 1]

Charlebois, Sylvain, Simon Somogyi, and Janet Music. "Plant-based dieting and meat attachment: Protein wars and the changing Canadian consumer (Preliminary Results)." Dalhousie University. October 30, 2018. https://cdn.dal.ca/content/dam/dalhousie/pdf/management/News/News%20%26%20Events/Charlebois%20Somogyi%20Music%20EN%20Plant-Based%20Study.pdf. [Chapter 3]

City of Calgary. "Acceptable compostable bags and liners." Accessed April 9, 2024. https://www.calgary.ca/waste/residential/compostable-bags-liners.html. [Chapter 6]

City of Calgary. "Contamination in carts." Accessed June 26, 2025. https://www.calgary.ca/waste/residential/cart-contamination.html. [Chapters 6, 7, and 15]

City of Calgary. "Household hazardous waste residential drop-off program." Accessed October 31, 2024. https://www.calgary.ca/waste/residential/household-hazardous-waste-drop-off-program.html. [Chapter 14]

City of Calgary. "Residential waste drop-off facilities: City Eco Centres." Accessed January 16, 2025. https://www.calgary.ca/waste/drop-off/eco-centres.html. [Chapter 15]

City of Calgary. "The Calgary Composting Facility." Accessed April 5, 2024. https://www.calgary.ca/waste/residential/how-composting-works.html. [Chapter 6]

City of Calgary. "Using your blue cart." Accessed September 3, 2024. https://www.calgary.ca/waste/residential/using-your-blue-cart.html. [Chapter 7]

City of Calgary. "What can't go in your blue cart." Accessed April 18, 2025. https://www.calgary.ca/waste/residential/what-cannot-go-in-blue-cart.html. [Chapter 7]

City of Calgary. "What can't go in your green cart." Accessed April 9, 2024. https://www.calgary.ca/waste/residential/what-cannot-go-in-green-cart.html. [Chapter 6]

City of Calgary. "What goes where." (Waste search tool). Accessed June 12, 2025. https://www.calgary.ca/waste/what-goes-where/default.html. [Chapters 6, 7, 8, 9, 11, 13, 14, and 15]

City of Calgary. "YardSmart Lawn alternatives and groundcovers." Accessed June 7, 2025. https://www.calgary.ca/water/programs/lawn-alternatives-and-groundcovers.html. [Chapter 12]

City of Edmonton. "Change Homes For Climate: Your Guide to an Energy Efficient and Sustainable Home." December 2023. https://www.edmonton.ca/city_government/environmental_stewardship/change-homes-for-climate-guide. [Chapters 13 and 15]

City of Edmonton. "Eco Station Accepted Items and Fees." Accessed January 16, 2025. https://www.edmonton.ca/programs_services/garbage_waste/eco-station-acceptable-items. [Chapter 15]

City of Edmonton. "What Goes Where?" WasteWise App. (Waste search tool). Accessed June 8, 2025. https://www.edmonton.ca/programs_services/apps_mobile/wastewise-app. [Chapters 6, 7, 9, 11, and 13]

City of Halifax. "FAQ." Compost Matters. Accessed April 9, 2024. https://www.shapeyourcityhalifax.ca/compost-matters/widgets/10061/faqs. [Chapter 6]

City of Halifax. "Green carts, leaf and yard material." Garbage, Recycling, & Green Cart. Accessed April 9, 2024. https://www.halifax.ca/home-property/garbage-recycling-green-cart/green-carts-leaf-yard-material. [Chapter 6]

City of Halifax. "What Goes Where?" Halifax Recycles App. (Waste search tool). Accessed June 12, 2025. https://www.halifax.ca/home-property/garbage-recycling-green-cart/recycling. [Chapters 6, 7, 8, 9, 11, 13, and 14]

City of Ottawa. "Waste Explorer." (Waste search tool). Accessed June 8, 2025. https://ottawa.ca/en/garbage-and-recycling/recycling/waste-explorer. [Chapters 6, 7, 9, 11, and 13]

City of Saskatoon. "Be Water Wise." Accessed May 2, 2024. https://www.saskatoon.ca/services-residents/power-water-sewer/smartutil/be-water-wise. [Chapter 12]

City of Saskatoon. "Boulevard Garden Guidelines." March 2024. https://www.saskatoon.ca/sites/default/files/documents/community-services/parks/Boulevard%20Gardens%20Update%20Final%202024.pdf. [Chapter 12]

City of Saskatoon. "City of Saskatoon 2023 to 2025 City-Wide Waste Characterization Study — Spring 2024." Waste Data & Studies. July 19, 2024. https://www.saskatoon.ca/environmental-initiatives/solid-waste/waste-data-studies. [Chapter 7]

City of Saskatoon. "Curbside Organics (Green Cart)." Accessed April 4, 2024. https://www.saskatoon.ca/services-residents/waste-recycling/organics-food-yard-waste/curbside-organics-green-cart. [Chapter 6]

City of Saskatoon. "Curbside Residential Recycling (Blue Cart)." Waste & Recycling. Accessed September 3, 2024. https://www.saskatoon.ca/services-residents/waste-recycling/recycling/curbside-residential-recycling-blue-cart. [Chapter 7]

City of Saskatoon. "Household Hazardous Waste." Accessed October 31, 2024. https://www.saskatoon.ca/services-residents/waste-recycling/household-hazardous-waste. [Chapter 14]

City of Saskatoon. "Native Plant Species List." March 2023. https://www.saskatoon.ca/sites/default/files/UE-SA_CentreMedian_SeedBooklet5.5x8.5_PRINT-Booklet2%20%281%29.pdf. [Chapter 12]

City of Saskatoon. "Plastic Containers: 1, 2, 3, 4, 5, 6, 7 (PET, HDPE, PVC, LDPE, PP, PS, Other)." Waste Wizard. (Waste search tool). Accessed July 24, 2024. https://www.saskatoon.ca/services-residents/waste-recycling/waste-wizard. [Chapter 7]

City of Saskatoon. "Recycling Market FAQ." Accessed July 25, 2024. https://www.saskatoon.ca/sites/default/files/documents/corporate-performance/environmental-corporate-initiatives/waste-minimization/recycling-opportunities/recycling_market_faq.pdf. [Chapter 7]

City of Saskatoon. "Saskatoon Regional Waste Management Centre." Accessed June 26, 2025. https://www.saskatoon.ca/services-residents/waste-recycling/garbage/saskatoon-regional-waste-management-centre. [Chapter 15]

City of Saskatoon. "Waste Wizard." (Waste search tool). Accessed June 12, 2025. https://www.saskatoon.ca/services-residents/waste-recycling/waste-wizard. [Chapters 6, 7, 8, 9, 10, 11 and 14]

City of Toronto and Ipsos Public Affairs. "Solid Waste Management: Coffee/Tea Pod Usage and Disposal Behaviours." March 2018. https://www.toronto.ca/wp-content/uploads/2018/04/9612-SWM-Coffee-Tea-Pod-Research-Report-Apr6.pdf. [Chapter 11]

City of Toronto. "Household Hazardous Waste." Accessed October 31, 2024. https://www.toronto.ca/services-payments/recycling-organics-garbage/household-hazardous-waste/. [Chapter 14]

City of Toronto. "The Benefits of the Green Bin." Accessed April 9, 2024. https://www.toronto.ca/services-payments/recycling-organics-garbage/houses/what-goes-in-my-green-bin/. [Chapter 6]

City of Toronto. "Waste Wizard." (Waste search tool). Accessed June 12, 2025. https://www.toronto.ca/services-payments/recycling-organics-garbage/waste-wizard/. [Chapters 6, 7, 8, 9, 11, 13, 14, and 15]

City of Toronto. "What Happens to Organics?" Accessed April 9, 2024. https://www.toronto.ca/services-payments/recycling-organics-garbage/houses/what-happens-to-organics/. [Chapter 6]

City of Vancouver. "Boulevard gardening guidelines." Accessed April 30, 2024. https://vancouver.ca/home-property-development/boulevard-gardening-guidelines.aspx. [Chapter 12]

City of Vancouver. "Waste Wizard." VanCollect. (Waste search tool). Accessed June 26, 2025. https://vancouver.ca/home-property-development/waste-wizard.aspx. [Chapters 6, 7, 8, 9, 11, 13, 14, and 15]

City of Whitehorse. "Waste Sorting App." (Waste search tool). Accessed June 26, 2025. https://www.whitehorse.ca/living-in-whitehorse/wasteservices/sorting/. [Chapters 6, 7, 9, 11, 13, and 15]

City of Winnipeg. "What goes where? Use the Recyclepedia." MyUtility. (Waste search tool). Accessed June 26, 2025. https://myutility.winnipeg.ca/UtilityPortal/RecyclingGarbageYardWaste/whatGoesWhere. [Chapters 7, 9, 11, 13, and 15]

Clark, Michael A., Nina G. G. Domingo, Kimberly Colgan, Sumil K. Thakrar, David Tilman, John Lynch, Inês L. Azevedo, and Jason D. Hill. "Global food system emissions could preclude achieving the 1.5° and 2°C climate change targets." *Science* 370, no. 6517 (2020): 705–708. DOI: 10.1126/science.aba7357. [What's Next?]

Clark, Michael, and David Tilman. "Comparative analysis of environmental impacts of agricultural production systems, agricultural input efficiency, and food choice." *Environmental Research Letters* 12, no. 6 (2017). DOI: 10.1088/1748-9326/aa6cd5. [Chapters 3 and 4]

CoffeeSock. "Basket Style." Hotbrew Filters. Accessed May 30, 2025. https://coffeesock.com/new-hotbrew/basket-style. [Chapter 11]

CoffeeSock. "Sock Care." Accessed May 30, 2025. https://coffeesock.com/sock-care. [Chapter 11]

Cole, Matthew, Alessio Gomiero, Adrián Jaén-Gil, Marte Haave, and Amy Lusher. "Microplastic and PTFE contamination of food from cookware." *Science of the Total Environment* 929 (2024). https://doi.org/10.1016/j.scitotenv.2024.172577. [Chapter 10]

Coltro, L., Mourad, A., Oliveira, P. *et al.* "Environmental Profile of Brazilian Green Coffee." *The International Journal of Life Cycle Assessment* 11 (2006): 16–21. http://dx.doi.org/10.1065/lca2006.01.230. [Chapter 11]

Compost Council of Canada. "Backyard Compost Handbook." Accessed April 2, 2024. https://www.compost.org/wp-content/uploads/2024/03/Backyard_Composting_Handbook.pdf. [Chapter 6]

Compost Education Centre. "Backyard Composting." Factsheet Series #1. Resources. Accessed April 12, 2024. https://compost.bc.ca/resources/factsheets/. [Chapter 6]

Compost Education Centre. "Bokashi." Factsheet Series #10. Resources. Accessed April 15, 2024. https://compost.bc.ca/resources/factsheets/. [Chapter 6]

Compost Education Centre. "Compost Ecology." Factsheet Series #8. Resources. Accessed April 12, 2024. https://compost.bc.ca/resources/factsheets/. [Chapter 6]

Compost Education Centre. "Grow Your Own Food." Factsheet Series #24. Resources. Accessed April 29, 2024. https://compost.bc.ca/resources/factsheets/. [Chapter 12]

Compost Education Centre. "Pollinator Stewardship." Factsheet Series #15. Resources. Accessed May 1, 2024. https://compost.bc.ca/resources/factsheets/. [Chapter 12]

Compost Education Centre. "Rainwater Harvesting." Factsheet Series #16. Resources. Accessed May 2, 2024. https://compost.bc.ca/resources/factsheets/. [Chapter 12]

Compost Education Centre. "Trench Composting." Factsheet Series #5. Resources. Accessed April 15, 2024. https://compost.bc.ca/resources/factsheets/. [Chapter 6]

Compost Education Centre. "Tumbler Composters." Factsheet Series #9. Resources. Accessed April 12, 2024. https://compost.bc.ca/resources/factsheets/. [Chapter 6]

Compost Education Centre. "Vermicomposting." Factsheet Series #2. Resources. Accessed April 11, 2025. https://compost.bc.ca/resources/factsheets/. [Chapter 6]

David Suzuki Foundation. "Does vinegar kill germs?" Living Green. Accessed October 30, 2024. https://davidsuzuki.org/living-green/does-vinegar-kill-germs/. [Chapter 14]

David Suzuki Foundation. "Environmentally friendly ingredients for DIY cleaning recipes." Living Green. Accessed October 30, 2024. https://davidsuzuki.org/living-green/environmentally-friendly-ingredients-for-diy-cleaning-recipes/. [Chapter 14]

David Suzuki Foundation. "Green Cleaning Recipes." Queen of Green. Accessed October 31, 2024. https://davidsuzuki.org/wp-content/uploads/2017/10/queen-of-green-green-cleaning-recipes.pdf. [Chapter 14]

David Suzuki Foundation. "How to choose eco-friendly kitchen tools." Living Green. Accessed August 29, 2024. https://davidsuzuki.org/living-green/choose-eco-friendly-kitchen-tools/. [Chapter 10]

David Suzuki Foundation. "How to dispose of household hazardous waste." Living Green. Accessed October 31, 2024. https://davidsuzuki.org/living-green/dispose-household-hazardous-waste/. [Chapter 14]

David Suzuki Foundation. "How to shop for green cleaners." Living Green. Accessed June 11, 2025. https://davidsuzuki.org/living-green/how-to-shop-for-green-cleaners/. [Chapter 14]

David Suzuki Foundation. "How to use castile soap." Living Green. Accessed October 30, 2024. https://davidsuzuki.org/living-green/how-to-use-castile-soap/. [Chapter 14]

David Suzuki Foundation. "Make every drop count: Water conservation tips." Living Green. Accessed October 8, 2024. https://davidsuzuki.org/living-green/make-every-drop-count-water-conservation-tips/. [Chapters 13 and 15]

David Suzuki Foundation. "Searching for a List of Ingredients in our Home Cleaning Products." Executive Summary. September 2012. https://davidsuzuki.org/science-learning-centre-article/executive-summary-searching-list-ingredients-home-cleaning-products/. [Chapter 14]

David Suzuki Foundation. "Understanding food, body care and cleaning eco-certifications and labels." Living Green. Accessed March 26, 2025. https://davidsuzuki.org/living-green/understanding-food-body-care-and-cleaning-eco-certifications-and-labels/. [Chapters 3, 4, and 14]

Dorwart, Meg. "Why relying so heavily on recycling isn't the answer." Saskatchewan Waste Reduction Council. December 15, 2023. https://www.saskwastereduction.ca/blog/green-living/2023/12/14/why-relying-so-heavily-on-recycling-isn't-the-answer/. [Chapter 7]

Dow. "1953 Saran Wrap® ad: 'The Most Amazing Food Wrap Ever Developed!'" Dow's Vintage Ads. Accessed October 1, 2024. https://corporate.dow.com/en-us/about-dow/company/history/vintage-chemical-advertising/portfolio/saran-wrap.html. [Chapter 10]

Dr. Bronner's. "Dilutions Cheat Sheet for Dr. Bronner's Pure-Castile Magic Soap." Accessed June 17, 2025. https://www.drbronner.com/pages/dilutions-cheat-sheet-for-castile-soap. [Chapter 14]

Dr. Bronner's. "Soapmaking the Dr. Bronner's way." Accessed June 17, 2025. https://www.drbronner.com/blogs/our-customers/making-the-best-soap. [Chapter 14]

Dr. Bronner's. "What Is Castile Soap? What Are Its Uses and Benefits?" Accessed October 30, 2024. https://www.drbronner.com/pages/what-is-castile-soap. [Chapter 14]

Ecojustice. "Greenwashing 101: What is it and why Ecojustice fights against it!" March 11, 2024. https://ecojustice.ca/news/greenwashing-101-what-is-it-and-why-ecojustice-fights-against-it/. [Chapter 14]

Ecojustice. "Words to watch: A marketer's guide to spotting greenwashing in Canada." March 18, 2024. https://ecojustice.ca/news/words-to-watch-a-marketers-guide-to-spotting-greenwashing-in-canada/. [Chapter 14]

Ekvall, Tomas, Christin Liptow, and Sofiia Miliutenko. "Single-use plastic bags and their alternatives: Recommendations from Life Cycle Assessments." United Nations Environment Programme. 2020. https://wedocs.unep.org/20.500.11822/31932. [Chapter 9]

Ellen MacArthur Foundation. "Fixing the economy to fix climate change." Accessed June 21, 2024. https://www.ellenmacarthurfoundation.org/topics/climate/overview. [Chapter 8]

Ellen MacArthur Foundation. "What is a circular economy?" Accessed June 21, 2024. https://www.ellenmacarthurfoundation.org/topics/circular-economy-introduction/overview. [Chapters 6 and 8]

Elton, Sarah. "Local Food Movement." The Canadian Encyclopedia. Last modified April 23, 2015. https://www.thecanadianencyclopedia.ca/en/article/local-food-movement. [Chapter 4]

Energy Star Help. "Are there ENERGY STAR certified coffee brewers?" Accessed January 14, 2025. https://energystarhelp.zendesk.com/hc/en-us/articles/34537181534227-Are-there-ENERGY-STAR-certified-coffee-brewers. [Chapter 15]

Energy Star Help. "Are there ENERGY STAR certified ovens, ranges, or microwave ovens?" Accessed June 21, 2025. https://energystarhelp.zendesk.com/hc/en-us/articles/34537209557907-Are-there-ENERGY-STAR-certified-ovens-ranges-or-microwave-ovens. [Chapter 15]

Energy Star Help. "Does using a microwave over a regular oven save energy?" Accessed January 14, 2025. https://energystarhelp.zendesk.com/hc/en-us/articles/34537172723731-Does-using-a-microwave-over-a-regular-oven-save-energy. [Chapter 15]

Energy Star. "2021-2022 Residential Induction Cooking Tops." Accessed January 14, 2025. https://www.energystar.gov/partner-resources/products_partner_resources/brand-owner/eta-consumers/res-induction-cooking-tops. [Chapter 15]

Energy Star. "About ENERGY STAR." Accessed January 13, 2025. https://www.energystar.gov/about. [Chapter 15]

Energy Star. "Energy Efficiency." Accessed January 13, 2025. https://www.energystar.gov/about/how-energy-star-protects-environment/energy-efficiency. [Chapter 15]

Energy Star. "ENERGY STAR Impacts." Accessed January 13, 2025. https://www.energystar.gov/about/impacts. [Chapter 15]

Energy Star. "ENERGY STAR International Partners." Accessed June 21, 2025. https://www.energystar.gov/partner-resources/international-partners. [Chapter 15]

Energy Star. "How ENERGY STAR Helps Reduce Emissions." Accessed January 13, 2025. https://www.energystar.gov/about/how-energy-star-protects-environment/how-energy-star-helps-reduce-emissions. [Chapter 15]

Energy Star. "How ENERGY STAR Works." Accessed January 13, 2025. https://www.energystar.gov/about/how-energy-star-works. [Chapter 15]

Environmental Working Group. "Decoding Labels." EWG's Guide to Healthy Cleaning. Accessed November 1, 2024. https://www.ewg.org/cleaners/content/decode/. [Chapter 14]

Environmental Working Group. "EWG's Guide to Healthy Cleaning." Search database. Accessed between October 2024 and July 2025. https://www.ewg.org/cleaners/. [Chapter 14]

Environmental Working Group. EWG's Guide to Healthy Cleaning. "About EWG Verified." Accessed November 1, 2024. https://www.ewg.org/cleaners/content/ewgverified/. [Chapter 14]

Environmental Working Group. EWG's Healthy Living: Home Guide. "About Us." Accessed June 11, 2025. https://www.ewg.org/healthyhomeguide/about-us/. [Chapter 14]

Ethical Tea Partnership. "Climate Change and Tea." Briefing Paper. October 2021. https://etp-global.org/resources/climate-change-and-tea-briefing-paper/. [Chapter 11]

European Bioplastics. "What are bioplastics?" Fact Sheet. January 2016. https://docs.european-bioplastics.org/2016/publications/fs/EUBP_fs_what_are_bioplastics.pdf. [Chapter 6]

Fairtrade America. "Fairtrade promotes organic farming." May 28, 2025. https://fairtrade.net/us-en/for-shoppers/organic-vs-fairtrade-standards.html. [Chapter 11]

Fairtrade Canada. "Coffee." What We Certify. Accessed June 4, 2024. https://fairtrade.ca/what-we-certify/coffee/. [Chapter 11]

Fairtrade Canada. "FAQs." Accessed May 28, 2025. https://fairtrade.ca/faq/. [Chapter 11]

Fairtrade Canada. "Tea." What We Certify. Accessed June 4, 2024. https://fairtrade.ca/what-we-certify/tea/. [Chapter 11]

Fairtrade Canada. "The Fairtrade Difference." Accessed June 4, 2024. https://fairtrade.ca/the-fairtrade-difference/. [Chapter 11]

Fairtrade Canada. "The Fairtrade Standards." Accessed June 4, 2024. https://fairtrade.ca/standards/. [Chapter 11]

Farnsworth, Tracy. "What Are The Easiest Materials to Recycle?" Recycle Nation. October 18, 2021. https://recyclenation.com/2021/10/what-are-the-easiest-materials-to-recycle/. [Chapter 7]

Farrell, Mary H.J. and Paul Hope. "How to Tell If a Pot or Pan Is Induction-Compatible." Consumer Reports. October 6, 2022. https://www.consumerreports.org/home-garden/cookware/how-to-tell-if-a-pot-or-pan-is-induction-compatible-a3637108643/. [Chapter 15]

Ferguson, Mark. "The state of water security in Canada: A water-rich nation prepares for the future after seasons of disaster." University of Saskatchewan, Global Institute for Water Security and Global Water Futures. March 22, 2022. https://news.usask.ca/media-release-pages/2022/the-state-of-water-security-in-canada-a-water-rich-nation-prepares-for-the-future-after-seasons-of-disaster.php. [Chapter 13]

Fetner, Hannah and Shelie A. Miller. "Environmental payback periods of reusable alternatives to single-use plastic kitchenware products." *The International Journal of Life Cycle Assessment* 26 (2021): 1521–1537. https://doi.org/10.1007/s11367-021-01946-6. [Chapter 9]

Fillman, Emma. "Comprehensive Right to Repair: The Fight Against Planned Obsolescence in Canada." *Dalhousie Journal of Legal Studies* 32, Article 5 (2023): 123–156. https://digitalcommons.schulichlaw.dal.ca/djls/vol32/iss1/5/. [Chapter 15]

Flashfood. "The app for grocery's best kept deals." Homepage. Accessed April 8, 2025. https://flashfood.com/. [Chapter 5]

Foley, Jonathan. "Regenerative grazing is overhyped as a climate solution. We should do it anyway." Project Drawdown. August 15, 2024. https://drawdown.org/insights/regenerative-grazing-is-overhyped-as-a-climate-solution-we-should-do-it-anyway. [Chapter 3]

Foley, Jonathan. "What's the best climate action you can take? You tell me." Project Drawdown. May 15, 2024. https://drawdown.org/insights/whats-the-best-climate-action-you-can-take-you-tell-me. [Introduction and What's Next?]

Food and Agriculture Organization of the United Nations. "Tea." Markets and Trade. Accessed May 26, 2025. https://www.fao.org/markets-and-trade/commodities-overview/beverages/tea/. [Chapter 11]

Food and Agriculture Organization of the United Nations. "The Status of Fishery Resources." The State of World Fisheries and Aquaculture 2022. Accessed January 23, 2025. https://openknowledge.fao.org/server/api/core/bitstreams/9df19f53-b931-4d04-acd3-58a71c6b1a5b/content/sofia/2022/status-of-fishery-resources.html. [Chapter 3]

Forbes, Hamish, Eloise Peacock, Nettie Abbot, and Michael Jones. "Food Waste Index Report 2024: Think Eat Save." United Nations Environment Programme. March 27, 2024. https://www.unep.org/resources/publication/food-waste-index-report-2024. [Chapter 1]

Forbes, Hamish, Tom Quested, and Clementine O'Connor. "Food Waste Index Report 2021." United Nations Environment Programme. March 4, 2021. https://www.unep.org/resources/report/unep-food-waste-index-report-2021. [Chapter 1]

Fraanje, Walter, and Tara Garnett. "Soy: food, feed, and land use change." Foodsource: Building Blocks. Food Climate Research Network, University of Oxford. January 30, 2020. https://www.doi.org/10.56661/47e58c32. [Chapter 3]

Frischmann, Chad and Crystal Chissell. "The powerful role of household actions in solving climate change." Project Drawdown. October 27, 2021. https://drawdown.org/insights/the-powerful-role-of-household-actions-in-solving-climate-change. [Introduction and What's Next?]

Gallego-Schmid, Alejandro, Joan Manuel F. Mendoza, and Adisa Azapagic. "Improving the environmental sustainability of reusable food containers in Europe." *Science of The Total Environment* 628–629 (2018): 979–989. https://doi.org/10.1016/j.scitotenv.2018.02.128. [Chapter 9]

GE Appliances. "How Induction Cooking Works." YouTube. January 28, 2010. Video, 2:05. https://www.youtube.com/watch?v=QPd963cCeec. [Chapter 15]

Gephart, Jessica A., Patrik J. G. Henriksson, Robert W. R., et al. "Environmental performance of blue foods." *Nature* 597 (2021): 360–365. https://doi.org/10.1038/s41586-021-03889-2. [Chapter 3]

Geyer, Roland, Jenna R. Jambeck, and Kara Lavender Law. "Production, use, and fate of all plastics ever made." *Science Advances* 3, no. 7 (2017). DOI: 10.1126/sciadv.1700782. [Chapters 7 and 10]

Glass Packaging Institute. "Glass Facts." Accessed July 29, 2024. https://www.gpi.org/facts-about-glass. [Chapter 7]

Global Forest Watch. "Topics: Commodities." Accessed March 26, 2024. https://www.globalforestwatch.org/topics/commodities/. [Chapter 3]

Government of Canada. "2030 Emissions Reduction Plan: Clean Air, Strong Economy." Accessed January 27, 2025. https://www.canada.ca/en/services/environment/weather/climatechange/climate-plan/climate-plan-overview/emissions-reduction-2030.html. [Introduction]

Government of Canada. "Be on the lookout for greenwashing." News Release. Competition Bureau Canada. January 26, 2022. https://www.canada.ca/en/competition-bureau/news/2022/01/be-on-the-lookout-for-greenwashing.html. [Chapter 14]

Government of Canada. "Buying ENERGY STAR certified products." Natural Resources Canada. Last modified March 19, 2025. https://natural-resources.canada.ca/energy-efficiency/energy-star/products/buy-energy-star. [Chapter 15]

Government of Canada. "Canada's Dietary Guidelines: for health professionals and policy makers." Health Canada. January 2019. https://food-guide.canada.ca/en/guidelines/. [Chapter 3]

Government of Canada. "Canada's water use in a global context." Environment and Climate Change Canada. Last modified March 23, 2016. https://www.canada.ca/en/environment-climate-change/services/environmental-indicators/water-use-global-context.html. [Chapter 13]

Government of Canada. "Canada's Zero Plastic Waste Agenda." Environment and Climate Change Canada. Last modified February 27, 2025. https://www.canada.ca/en/environment-climate-change/services/managing-reducing-waste/reduce-plastic-waste/canada-action.html. [Chapter 10]

Government of Canada. "Change is here: Canada's ban on certain harmful single-use plastics starts to take effect this month." News release. Environment and Climate Change Canada. Last modified December 19, 2022. https://www.canada.ca/en/environment-climate-change/news/2022/12/change-is-here-canadas-ban-on-certain-harmful-single-use-plastics-starts-to-take-effect-this-month.html. [Chapters 9 and 10]

Government of Canada. "Consultation paper: Towards Canada-wide rules to strengthen recycling and composting of plastics through accurate labelling." Environment and Climate Change Canada. July 2022. https://www.canada.ca/en/environment-climate-change/services/canadian-environmental-protection-act-registry/consultation-rules-recycling-composting-plastics-labelling.html. [Chapters 6 and 7]

Government of Canada. "Cooking appliances." Natural Resources Canada. Last modified January 14, 2025. https://natural-resources.canada.ca/energy-efficiency/product-energy-ratings/cooking-appliances. [Chapter 15]

Government of Canada. "Definitions." Transport Canada. Last modified November 28, 2016. https://tc.canada.ca/en/dangerous-goods/definitions-0. [Chapter 7]

Government of Canada. "Dishwashers." Natural Resources Canada. Last modified March 19, 2025. https://natural-resources.canada.ca/energy-efficiency/energy-star/products/list-certified-products/dishwashers. [Chapter 15]

Government of Canada. "ENERGY STAR Most Efficient." Natural Resources Canada. Last modified March 19, 2025. https://natural-resources.canada.ca/energy-efficiency/energy-star/products/energy-star-most-efficient. [Chapter 15]

Government of Canada. "ENERGY STAR® rebates and incentives directory – Search." (Search tool). Natural Resources Canada. Accessed June 23, 2025. https://oee.nrcan.gc.ca/energy/products/energystar/why-buy/programs.cfm. [Chapter 15]

Government of Canada. "Energy Use in the Residential Sector." Natural Resources Canada. Accessed January 13, 2025. https://oee.nrcan.gc.ca/publications/statistics/trends/2019/residential.cfm. [Chapter 15]

Government of Canada. "Environmental claims and greenwashing." Competition Bureau Canada. Last modified June 5, 2025. https://competition-bureau.canada.ca/en/how-we-foster-competition/education-and-outreach/environmental-claims-and-greenwashing. [Chapter 14]

Government of Canada. "Estimating, Measuring and Monitoring Landfill Methane Technical Guidance Document." Environment and Climate Change Canada. Accessed March 21, 2025. [Chapters 1 and 6]

Government of Canada. "Faster and Further: Canada's Methane Strategy." Environment and Natural Resources. Last modified November 8, 2022. https://www.canada.ca/en/services/environment/weather/climatechange/climate-plan/reducing-methane-emissions/faster-further-strategy.html. [Chapter 6]

Government of Canada. "Food loss and waste." Waste Reduction and Management Division, Environment and Climate Change Canada. Last modified February 9, 2024. https://www.canada.ca/en/environment-climate-change/services/managing-reducing-waste/food-loss-waste.html. [Chapter 1]

Government of Canada. "Food safety and you." Health Canada. Last modified June 29, 2021. https://www.canada.ca/en/health-canada/services/general-food-safety-tips/food-safety-you.html#a6. [Chapter 2]

Government of Canada. "Food safety tips for leftovers." Health Canada. Last modified July 17, 2024. https://www.canada.ca/en/health-canada/services/general-food-safety-tips/food-safety-tips-leftovers.html. [Chapter 2]

Government of Canada. "Government of Canada launches consultation on right to repair to better meet Canadian consumers' needs." News release. Innovation, Science and Economic Development Canada. June 28, 2024. https://www.canada.ca/en/

innovation-science-economic-development/news/2024/06/government-of-canada-launches-consultation-on-right-to-repair-to-better-meet-canadian-consumers-needs.html. [Chapter 15]

Government of Canada. "Greenhouse gas sources and sinks in Canada: executive summary 2025." Environment and Climate Change Canada. Last modified March 21, 2025. https://www.canada.ca/en/environment-climate-change/services/climate-change/greenhouse-gas-emissions/sources-sinks-executive-summary-2025.html. [Chapters 1 and 3]

Government of Canada. "Household guide to water efficiency." Catalogue number: NH15-362/2014E-PDF. Canada Mortgage and Housing Corporation. 2014. https://publications.gc.ca/site/eng/9.825739/publication.html. [Chapter 13]

Government of Canada. "List of ENERGY STAR certified products." Natural Resources Canada. Last modified June 16, 2025. https://natural-resources.canada.ca/energy-efficiency/energy-star/products/list-certified-products. [Chapter 15]

Government of Canada. "Management of Canadian Aquaculture: Canadian Environmental Sustainability Indicators." Environment and Climate Change Canada. February 2023. https://www.canada.ca/en/environment-climate-change/services/environmental-indicators/management-canadian-aquaculture.html. [Chapter 3]

Government of Canada. "Net-zero emissions by 2050." Accessed January 27, 2025. https://www.canada.ca/en/services/environment/weather/climatechange/climate-plan/net-zero-emissions-2050.html. [Introduction]

Government of Canada. "Organic equivalency arrangements with other countries." Canadian Food Inspection Agency. Last modified August 12, 2024. https://inspection.canada.ca/en/food-labels/organic-products/equivalence-arrangements. [Chapter 4]

Government of Canada. "Organic production systems: General principles and management standards." Canadian General Standards Board, Standards Council of Canada. March 2021. https://www.publications.gc.ca/site/eng/9.894375/publication.html. [Chapter 4]

Government of Canada. "Organic production systems: Permitted substances lists." Canadian General Standards Board, Standards Council of Canada. March 2021. https://www.publications.gc.ca/site/eng/9.894398/publication.html. [Chapter 4]

Government of Canada. "Plastic waste and pollution reduction." Environment and Climate Change Canada. Last modified July 12, 2024. https://www.canada.ca/en/environment-climate-change/services/managing-reducing-waste/reduce-plastic-waste.html. [Chapter 7]

Government of Canada. "Pollinator protection." Health Canada. Last modified July 29, 2024. https://www.canada.ca/en/health-canada/services/consumer-product-safety/pesticides-pest-management/growers-commercial-users/pollinator-protection.html. [Chapter 12]

Government of Canada. "Provincial and Territorial Energy Profiles." Canada Energy Regulator. Last modified September 6, 2024. https://www.cer-rec.gc.ca/en/data-analysis/energy-markets/provincial-territorial-energy-profiles/. [Chapter 15]

Government of Canada. "Recipes for energy savings in your kitchen." Natural Resources Canada. Last modified June 10, 2025. https://natural-resources.canada.ca/stories/spotlight-energy-efficiency/recipes-energy-savings-your-kitchen. [Chapter 15]

Government of Canada. "Reducing methane emissions from Canada's municipal solid waste landfills: discussion paper." Canadian Environmental Protection Act Registry. Environment and Climate Change Canada. Last modified January 28, 2022. https://www.canada.ca/en/environment-climate-change/services/canadian-environmental-protection-act-registry/reducing-methane-emissions-canada-municipal-solid-waste-landfills-discussion.html. [Chapter 6]

Government of Canada. "Refrigerators." Natural Resources Canada. Last modified March 19, 2025. https://natural-resources.canada.ca/energy-efficiency/energy-star/products/list-certified-products/refrigerators. [Chapter 15]

Government of Canada. "Residential electric cooking products." Natural Resources Canada. Last modified March 19, 2025. https://natural-resources.canada.ca/energy-efficiency/energy-star/products/list-certified-products/residential-electric-cooking-products. [Chapter 15]

Government of Canada. "Right to Repair Consultation Document." Innovation, Science and Economic Development Canada. Last modified September 27, 2024. https://ised-isde.canada.ca/site/ised/en/right-repair-consultation-document. [Chapter 15]

Government of Canada. "Right to Repair Consultation." Innovation, Science and Economic Development Canada. Last modified December 12, 2024. https://ised-isde.canada.ca/site/ised/en/right-repair-consultation. [Chapter 15]

Government of Canada. "Safe food storage." Health Canada. Last modified April 11, 2024. https://www.canada.ca/en/health-canada/services/general-food-safety-tips/safe-food-storage.html. [Chapters 1 and 2]

Government of Canada. "Safely defrosting foods." Health Canada. Last modified June 9, 2017. https://www.canada.ca/en/health-canada/services/general-food-safety-tips/defrosting-safety.html. [Chapter 13]

Government of Canada. "Scare the phantom power out of your home." Natural Resources Canada. Last modified June 10, 2025. https://natural-resources.canada.ca/stories/spotlight-energy-efficiency/scare-phantom-power-out-your-home. [Chapter 15]

Government of Canada. "Single-use Plastics Prohibition Regulations – Overview." Environment and Climate Change Canada. Last modified April 18, 2023. https://www.canada.ca/en/environment-climate-change/services/managing-reducing-waste/reduce-plastic-waste/single-use-plastic-overview.html. [Chapter 10]

Government of Canada. "Solid waste diversion and disposal." Environment and Climate Change Canada. Last modified November 28, 2024. https://www.canada.ca/en/environment-climate-change/services/environmental-indicators/solid-waste-diversion-disposal.html. [Chapters 6 and 8]

Government of Canada. "Taking Stock: Reducing Food Loss and Waste in Canada." Waste Reduction and Management Division, Environment and Climate Change Canada. June 2019. https://www.canada.ca/en/environment-climate-change/services/managing-reducing-waste/food-loss-waste/taking-stock.html. [Chapter 1]

Government of Canada. "The EnerGuide label." Natural Resources Canada. Last modified December 23, 2024. https://natural-resources.canada.ca/energy-efficiency/product-energy-ratings/energuide/energuide-label. [Chapter 15]

Government of Canada. "The safe use of cookware and bakeware." Health Canada. Last modified December 4, 2024. https://www.canada.ca/en/health-canada/services/household-products/safe-use-cookware.html. [Chapter 9]

Government of Canada. "Understanding the date labels on your food." Canadian Food Inspection Agency. Last modified August 23, 2023. https://inspection.canada.ca/en/food-labels/labelling/consumers/understanding-date-labels-your-food. [Chapter 1]

Government of Canada. "Waste and greenhouse gases: Canada's actions." Waste Reduction and Management Division, Environment and Climate Change Canada. Last modified October 29, 2024. https://www.canada.ca/en/environment-climate-change/services/managing-reducing-waste/municipal-solid/waste-greenhouse-gases-canada-actions.html. [Chapters 1 and 6]

Government of Canada. "Zero plastic waste: the need for action." Environment and Climate Change Canada. Last modified February 12, 2025. https://www.canada.ca/en/environment-climate-change/services/managing-reducing-waste/reduce-plastic-waste/need-action.html. [Chapter 10]

Habib, Rishad, Katherine White, David J. Hardisty, and Jiaying Zhao. "Shifting consumer behavior to address climate change." *Current Opinion in Psychology* 42 (2021): 108–113. https://doi.org/10.1016/j.copsyc.2021.04.007. [Introduction]

Hansen, Naomi. "5 Ways To Reduce Food Waste At Thanksgiving." *Chatelaine*. Last modified November 23, 2023. https://chatelaine.com/food/how-to/reduce-thanksgiving-food-waste/. [Chapter 1]

Hansen, Naomi. "How to prevent food waste at home?" *Canadian Living*. April 27, 2022. https://www.canadianliving.com/home-and-garden/eco-friendly-living/article/how-to-prevent-food-waste-at-home. [Chapter 1]

Hansen, Naomi. "How To Shop At A Zero-Waste Grocery Store." *Chatelaine*. Last modified June 21, 2023. https://chatelaine.com/food/zero-waste-grocery-store-how-to/. [Chapter 5]

Hansen, Naomi. "Is There Such A Thing As Sustainable Beef?" *Chatelaine*. Last modified May 5, 2022. https://chatelaine.com/health/sustainable-beef-in-canada/. [Chapter 3]

Hansen, Naomi. "Sorry, Compostable Plastic Isn't Really Compostable (Or Recyclable). Here's Why." *Chatelaine*. Last modified August 12, 2024. https://chatelaine.com/living/compostable-plastic/. [Chapter 6]

Harris, Sophia. "We're drowning in reusable bags. Are bag profits preventing big grocers from adopting solutions?" *CBC News*. Last modified October 4, 2024. https://www.cbc.ca/news/business/reusable-bags-profits-1.7338237. [Chapter 9]

Harris, Sophia. "We're still stockpiling reusable bags. Big grocers have adopted solutions, but experts have concerns." *CBC News*. Last modified April 22, 2024. https://www.cbc.ca/news/business/reusable-bags-grocers-walmart-1.7178439. [Chapter 9]

Hawes, Jason K., Benjamin P. Goldstein, Joshua P. Newell, Erica Dorr, Silvio Caputo, Runrid Fox-Kämper, Baptiste Grard, Rositsa T. Ilieva, Agnès Fargue-Lelièvre, Lidia Poniży, Victoria Schoen, Kathrin Specht, and Nevin Cohen. "Comparing the carbon footprints of urban and conventional agriculture." *Nature Cities* 1 (2024): 164–173. https://doi.org/10.1038/s44284-023-00023-3. [Chapters 6 and 12]

Heard, Brent R., Mayur Bandekar, Benjamin Vassar, and Shelie A. Miller. "Comparison of life cycle environmental impacts from meal kits and grocery store meals." *Resources, Conservation and Recycling* 147 (2019): 189–200. https://doi.org/10.1016/j.resconrec.2019.04.008. [Chapter 5]

Heller, Martin. "Food Product Environmental Footprint Literature Summary: Coffee." Food Footprints Factsheets. Center for Sustainable Systems, University of Michigan. September 2017. https://css.umich.edu/publications/factsheets/food/food-footprints. [Chapter 11]

Herberz, Timo, Claire Y. Barlow, and Matthias Finkbeiner. "Sustainability Assessment of a Single-Use Plastics Ban." *Sustainability* 12 (2020). https://doi.org/10.3390/su12093746. [Chapter 9]

Hernandez, Laura M., Elvis Genbo Xu, Hans C. E. Larsson, Rui Tahara, Vimal B. Maisuria, and Nathalie Tufenkji. "Plastic Teabags Release Billions of Microparticles and Nanoparticles into Tea." *Environmental Science & Technology* 53, no. 21 (2019): 12300–12310. https://doi.org/10.1021/acs.est.9b02540. [Chapter 11]

Hounsell, Kayla. "Canadian municipalities struggling to find place for recyclables after China restricts foreign waste." *CBC News*. March 29, 2018. https://www.cbc.ca/news/science/garbage-recycling-china-plastics-canada-1.4586602. [Chapter 7]

Huismans, Mathilde and Fabian Voswinkel. "Electrification." The International Energy Agency. Last modified July 11, 2023. https://www.iea.org/energy-system/electricity/electrification. [Chapter 15]

Intergovernmental Panel on Climate Change (IPCC), ed. "Demand, Services and Social Aspects of Mitigation." In *Climate Change 2022 – Mitigation of Climate Change: Working Group III Contribution to the Sixth Assessment Report of the Intergovernmental Panel on Climate Change*, 503–612. Cambridge: Cambridge University Press, 2023. DOI: 10.1017/9781009157926.007. [Chapters 3, 7, 15, and What's Next?]

Inuvik Community Greenhouse. "About Us." Accessed March 31, 2025. https://inuvikgreenhouse.square.site/about-us. [Chapter 4]

IPBES. "Summary for Policymakers of the Global Assessment Report on Biodiversity and Ecosystem Services." Zenodo. November 25, 2019. https://doi.org/10.5281/zenodo.3553579. [Chapters 3 and 12]

"IPCC, 2023: Summary for Policymakers." In *Climate Change 2023: Synthesis Report. Contribution of Working Groups I, II and III to the Sixth Assessment Report of the Intergovernmental Panel on Climate Change*, ed. Hoesung Lee and José Romero, 1–34. Geneva: IPCC, 2023. DOI: 10.59327/IPCC/AR6-9789291691647.001. [Introduction]

Island Waste Management Corporation Prince Edward Island. "What Goes Where?" Interactive Sorting Guide. (Waste search tool). Accessed April 26, 2024. https://iwmc.pe.ca/sort/. [Chapter 6]

Jambeck, Jenna R., Roland Geyer, Chris Wilcox, et al. "Plastic waste inputs from land into the ocean." *Science* 347, no. 6223 (2015): 768–771. DOI: 10.1126/science.1260352. [Chapter 10]

Johnson, Bea. *Zero Waste Home: The Ultimate Guide to Simplifying Your Life by Reducing Your Waste.* New York: Scribner, 2013. [Chapters 8 and 14]

Kellogg, Kathryn. *101 Ways To Go Zero Waste.* New York: The Countryman Press, 2019. [Chapter 14]

Keurig. "Sustainability: For the Love of Coffee Today and Tomorrow." Accessed May 30, 2024. https://www.keurig.ca/sustainability. [Chapter 11]

Kumar, Amit and Maria Holuszko. "Electronic Waste and Existing Processing Routes: A Canadian Perspective." *Resources* 5, no. 4 (2016). https://doi.org/10.3390/resources5040035. [Chapter 15]

Kumar, Sunil, Kun-Yi Andrew Lin, Young-Kwon Park, et al. "Food loss and waste: A carbon footprint too big to be ignored." *Sustainable Environment* 8, no. 1 (2022). https://doi.org/10.1080/27658511.2022.2115685. [Chapter 1]

Kuschnig, Nikolas, Jesús Crespo Cuaresma, Tamás Krisztin, and Stefan Giljum. "Unveiling Drivers of Deforestation: Evidence from the Brazilian Amazon." Ecological Economic Papers, no. 32 (2019). https://doi.org/10.57938/dfd9efb0-c0b3-40fb-9f62-87963724da40. [Chapter 3]

Kustar, Anna, and Dalia Patino-Echeverri. "A Review of Environmental Life Cycle Assessments of Diets: Plant-Based Solutions Are Truly Sustainable, even in the Form of Fast Foods." *Sustainability* 13 (2021). https://doi.org/10.3390/su13179926. [Chapter 3]

Level Ground Coffee Róasters. "About Level Ground." Accessed August 8, 2024. https://levelground.com/pages/about-level-ground. [Chapter 11]

Level Ground Coffee Roasters. "Looking to get a question answered?" Accessed May 28, 2025. https://levelground.com/pages/q-and-a. [Chapter 11]

Life Without Plastic. "Silicone." Accessed September 28, 2024. https://lifewithoutplastic.com/silicone/. [Chapter 9]

London Drugs. "Recycling." London Green. Accessed June 26, 2025. https://www.londondrugs.com/believe-in-better/london-green/recycling. [Chapters 13 and 15]

Loraas Organics. "Our Compost." Accessed June 3, 2025. https://loraas.ca/compost. [Chapter 12]

Loraas Organics. "Our Facility." Accessed April 10, 2025. https://loraas.ca/our-facility-1. [Chapter 6]

Loraas Recycle. "Our Facility." Accessed April 15, 2025. https://loraas.ca/our-facility. [Chapter 7]

Love Food Hate Waste Canada. "Food Waste in the Home." FoodMesh. Accessed March 15, 2024. https://lovefoodhatewaste.ca/about/food-waste/. [Chapter 1]

Marsh, Kenneth and Betty Bugusu. "Food Packaging—Roles, Materials, and Environmental Issues." *Journal of Food Science* 72, no. 3 (2007): R39–R55. https://doi.org/10.1111/j.1750-3841.2007.00301.x. [Chapter 7]

Martinez-Porchas, Marcel, and Luis R Martinez-Cordova. "World Aquaculture: Environmental Impacts and Troubleshooting Alternatives." *The Scientific World Journal* vol. 2012 (2012). DOI: 10.1100/2012/389623. [Chapter 3]

Mathias, James A., Kimberly M. Juenger, and Jennifer J. Horton. "Advances in the energy efficiency of residential appliances in the US: A review." *Energy Efficiency* 16, no. 34 (2023). https://doi.org/10.1007/s12053-023-10114-8. [Chapter 15]

Melrose, Janet, and Sheryl Normandeau. *The Prairie Gardener's Go-To for Pests and Diseases*. British Columbia: TouchWood Editions, 2020. [Chapter 12]

Merriam-Webster, s.v. "biodiversity (noun)." Accessed November 14, 2024. https://www.merriam-webster.com/dictionary/biodiversity. [Chapter 3]

Merriam-Webster, s.v. "carbon sink (noun)." Accessed November 14, 2024. https://www.merriam-webster.com/dictionary/carbon%20sink. [Chapter 3]

Merriam-Webster, s.v. "incinerate (verb)." Accessed April 21, 2025. https://www.merriam-webster.com/dictionary/incinerate. [Chapter 8]

Merriam-Webster, s.v. "journey (noun)." Accessed June 29, 2025. https://www.merriam-webster.com/dictionary/journey. [What's Next?]

Merriam-Webster, s.v. "rewilding (noun)." Accessed June 6, 2025. https://www.merriam-webster.com/dictionary/rewilding. [Chapter 12]

Merriam-Webster, s.v. "ruminant (noun)." Accessed March 26, 2025. https://www.merriam-webster.com/dictionary/ruminant. [Chapter 3]

Merriam-Webster, s.v. "sustainable (adjective)." Accessed January 27, 2025. https://www.merriam-webster.com/dictionary/sustainable. [Introduction]

Merriam-Webster, s.v. "sustained (adjective)." Accessed January 27, 2025. https://www.merriam-webster.com/dictionary/sustained. [Introduction]

Metro Vancouver and National Zero Waste Council. "Circular Economy: The Issue." Accessed June 21, 2024. https://nzwc.ca/focus-areas/circular-economy/issue/Pages/default.aspx. [Chapters 6 and 8]

Metro Vancouver. "What to Do With Confusing Items: Food Scraps Recycling." Accessed April 29, 2025. https://metrovancouver.org/foodscraps/confusing-items. [Chapter 9]

Middle Tennessee State University. "The Origin of the Recycling Symbol." Center for Energy Efficiency. Accessed April 14, 2025. https://cee.mtsu.edu/3rs/. [Chapter 7]

Miller, Shelie A. "Five Misperceptions Surrounding the Environmental Impacts of Single-Use Plastic." *Environmental Science & Technology* 54, no. 22 (2020): 14143–14151. https://doi.org/10.1021/acs.est.0c05295. [Chapters 3, 5, and 9]

Minogue, Kristen. "Do We Live in the Plasticene? 12 Words to Know for the Age of Plastics." *Shorelines*. Smithsonian Environmental Research Center. January 15, 2020. https://sercblog.si.edu/do-we-live-in-the-plasticene-12-words-to-know-for-the-age-of-plastics/. [Chapter 10]

Monterey Bay Aquarium Seafood Watch. "The Super Green List of seafood no-brainers." Accessed January 23, 2025. https://www.seafoodwatch.org/seafood-basics/sustainable-healthy-fish. [Chapter 3]

Montgomery, Wren, Tom Lyon, Julian Barg, and Matthew Lynch. "Greenwashing 3.0." Issue Brief. Ivey Centre for Building Sustainable Value and University of Michigan Erb Institute. October 2023. https://online.flippingbook.com/view/175998623/. [Chapter 14]

Morgan, John P. "Gardening with Native Canadian Plants." Canadian Wildlife Federation. Accessed September 26, 2024. https://cwf-fcf.org/en/news/articles/gardening-with-native-canadian-plants.html. [Chapter 12]

Moseman, Andrew and Jessika Trancik. "Why do we compare methane to carbon dioxide over a 100-year timeframe? Are we underrating the importance of methane emissions?" Ask MIT Climate. MIT Climate Portal. Last modified January 4, 2024. https://climate.mit.edu/ask-mit/why-do-we-compare-methane-carbon-dioxide-over-100-year-timeframe-are-we-underrating. [Chapter 1]

Mukhopadhyay, Mainaak and Tapan Kumar Mondal. "Cultivation, Improvement, and Environmental Impacts of Tea." *Oxford Research Encyclopedia of Environmental Science.* April 26, 2017. https://doi.org/10.1093/acrefore/9780199389414.013.373. [Chapter 11]

National Oceanic and Atmospheric Administration. "What is nutrient pollution?" National Ocean Service. Last modified June 16, 2024. https://oceanservice.noaa.gov/facts/nutpollution.html. [Chapter 12]

National Zero Waste Council and Love Food Hate Waste Canada. "Food Waste in Canadian Homes: A Snapshot of Current Consumer Behaviours and Attitudes." September 2020. [Chapter 1]

National Zero Waste Council and Metro Vancouver. "Focus Areas: Circular Economy." Accessed June 21, 2024. https://nzwc.ca/focus-areas/circular-economy/Pages/default.aspx. [Chapter 8]

NatureBee. "Beeswax Wrap Variety Set." Accessed January 5, 2024. https://www.naturebeewraps.ca/collections/beeswax-wraps/products/beeswax-wrap-variety-set-pink-nature-bee. [Chapter 9]

Nayanathara Thathsarani Pilapitiya, P.G.C. and Amila Sandaruwan Ratnayake. "The world of plastic waste: A review." *Cleaner Materials* 11 (2024). https://doi.org/10.1016/j.clema.2024.100220. [Chapter 10]

Nazari, Laleh, Chunbao (Charles) Xu, and Madhumita B. Ray. *Advanced and Emerging Technologies for Resource Recovery from Wastes.* Green Chemistry and Sustainable Technology. Springer Nature Singapore, 2021. https://doi.org/10.1007/978-981-15-9267-6_2. [Chapters 6, 7, and 8]

Nespresso. "Our Commitment to Recycling & Circularity." Accessed May 30, 2024. https://www.nespresso.com/ca/en/sustainability/capsule-recycle. [Chapter 11]

Nespresso. "The Nespresso Recycling Program." Accessed May 30, 2024. https://www.nespresso.com/ca/en/irecycle. [Chapter 11]

NU Grocery. "How it works." Accessed April 8, 2025. https://nugrocery.com/pages/how-it-works. [Chapter 5]

O'Connor, Liam. "Sarcan now taking flexible plastics and foam packaging at depots." *CBC News Saskatchewan.* December 4, 2024. https://www.cbc.ca/news/canada/saskatchewan/sarcan-accepting-flexible-plastics-foam-packaging-1.7400672. [Chapter 7]

O'Connor, Ryan. "Blue Box." The Canadian Encyclopedia. Last modified July 13, 2021. https://www.thecanadianencyclopedia.ca/en/article/blue-box. [Chapter 7]

Odd Bunch. "Our Story." Accessed April 8, 2025. https://www.oddbunch.ca/pages/about. [Chapter 5]

Organic Council of Ontario. "Canada Organic vs. USDA Organic." August 29, 2019. https://organiccouncil.ca/canada-organic-vs-usda-organic/. [Chapter 4]

Organic Council of Ontario. "Why is Organic Food More Expensive?" August 22, 2017. https://organiccouncil.ca/9171/. [Chapter 4]

Original Family Farm. "A long history of farming in Saskatchewan." Accessed November 11, 2024. https://www.originalfamilyfarm.com/about/index. [Chapter 4]

Original Family Farm. "Products." Accessed November 11, 2024. https://www.originalfamilyfarm.com/products/index. [Chapter 4]

Our World in Data. "Grocery bag comparisons for greenhouse gas emissions." Accessed January 16, 2024. https://ourworldindata.org/grapher/grocery-bag-comparisons-ghg. [Chapter 9]

Pedersen, Katie, Eric Szeto, David Common, and Luke Denne. "We asked 3 companies to recycle Canadian plastic and secretly tracked it. Only 1 company recycled the material." *CBC News.* Last modified October 9, 2019. https://www.cbc.ca/news/science/marketplace-recycling-trackers-b-c-blue-box-1.5299176. [Chapter 7]

Petruzzello, Melissa. "water scarcity." *Encyclopedia Britannica.* Last modified June 10, 2025. https://www.britannica.com/topic/water-scarcity. [Chapter 13]

Pollinator Partnership Canada. "About Pollinators." Accessed May 1, 2024. https://pollinatorpartnership.ca/en/about-pollinators. [Chapter 12]

Pollinator Partnership Canada. "Find Your Roots." (Search tool). Accessed May 4, 2024. https://pollinatorpartnership.ca/en/find-your-roots. [Chapter 12]

Pollinator Partnership Canada. "Threats to pollinators." Accessed May 1, 2024. https://pollinatorpartnership.ca/en/threats-to-pollinators. [Chapter 12]

Pollinator Partnership Canada. "Who Are The Pollinators?" Accessed May 1, 2024. https://pollinatorpartnership.ca/en/who-are-the-pollinators. [Chapter 12]

Poore, J., and T. Nemecek. "Reducing food's environmental impacts through producers and consumers." *Science* 360, no. 6392 (2018): 987–992. DOI: 10.1126/science.aaq0216. [Chapters 3, 4, 5, and 11]

Porras, Gabriela, Gregory Keoleian, Geoffrey Lewis, and Nagapooja Seeba. "A guide to household manual and machine dishwashing through a life cycle perspective." *Environmental Research Communications* 2, no. 2 (2020). https://doi.org/10.1088/2515-7620/ab716b. [Chapter 13]

Poskin, Ashley. "We Tried 5 Methods for Removing Sticky Stickers — And We Were Blown Away by the Winner." The Kitchn. Last modified October 24, 2023. https://www.thekitchn.com/best-way-remove-sticky-stickers-23201250. [Chapter 14]

Project Drawdown. "About Project Drawdown." Accessed March 19, 2025. https://drawdown.org/about. [Introduction]

Project Drawdown. "Advancing science-based solutions and sharing insights at the intersection of food, agriculture, land use, and climate change." Drawdown Food. Accessed November 7, 2024. https://drawdown.org/programs/drawdown-science/food. [Chapter 3]

Project Drawdown. "Table of Solutions." Accessed January 21, 2025. https://drawdown.org/solutions/table-of-solutions. [Introduction and What's Next?]

Quon, Alexander. "Regina to roll out green bins as it prepares to launch organic waste program in September." *CBC News Saskatchewan.* August 5, 2023. https://www.cbc.ca/news/canada/saskatchewan/regina-organic-waste-green-bins-1.6928127. [Chapter 6]

RainBarrel.ca. "Mission Statement." Accessed June 4, 2025. https://rainbarrel.ca/about-us/#mission. [Chapter 12]

RainBarrel.ca. "Rain Barrel Assembly, Installation, Maintenance and Warranty." Accessed June 4, 2025. https://rainbarrel.ca/instructions/#assembly. [Chapter 12]

Recycle BC. "10 Years of Impact: 2023 Annual Report." Accessed July 31, 2024. https://recyclebc.ca/about/annual-reports/. [Chapter 7]

Recycle BC. "More on Recycling Coffee Cups and Cartons." August 20, 2015. https://recyclebc.ca/more-on-recycling-coffee-cups-and-cartons/. [Chapter 11]

Recycle My Electronics. "What Can I Recycle?" Nova Scotia. Last modified June 1, 2024. https://recyclemyelectronics.ca/ns/what-can-i-recycle. [Chapter 15]

Rehak, Melanie. "Who Made That Ziploc Bag?" *The New York Times Magazine.* July 25, 2014. https://www.nytimes.com/2014/07/27/magazine/who-made-that-ziploc-bag.html. [Chapter 10]

Repair Cafe. "About." Accessed January 14, 2025. https://www.repaircafe.org/en/about/. [Chapter 15]

Repair Cafe. "Repair guides." Accessed January and February 2025. https://www.repaircafe.org/en/community/repair-guides/. [Chapter 15]

Repair Cafe. "Visit." (Interactive map). Accessed June 26, 2025. https://www.repaircafe.org/en/visit/. [Chapter 15]

Reroute. "Our Services." Accessed May 1, 2025. https://www.reroutesk.ca/services. [Chapter 9]

Ritchie, Hannah, and Max Roser. "Fish and Overfishing." Our World in Data. Last modified March 2024. https://ourworldindata.org/fish-and-overfishing. [Chapter 3]

Ritchie, Hannah, Pablo Rosado, and Max Roser. "Environmental Impacts of Food Production." Our World in Data. Accessed June 7, 2025. https://ourworldindata.org/environmental-impacts-of-food. [Chapters 3, 5, 11 and 12]

Ritchie, Hannah, Pablo Rosado, and Max Roser. "Meat and Dairy Production." Our World in Data. Last modified December 2023. https://ourworldindata.org/meat-production. [Chapter 3]

Ritchie, Hannah. "Dairy vs. plant-based milk: what are the environmental impacts?" Our World in Data. January 19, 2022. https://ourworldindata.org/environmental-impact-milks. [Chapter 3]

Ritchie, Hannah. "Drivers of Deforestation." Our World in Data. Last modified May 2024. https://ourworldindata.org/drivers-of-deforestation. [Chapter 3]

Ritchie, Hannah. "FAQs on plastics." Our World in Data. September 2, 2018. https://ourworldindata.org/faq-on-plastics. [Chapters 7 and 10]

Ritchie, Hannah. "Food production is responsible for one-quarter of the world's greenhouse gas emissions." Our World in Data. November 6, 2019. https://ourworldindata.org/food-ghg-emissions. [Chapter 3]

Ritchie, Hannah. "Is organic really better for the environment than conventional agriculture?" Our World in Data. October 19, 2017. https://ourworldindata.org/is-organic-agriculture-better-for-the-environment. [Chapters 4 and 12]

Ritchie, Hannah. "Less meat is nearly always better than sustainable meat, to reduce your carbon footprint." Our World in Data. February 4, 2020. https://ourworldindata.org/less-meat-or-sustainable-meat. [Chapter 3]

Ritchie, Hannah. "Very little of global food is transported by air; this greatly reduces the climate benefits of eating local." Our World in Data. January 28, 2020. https://ourworldindata.org/food-transport-by-mode. [Chapter 4]

Ritchie, Hannah. "You want to reduce the carbon footprint of your food? Focus on what you eat, not whether your food is local." Our World in Data. January 24, 2020. https://ourworldindata.org/food-choice-vs-eating-local. [Chapters 3 and 11]

Roux, Katie. "Baked Potatoes (Without Foil)." Wholefood Soulfood Kitchen. Last modified September 13, 2022. https://wholefoodsoulfoodkitchen.com/baked-potatoes-without-foil/. [Chapter 9]

Sanderson, Kim, Michael Gertler, Diane Martz, and Ramesh Mahabir. "Farmers' Markets in North America: A Background Document." Community-University Institute for Social Research, University of Saskatchewan (2005). [Chapter 4]

Saskatchewan Waste Reduction Council. "Compost." Accessed April 5, 2024. https://www.saskwastereduction.ca/recycle/resources/composting/. [Chapter 6]

Saskatchewan Waste Reduction Council. "Waste Reduction Hub." (Waste search tool). Accessed April 18, 2025. https://www.saskwastereduction.ca/recycle/. [Chapters 7, 10, 13 and 15]

Saskatchewan Waste Reduction Council. "Who we are." About. Accessed April 18, 2025. https://www.saskwastereduction.ca/about/. [Chapter 7]

Schildgen, Bob. "Ask Mr. Green: Paper Towels or Rags?" *Sierra Magazine*. The Sierra Club. Accessed September 6, 2024. https://www.sierraclub.org/sierra/green-life/2014/03/ask-mr-green-paper-towels-or-rags-0. [Chapter 9]

Seasonal Food Guide. "Why Eat Seasonally?" Accessed November 11, 2024. https://www.seasonalfoodguide.org/why-eat-seasonally. [Chapter 4]

Second Harvest. "Still Good to Eat: A guide to reducing food waste at home & saving on your grocery bill." Accessed December 4, 2023. https://www.secondharvest.ca/resources/still-good. [Chapter 1]

Siddiqua, Ayesha, John N. Hahladakis, and Wadha Ahmed K A Al-Attiya. "An overview of the environmental pollution and health effects associated with waste landfilling and open dumping." *Environmental Science and Pollution Research* 29 (2022): 58514–58536. https://doi.org/10.1007/s11356-022-21578-z. [Chapter 8]

SK Recycles. "Transitioning to Full EPR." Accessed December 16, 2024. https://skrecycles.ca/learn/transitioning-to-full-epr/. [Chapter 7]

SK Recycles. "What Can I Recycle?" Accessed December 16, 2024. https://skrecycles.ca/what-can-i-recycle/. [Chapter 7]

Smith, Pete, Dave Reay, and Jo Smith. "Agricultural methane emissions and the potential for mitigation." *Philosophical Transactions of the Royal Society A: Mathematical, Physical and Engineering Sciences* 379, no. 2210 (2021): 1–16. https://doi.org/10.1098/rsta.2020.0451. [Chapter 3]

Smithsonian's National Zoo & Conservation Biology Institute. "About Bird Friendly Coffee." Accessed June 4, 2024. https://nationalzoo.si.edu/migratory-birds/about-bird-friendly-coffee. [Chapter 11]

Smithsonian's National Zoo & Conservation Biology Institute. "Ecological Benefits of Shade-grown Coffee." Accessed June 4, 2024. https://nationalzoo.si.edu/migratory-birds/ecological-benefits-shade-grown-coffee. [Chapter 11]

Smithsonian's National Zoo & Conservation Biology Institute. "Find a Bird Friendly Coffee Retailer Near You." (Search tool). Accessed May 28, 2025. https://nationalzoo.si.edu/migratory-birds/find-bird-friendly-coffee-retailer-near-you. [Chapter 11]

Smithsonian's National Zoo & Conservation Biology Institute. "Migratory Bird Center." Accessed May 28, 2025. https://nationalzoo.si.edu/migratory-birds. [Chapter 11]

Smithsonian's National Zoo & Conservation Biology Institute. "Smithsonian Bird Friendly®." Accessed June 4, 2024. https://nationalzoo.si.edu/migratory-birds/bird-friendly. [Chapter 11]

Snekkevik, Vilde K., Matthew Cole, Alessio Gomiero, Marte Haave, Farhan R. Khan, and Amy L. Lusher. "Beyond the food on your plate: Investigating sources of microplastic contamination in home kitchens." *Heliyon* 10, no. 15 (2024). DOI: 10.1016/j.heliyon.2024.e35022. [Chapters 10 and 14]

Springle, Nadia, Belinda Li, Tammara Soma, and Tamara Shulman. "The complex role of single-use compostable bioplastic food packaging and foodservice ware in a circular economy: Findings from a social innovation lab." *Sustainable Production and Consumption* 33 (2022): 664-673. https://doi.org/10.1016/j.spc.2022.08.006. [Chapters 6, 7, and 8]

St. Pierre, Michelle. "Canada's farms are adjusting the ways they sell their products to consumers." Canadian Agriculture at a Glance. Statistics Canada. Last modified February 9, 2023. https://www150.statcan.gc.ca/n1/pub/96-325-x/2021001/article/00014-eng.htm. [Chapter 4]

Stasher. "FAQ." Accessed September 6, 2024. https://www.stasherbag.com/pages/faq. [Chapter 9]

Stasher. "How to Cook in a Stasher." September 14, 2021. https://www.stasherbag.com/blogs/stasher-life/how-to-cook-in-stasher-bag. [Chapter 9]

Statistics Canada. "Composting practices of Canadian households." Table: 38-10-0128-01. December 8, 2023. https://doi.org/10.25318/3810012801-eng. [Chapter 6]

Statistics Canada. "Homegrown fruit, herbs, vegetables and flowers." Table: 38-10-0025-01. Last modified June 7, 2025. https://www150.statcan.gc.ca/t1/tbl1/en/tv.action?pid=3810002501. [Chapter 12]

Statistics Canada. "Human Activity and the Environment: Waste management in Canada." Catalogue no. 16-201-X. September 2012. https://www150.statcan.gc.ca/n1/en/pub/16-201-x/16-201-x2012000-eng.pdf?st=iSC-Y0mi. [Chapter 8]

Statistics Canada. "Survey of Drinking Water Plants, 2021." *The Daily*. November 14, 2023. https://www150.statcan.gc.ca/n1/daily-quotidien/231114/dq231114d-eng.htm. [Chapter 13]

Statistics Canada. "Survey on Local Food and Beneficial Management Practices, 2022." *The Daily*. Last modified September 5, 2023. https://www150.statcan.gc.ca/n1/daily-quotidien/230905/dq230905a-eng.htm. [Chapter 4]

Statistics Canada. "The dirt on composting." StatsCAN Plus. Last modified July 5, 2022. https://www.statcan.gc.ca/o1/en/plus/1327-dirt-composting. [Chapter 6]

Streit-Bianchi, Marilena, Margarita Cimadevila, and Wolfgang Trettnak, eds. *Mare Plasticum – The Plastic Sea: Combatting Plastic Pollution Through Science and Art.* Springer Nature Switzerland, 2020. https://doi.org/10.1007/978-3-030-38945-1. [Chapters 7 and 10]

Sustainability Directory. "Wish-Cycling." Term. April 11, 2025. https://sustainability-directory.com/term/wish-cycling/. [Chapter 7]

Switch to Renewable. "Renewable Energy in Canada." Earth Day Canada. Accessed June 20, 2025. https://switchtorenewable.ca/. [Chapter 15]

Thapa, Pradeep, MD Tanvir Hasnine, Ali Zoungrana, Sandeep Thakur, and Qiuyan Yuan. "Food Waste Treatments and the Impact of Composting on Carbon Footprint in Canada." *Fermentation* 8, no. 10 (2022). https://doi.org/10.3390/fermentation8100566. [Chapter 6]

The Aluminum Association. "Infinitely Recyclable." Accessed July 29, 2024. https://www.aluminum.org/Recycling. [Chapter 7]

The Britannica Dictionary, s.v. "ruminant (noun)." Accessed November 19, 2024. https://www.britannica.com/dictionary/ruminant. [Chapter 3]

The Canadian Real Estate Association and Natural Resources Canada. "A Homeowner's Guide to Energy Efficiency." Accessed January 13, 2025. https://www.crea.ca/files/publications/english/Homeowners-Guide_Energy-Efficiency_En_DM_WEB.pdf. [Chapter 15]

The EAT-Lancet Commission. "EAT-Lancet Commission Brief for Everyone." Accessed March 1, 2024. https://eatforum.org/lancet-commission/eatinghealthyandsustainable/. [Chapters 3 and 4]

The EAT-Lancet Commission. "Healthy Diets from Sustainable Food Systems: Food Planet Health." EAT-Lancet Commission Summary Report 2019. Accessed February 29, 2024. https://eatforum.org/eat-lancet-commission/eat-lancet-commission-summary-report/. [Chapter 3]

The Environmental Research & Education Foundation of Canada. "State of the Practice of Organic Waste Management and Collection in Canada." Data & Policy Program. June 2021. https://www.eref.ca/reports. [Chapter 6]

The International Aluminium Institute. "Aluminium Recycling Factsheet." October 2020. https://international-aluminium.org/resources/aluminium-recycling-fact-sheet/. [Chapter 7]

The National Aeronautics and Space Administration (NASA). "Global Temperature." Accessed September 2, 2025. https://climate.nasa.gov/vital-signs/global-temperature/. [Introduction]

The National Aeronautics and Space Administration (NASA). "Methane." Accessed March 21, 2025. https://climate.nasa.gov/vital-signs/methane/. [Chapter 1]

The Paper and Paperboard Packaging Environmental Council. "2022 PPEC Recycled Content Survey." 2022. https://ppec-paper.com/recycled-content/. [Chapter 7]

The Paper and Paperboard Packaging Environmental Council. "Circular Economy." Accessed July 30, 2024. https://ppec-paper.com/paper-packaging-circular-economy/. [Chapter 7]

The Wandering Market. "Food Producer Application and Information." Accessed December 2, 2024. [Chapter 4]

The Wandering Market. "Where Does The Food Come From?" Accessed April 2, 2025. https://www.thewanderingmarket.com/https/wwwcognitoformscom/thewanderingmarket/foodproducerswewanttoknowallaboutyou. [Chapter 4]

Thunberg, Greta. *The Climate Book: The Facts and the Solutions.* USA: Penguin Books, 2022. [Introduction, Chapter 3, and What's Next?]

Tiny Waste Blog. "The Environmental Impact of Paper Towels." Accessed September 6, 2024. https://tiny-waste.com/environmental-impact-of-paper-towels.html. [Chapter 9]

Tizzard, Christine. *Cook More, Waste Less: Zero-Waste Recipes to Use Up Groceries, Tackle Food Scraps, and Transform Leftovers.* Canada: Appetite, 2021. [Chapter 2]

Town of Inuvik Northwest Territories. "Inuvik Community Greenhouse." Accessed November 28, 2024. https://www.inuvik.ca/en/discovering-inuvik/Inuvik-Community-Greenhouse.asp. [Chapter 4]

Tuck, Sean L., Camilla Winqvist, Flávia Mota, Johan Ahnström, Lindsay A. Turnbull, and Janne Bengtsson. "Land-use intensity and the effects of organic farming on biodiversity: a hierarchical meta-analysis." *Journal of Applied Ecology* 51, no. 3 (2014): 746–755. https://doi.org/10.1111/1365-2664.12219. [Chapter 4]

U.S. National Park Service, Mote Marine Lab and the National Oceanic and Atmospheric Administration Marine Debris Program. "Approximate Time it Takes for Garbage to Decompose in the Environment." Accessed May 5, 2025. https://www.des.nh.gov/organization/divisions/water/wmb/coastal/trash/documents/Marine_debris.pdf. [Chapter 10]

United Nations Development Programme Climate Promise. "The Climate Dictionary: An everyday guide to climate change." February 2, 2023. https://climatepromise.undp.org/news-and-stories/climate-dictionary-everyday-guide-climate-change. [Introduction and What's Next?]

United Nations Environment Programme and Secretariat of the Basel, Rotterdam and Stockholm Conventions. "Chemicals in Plastics – A Technical Report." May 3, 2023. https://www.unep.org/resources/report/chemicals-plastics-technical-report. [Chapter 10]

United Nations Environment Programme. "About water." Accessed December 9, 2024. https://www.unep.org/explore-topics/water/about-water. [Chapter 13]

United Nations Environment Programme. "From birth to ban: A history of the plastic shopping bag." Chemicals and Pollution Action. December 20, 2021. https://www.unep.org/news-and-stories/story/birth-ban-history-plastic-shopping-bag. [Chapter 10]

United Nations Environment Programme. "From Pollution to Solution: A global assessment of marine litter and plastic pollution." October 21, 2021. https://www.unep.org/resources/pollution-solution-global-assessment-marine-litter-and-plastic-pollution. [Chapter 10]

United Nations Environment Programme. "Plastic planet: How tiny plastic particles are polluting our soil." Nature Action. December 22, 2021. https://www.unep.org/news-and-stories/story/plastic-planet-how-tiny-plastic-particles-are-polluting-our-soil. [Chapter 10]

United Nations Environment Programme. "Single-use beverage cups and their alternatives: Recommendations from Life Cycle Assessments." Life Cycle Initiative. February 2021. https://www.lifecycleinitiative.org/library/single-use-beverage-cups-and-their-alternatives-lca/. [Chapter 11]

United Nations Environment Programme. "Single-Use Plastics: A Roadmap for Sustainability." Rev. 2. 2018. https://www.unep.org/ietc/resources/publication/single-use-plastics-roadmap-sustainability. [Chapters 9 and 10]

United Nations Environment Programme. "Synthesis Report on the Environmental and Health Impacts of Pesticides and Fertilizers and Ways to Minimize Them." January 24, 2021. https://www.unep.org/resources/report/environmental-and-health-impacts-pesticides-and-fertilizers-and-ways-minimizing. [Chapters 4 and 12]

United Nations. "1.5°C: what it means and why it matters." Climate Action. Accessed January 20, 2025. https://www.un.org/en/climatechange/science/climate-issues/degrees-matter. [Introduction]

United Nations. "Actions for a healthy planet." Act Now. Accessed January 15, 2025. https://www.un.org/en/actnow/ten-actions. [Chapter 15]

United Nations. "Climate change: World likely to breach 1.5°C limit in next five years." UN News. Accessed September 2, 2025. https://news.un.org/en/story/2025/05/1163751. [Introduction]

United Nations. "Facts and Figures." Act Now. Accessed April 21, 2025. https://www.un.org/en/actnow/facts-and-figures. [Chapter 8]

United Nations. "Food and Climate Change: Healthy diets for a healthier planet." Climate Action. Accessed March 1, 2024. https://www.un.org/en/climatechange/science/climate-issues/food. [Chapter 3]

United Nations. "Food." Act Now, Facts and Figures. Accessed January 22, 2024. https://www.un.org/en/actnow/facts-and-figures. [Chapter 3]

United Nations. "For a livable climate: Net-zero commitments must be backed by credible action." Climate Action. Accessed January 27, 2025. https://www.un.org/en/climatechange/net-zero-coalition. [Introduction]

United Nations. "In Images: Plastic is Forever." Exhibits. June 2021. https://www.un.org/en/exhibits/exhibit/in-images-plastic-forever. [Chapter 10]

United Nations. "Myth Busters: The facts on climate and energy." Climate Action. Accessed January 27, 2025. https://www.un.org/en/climatechange/science/mythbusters. [Introduction]

United Nations. "Renewable energy – powering a safer future." Climate Action. Accessed January 15, 2025. https://www.un.org/en/climatechange/raising-ambition/renewable-energy. [Chapter 15]

United Nations. "Sustainability." Academic Impact. Accessed January 27, 2025. https://www.un.org/en/academic-impact/sustainability. [Introduction]

United Nations. "The Paris Agreement." Climate Action. Accessed January 27, 2025. https://www.un.org/en/climatechange/paris-agreement. [Introduction]

United Nations. "What Is Climate Change?" Climate Action. Accessed January 20, 2025. https://www.un.org/en/climatechange/what-is-climate-change. [Introduction]

United Nations. "What is renewable energy?" Climate Action. Accessed January 15, 2025. https://www.un.org/en/climatechange/what-is-renewable-energy. [Chapter 15]

United Nations. "Your guide to climate action: Home Energy." Act Now. Accessed January 15, 2025. https://www.un.org/en/actnow/home-energy. [Chapter 15]

United States Environmental Protection Agency. "Approaches to Composting." Sustainable Management of Food. Last modified January 17, 2025. https://www.epa.gov/sustainable-management-food/approaches-composting. [Chapter 6]

United States Environmental Protection Agency. "Basics of Climate Change." Last modified November 7, 2024. https://www.epa.gov/climatechange-science/basics-climate-change. [Introduction]

United States Environmental Protection Agency. "Climate Change Terms." Office of Air and Radiation, Office of Atmospheric Protection, Climate Change Division. Last modified September 9, 2013. https://sor.epa.gov/sor_internet/registry/termreg/searchandretrieve/glossariesandkeywordlists/search.do;jsessionid=xcGokXS_bnq8EyKCupLC9VDMrcpC0p0vmNgHnPen2TfGfaPdw1Fm!-896804482?details=&vocabName=Glossary%20Climate%20Change%20Terms#formTop. [Introduction]

United States Environmental Protection Agency. "Frequently Asked Questions about Plastic Recycling and Composting." Trash-Free Waters. Last modified November 21, 2024. https://www.epa.gov/trash-free-waters/frequently-asked-questions-about-plastic-recycling-and-composting. [Chapter 6]

United States Environmental Protection Agency. "Frequent Questions on Recycling." Reduce, Reuse, Recycle. Last modified February 11, 2025. https://www.epa.gov/recycle/frequent-questions-recycling. [Chapter 7]

United States Environmental Protection Agency. "Greenhouse Gas Equivalencies Calculator." Last modified November 2024. https://www.epa.gov/energy/greenhouse-gas-equivalencies-calculator. [Chapter 3]

United States Environmental Protection Agency. "How We Use Water." WaterSense. Last modified September 12, 2024. https://www.epa.gov/watersense/how-we-use-water. [Chapter 13]

United States Environmental Protection Agency. "Identifying Greener Cleaning Products." Sustainable Marketplace: Greener Products and Services. Last modified April 6, 2025. https://www.epa.gov/greenerproducts/identifying-greener-cleaning-products. [Chapter 14]

United States Environmental Protection Agency. "Importance of Methane." Global Methane Initiative. Last modified March 3, 2025. https://www.epa.gov/gmi/importance-methane. [Chapter 1]

United States Environmental Protection Agency. "Learn About Sustainability." Last modified October 1, 2024. https://www.epa.gov/sustainability/learn-about-sustainability. [Introduction]

United States Environmental Protection Agency. "Microplastics Research." Water Research. Last modified July 22, 2024. https://www.epa.gov/water-research/microplastics-research. [Chapter 10]

United States Environmental Protection Agency. "Overview of Greenhouse Gases." Last modified January 16, 2025. https://www.epa.gov/ghgemissions/overview-greenhouse-gases. [Introduction]

United States Environmental Protection Agency. "Recycling Basics and Benefits." Reduce, Reuse, Recycle. Last modified February 14, 2025. https://www.epa.gov/recycle/recycling-basics-and-benefits. [Chapter 7]

United States Environmental Protection Agency. "Reducing and Reusing Basics." Reduce, Reuse, Recycle. Last modified February 6, 2025. https://www.epa.gov/recycle/reducing-and-reusing-basics. [Chapters 7 and 8]

United States Environmental Protection Agency. "What Can You Do to Protect Local Waterways?" December 2002. https://www3.epa.gov/npdes/pubs/centralized_brochure.pdf. [Chapter 14]

University of Michigan. "Fighting climate change at the sink: A guide to greener dishwashing." *Michigan News*. February 12, 2020. https://news.umich.edu/fighting-climate-change-at-the-sink-a-guide-to-greener-dishwashing/. [Chapter 13]

University of New Hampshire. "Are organic pesticides safer for my garden?" Yard and Garden Infoline. July 19, 2019. https://extension.unh.edu/blog/2019/07/are-organic-pesticides-safer-my-garden. [Chapter 12]

University of Plymouth. "Why are artificial lawns bad for the environment?" Accessed June 7, 2025. https://www.plymouth.ac.uk/discover/why-are-artificial-lawns-bad-for-the-environment. [Chapter 12]

University of Saskatchewan. "Creating Biodiversity in Your Yard: A How-To Guide." College of Agriculture and Bioresources, Gardening at USask. February 2, 2018. https://gardening.usask.ca/articles-and-lists/articles-how-to/creating-biodiversity-in-your-yard.php. [Chapter 12]

University of Saskatchewan. "Lawns and alternatives." Gardening at USask. Accessed June 6, 2025. https://gardening.usask.ca/gardening-advice/sorted-by-plant/lawns.php. [Chapter 12]

University of Saskatchewan. "Mulch & More: A How-To Guide to a Healthy Yard." Gardening at USask. December 27, 2022. https://gardening.usask.ca/articles-and-lists/articles-healthysoils/mulch--more.php. [Chapter 12]

University of Saskatchewan. "Plants from Saskatchewan's prairies, aspen parkland and boreal forest." Patterson Garden Arboretum. Accessed June 7, 2025. https://patterson-arboretum.usask.ca/featured%20lists/saskatchewan-native-plants.php. [Chapter 12]

University of Saskatchewan. "Turning grass into gardens." Gardening at USask. April 27, 2022. https://gardening.usask.ca/articles-and-lists/articles-how-to/making-a-new-vegetable-or-flower-garden.php. [Chapter 12]

University of Saskatchewan. "Water Security for Canadians: Solutions for Canada's Emerging Water Crisis." Global Water Futures. April 2019. https://gwf.usask.ca/documents/meetings/water-security-for-canada/WaterSecurityForCanada_April-25-2019-2pg1.pdf. [Chapter 13]

Urban, Rylan. "Cost of Solar Power In Canada 2024." Energyhub.org. Last modified September 3, 2023. https://www.energyhub.org/cost-solar-power-canada/. [Chapter 15]

Vancouver Public Library. "Kill A Watt EZ." Accessed February 7, 2025. https://www.vpl.ca/lendable/kill-watt-ez. [Chapter 15]

Vancouver Public Library. "Power Meter Instructions." Accessed June 21, 2025. https://www.vpl.ca/guide/power-meter-instructions. [Chapter 15]

Vintage Fanatic. "Saran Plastic Wrap Commercial 1953." YouTube. May 24, 2013. Video, 1:38. https://www.youtube.com/watch?v=hiXGiCaBxtM. [Chapter 10]

Wallender, Lee. "What Is a Faucet Aerator? Purpose, Cleaning, and Replacing." *The Spruce*. Last modified August 27, 2024. https://www.thespruce.com/why-you-need-to-install-faucet-aerators-1821314. [Chapter 13]

Weber, Christopher L., and H. Scott Matthews. "Food-Miles and the Relative Climate Impacts of Food Choices in the United States." *Environmental Science & Technology* 42, no. 10 (2008): 3508–3513. https://doi.org/10.1021/es702969f. [Chapters 3 and 4]

Weisse, Mikaela, Elizabeth Goldman, and Sarah Carter. "Forest Pulse: The Latest on the World's Forests." World Resources Institute Global Forest Review. Last modified April 4, 2024. https://gfr.wri.org/latest-analysis-deforestation-trends. [Chapter 3]

Westbroek, Coenraad D., Jennifer Bitting, Matteo Craglia, José M. C. Azevedo, and Jonathan M. Cullen. "Global material flow analysis of glass: From raw materials to end of life." *Journal of Industrial Ecology* 25, no. 2 (2021): 333–343. https://doi.org/10.1111/jiec.13112. [Chapter 7]

West Coast Seeds. "Vegetable Seeds." (Search tool). Accessed September 24, 2024. https://www.westcoastseeds.com/collections/vegetable-seeds. [Chapter 12]

Wilson, Aaron. "Sustainability Series: What is sustainability and why is it important?" ECO Canada. April 7, 2021. https://eco.ca/blog/what-is-sustainability-and-why-is-it-important/. [Introduction]

World Coffee Research. "About Us." Accessed May 26, 2025. https://worldcoffeeresearch.org/about. [Chapter 11]

World Coffee Research. "F1 Hybrid Trials." Accessed June 20, 2024. https://worldcoffeeresearch.org/programs/next-generation-f1-hybrid-varieties. [Chapter 11]

World Meteorological Organization (WMO). "WMO Global Annual to Decadal Climate Update 2025-2029." May 26, 2025. https://wmo.int/files/wmo-global-annual-decadal-climate-update-2025-2029. [Introduction]

World Wildlife Fund Australia. "The Lifecycle of Plastics." July 1, 2021. https://wwf.org.au/blogs/the-lifecycle-of-plastics/. [Chapter 10]

Wynes, Seth, and Kimberly A Nicholas. "The climate mitigation gap: education and government recommendations miss the most effective individual actions." *Environmental Research Letters* 12, no. 7 (2017). https://doi.org/10.1088/1748-9326/aa7541. [Chapter 3 and What's Next?]

Zero Waste Canada. "Zero Waste Cleaning Guide." Accessed October 31, 2024. https://www.zerowastecanada.ca/education-resources-and-guides. [Chapter 14]

LIST OF INTERVIEWEES

Alisha Drinkwater, Communications Specialist, Metro Vancouver
Angie Bugg, Energy Conservation Engineer, Saskatchewan Environmental Society
Anne-Marie Bonneau, Author, *Zero-Waste Chef*
Ashley Esakin, Founder, Gardening In Canada
Becca Kram-Dos Santos, Communications and Engagement Specialist, David Suzuki Foundation
Belinda Li, Director of Innovation, Food Systems Lab, Simon Fraser University
Dr. Bettina Liverant, Adjunct Assistant Professor, Department of History, University of Calgary
Brianne Miller, Founder and CEO, Nada Grocery
Dr. Calvin Lakhan, Project Director, Circular Innovation Hub, York University
Cassie Barker, Senior Program Manager, Toxics, Environmental Defence Canada
Catalina Nadeau-Bonilla, Leader, Operational Performance, Wastewater Treatment, The City of Calgary
Catherine Clark, Executive Director, Farmers' Markets Ontario
Dr. Charles Z. Levkoe, Director, Sustainable Food Systems Lab, Lakehead University
Chet Neufeld, Executive Director, Native Plant Society of Saskatchewan
Christine Tizzard, Author, *The Zero Waste Kitchen*
Claire Remington, Executive Director, Greater Victoria Compost Education Centre
Dr. Claudia Wagner-Riddle, Professor, School of Environmental Sciences, University of Guelph
Dale Schmidt, Recycle Manager, Loraas Recycle
Darrin Qualman, Director of Climate Crisis Policy and Action, National Farmers Union
Dr. Deborah Lawrence, Chief Scientist and Director of Forest and Land, Calyx Global
Denise Philippe, Senior Policy Advisor, National Zero Waste Council
Divyansh Ojha, Founder and CEO, Odd Bunch
Dr. Elizabeth A. Bennett, Associate Professor, International Affairs, Lewis & Clark College
Emilia Umaña, Nursery Development Program Manager, World Coffee Research
Emily Robinson, Food Education Manager, School of Hospitality, Food and Tourism Management, University of Guelph
FluxLab at St. Francis Xavier University: Dr. Dave Risk, Chelsie Hall, Rebecca Martino, Jordan Stuart, and Farnaz Farjami
Getty Stewart, Food Educator & Professional Home Economist, GettyStewart.com
Henrietta Lovell, CEO and Founder, Rare Tea Company
Janet Melrose, Author and Garden Educator, Calgary's Cottage Gardener
Dr. Jason Hawes, Assistant Professor, School of Computing, University of Wyoming
Jason Ofield, President and CEO, Bulk Barn Foods Limited
Jay Sinha, Co-Founder and Author, *Life Without Plastic*

Jen Humphries, Chair, Inuvik Community Greenhouse
Joanne Fedyk, Executive Director, Saskatchewan Waste Reduction Council
Joanne Gauci, Senior Policy Advisor, Metro Vancouver
Dr. Josh Lepawsky, Professor, Department of Geography, Memorial University of Newfoundland
Karen Murchison, Executive Director, Canadian Organic Growers
Karen Storry, Senior Engineer, Zero Waste Implementation, Metro Vancouver
Karen Wirsig, Senior Program Manager, Plastics, Environmental Defence Canada
Karli Fleury, Director, Workforce & Destination Initiatives, Banff & Lake Louise Hospitality Association
Kate Pepler, CEO and Owner, The Tare Shop
Dr. Kathleen Kevany, Professor, Department of Business & Social Sciences, Dalhousie University
Katie Burns, Community Leadership & Program Development Manager, The City of Saskatoon
Kelsey Meyer, Director, Environmental Policy and Public Affairs, Clear Strategy Inc.
Kirk Symonds, Manager for Education and Promotion, Solid Waste Resources, The City of Halifax
Kylene Goodman, Organics and Landfill Supervisor, Loraas Disposal North
Lindsay Coulter, Program Coordinator, Victoria Nature School
Lisa Bronner, Consumer Educator and Author, Dr. Bronner's Magic Soaps
Lisa Howse, Compost Education Coordinator, Saskatchewan Waste Reduction Council
Dr. Love-Ese Chile, Principal Researcher and Consultant, Grey to Green Sustainable Solutions
Maeve Holler, Industry Communications Manager, World Coffee Research
Maja Rusinowska, Manager, Stakeholder Relations, Western Canada, Recycle BC
Dr. Maria T. (Maite) Maldonado, Professor, Earth, Ocean & Atmospheric Sciences, University of British Columbia
Matt Hulse, Lawyer, Ecojustice Canada
Dr. Megan Bailey, Associate Professor, Marine Affairs Program, Dalhousie University
Meg Dorwart, Communications Coordinator, Saskatchewan Waste Reduction Council
Michael Zarbl, Executive Director, Major Appliance Recycling Roundtable
Munu Hicken-Gaberria, CEO and Founder, Live for Tomorrow
Dr. Myra Hird, Professor, School of Environmental Studies, Queen's University
Nadine LeBean, Co-Creator, The Wandering Market
Dr. Neil Rooney, Associate Professor, School of Environmental Sciences, University of Guelph
Dr. Paul West, Senior Scientist, Ecosystems & Agriculture, Project Drawdown
Dr. Pradeep Sambyal, Postdoctoral Fellow, Plastic Recycling Research Cluster, University of British Columbia
Rachel Cracknell, Environment and Climate Lead, Ethical Tea Partnership
Dr. Rafaela F. Gutierrez, Program Lead, Social Science and Educational Programs, University of Toronto Trash Team
Rebecca Carroll, Operations Services Technologist, Town of Cochrane
Rebecca Kolarich, Program Manager, Water, Environmental Defence Canada
Rebecca Veenhuis, Program Assistant, Organic Agriculture Centre of Canada, Dalhousie University
Rhodes Yepsen, Executive Director, Biodegradable Products Institute
Richard Alexander, Executive Vice President, Government Relations & Public Affairs, Restaurants Canada

Dr. Sadaf Mollaei, Assistant Professor, School of Hospitality, Food & Tourism Management, University of Guelph

Sarah Coulber, Education Specialist, Canadian Wildlife Federation

Sarah Riddell, Policy Research Associate, Clean Heat, Efficiency Canada

Shanna Farrell, Author, *A Good Drink*

Sharon Howland, Leader, Program Management, Waste & Recycling Services, The City of Calgary

Shira Blustein, Founder, The Acorn Restaurant

Stephen Thomas, Clean Energy Manager, David Suzuki Foundation

Dr. Stuart McCook, Professor, College of Arts, University of Guelph

Sue Maxwell, Chair, Zero Waste BC

Susan Antler, Executive Director, The Compost Council of Canada

Dr. Tammara Soma, Director of Research, Food Systems Lab, Simon Fraser University

Tippi Thole, Blogger, Tiny Trash Can

Dr. Victoria Wojcik, Director, Pollinator Partnership Canada

Dr. Virginia Maclaren, Associate Emerita Professor, Department of Geography and Planning, University of Toronto

Dr. William Knight, Curator, Agriculture and Fisheries, Ingenium: Canada's Museums of Science and Innovation

Dr. Wren Montgomery, Associate Professor, Ivey Business School, Western University

Dr. Zahra Kassam, Co-Founder and Director, Plant-Based Canada

A special thanks to the following people who answered questions and/or provided contacts via email:

Andrew Telfer, Director, Circular Innovation Council

Bret Sloboshan, Co-Owner, Original Family Farm

Gavin Robertson, Instructor, The School of Wine, Beer and Spirits, Niagara College

Julie Craves, Ecologist and Writer, Coffee & Conservation

LIST OF FIGURES

INDEX

C

G

H

M

N

O

Y

Z

Naomi Hansen is an award-winning author. Her debut book, *Only in Saskatchewan: Recipes & Stories from the Province's Best-Loved Eateries*, was published in 2022. She is a contributor to many publications, including CBC, *Chatelaine*, and *Canadian Living*. *Building a Sustainable Kitchen* is her second book. She lives on Treaty 6 Territory in Saskatoon, Saskatchewan with her partner, Paul, and their dog, Rue. Find her online at *naomihansen.ca*.